Learning Vaadin

Master the full range of web development features
powered by Vaadin-built RIAs

Nicolas Fränkel

[PACKT] open source ✳
PUBLISHING   community experience distilled

BIRMINGHAM - MUMBAI

Learning Vaadin

First published: October 2011

Production Reference: 1141011

Published by Packt Publishing Ltd.
Livery Place
35 Livery Street
Birmingham B3 2PB, UK.

ISBN 978-1-84951-522-1

www.packtpub.com

Cover Image by Grand-Duc, Wikipedia
(https://secure.wikimedia.org/wikipedia/en/wiki/User:Grand-Duc)

Credits

Author
Nicolas Fränkel

Reviewers
Phil Barrett
Jouni Lehto
Risto Yrjänä

Acquisition Editor
Chaitanya Apte

Development Editor
Kartikey Pandey
Meeta Rajani

Technical Editors
Azharuddin Sheikh
Kavita Iyer

Project Coordinator
Joel Goveya

Proofreader
Mario Cecere

Indexers
Tejal Daruwale
Hemangini Bari

Graphics
Nilesh Mohite
Valentina D'silva

Production Coordinator
Aparna Bhagat

Cover Work
Aparna Bhagat

Foreword

When we started designing Vaadin Framework in year 2000—then called Millstone Framework—we had a clear vision of creating a platform that would make building web applications fast, easy, and modular. Something that we wanted to use by ourselves in the process of building business oriented web applications. We envisioned a full stack of technologies starting from a web server, an object relationship-mapping tool, rich set of user interface components, and extensible theme system. Everything built from scratch with a tiny team with no funding and little experience. Fortunately, we did not have a clue on the size and complexity of the task or the lack of our experience; otherwise, we would have never dared to start working on such a huge task. Finally, it took two years and three complete rewrites to understand the value of focusing solely on the user interface layer and being able to release something solid that has outgrown all the expectations we had.

Now when I look back to the design principles we chose for Vaadin, three principles in particular seem to have contributed to the longevity of the framework. First, we reasoned that the diversity and incompatibility of web browsers we experienced back in year 2000 was not going away—quite the contrary. While the Web has gained more and more popularity as a platform for building interactive application user interfaces, the features in web browsers have exploded and the number of web browsers have grown to include smartphones and tablets in addition to 5-10 desktop browsers that should be supported. Therefore, we chose to embrace this diversity and abstract away from the browser to make it easier for developers to support "all" browsers at once. Secondly, we set our optimization target to be developer efficiency what could in most cases be roughly measured by the number of code lines in the user interface layer of the program. This has been a good choice as developers continue to be more expensive resource in business application projects than servers are. Finally, we recognized the need to support heterogeneous teams where some developers might be more experienced than others. Some of the mechanisms to support teams include theme packaging, multiple levels of abstraction, support for data bindings side-by-side with internal data in components, deep inheritance hierarchies for user interface components to name a few.

I have always been a huge fan of open source being introduced to it by starting to play around with Linux kernel 0.3 and early Linux distributions. Working on, living in, and breathing open source did make it natural to choose to release Vaadin with an open source license and to build community around it. After years of trying and failing to build impactful community, all pieces finally clicked together in 2009 with the release of Vaadin 6. Seeing how people all over the world started to use Vaadin for building applications their businesses depend on for years to come had been great. What have been even more amazing is how people have started to contribute back to Vaadin—in the terms of add-on components, helping each other on the forums, and promoting the framework to their peers have been amazing. At the end of the day, lively and friendly community and ecosystem around Vaadin has been the key to the rapid growth of adoption.

I think that I first heard of Nicolas Frankel by reading one of his many insightful blog posts couple of years back. Also, remember him being one of the more active Vaadin community members helping others on the forum. One year ago, Nicolas was working on a really interesting project for a multinational organization. He invited me on a really nice dinner in Geneva where I was visiting Soft-Shake conference to discuss of Vaadin and overeat excellent Swiss fondue. During the dinner, we ended up talking about the need for a book that would tutor beginners through Vaadin and would introduce them to common patterns for Vaadin development. I remembered being contacted by Packt Publishing about getting in touch with potential authors for such a book. Nicolas had quite a lot of Vaadin experience and I asked if he would be interested in considering writing the book. To my surprise, he agreed.

You might be familiar with Book of Vaadin—a free book about Vaadin. While being a complete reference of Vaadin and anything related to it, the amount of contents and the referential approach can make it overwhelming for a beginner. This book takes another approach. Instead of trying to be a reference, it teaches the reader about Vaadin concepts by introducing them one by one in an order natural for learning. It is written as a journey of building a simple Twitter client while learning the most important aspects of Vaadin—one by one.

In conclusion, I would like to give my deep thanks to Nicolas for taking the challenge of writing this book which I am sure will help many people to get a quick start for writing Vaadin based applications. I hope that these applications will benefit the companies investing in them, as well as save a lot of time and frustration from the end users. However, at the end of the day—it is the most important to me—and I am sure that Nicolas shares this thought—that you as a developer of those applications will save your time and frustration and be able to accomplish something that would not be possible otherwise.

Dr. Joonas Lehtinen
Vaadin, CEO and Founder

About the Author

Nicolas Fränkel comes from a rather unorthodox background, as he holds an MSc in both Architecture and Civil Engineering. Now a Sun Certified professional, he operates as a successful Java/Java EE architect with more than 10 years of experience in consulting for different clients.

Based in France, he also practices (or practiced) as WebSphere Application Server administrator, certified Valtech trainer, and part-time lecturer in different French universities, so as to broaden his understanding of software craftsmanship.

His interests in computer software are diversified, ranging from Rich Client Application, to Quality Processes through open source software. When not tinkering with new products, or writing blog posts, he may be found practicing sports: squash, kickboxing, and skiing at the moment. Other leisure activities include reading novels, motorcycles, photography, and drawing, not necessarily in that order.

I would like to thank my wonderful wife, Corinne, for letting me throw myself in the formidable task of writing a book, fully knowing the time it takes. I love you, deeply.

I would like to thank my son, Dorian, for making me proud to be a father.

I would like to thank Joonas Lehtinen, Vaadin's creator, for letting me ask him so many questions and always having time to answer them all and in detail despite his many responsibilities. I would also like to thank the Vaadin team as a whole: Artur, Sami, Vile, Fredrik, and countless others I don't know of, but who made Vaadin possible by their work and their dedication to the framework.

About the Reviewers

Phil Barrett, father of two, living abroad. He is an open source addict who still lives with the vague belief that HashMaps are the answer.

Jouni Lehto has over 10 years of experience on different kinds of web technologies and has been involved in a few projects where Vaadin has been the choice.

Risto Yrjänä is currently working as Vaadin Expert at Vaadin Ltd. He has several years of experience in software design and development, as well as maintaining Vaadin projects for both the company and their clients. Risto is particularly interested in UI-design, RIA, and lean methodologies.

www.PacktPub.com

Support files, eBooks, discount offers and more

You might want to visit www.PacktPub.com for support files and downloads related to your book.

Did you know that Packt offers eBook versions of every book published, with PDF and ePub files available? You can upgrade to the eBook version at www.PacktPub.com and as a print book customer, you are entitled to a discount on the eBook copy. Get in touch with us at service@packtpub.com for more details.

At www.PacktPub.com, you can also read a collection of free technical articles, sign up for a range of free newsletters and receive exclusive discounts and offers on Packt books and eBooks.

http://PacktLib.PacktPub.com

Do you need instant solutions to your IT questions? PacktLib is Packt's online digital book library. Here, you can access, read and search across Packt's entire library of books.

Why Subscribe?

Fully searchable across every book published by Packt

Copy and paste, print and bookmark content

On demand and accessible via web browser

Free Access for Packt account holders

If you have an account with Packt at www.PacktPub.com, you can use this to access PacktLib today and view nine entirely free books. Simply use your login credentials for immediate access.

Table of Contents

Preface

Vaadin is a new Java web framework for making applications look great and perform well, making your users happy. Vaadin promises to make your user interfaces attractive and usable while easing your development efforts and boosting your productivity. With this book in hand, you will be able to utilize the full range of development and deployment features offered by Vaadin while thoroughly understanding the concepts.

Learning Vaadin is a practical systematic tutorial to understand, use, and master the art of RIA development with Vaadin. You will learn about the fundamental concepts that are the cornerstones of the framework, at the same time making progress on building your own web application. The book will also show you how to integrate Vaadin with other popular frameworks and how to run it on top of internal, as well as externalized infrastructures.

This book will show you how to become a professional Vaadin developer by giving you a concrete foundation through diagrams, practical examples, and ready-to-use source code. It will enable you to grasp all the notions behind Vaadin one-step at a time: components, layouts, events, containers, and bindings. You will learn to build first-class web applications using best-of-breed technologies. You will find detailed information on how to integrate Vaadin's presentation layer on top of other widespread technologies, such as Spring, CDI, and Hibernate. Finally, the book will show you how to deploy on different infrastructures, such as Liferay portlet container and Google App Engine.

This book is an authoritative and complete systematic tutorial on how to create top-notch web applications with the RIA Vaadin framework.

What this book covers

Chapter 1, Vaadin and its context is an introduction to Vaadin, its features, its philosophy, and the environment surrounding it.

Chapter 2, Environment Setup is a detailed how-to that describes how to set up the development environment, whether using Eclipse or NetBeans.

Chapter 3, Hello Vaadin is the creation of a basic Vaadin project, and the explanation of what happens under the hood.

Chapter 4, Components and Layouts presents the building blocks of any Vaadin application worth its salt.

Chapter 5, Event Listener Model illustrates the interactions between users and your application and the way they are implemented in Vaadin.

Chapter 6, Containers and Related Widgets explains not only widgets presenting collections of beans, but also the ways they can be bound to the underlying data.

Chapter 7, Advanced Features portrays real-life problems and how to resolve them, such as accessing the request/response from inside Vaadin, running Vaadin applications inside legacy ones and customizing error handling.

Chapter 8, Creating Custom Components depicts the strategies available to create your own reusable components.

Chapter 9, Integrating with Third-party Products details how to run Vaadin on top of other frameworks such as Spring, CDI and Hibernate.

Chapter 10, Beyond Application Servers describes how to deploy Vaadin applications in other contexts: GateIn for portals, Glassfish for OSGi and finally Cloud Foundry for "the cloud".

What you need for this book

In order to get the most out of this book, it is advised to have a computer, a Java Developer Kit 6 installed on it, as well as Internet access.

Who this book is for

If you are a Java developer with some experience in Java web development and want to enter the world of Rich Internet Applications, then this technology and book are ideal for you. Learning Vaadin will be perfect as your next step towards building eye-candy dynamic web applications on a Java-based platform.

Conventions

In this book, you will find a number of styles of text that distinguish between different kinds of information. Here are some examples of these styles, and an explanation of their meaning.

Code words in text are shown as follows: "We can include other contexts through the use of the `include` directive."

A block of code is set as follows:

```
import com.vaadin.Application;
import com.vaadin.ui.*;

public class HelloWorldApp extends Application

  public void init() {

    Window mainWindow = new Window("Hello World Application");
    Label label = new Label("Greetings, Vaadin user!");
    mainWindow.addComponent(label);
    setMainWindow(mainWindow);
  }
}
```

When we wish to draw your attention to a particular part of a code block, the relevant lines or items are set in bold:

```
<servlet>
  <servlet-name>Spring Integration</servlet-name>
  <servlet-class>
    com.packtpub.vaadin.SpringApplicationServlet
  </servlet-class>
  <init-param>
    <param-name>applicationBeanName</param-name>
    <param-value>app</param-value>
  </init-param>
</servlet>
```

Any command-line input or output is written as follows:

```
Welcome to Apache Felix Gogo

g! help
```

New terms and **important words** are shown in bold. Words that you see on the screen, in menus or dialog boxes for example, appear in the text like this: "Right-click on the **Server** tab and select **New | Server**".

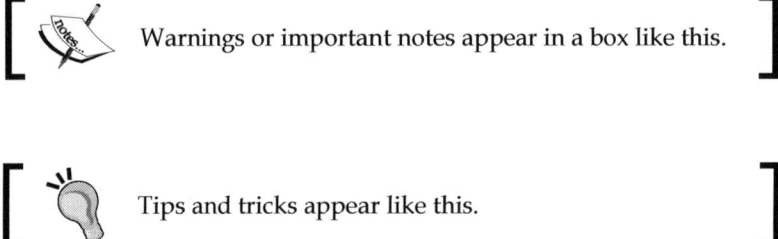

Warnings or important notes appear in a box like this.

Tips and tricks appear like this.

Reader feedback

Feedback from our readers is always welcome. Let us know what you think about this book—what you liked or may have disliked. Reader feedback is important for us to develop titles that you really get the most out of.

To send us general feedback, simply send an e-mail to feedback@packtpub.com, and mention the book title via the subject of your message.

If there is a book that you need and would like to see us publish, please send us a note in the **SUGGEST A TITLE** form on www.packtpub.com or e-mail suggest@packtpub.com.

If there is a topic that you have expertise in and you are interested in either writing or contributing to a book, see our author guide on www.packtpub.com/authors.

Customer support

Now that you are the proud owner of a Packt book, we have a number of things to help you to get the most from your purchase.

Downloading the example code for this book

You can download the example code files for all Packt books you have purchased from your account at http://www.PacktPub.com. If you purchased this book elsewhere, you can visit http://www.PacktPub.com/support and register to have the files e-mailed directly to you.

Errata

Although we have taken every care to ensure the accuracy of our content, mistakes do happen. If you find a mistake in one of our books—maybe a mistake in the text or the code—we would be grateful if you would report this to us. By doing so, you can save other readers from frustration and help us improve subsequent versions of this book. If you find any errata, please report them by visiting http://www.packtpub.com/support, selecting your book, clicking on the **errata submission form** link, and entering the details of your errata. Once your errata are verified, your submission will be accepted and the errata will be uploaded on our website, or added to any list of existing errata, under the Errata section of that title. Any existing errata can be viewed by selecting your title from http://www.packtpub.com/support.

Piracy

Piracy of copyright material on the Internet is an ongoing problem across all media. At Packt, we take the protection of our copyright and licenses very seriously. If you come across any illegal copies of our works, in any form, on the Internet, please provide us with the location address or website name immediately so that we can pursue a remedy.

Please contact us at copyright@packtpub.com with a link to the suspected pirated material.

We appreciate your help in protecting our authors, and our ability to bring you valuable content.

Questions

You can contact us at questions@packtpub.com if you are having a problem with any aspect of the book, and we will do our best to address it.

1
Vaadin and its context

Developing Java applications and more specifically, developing Java web applications should be fun. Instead, most projects are a mess of sweat and toil, pressure and delays, costs and cost cutting. Web development has lost its appeal. Yet, among the many frameworks available, there is one in particular that draws our attention because of its ease of use and its original stance. It has been around since the past decade and has begun to grow in importance. The name of this framework is **Vaadin**. The goal of this book is to see, step-by-step, how to develop web applications with Vaadin.

 Vaadin is the Finnish word for a female reindeer. This piece of information will do marvels to your social life as you are now one of the few people on Earth who know this (outside Finland).

We are going to see Vaadin in detail in later chapters; the following is a preview of what it is:

- A component-based approach that really works, and provides a bunch of out-of-the-box components
- Full web compatibility, in addition to Google Web Toolkit
- All development is made completely in Java
- Integration with Eclipse and NetBeans IDEs
- And much, much more

Before diving right into Vaadin, it is important to understand what led to its creation. Readers who already have this information (or who don't care) should go directly to *Chapter 2, Environment Setup*.

In this chapter, we will look into the following:

- The evolution from mainframe toward the rich client
  - ° The concept of application tier
  - ° The many limits of the thin-client approach
  - ° What stands beyond those limits
- Why choose Vaadin today?
  - ° The state of the market
  - ° Vaadin's place in the market
  - ° A preview of what other frameworks Vaadin can be integrated with and what platforms it can run on

Rich applications

Vaadin is often referred to as a **Rich Internet Application (RIA)**. Before explaining why, we need to first define some terms which will help us describe the framework. In particular, we will have a look at application tiers, the different kind of clients and their history.

Application tiers

Some software run locally, that is, on the client machine and some run remotely, such as on a server machine. Some applications also run on both the client and the server. For example, when requesting an article from a website, we interact with a browser on our client but the order itself is passed on a server.

Traditionally, all applications can be logically separated into tiers, each having different responsibilities as follows:

- **Presentation**: The presentation tier is responsible for displaying the end-user information and interaction. It is the realm of the user interface.
- **Business Logic**: The logic tier is responsible for controlling the application logic and functionality. It is also known as the application tier, or the middle tier as it is the glue between the other two surrounding tiers, thus leading to the term middleware.
- **Data**: The data tier is responsible for storing and retrieving data. This backend may be a file system. In most cases, it is a database, whether relational, flat, or even an object-oriented one.

This categorization not only naturally corresponds to specialized features, but also allows you to physically separate your system into different parts, so that you can change a tier with reduced impact on adjacent tiers and no impact on non-adjacent tiers.

Tiers migration

In the history of computers and computer software, these three tiers have moved back and forth between the server and the client.

Mainframes

When computers were mainframes, all tiers were handled by the server. Mainframes stored data, processed it, and were also responsible for the layout of the presentation. Clients were dumb terminals, suited only for displaying characters on the screen and accepting the user input.

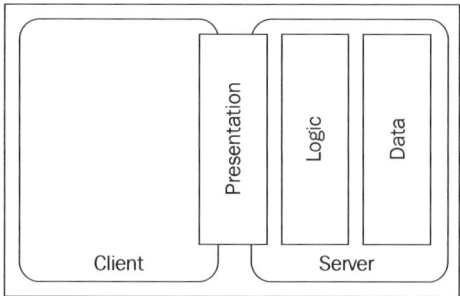

Client server

Not many companies could afford the acquisition of a mainframe (and many still cannot). Yet, those same companies could not do without computers at all, because the growing complexity of business processes needed automation. This development in personal computers led to a decrease in their cost. With the need to share data between them, the network traffic rose.

This period in history saw the rise of the personal computer, as well as the **Client server** term, as there was now a true client. The presentation and logic tier moved locally, while shared databases were remotely accessible, as shown in the following diagram:

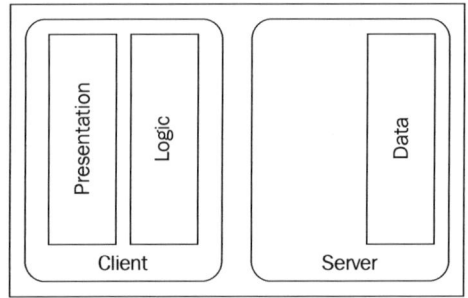

Thin clients

The big enterprises migrating from mainframes to fat clients thought that deploying software on ten client machines at the same site was relatively easy and could be done in a few hours. However, they quickly became aware of the fact that with the number of machines growing in a multi-site business, it could quickly become a nightmare.

Enterprises also found that it was not only the development phase that had to be managed like a project, but also the installation phase. When upgrading either the client or the server, you most likely found that the installation time was high, which in turn led to downtime and that led to additional business costs.

It was some time ago that Sir Tim Berners-Lee invented the **Hyper Text Markup Language**, better known as **HTML**. Some people considered tweaking its original use, which is to navigate between documents, to make web applications. This solved the deployment problem as the logic tier was run on a single-server node (or a cluster), and each client connected to this server. A deployment could be done in a matter of minutes, at worst overnight, which was a huge improvement. The presentation layer was still hosted on the client, with the browser responsible for displaying the user interface and handling user interaction.

This new approach brought new terms, which are as follows:

- The old client-server architecture was now referred to as **fat client**
- The new architecture was coined as **thin client**:

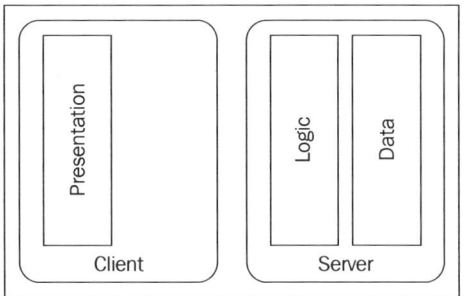

Limitations of the thin-client applications approach

Unfortunately, this evolution was made for financial reasons and did not take into account some very important drawbacks of the thin client.

Poor choice of controls

HTML does not support many controls, and what is available is not on par with fat client technologies. Consider, for example, the list box: in any fat client, choices displayed to the user can be filtered according to what is typed in the control. In HTML, there's no such feature and all lines are displayed in all cases. This is a usability disaster if you need to display the list of countries (more than 200 entries!). As such, ergonomics of true thin clients have nothing to do with their fat client ancestors.

Many unrelated technologies

Developers of fat client applications have only to learn two languages: SQL and the technology's language, such as Visual Basic, Java, and so on.

Web developers, on the contrary, have to learn an entire stack of technologies, both on the client side and on the server side.

On the client side, the following are the requirements:

- First, of course, is HTML. It is the basis of all web applications, and although some do not consider it a language per se, every web developer must learn it so that they can create content to be displayed by browsers.

- In order to apply some sense of unity into your application, one will probably have to learn the **Cascading Style Sheets (CSS)** technology. CSS is available in three main versions, each version being more or less supported by browser version combinations (see Browser compatibility).

- Most of the time, it is nice to have some interactivity on the client side, like pop-up windows or others. In this case, we will need a scripting technology such as **ECMAScript**.

ECMAScript is the real name of JavaScript, standardized by the ECMA organization. See `http://www.ecma-international.org/publications/standards/Ecma-262.htm` for more information on the subject

- Finally, one will probably need to update the structure of the HTML page, a healthy dose of knowledge of the **Document Object Model (DOM)** is necessary.

As a side note, consider that HTML, CSS, and DOM are W3C specifications and ECMAScript is an ECMA standard.

From a Java point-of-view and on the server side, the following are the requirements:

- As servlets are the basis of all human user interactions in Java EE, every developer worth his salt has to know both the Servlet specification and the Servlet API.

- Moreover, most web applications tend to enforce the Model-View-Controller paradigm. As such, the Java EE specification enforces the use of servlets for controllers and **JavaServer Pages (JSP)** for views. As JSP are intended to be templates, developers who create JSP have an additional syntax to learn, even though they offer the same features as servlets.

- JSP accept scriptlets, that is Java code snippets, but good coding practices tend to frown upon this as Java code can contain any feature, including some that should not be part of views—database access code for example. Therefore, a completely new technology stack is proposed in order to limit code included in JSP: the Tag libraries. These tag libraries also have a specification and API, and that is another stack to learn.

However, these are a few of the standard requirements that you should know in order to develop web applications in Java. Most of the time, in order to boost developer productivity, one has to use frameworks. These frameworks are available in most of the previously cited technologies. Some of them are supported by Oracle, such as Java Server Faces, others are open source, such as Struts.

Knowing so much has negative effects, a few are as follows:

- On the technical side, as web developers have to manage so many different technologies, web development is more complex than fat-client development, potentially leading to more bugs

- On the human resources side, different meant either different profiles were required or more resources, either way it added to the complexity of human resource management

- On the project management side, increased complexity caused lengthier projects: developing a web application was potentially taking longer than developing a fat client application

All of these factors tend to make the thin client development cost much more than fat-client, albeit the deployment cost was close to zero.

Browser compatibility

The Web is governed by standards, most of them upheld by the World Wide Web Consortium. Browsers more or less implement these standards, depending on the vendor and the version. The ACID test, now in version 3, is a test for browser compatibility with web standards. The following summary speaks for itself:

Browser	Version	Score
Google Chrome	5.0	100
Apple Safari	4.0	100
Mozilla Firefox	4.0	97
Internet Explorer	9.0	95
Mozilla Firefox	3.6	94
Netscape Navigator	9.0	52
Internet Explorer	6.0	12

Some browsers even make the standards evolve, such as Microsoft which implemented the XmlHttpRequest object in Internet Explorer and thus formed the basis for Ajax.

One should be aware of the combination of the platform, browser, and version. As some browsers cannot be installed with different versions on the same platform, testing can quickly become a mess (which can fortunately be mitigated with virtual machines). Applications should be developed with browser combinations in mind, and then tested in order to ensure application compatibility.

For intranet applications, the number of supported browsers is normally limited. For Internet applications, however, most common combinations must be supported in order to increase availability. If this wasn't enough, then the same browser in the same version may run differently on different operating systems. At least one such difference has been detected by the Vaadin team when running Firefox 3.0.0 on Linux/OSX/Windows.

In all cases, each combination has an exponential impact on the application's complexity, and therefore, on cost.

Page flow paradigm

Fat-client applications manage windows. Most of the time, there's a main window. Actions are mainly performed in this main window, even if sometimes managed windows or pop-up windows are used.

As web applications are browser-based and use HTML over HTTP, things are managed differently. In this case, the presentation unit is not the window but the page. This is a big difference that entails a performance problem: indeed, each time the user clicks on a submit button, the request is sent to the server, processed by it, and the HTML response is sent back to the client.

For example, when a client submits a complex registration form, the entire page is recreated on the server side and sent back to the browser even if there is a minor validation error, even though the required changes to the registration form would have been minimal.

Beyond the limits

Over the last few years, users have been applying some pressure in order to have user interfaces that offer the same richness as good old fat-client applications. IT managers, however, are unwilling to go back to the old deploy-as-a-project routine and its associated costs and complexity. They push towards the same deployment process as thin-client applications. It is no surprise that there are different solutions in order to solve this dilemma.

What are rich clients?

All the following solutions are globally called rich clients, even if the approach differs. They have something in common though: all of them want to retain the ease of deployment of the thin-client and solve some or all of the problems mentioned above.

Rich clients fulfill the fourth quadrant of the following schema, which is like a dream come true, as shown in the following diagram:

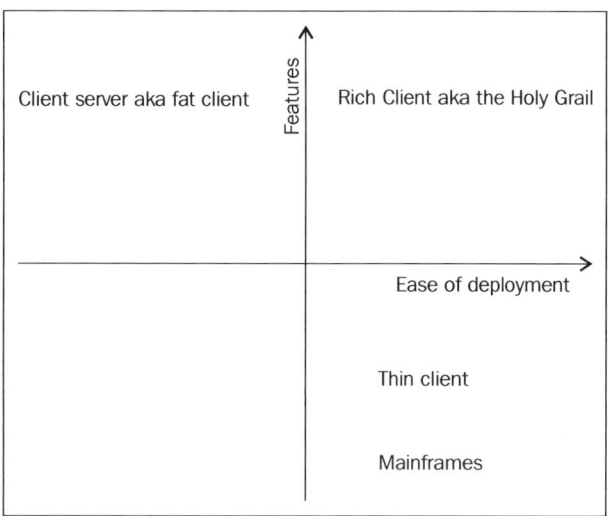

Some rich client approaches

The following solutions are strategies that deserve the rich client label.

Ajax

Ajax was one of the first successful rich-client solutions. The term means **Asynchronous JavaScript with XML**. In effect, this browser technology enables sending asynchronous requests. When receiving the response, the handling script manipulates the DOM representing the web page according to the data in the response, and updates parts of the former.

Ajax addresses the richness of controls and the page flow paradigm. Unfortunately:

- It aggravates browser-compatibility problems as Ajax is not done the same way in all browsers.
- It has problems unrelated directly to the technologies, which are as follows:
  - Either, one learns all the necessary technologies to do Ajax on its own, that is, JavaScript, Document Object Model, and JSON/XML, to communicate with the server and write all common features such as error handling from scratch.
  - Alternatively, one uses an Ajax framework, and thus, one has to learn another technology stack.

Richness through a plugin

The oldest way to bring richness to the user's experience is to execute the code on the client side and more specifically, in the browser's plugin. Sun—now Oracle—proposed the applet technology, whereas Microsoft proposed ActiveX. The latest technology using this strategy is Flash.

Both were commercial failures due to technical problems, including performance lags, security holes, and plain-client incompatibility.

There is an interesting try to revive the applet with the Apache Pivot project, as shown in the following screenshot (`http://pivot.apache.org/`), but it hasn't made a huge impact yet.

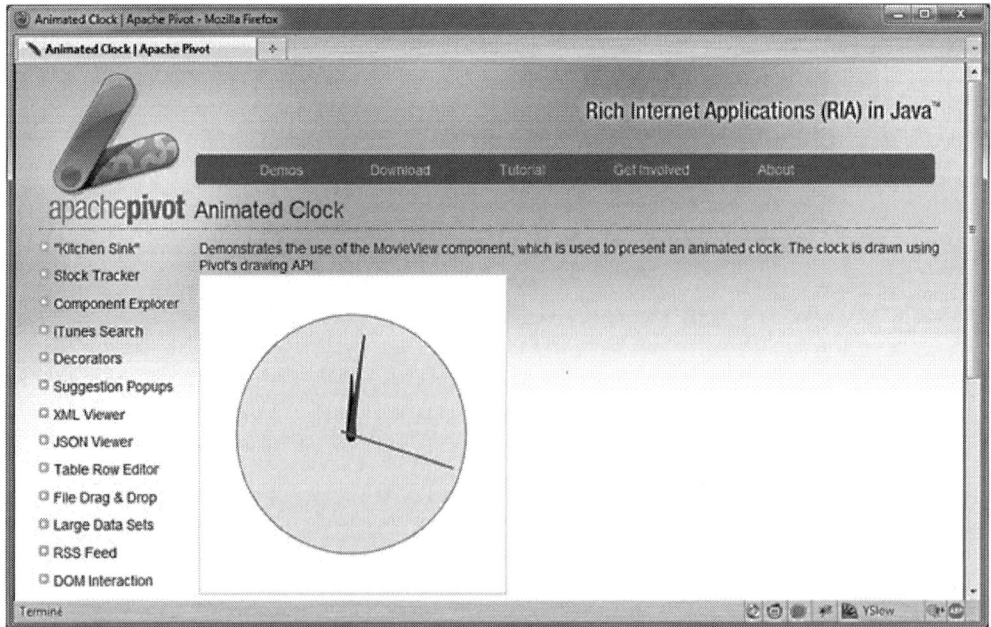

A more recent and successful attempt at executing code on the client side through a plugin is through Adobe's Flex. A similar path was taken by Microsoft's Silverlight technology.

Flex is a technology where static views are described in XML and dynamic behavior in ActionScript. Both are transformed at compile time in Flash format. As the penetration rate for the Flash plugin was found to be near 99% in March 2011. See `http://www.adobe.com/products/player_census/flashplayer/`. Flex is one of the de facto standards for rich-client applications. Readers wanting more information on this technology should read *Flex 3 with Java, Satish Kore, Packt Publishing.* `https://www.packtpub.com/flex-3-with-java/book`

Deploying and updating fat-client from the web

The most direct way toward rich-client applications is to deploy (and update) a fat-client application from the web.

Java Web Start

Java Web Start (JWS), available at `http://download.oracle.com/javase/1.5.0/docs/guide/javaws/`, is a proprietary technology invented by Sun. It uses a deployment descriptor in **Java Network Launching Protocol (JNLP)** that takes the place of the manifest inside a JAR file and supplements it. For example, it describes the main class to launch, the classpath, and also additional information such as the minimum Java version, icons to display on the user desktop, and so on.

This descriptor file is used by the `javaws` executable, which is bundled in the Java Runtime Environment. It is `javaws`'s responsibility to read the JNLP file and do the right thing according to it. In particular, when launched, `javaws` will download the updated JAR.

The detailed process goes something like the following:

1. The user clicks on a JNLP file
2. The JNLP file is downloaded on the user machine, and interpreted by the local `javaws` application
3. The file references JARs that `javaws` can download

4. Once downloaded, JWS reassembles the different parts, creates the classpath, and launches the main class described in the JNLP

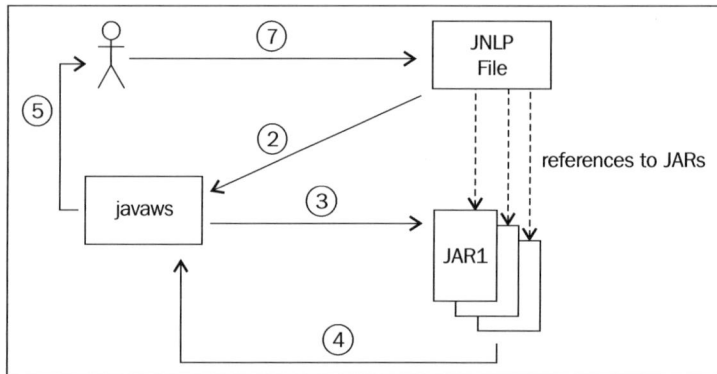

JWS correctly tackles all problems posed by the thin-client approach. Yet, it never reaches critical mass for a number of reasons:

- First time installations are time-consuming because typically lots of megabytes need to be transferred on the wire before the users can even start using the app. This is a mere annoyance for Intranet applications, but a complete no go for Internet apps.
- Some persistent bugs weren't fixed across major versions.
- Finally, the lack of commercial commitment by Sun was the final straw.

A good example of a successful JWS application is JDiskReport (`http://www.jgoodies.com/download/jdiskreport/jdiskreport.jnlp`), a disk space analysis tool by Karsten Lentzsch, which is available on the Web for free.

Update sites

Updating software through update sites is a path taken by both **Integrated Development Environment (IDE)** leaders, NetBeans and Eclipse. In short, once the software is initially installed, updates and new features can be downloaded from the application itself.

Both IDEs also propose an API to build applications.

This approach also handles all problems posed by the thin-client approach. However, like JWS, there's no strong trend to build applications based on these IDEs. This can probably be attributed to both IDEs using the OSGI standard whose goal is to address some of Java's shortcomings but at the price of complexity.

Google Web Toolkit

Google Web Toolkit (GWT) is the framework used by Google to create its own applications, such as Wave. Its point of view is very unique among the technologies presented here. It lets you develop in Java, and then the GWT compiler transforms your code to JavaScript, which in turn generates HTML. It's GWT's responsibility to handle browser compatibility. This approach also solves the other problems of the pure thin-client approach.

Yet, GWT does not shield developers from all the dirty details. In particular, the developer still has to write the code to handle the server-client communication, and he has to deal with DOM manipulation through JavaScript.

Why Vaadin?

Vaadin is a solution evolved from a decade of problem-solving approach, provided by a Finnish company named Vaadin, formerly IT Mill.

Therefore, having so many solutions available, one could question the use Vaadin instead of Flex or GWT? Let's first have a look at the state of the market for web application frameworks in Java, then detail what makes Vaadin so unique in this market.

State of the market

Despite all the cons of the thin-client approach, an important share of applications developed today uses this paradigm, most of the time with a touch of Ajax augmentation.

Unfortunately, there is no clear leader for web applications. Some reasons include the following:

- Flex would be a good candidate, as the technology is mature and Adobe a commercial force to be reckoned with, but Apple did not add the Flash player to its iOS platforms. Thus, surfing mobile with these devices cuts you from Flex content.

- Most developers know how to develop plain old web applications, with enough Ajax added in order to make them usable by users.

- GWT, although new and original, is still complex and needs seasoned developers in order to be effective.

From a Technical Lead or an IT Manager's point of view, this is a very fragmented market where it is hard to choose a solution that will meet users' requirements as well as offering guarantees to be maintained in the years to come.

Importance of Vaadin

Vaadin is a unique framework in the current ecosystem; its differentiating features include the following:

- There is no need to learn different technology stacks, as the coding is solely in Java. The only thing to know beside Java is Vaadin's own API, which is easy to learn. This means:
    - The UI code is fully object-oriented
    - There's no spaghetti JavaScript to maintain
    - Furthermore, the IDE's full power is in our hands with refactoring and code completion

- No plugin to install on the client's browser, ensuring all users that browse our application will be able to use it "as is".

- As Vaadin uses GWT under the cover, it supports all browsers that GWT also supports. Therefore, we can develop a Vaadin application without paying attention to the browsers and let GWT handle the differences. Our users will interact with our application in the same way, whether they use an outdated version (such as Firefox 3.5), or a niche browser (like Opera).

- Moreover, Vaadin uses an abstraction over GWT so that, in theory, you can use another rendering engine, even Swing! This architecture works toward alleviating risks of GWT becoming a closed source in the future and the Vaadin team is committed to open source.

- Finally, Vaadin conforms to standards such as HTML and CSS, making the technology future proof. For example, many applications created with Vaadin run seamlessly on mobile devices although they were not initially designed to do so.

Vaadin's integration

In today's environment, integration features of a framework are very important as normally every enterprise has rules about which framework is to be used in some context. Vaadin is about the presentation layer and runs on any servlet container capable environment.

Integrated frameworks

A whole chapter (see *Chapter 9, Integration with Third-party Products*) is dedicated to the details of how Vaadin can be integrated with some third-party frameworks and tools. There are three integration levels possible which are as follows:

- Level 1: out-of-the-box or available through an add-on, no effort required save reading the documentation
- Level 2: more or less documented
- Level 3: possible with effort

The following are examples of such frameworks and tools with their respective integration estimated effort:

- **Level 1**:
  - ° **Java Persistence API (JPA)**: JPA is the Java EE 5 standard for all things related to persistence. An add-on exists that lets us wire existing components to a JPA backend. Other persistence add-ons are available in the Vaadin directory, such as a container for Hibernate, one of the leading persistence frameworks available in the Java ecosystem.
  - ° A bunch of widget add-ons, such as tree tables, popup buttons, contextual menus, and many more.

- **Level 2**:
  - ° Spring is a framework which is based on **Inversion of Control (IoC)** that is the de facto standard for Dependency Injection. Spring can easily be integrated with Vaadin, and different strategies are available for this. We will see those strategies in detail in *Chapter 9*.
  - ° **Context Dependency Injection (CDI)**: CDI is an attempt at making IoC a standard on the Java EE platform. Whatever can be done with Spring can be done with CDI.
  - ° Any GWT extensions such as Ext-GWT or Smart GWT can easily be integrated in Vaadin as Vaadin is built upon GWT's own widgets. This will be seen in complete detail in *Chapter 8, Creating Custom Components* where we will create such new components.

- **Level 3**:
  - ° We can use another entirely new persistence framework such as Apache iBatis, and integrate it with Vaadin.

Integration platforms

Vaadin provides an out-of-the-box integration with two important third-party platforms:

- Liferay is an open source enterprise portal backed by Liferay Inc. Vaadin provides a specialized portlet that enables us to develop Vaadin applications as portlets that can be run on Liferay.

- **Google Application Engine (GAE)**: Google provides us with limited Java EE hosting in the cloud. Pricing depends on many factors, but suffice to say that basic levels are available for free, making GAE an environment of choice for deploying test applications. Like Liferay, a specialized servlet takes care of all gruesome details, letting us deploy our Vaadin application on GAE.

Using Vaadin in the real world

If you embrace Vaadin, then chances are that you will want to go beyond toying with the Vaadin framework and develop real-world applications.

Concerns about using a new technology

Although it is okay to use the latest technology for a personal or academic project, projects that have business objectives should just run and not be riddled with problems from third-party products. In particular, most managers are very wary when confronted by a new product (or even a new version), and developers should be too.

The following are some of the reasons to be cautious of new technologies, and why they don't apply to Vaadin:

- Product being bug-ridden: The Vaadin team has done rigorous testing throughout their automated build process. Currently, it consists of more than 8,000 unit tests. Moreover, in order to guarantee full compatibility between versions, some tests include pixel-level regression testing.

- Lack of support:
    - Commercial: Although completely committed to open source, Vaadin Limited offer commercial support for their product. Check their Pro Account offering.

- ° User forums: A Vaadin user forum is available. Anyone registered can post questions and see them answered by a member of the team or of the community.

 Note that Vaadin registration is free, as well as hassle-free: you will just be sent the newsletter once a month.

- Incompatible changes from version to version:
    - ° API: The server-side API is very stable, version after version, and has survived major client-engines rewrite.
    - ° Architecture: Vaadin's architecture favors abstraction and is at the root of it all.

- No documentation available:
    - ° Product documentation: Vaadin's site provides three levels of documentation regarding Vaadin: a 5-minute tutorial, a one-hour tutorial, and the famed Book of Vaadin.
    - ° Tutorials
    - ° API documentation: The Javadocs are available online; there is no need to build the project locally.

- No course/webinar offerings: Vaadin Ltd currently provides four different courses, which tackle all the needed skills for a developer to be proficient in the framework.

- Absence of community around the product: There is a community gathering, which is ever growing and actively using the product. There are plenty of blogs and articles online on Vaadin. Furthermore, there are already many enterprises using Vaadin for their applications.

- Lack of competent resources: There are more and more people learning Vaadin. Moreover, if no developer is available, the framework can be learnt in a few days.

- No integration with existing product/platforms: Vaadin is built to be easily integrated with other products and platforms. The Book of Vaadin describes how to integrate with Liferay and Google App Engine.

More reasons

Vaadin has answers for each of the previous concerns, but management's fears mainly focus around Vaadin being new and that the enterprise will be the first to experience bugs.

Vaadin is 10 years old

The latest version of Vaadin, at the time of this writing, is 6.7. It shouldn't be considered the latest trend, but managers being managers, they will probably check and double-check, just in case. Doing that, they will encounter no prior version! Does it mean that Vaadin 6 was the first version? The answer is yes, but only because of a name change.

In fact, the following are the major steps in the history of Vaadin:

- At first, a Finnish company named IT Mill created applications for their customers. In order to be more productive, they developed a framework. In 2001, the first internal version was ready.
- In 2002, they released it to the public under the name Millstone 3 and with an open source license.
- In 2005, Millstone 3 was deemed too static and enhanced with Ajax features built on top of it. The client-side engine was rewritten, as well as the server-side API (the latter looks like the one available today and has only marginally changed since this version).
- In 2006, there was another major change on the client side in order to blend in Ajax features. It was released as the IT Mill Toolkit 4. However, it included a lot of proprietary JavaScript and was difficult to extend.
- In 2007, the choice was made to remove those proprietary implementations and instead run on top of GWT. This led to a complete client side rewriting and the release of IT Mill Toolkit 5.
- In 2009, IT Mill released the sixth version of the toolkit and changed its name to Vaadin.
- Finally, in 2010, Vaadin overshadowed IT Mill in terms of public recognition and the company IT Mill was renamed Vaadin, confirming the company's long-term commitment to the product.

Others already use Vaadin

Upon reading this, managers and developers alike should realize Vaadin is mature and is used on real-world applications around the world. If you still have any doubts, then you should check `http://vaadin.com/who-is-using-vaadin` and be assured that big businesses trusted Vaadin before you.

Summary

In this chapter, we saw the migration of application tiers in the software architecture between the client and the server.

We saw that each step resolved the problems in the previous architecture:

- Client-server used the power of personal computers in order to decrease mainframe costs
- Thin clients resolved the deployment costs and delays

Thin clients have numerous drawbacks. For the user, a lack of usability due to poor choice of controls, browser compatibility issues, and the navigation based on page flow; for the developer, many technologies to know.

As we are at the crossroad, there is no clear winner in all the solutions available: some only address a few of the problems, some aggravate them.

Vaadin is an original solution that tries to resolve many problems at once:

- It provides rich controls
- It uses GWT under the cover that addresses most browser compatibility issues
- It has abstractions over the request response model, so that the model used is application-based and not page based
- The developer only needs to know one programming language: Java, and Vaadin generates all HTML, JavaScript, and CSS code for you

Now, we can go on and create our first Vaadin application!

2
Environment Setup

In this chapter, we will set up our IDE in order to ease the use of Vaadin and create new projects using this framework.

In particular, we will see how to:

- Download and install the right distribution of the IDE
- Check that your currently installed IDE is the right distribution
- Install the Vaadin plugin in your IDE
- Create a new Vaadin project using our now enhanced IDE

The first section is dedicated to Eclipse from the Eclipse Foundation, the second to the NetBeans from Oracle (formerly Sun).

Note that at the time of this writing, there is no support for IntelliJ IDEA. A ticket is open in the Vaadin's tracking system at http://dev.vaadin.com/ticket/4420. Users who strive to code with IntelliJ IDEA above all else should subscribe to this ticket; there is hope! Depending on your own personal taste, you can go directly to your preferred section and ignore the other one or browse both.

Finally, we will look at the configuration performed by the Vaadin plugin when we create a new Vaadin project if you want to configure your project in other IDEs or manually.

Vaadin in Eclipse

In order to add Vaadin capabilities to Eclipse IDE, we will first need to have the Web Tools Platform (or WTP for short). Eclipse's WTP concerns itself with all that is centered on web standards in the Java ecosystem: servlets, JSP, HTML, JavaScript, and so on. As everything is a plugin in Eclipse, WTP itself is available as a collection of plugins.

Setting up Eclipse

If you already have Eclipse installed on your system, chances are that it already contains WTP and its dependencies. If not, you could want to start from scratch and install an Eclipse bundled with WTP (*aka* Eclipse for Java EE developers) or just have WTP and its dependencies added to your existing installation.

 Note that the recommended way is to install the complete Java EE bundle, not only because it is recommended by Vaadin but also because manual handling of WTP dependencies can be a bore.

When Eclipse is not installed

A more straightforward way to download an Eclipse bundled with WTP is to go to the Eclipse downloads website at `http://www.eclipse.org/downloads/` and choose Eclipse IDE for Java EE Developers. The exact URL changes with each Eclipse major release. At the time of this writing, it references the Indigo (Eclipse 3.7) release: `http://www.eclipse.org/downloads/packages/eclipse-ide-java-ee-developers/indigor`.

 Astute readers will note, and rightly so, that the "Eclipse IDE for Java EE Developers" distribution contains much more than simply the Eclipse IDE and WTP; EJB features for example. Although those features are unnecessary, it is the simplest way to have the WTP features.

Now choose your OS carefully on the right panel of the screen and click on the proposed distribution site, as shown in the following screenshot:

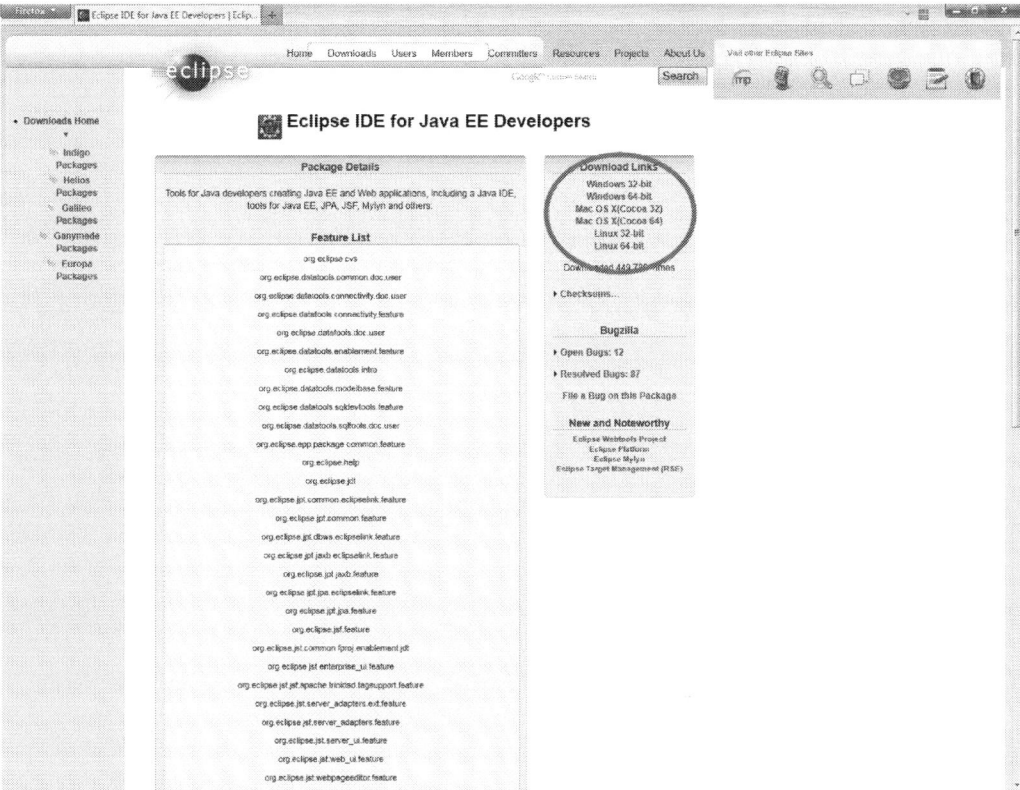

Installing the Vaadin plugin

Carry out the following steps:

1. In Eclipse, go to the **Help menu | Install new software**.

2. Click on the **Add** button. You will be presented with a dialog prompting you for a name and an update site's location. So, type `Vaadin` in the first field and `http://vaadin.com/eclipse` in the second.

Naturally, you can name the update site any way you choose, prudence would suggest you make this name relevant.

3. Click on **Next** and complete the wizard as follows:

    ° Select the Vaadin item: It should include both **Book of Vaadin** and **Vaadin plug-in for Eclipse** (the former being Vaadin's documentation), as shown in the following screenshot:

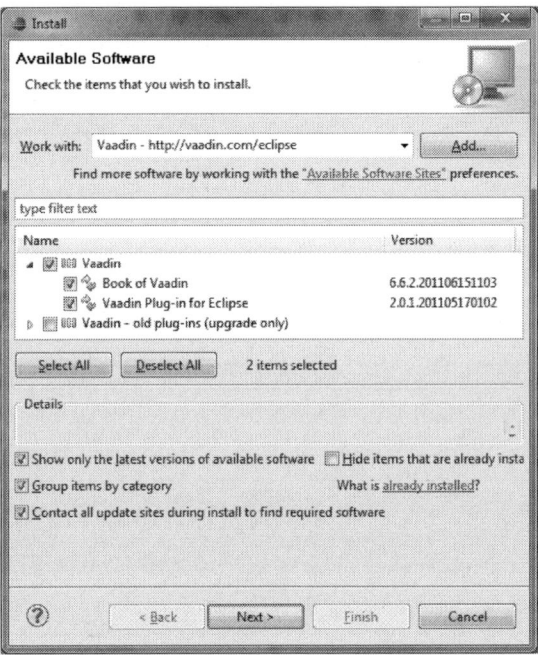

    ° Review the choices

    ° Accept the terms of the license agreement

    ° Finally restart Eclipse in order to have the Vaadin features

4. Now, we can check the installed features: go to the menu **Help | About Eclipse**. The opening pop up should display the Vaadin logo, as shown in the following screenshot:

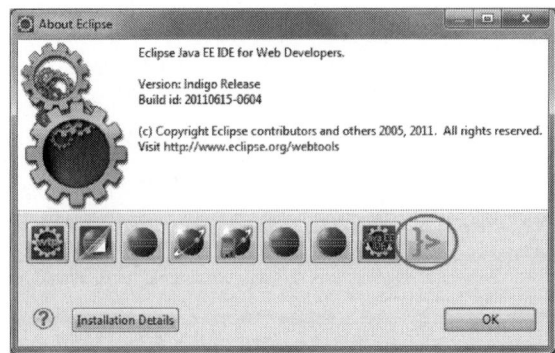

Troubleshooting

If Vaadin does not appear in the plugins list, then restart Eclipse.

Congratulations, now we have completed the IDE setup. It is now time to create our first Vaadin project!

Creating a server runtime

Before creating the project itself, we need a server to run it on. Therefore, carry out the following steps:

1. On the **Server** tab, right-click and select **New Server**. The following screen should then pop up:

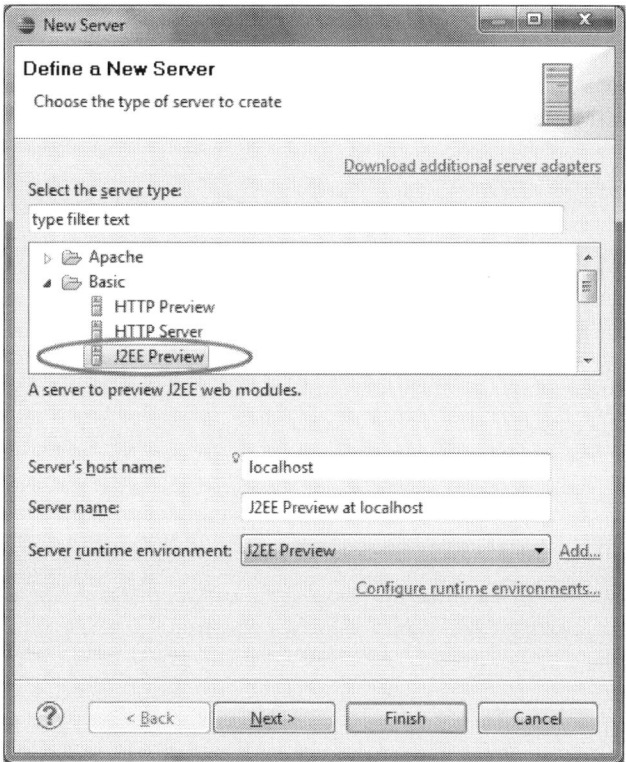

5. On the opening window, select **J2EE Preview**, as it is the simplest server Vaadin can run on. Click on **Finish** and the newly created server should appear in the **Server** tab.

Creating our first Eclipse Vaadin project

Carry out the following steps:

1. Go to the menu **File | New | Vaadin Project**.
2. Set the project name as you wish, `MyFirstVaadinApp` for example.
3. Choose the previously created J2EE preview as the target runtime.
4. We will update the configuration slightly (those are Eclipse facets for Eclipse experts): click on **Modify**. A pop up opens with the following options:
   - ° Check Dynamic Web Module and choose **2.5**
   - ° Check Java and choose **1.6**
   - ° Check Vaadin

 If you followed the previous instructions, then all three components should be checked from the start. The only thing to do is to select the right version.

   - ° Click on the **OK** button.

5. Now let's get back to our previous window. Keep **Servlet (default)** for the server configuration. The Vaadin version should be set to the latest stable release by default. The steps are depicted in the following screenshot:

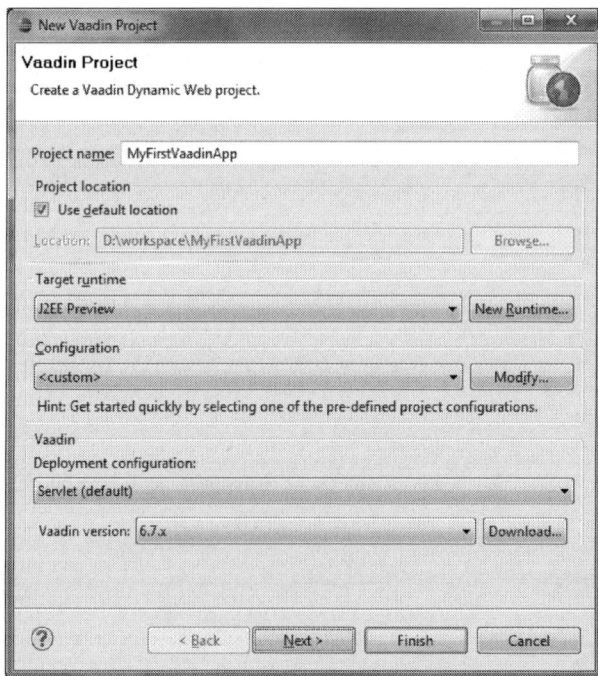

6. Click on the **Next** button. On the Java step, keep the source and the build folders as they are and click on **Next**.

7. On the Web Module step, change the context root to `myfirstvaadinapp` and click on **Next**.

 Context roots are used to separate multiple web applications installed in the same servlet container and accessible on the same port.

8. In the last step, change the values as follow:
   - `My First Vaadin Application` for the Application name
   - `com.packt.learnvaadin` for the Base package name
   - `MyApplication` for the Application class name

9. Finally, click on **Finish**. The project should look something similar to the one shown on the following screenshot in the **Project Explorer** Tab, when expanded:

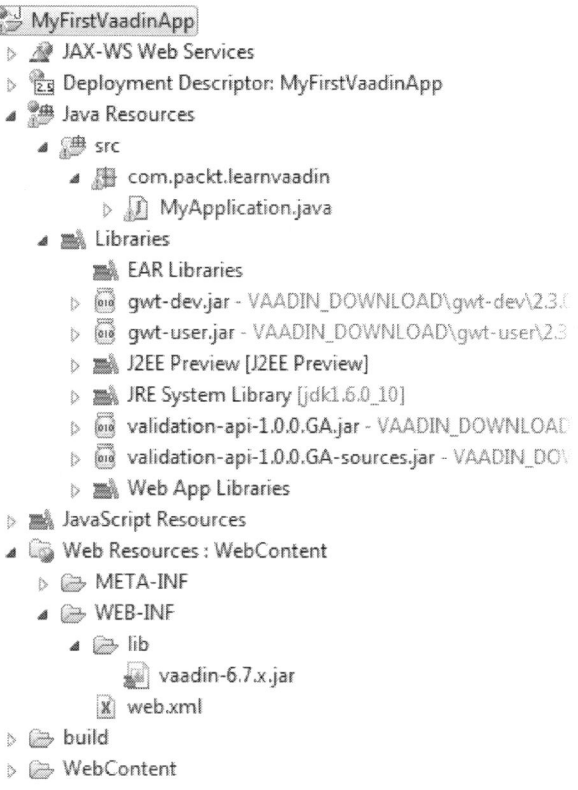

Note that although Eclipse adds a bunch of libraries, Vaadin does not need JAX-WS Web Services, EAR libraries nor JavaScript resources. These can be safely removed from the project classpath, even though they are provided by default.

There is one last action to complete our project. Open the `web.xml` deployment descriptor and search for `servlet-mapping`:

```
<servlet-mapping>
  <servlet-name>My First Vaadin Application</servlet-name>
  <url-pattern>/*</url-pattern>
</servlet-mapping>
```

Downloading the example code for this book

You can download the example code files for all Packt books you have purchased from your account at http://www.PacktPub.com. If you purchased this book elsewhere, you can visit http://www.PacktPub.com/support and register to have the files e-mailed directly to you.

In order to be fully generic:

- Change the URL pattern from `/*` to `/app/*` as follows:

```
<servlet-mapping>
  <servlet-name>My First Vaadin Application</servlet-name>
  <url-pattern>/app/*</url-pattern>
</servlet-mapping>
```

- Add the `/VAADIN/*` mapping as follows:

```
<servlet-mapping>
  <servlet-name>My First Vaadin Application</servlet-name>
  <url-pattern>/VAADIN/*</url-pattern>
</servlet-mapping>
```

The rationale behind these changes can be found later in the *Declaring the servlet mapping* section in this chapter.

Testing our application

Finally, select the project, right-click and on the contextual menu, select **Run As | Run on Server**.

It should display a welcome message for us in Eclipse's internal browser, as shown in the following screenshot:

That is it. Congratulations, your first project just runs!

Alternatives

There are a few alternatives in the process we have just seen. The first approach consists of using a vendor-specific distribution, the second of adding the Web Tools Project plugin to an existing distribution devoid of it.

Vendor-specific distribution

Some vendors provide distribution, which contains WTP along some of its specific plugins in one big download package.

Spring Source, which is the provider of the well-known Spring framework gives away such a distribution. It is known as the **Spring Source Tools Suite** (or **STS** for short). STS is free—but not open source—provided you first register yourself and accept the license terms. The download is available, at the time of this writing, from the following URL:

```
http://www.springsource.com/landing/best-development-tool-enterprise-
java.
```

 Choosing STS is the right choice if you also intend to use Spring intensively with Vaadin (or without for that matter) or Cloud Foundry as will be seen in *Chapter 9, Integration with Third-party Products*. If in doubt, stick with Eclipse and WTP, plugins are also available to help with the Spring development.

When Eclipse is already installed

If you already have Eclipse installed and want to use this existing installation, then the first thing to do is to check whether WTP is present, as it is a dependency of the Vaadin plugin.

Checking if WTP is present

In order to check whether an Eclipse installation has WTP, you have to launch it and open the menu **Help | About Eclipse**. The pop up that opens will show some information along with an icon list. Check the **wtp** icon, as can be seen in the following screenshot, to know whether WTP is installed:

If you have WTP installed, then head back to the section named *Installing the Vaadin plugin* in this chapter, otherwise, please first follow the instructions in the following section.

Adding WTP to Eclipse

In Eclipse, adding additional features to the core is done through a two-step process, which is as follows:

1. Add an update site which is an URL that describes the deployment of additional components.

2. Use the update site to download and install them.

In order to add the WTP features to an existing Eclipse installation, we will first add an update site. As seen in the *Installing the Vaadin plugin* section in this chapter, go to the **Help menu | Install new software** and carry out the following steps:

1. Click on the **Add** button. You will be presented with a dialog prompting you for a name and an update site's location (as shown in the following screenshot). So, type WTP in the first field and `http://download.eclipse.org/webtools/repository/indigo/` in the second (the last part of the URL depending on the particular Eclipse release).

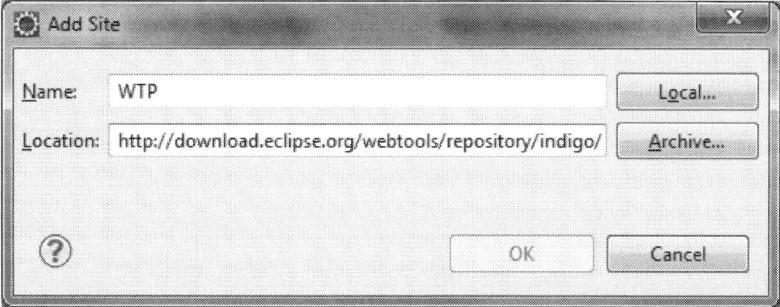

2. Clicking on **OK** will populate the preceding window. For the purpose of using Vaadin, we only need the latest version that does not include the SDK (at the time of this writing, it is Version 3.3.0).

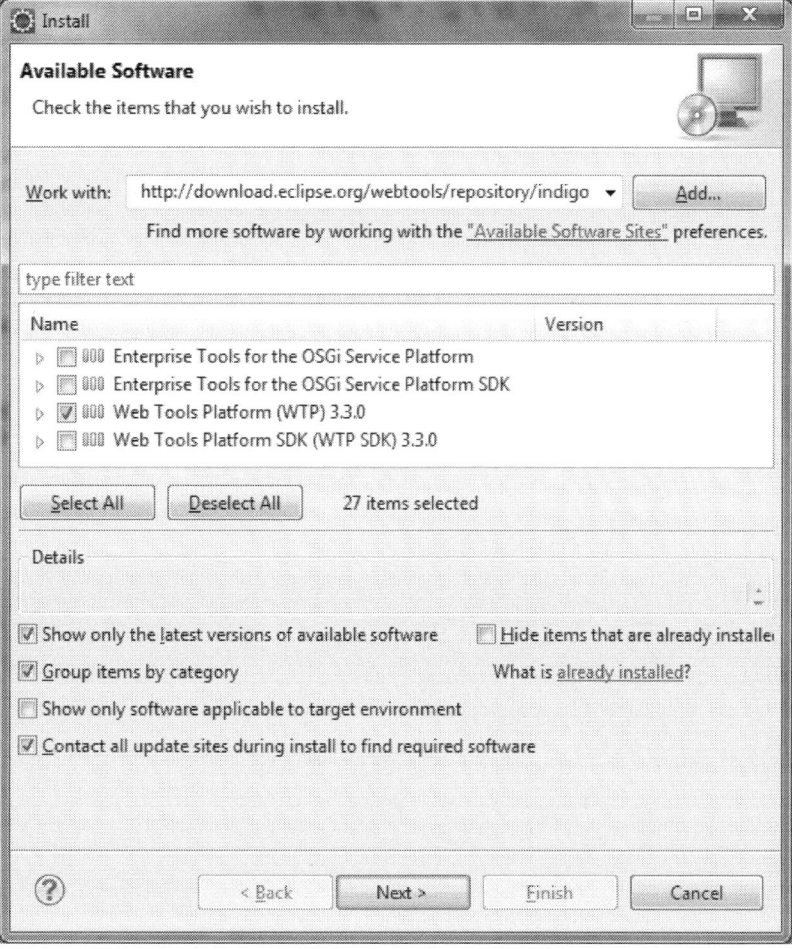

The SDK is only required when writing WTP plugins, which is not the case. The bare version is preferable as it is much lighter (thus, faster to download).

 Dependencies

Depending on the exact Eclipse installation and the precise WTP version, there may be some need to download additional WTP dependencies. As such, it is very important to select the option **Contact all update sites during install to find required software** to let Eclipse do just that.

3. Click on **Next** and complete the wizard as follows:
   - Review your choices
   - Accept the license agreement
   - Finally, restart Eclipse with our much wanted WTP features

4. Once restarted, you should see WTP installed as described in the preceding section named *Checking if WTP is present*.

 **Troubleshooting**

If WTP still does not appear in the plugins list or behaves strangely, then make sure to restart Eclipse. Using a freshly installed Eclipse without restarting may well have unpredicted side effects, such as leaving Eclipse in an unstable state. Therefore, it is a good practice to always restart it just after having installed a new plugin or a new version of the plugin.

Vaadin in NetBeans

If you do not intend to use NetBeans, then you can safely skip this NetBeans-specific part and go to the *Vaadin and other IDEs* section.

Setting up NetBeans

Like in Eclipse, there is a plugin available for NetBeans. This plugin is not provided by the Vaadin team, but personally by Geertjan Wielenga and Sami Ekblad (the latter from the Vaadin team). As such, we don't get to choose the version of Vaadin we want to use like in Eclipse, but it is set at 6.1.3. We will need to tweak this behavior a bit, as this is not the one we want.

At the time of this writing, the latest NetBeans version is 7.0. There are a few different distributions available. You can download them from the following URL:

```
http://netbeans.org/downloads/index.html
```

The distribution needed to create a Vaadin project, is the one named **Java EE** which provides servlet capabilities, as shown in the following screenshot:

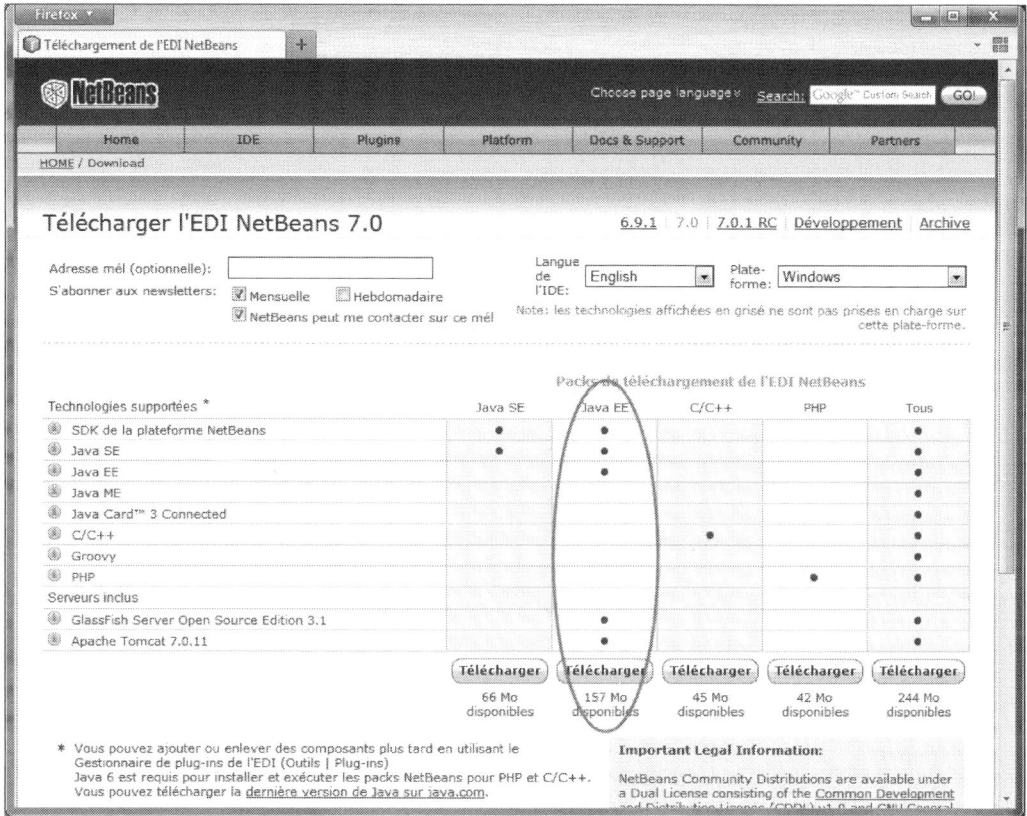

1. Install the product, choosing Tomcat 7.0.11, as shown in the following screenshot. We can safely replace the **GlassFish** Server by Tomcat, as Vaadin only needs a simple servlet container to run on. We can also keep GlassFish or install both; it all depends on one's personal taste regarding application servers.

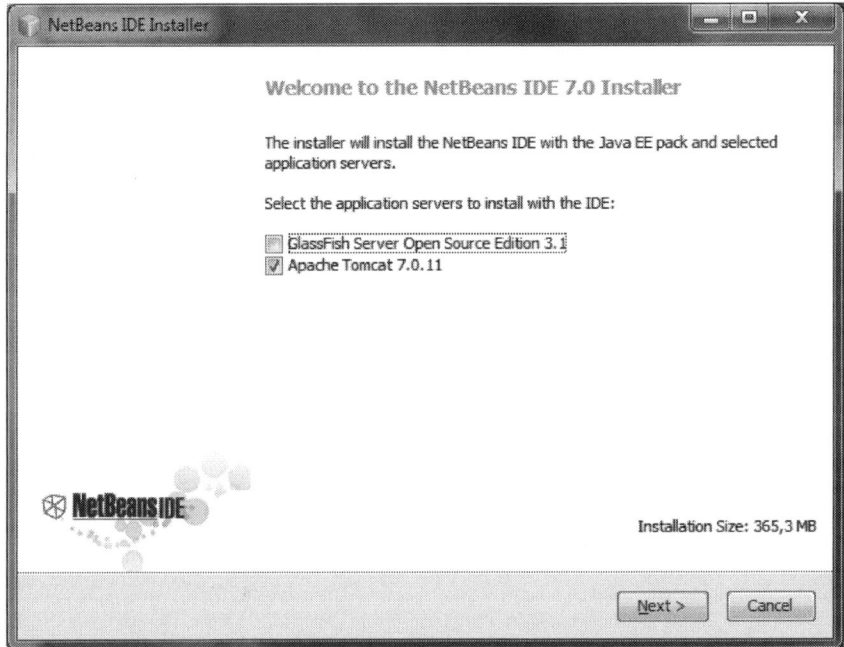

 In this book, we will use either Eclipse's internal servlet container or Tomcat as they are the simplest containers able to run Vaadin. You may however use your favorite servlet container such as **Jetty**, or more advanced application server, such as Red Hat JBoss Application Server or OW2 JOnAS. In most cases, this won't matter however.

2. Click on **Next** and accept the license agreement.

3. Click on **Next** and accept the license agreement to use JUnit.

4. Click on **Next** and choose:
   - NetBeans folder location
   - The JDK 7 folder location

5. Click on **Next** and choose **Tomcat 7.0** folder location. Finally, click on **Install** to begin the installation process.

Go have a coffee during the installation process; it may take some time depending on each specific machine.

A final screen asks for permission to use our usage data anonymously: choose depending on your own personal taste and click on **Finish**.

Checking if Java Web features are present

Launch NetBeans and go to the menu **Tools | Plugin**. Select the **Installed** tab, type web in the **Search** field, and then press *Enter*.

If the Java Web Applications plugin appears, it is installed and you should check if the Vaadin plugin is already installed (see the following section). If not, then either install a compatible version as described above or install the Java Web Applications plugin from inside NetBeans.

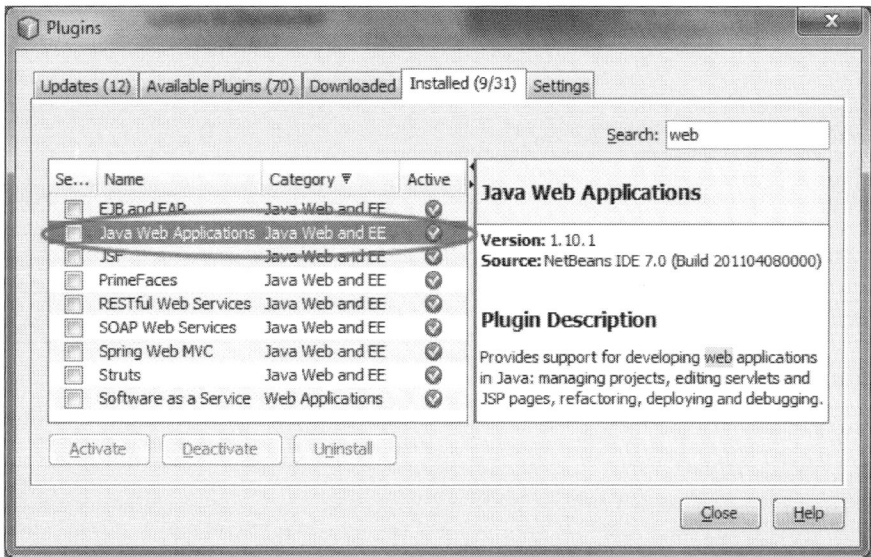

Checking if the Vaadin plugin is installed

Launch NetBeans and go to the menu **Tools | Plugin**. Select the **Installed** tab, type `Vaadin` in the **Search** field, and then press *Enter*.

If the Vaadin plugin appears, it is installed, if not, then go to the section aptly named *Installing the Vaadin plugin* in this chapter.

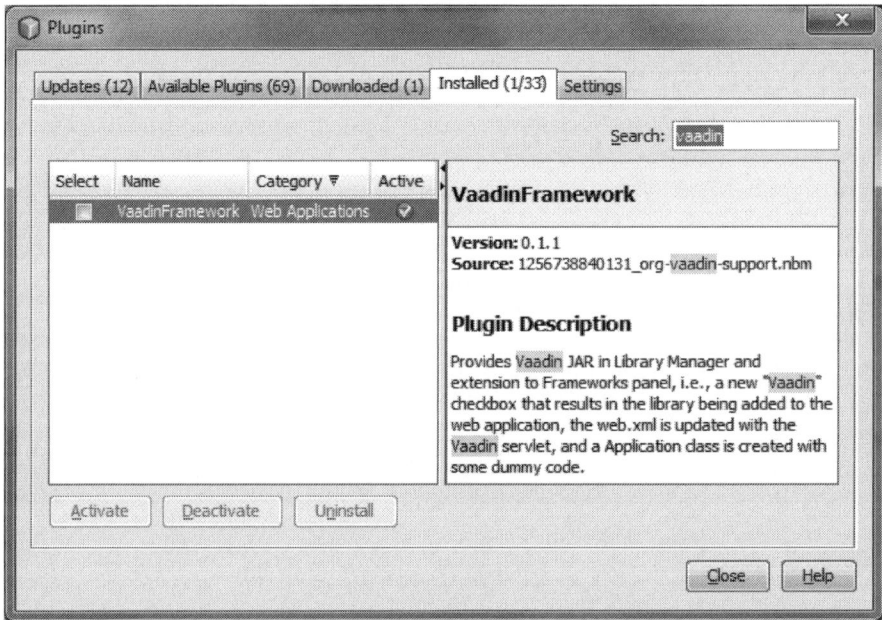

Installing the Vaadin plugin

Go to the Vaadin plugin homepage at `http://plugins.netbeans.org/PluginPortal/faces/PluginDetailPage.jsp?pluginid=21965`. Click on the **Download** button and save the NBM file on your hard drive.

 The plugin was developed with NetBeans 6.8 in mind. However, luckily it is also compatible with 7.0.

Now, in NetBeans, go to the menu **Tools | Plugin**. Select the **Downloaded** tab and click on the **Add Plugins** button. Select the previous NBM file.

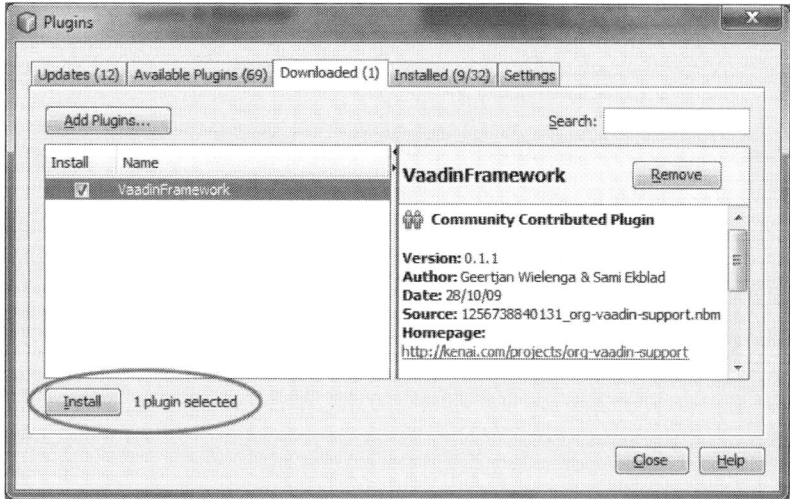

Finally, click on **Install**, at the bottom left corner: accept the license agreement and confirm that the plugin is not signed.

Creating our first NetBeans Vaadin project

Go to the menu **File | New Project**. It opens a multi-step window.

1. Step 1: Choose Project: Choose Java Web project, and then Web Application and click on **Next**.

Troubleshooting:
If Java Web project does not appear in the categories list, then first check that the Java Web features are installed, as seen in preceding section named *Checking if you have Java Web features*.

2. Step 2: Name and location. Fill the name, application, and folder fields according to your preferences and click on **Next**.

3. Step 3: Server and settings. For server, select the server you installed during the NetBeans setup, or if you installed both GlassFish and Tomcat, select the server with which you are most comfortable. If you don't know which one to choose, then select Tomcat as it is the simplest.

For the Java EE version, keep Java EE 5. For context path, choose /my-firstvaadinapp and click on **Next**.

 Just so you know, Vaadin can run in a J2EE 1.4 compatible web container so we can also choose this particular version if we want.

4. Step 4: Frameworks: Scroll down and select **Vaadin 6.1.3**. Don't worry; we will change to the desired version in the next section.

   Keep /vaadin/* as the servlet URL pattern and MyApplication as the Vaadin application class name. Finally, change the main package to com.packt.learnvaadin.

 Troubleshooting:

If Vaadin does not appear in the framework list, then check that the plugin is installed first, as seen in the preceding section named *Checking if you have the Vaadin plugin installed*.

Clicking on **Finish** should create the project. The **Projects** tab should look similar to the one shown in the following screenshot:

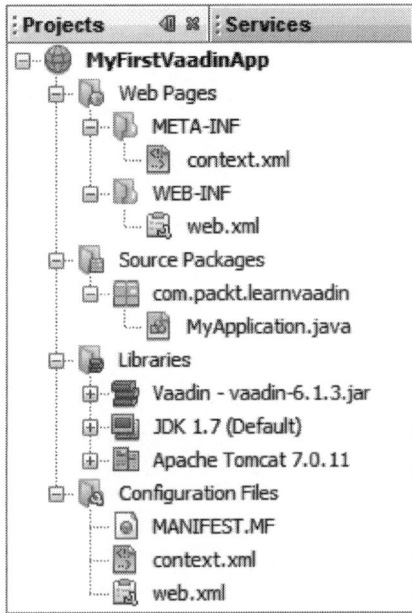

Changing the Vaadin version

As was said before, there is a slight problem with the NetBeans Vaadin plugin in its current form: we are stuck with using the version configured in it, which is 6.1.3. As we want the latest 6 version (at the time of this writing, it is 6.7), we have to download it manually.

Just go to `http://vaadin.com/releases` and select **Download Vaadin-6.7.x.jar**. This will download the latest version.

Now carry out the following steps:

1. Save the JAR to `<APP_ROOT>/build/web/WEB-INF/lib` where `APP_ROOT` references the root of our MyFirstVaadinApp project. There should already be `vaadin-6.1.3.jar` at this location.

2. In NetBeans, right click on `vaadin-6.1.3.jar` and choose **remove**.

3. In NetBeans, right click on the **Library** folder and choose **Add JAR/Folder**. Select the previously downloaded JAR in `<APP_ROOT>/build/web/WEB-INF/lib`.

4. We can now safely remove `vaadin-6.1.3.jar` from the file system.

This should yield the following structure:

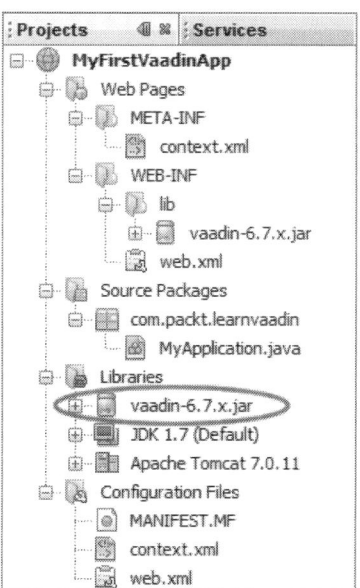

To be frank, this is not really an easy setup, yet, it is the only one that gets us the right result, apart from doing everything manually.

Readers that have good proficiency in creating NetBeans plugins are encouraged to get in touch with the plugin lead committer in order to ease the setup of Vaadin projects under NetBeans. The plugin site is located on project Kenai at http://kenai.com/projects/org-vaadin-support/ where all relevant information can be found including the mailing list, chat rooms, and the lead committer.

Testing the application

In order to test the application, right click on the newly created project and select **Run**. It should display a welcome message for us in our default browser, as shown in the following screenshot:

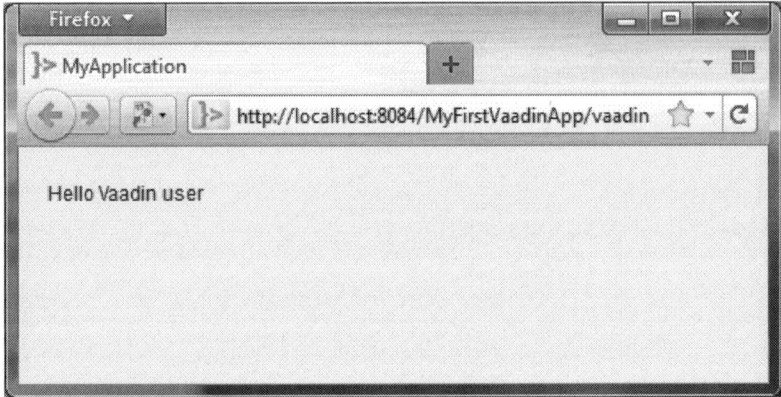

Vaadin and other IDEs

In both IDEs, the Vaadin plugin helps us jumpstart a project in a matter of minutes. However, it may be interesting to understand what is really done in the created project by the plugin in case we need to do it manually in other IDEs which don't have such plugins.

Adding the Vaadin library

First, we should add the Vaadin library to the web application's WEB-INF/lib folder. According to Java EE specifications, this means that our code can now access the Vaadin JAR as it is on the web application's classpath.

Creating the application

Then, we also need to create a class named `com.packt.vaadin.MyApplication` as defined in our preceding sample application. Now, if we look at this class, we can see that it inherits from `com.vaadin.Application`.

For now, suffice to say that `Application` is the entry point of all what we code in Vaadin. For example, it lets us:

- Reference and open "main" windows, that is, windows that fit the whole screen
- Manage the application lifecycle and more specifically, the closing of the application
- Change the application's theme

Adding the servlet mapping

The last thing the plugin does is updating the `WEB-INF/web.xml` file, also known as the web deployment descriptor.

Looking at the file, we see the following Vaadin-specific lines:

```xml
<?xml version="1.0" encoding="UTF-8"?>
<web-app version="2.5" xmlns="http://java.sun.com/xml/ns/javaee"
  xmlns:xsi="http://www.w3.org/2001/XMLSchema-instance"
  xsi:schemaLocation="http://java.sun.com/xml/ns/javaee
    http://java.sun.com/xml/ns/javaee/web-app_2_5.xsd">
  <servlet>
    <servlet-name>VaadinApplication</servlet-name>
    <servlet-class>
      com.vaadin.terminal.gwt.server.ApplicationServlet
    </servlet-class>
    <init-param>
      <param-name>application</param-name>
      <param-value>
        com.packt.learnvaadin.MyApplication
      </param-value>
    </init-param>
  </servlet>
  <servlet-mapping>
    <servlet-name>VaadinApplication</servlet-name>
    <url-pattern>/app/*</url-pattern>
  </servlet-mapping>
```

```
<servlet-mapping>
  <servlet-name>VaadinApplication</servlet-name>
  <url-pattern>/VAADIN/*</url-pattern>
</servlet-mapping>
</web-app>
```

Declaring the servlet class

The first thing to do is to declare the servlet. For servlet containers and full application servers, the servlet is provided by Vaadin and is `com.vaadin.terminal.gwt.server.ApplicationServlet`. We will see in *Chapter 10, Beyond Application Servers* that for more exotic platforms such as portlet `containers` and other classes are provided.

The servlet class is of utmost importance as it is the entry point of HTTP (as well as HTTPS) requests, as well as the exit point of their respective responses in Java Web Applications. The good news is that Vaadin takes care of handling requests (and sending responses) for us. However, we can inherit from `ApplicationServlet` or its parent class `AbstractApplicationServlet` in order to respectively supplement or override the Vaadin's default behavior.

Declaring the Vaadin's entry point

We saw in the preceding section named *Creating an application* that the real entry point in Vaadin is not the servlet anymore, but a class that extends Vaadin's `Application`. We should make the servlet aware of this entry point and this is done with the servlet initialization parameter named `application`.

This parameter is not optional and Vaadin will vigorously complain if this parameter is omitted with the following explicit message:

javax.servlet.ServletException: Application not specified in servlet parameters

Application not specified in servlet parameters

If you ever encounter such a message, then your first reflex should be to check the deployment descriptor for the missing `application` servlet initialization parameter.

Declaring the servlet mapping

Like in any Java Web Application, we should make our servlet available through a mapping that represents the URL part after the protocol, domain name, port (optional), and context-root that will activate the Vaadin servlet.

Refresher: in `http://packtpub.com:80/vaadin`, `packtpub.com` is the domain, `80` is the port, and `vaadin` is the context-root. The context-root we set up previously in the project is `/myfirstvaadinapp`.

In our previous setup, we configured the web application creation wizard to use the `/app/*` mapping.

Apart from specific cases, it is a bad idea to use the `/*` mapping for Vaadin servlet. That would mean that Vaadin servlet would have to handle every request in our application, including static resources, JAAS login form, and so on. We definitely don't want that.

Moreover, we will see later in *Chapter 7, Advanced Features* that it is also necessary in order to properly close Vaadin applications.

The second servlet mapping is added because the internal Vaadin's themes and resources are referenced under `<context-root>/VAADIN/*` and thus, should be handled by the Vaadin servlet. As a developer, you can safely ignore this part (but don't remove it!).

Alternatively, we can also provide access to themes and resources ourselves, but this is the simplest option.

If you run the Vaadin servlet under the more general `/*` mapping, then there is no need for this additional mapping.

Summary

In this chapter, we have seen how to:

- Correctly set up our IDE, depending on whether it is already present on our system or not
- Enhance our IDE with specific Vaadin features, to make our project set up faster
- Create a new project, using the plugin's help.
- Add the Vaadin framework to a project when no plugin is available

This chapter forms the basis of all your future work with Vaadin, be sure to grasp all the concepts explained in it. After having created a basic "Hello World" project, the next chapter will detail Vaadin internals, as well as how to deploy our project outside the IDE.

3

Hello Vaadin!

In this chapter, we will:

- Learn key concepts behind the Vaadin framework
- Have an overview of its internal architecture
- See how to deploy a Vaadin application to a servlet container, be it in an IDE or outside it
- See how to update the previously developed application with a very simple interaction in order to display "Hello Vaadin!"

 In the rest of this book, we will use the Eclipse IDE for detailed explanations and screenshots. However, there are enough similarities between Eclipse and NetBeans such that those same explanations can safely be used in NetBeans.

Now enough with the talk, let's begin.

Understanding Vaadin

In order to understand Vaadin, we should first understand what is its goal regarding the development of web applications.

Vaadin's philosophy

Classical HTML over HTTP application frameworks are coupled to the inherent request/response nature of the HTTP protocol. This simple process translates as follows:

1. The client makes a request to access an URL.
2. The code located on the server parses request parameters (optional).

3. The server writes the response stream accordingly.

4. The response is sent to the client.

All major frameworks (and most minor ones, by the way) do not question this model: Struts, Spring MVC, Ruby on Rails, and others, completely adhere to this approach and are built upon this request/response way of looking at things. It is no mystery that HTML/HTTP application developers tend to comprehend applications through a page-flow filter.

On the contrary, traditional client-server application developers think in components and data binding because it is the most natural way for them to design applications (for example, a select-box of countries or a name text field).

A few recent web frameworks, such as JSF, tried to cross the bridge between components and page-flow, with limited success. The developer handles components, but they are displayed on a page, not a window, and he/she still has to manage the flow from one page to another.

The Play Framework (`http://www.playframework.org/`) takes a radical stance on the page-flow subject, stating that the Servlet API is a useless abstraction on the request/response model and sticks even more to it.

Vaadin's philosophy is two-fold:

- It lets developers design applications through components and data bindings
- It isolates developers as much as possible from the request/response model in order to think in screens and not in windows

This philosophy lets developers design their applications the way it was before the web revolution. In fact, fat client developers can learn Vaadin in a few hours and start creating applications in no time.

The downside is that developers, who learned their craft with the thin client and have no prior experience of fat client development, will have a hard time understanding Vaadin as they are inclined to think in page-flow. However, they will be more productive in the long run.

Vaadin's architecture

In order to achieve its goal, Vaadin uses an original architecture. The first fact of interest is that it is comprised of both a server and a client side.

- The client side manages thin rendering and user interactions in the browser

- The server side handles events coming from the client and sends changes made to the user interface to the client
- Communication between both tiers is done over the HTTP protocol

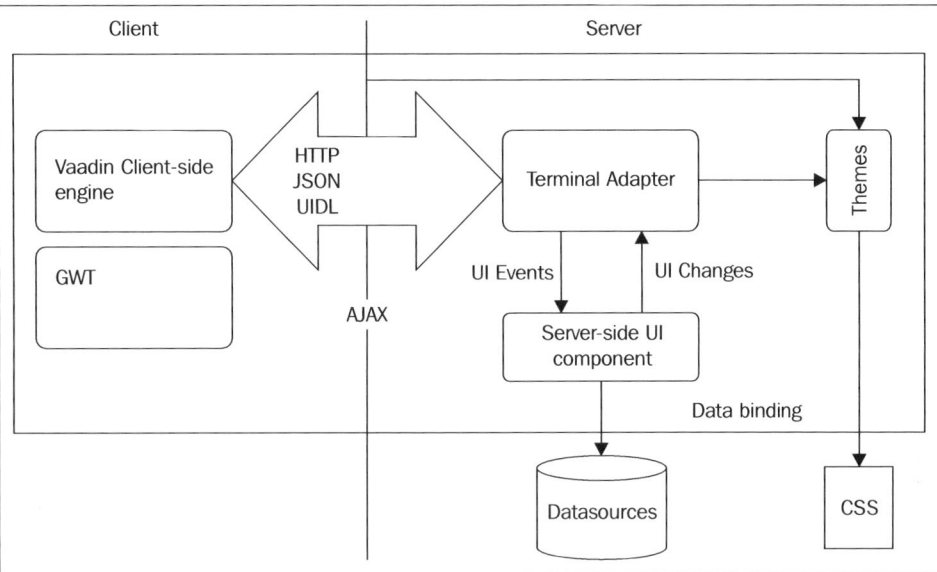

We will have a look at each of these tiers.

Client server communication

Messages in Vaadin use three layers: HTTP, **JSON**, and **UIDL**. The former two are completely un-related to the Vaadin framework and are supported by independent third parties; UIDL is internal.

HTTP protocol

Using the HTTP protocol with Vaadin has the following two main advantages:

1. There is no need to install anything on the client, as browsers handle HTTP (and HTTPS for that matter) natively.
2. Firewalls that let pass the HTTP traffic (a likely occurrence) will let Vaadin applications function normally.

JSON message format

Vaadin messages between the client and the server use **JavaScript Objects Notation (JSON)**. JSON is an alternative to XML that has the following several differences:

- First of all, the JSON syntax is lighter than the XML syntax. XML has both a start and an end tag, whereas JSON has a tag coupled with starting brace and ending brace. For example, the following two code snippets convey the same information, but the first requires 78 characters and the second only 63. For a more in depth comparison of JSON and XML, refer to the following URL:

```
http://json.org/xml.html
<person>
  <firstName>John</firstName>
  <lastName>Doe</lastName>
</person>

{"person" {
  {"firstName": "John"},
  {"lastName": "Doe"}
}
```

  The difference varies from message to message, but on an average, it is about 40%. It is a real asset only for big messages, and if you add server GZIP compression, size difference starts to disappear. The reduced size is no disadvantage though.

- Finally, XML designers go to great length to differentiate between child tags and attributes, the former being more readable to humans and the latter to machines. JSON messages design is much simpler as JSON has no attributes.

UIDL "schema"

The last stack that is added to JSON and HTTP is the **User Interface Definition Language (UIDL)**. UIDL describes complex user interfaces with JSON syntax.

The good news about these technologies is that Vaadin developers won't be exposed to them.

The client part

The client tier is a very important tier in web applications as it is the one with which the end user directly interacts.

In this endeavor, Vaadin uses the excellent **Google Web Toolkit (GWT)** framework. GWT has been mentioned in *Chapter 1, Vaadin and its Context*. However, we will need to go deeper to understand how it is used in Vaadin.

In the GWT development, there are the following mandatory steps:

1. The code is developed in Java.
2. Then, the GWT compiler transforms the Java code in JavaScript.
3. Finally, the generated JavaScript is bundled with the default HTML and CSS files, which can be modified as a web application.

Although novel and unique, this approach provides interesting key features that catch the interest of end users, developers, and system administrators alike:

- Disconnected capability, in conjunction with HTML 5 client-side data stores
- Displaying applications on small form factors, such as those of handheld devices
- Development only with the Java language
- Excellent scalability, as most of the code is executed on the client side, thus freeing the server side from additional computation

On the other hand, there is no such thing as a free lunch! There are definitely disadvantages in using GWT, such as the following:

- The whole coding/compilation/deployment process adds a degree of complexity to the standard Java web application development.
- Although a Google GWT plugin is available for Eclipse and NetBeans, IDEs do not provide standard GWT development support. Using GWT development mode directly or through one such plugin is really necessary, because without it, developing is much slower and debugging almost impossible.

> For more information about GWT dev mode, please refer to the following URL:
>
> `http://code.google.com/intl/en/webtoolkit/`
> `doc/latest/DevGuideCompilingAndDebugging.html.`

- There is a consensus in the community that GWT has a higher learning curve than most classic web application frameworks; although the same can be said for others, such as JSF.
- If the custom JavaScript is necessary, then you have to bind it in Java with the help of a stack named **JavaScript Native Interface (JSNI)**, which is both counter-intuitive and complex.

- With pure GWT, developers have to write the server-side code themselves (if there is any).

- Finally, if ever everything is done on the client side, it poses a great security risk. Even with obfuscated code, the business logic is still completely open for inspection from hackers.

Vaadin uses GWT features extensively and tries to downplay its disadvantages as much as possible. This is all possible because of the Vaadin server part.

The server part

Vaadin's server-side code plays a crucial role in the framework.

The biggest difference in Vaadin compared to GWT is that developers do not code the client side, but instead code the server side that generates the former. In particular, in GWT applications, the browser loads static resources (the HTML and associated JavaScript), whereas in Vaadin, the browser accesses the servlet that serves those same resources from a JAR (or the WEB-INF folder).

The good thing is that it completely shields the developer from the client-code, so he/she cannot make unwanted changes. It may be also seen as a disadvantage, as it makes the developer unable to change the generated JavaScript before deployment.

 It is possible to add custom JavaScript, although it is rarely necessary.

In Vaadin, you code only the server part!

There are two important tradeoffs that Vaadin makes in order achieve this:

1. As opposed to GWT, the user interface related code runs on the server, meaning Vaadin applications are not as scalable as pure GWT ones. This should not be a problem in most applications, but if you need to, you should probably leave Vaadin for some less intensive part of the application; stick to GWT or change an entirely new technology.

 While Vaadin applications are not as scalable as applications architecture around a pure JavaScript frontend and a SOA backend, a study found that a single Amazon EC2 instance could handle more than 10,000 concurrent users per minute, which is much more than your average application. The complete results can be found at the following URL:

```
http://vaadin.com/blog/-/blogs/vaadin-scalability-
study-quicktickets
```

2. Second, each user interaction creates an event from the browser to the server. This can lead to changes in the user interface's model in memory and in turn, propagate modifications to the JavaScript UI on the client. The consequence is that Vaadin applications simply cannot run while being disconnected from the server! If your requirements include the offline mode, then forget Vaadin.

Terminal and adapter

As in any low-coupled architecture, not all Vaadin framework server classes converse with the client side. In fact, this is the responsibility of one simple interface: `com.vaadin.terminal.Terminal`.

In turn, this interface is used by a part of the framework aptly named as the **Terminal Adapter**, for it is designed around the **Gang of Four Adapter** (`http://www.vincehuston.org/dp/adapter.html`) pattern.

This design allows for the client and server code to be completely independent of each other, so that one can be changed without changing the other. Another benefit of the Terminal Adapter is that you could have, for example, other implementations for things such as Swing applications. Yet, the only terminal implementation provided by the current Vaadin implementation is the web browser, namely `com.vaadin.terminal.gwt.server.WebBrowser`.

 However, this does not mean that it will always be the case in the future. If you are interested, then browse the Vaadin add-ons directory (see *Chapter 7, Advanced Features*) regularly to check for other implementations, or as an alternative, create your own!

Client server synchronization

The biggest challenge when representing the same model on two heterogeneous tiers is synchronization between each tier. An update on one tier should be reflected on the other or at least fail gracefully if this synchronization is not possible (an unlikely occurrence considering the modern day infrastructure).

Vaadin's answer to this problem is a synchronization key generated by the server and passed on to the client on each request. The next request should send it back to the server or else the latter will restart the current session's application.

This may be the cause of the infamous and sometimes frustrating "Out of Sync" error, so keep that in mind.

Session Expired
Take note of any unsaved data, and <u>click here</u> to continue.

Deploying a Vaadin application

Now, we will see how we can put what we have learned to good use.

Vaadin applications are primarily web applications and they follow all specifications of Web Archive artifacts (WARs). As such, there is nothing special about deploying Vaadin web applications. Readers who are familiar with the WAR deployment process will feel right at home!

 **WAR** deployment is dependent on the specific application server (or servlet/JSP container).

Inside the IDE

In the last chapter, we smoke tested our brand-new Vaadin application with Eclipse's mock servlet container. In most cases, we will need features not available on the latter, for example, data sources management.

Creating an IDE-managed server

Although it is possible to export our project as a WAR file and deploy it on the available servlet container, the best choice is to use a server managed by the IDE. It will let us transparently debug our Vaadin application code.

The steps are very similar to what we did with the mock servlet container in *Chapter 2, Environment Setup*.

Selecting the tab

First of all, if the **Server** tab is not visible, then go to the menu **Window | Open perspective | Other**... and later choose **Java EE**.

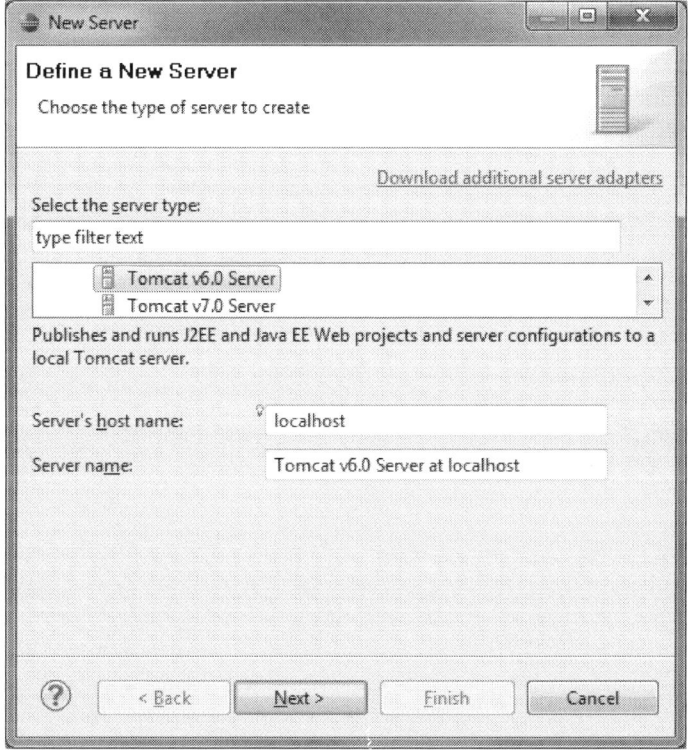

Creating a server

In order to be as simple as possible, we will use Tomcat. Tomcat is a servlet container, as opposed to a full-fledged application server, and only implements the servlet specifications, not the full Java EE stack. However, what it does, it does it so well that Tomcat was the servlet API reference implementation.

Right-click on the **Server** tab and select **New | Server**. Open Apache and select **Tomcat 6.0 Server**. Keep both **Server's host name** and **Server name** values and click on **Next**.

> For running Vaadin applications, Tomcat 6.0 is more than enough as compared to Tomcat 7.x. In fact, it can be downloaded and installed with just a push button. If you want to use Tomcat 7.x, then the process is similar, but you will have to download it separately out of Eclipse. Download it from the following URL:
>
> `http://tomcat.apache.org/download-70.cgi`.
>
> However, beware that the first stable version of the 7.x branch is 7.0.6.

Now, the following two options are possible:

1. If you don't have Tomcat 6 installed, then click on **Download and install**. Accept the license agreement and then select the directory where you want to install it as shown in the following screenshot:

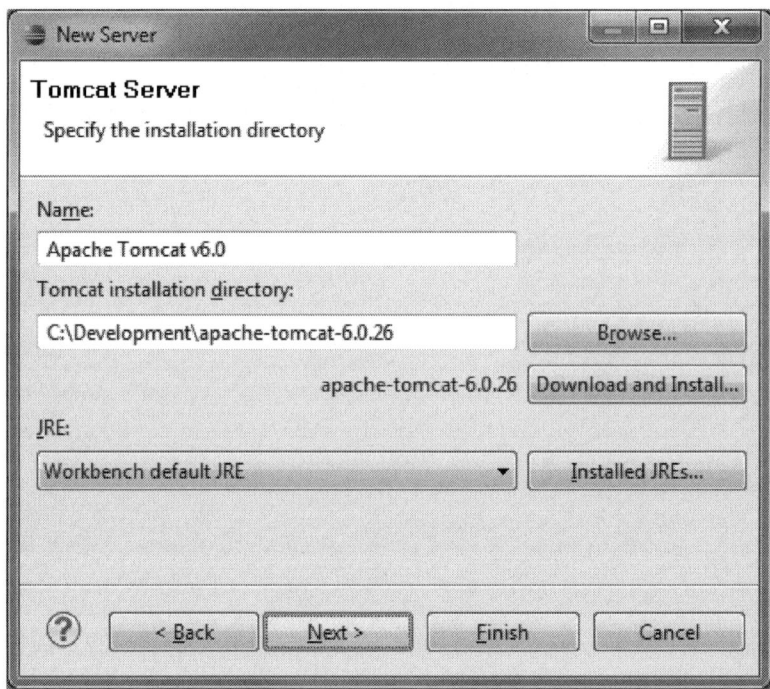

2. If you already do, just point to its root location in the **Tomcat installation directory** field.

By default, you should see a warning message telling you that Tomcat needs a **Java Development Kit (JDK)** and not a **Java Runtime Environment (JRE)**.

 A JRE is a subset of the JDK as it lacks the javac compiler tool (along with some other tools such as javap, a decompiler tool). As JSPs are compiled into servlets at runtime and most regular web applications make heavy use of them, it is a standard to choose a JDK to run Tomcat.

The good thing about Vaadin is that it does not use JSP, so we can simply ignore the warning.

Click on the **Finish** button.

Verifying the installation

At the end of the wizard, there should be a new Tomcat 6.0 server visible under the **Servers** tab, as shown in the following screenshot. Of course, if you chose another version or another server altogether, that will be the version or server displayed.

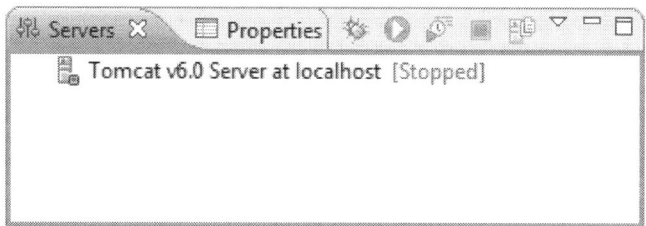

Adding the application

As Vaadin applications are web applications, there is no special deployment process.

Right-click on the newly created server and click on the **Add and Remove** menu entry. A pop-up window opens. On the left side, there is the list of available web application projects that are valid candidates to be deployed on your newly created server. On the right side, there is the list of currently deployed web applications.

Select **MyFirstVaadinApp** project we created in *Chapter 2* and click on the **Add** button. Then, click on **Finish**.

The application should now be visible under the server.

Launching the server

Select the server and right-click on it. Select the **Debug** menu entry. Alternatively, you can:

- Click on the **Debug** button (the one with the little bug) on the **Server** tab header
- Press *Ctrl + Alt + d*

Each IDE has its own menus, buttons, and shortcuts. Know them and you will enjoy a huge boost in productivity.

The **Console** tab should display a log similar to the following:

12 janv. 2011 21:14:36 org.apache.catalina.core.AprLifecycleListener init

INFO: The APR based Apache Tomcat Native library which allows optimal performance in production environments was not found on the java.library.path: ...

12 janv. 2011 21:14:36 org.apache.tomcat.util.digester.SetPropertiesRule begin

ATTENTION: [SetPropertiesRule]{Server/Service/Engine/Host/Context} Setting property 'source' to 'org.eclipse.jst.jee.server:MyFirstVaadinApp' did not find a matching property.

12 janv. 2011 21:14:36 org.apache.coyote.http11.Http11Protocol init

INFO: Initialisation de Coyote HTTP/1.1 sur http-8080

12 janv. 2011 21:14:36 org.apache.catalina.startup.Catalina load

INFO: Initialization processed in 484 ms

12 janv. 2011 21:14:36 org.apache.catalina.core.StandardService start

INFO: Démarrage du service Catalina

12 janv. 2011 21:14:36 org.apache.catalina.core.StandardEngine start

INFO: Starting Servlet Engine: Apache Tomcat/6.0.26

12 janv. 2011 21:14:37 org.apache.coyote.http11.Http11Protocol start

INFO: Démarrage de Coyote HTTP/1.1 sur http-8080

12 janv. 2011 21:14:37 org.apache.jk.common.ChannelSocket init

INFO: JK: ajp13 listening on /0.0.0.0:8009

12 janv. 2011 21:14:37 org.apache.jk.server.JkMain start

INFO: Jk running ID=0 time=0/21 config=null

12 janv. 2011 21:14:37 org.apache.catalina.startup.Catalina start

INFO: Server startup in 497 ms

This means Tomcat started normally.

Outside the IDE

In order to deploy the application outside the IDE, we should first have a deployment unit.

Creating the WAR

For a servlet container, such as Tomcat, the deployment unit is a **Web Archive**, better known as a WAR.

Right-click on the project and select the **Export** menu | **WAR** file. In the opening pop up, just update the location of the exported file: choose the webapps directory where we installed Tomcat and name it myfirstvaadinapp.war.

Launching the server

Open a prompt command. Change the directory to the bin subdirectory of the location where we installed Tomcat and run the startup script.

Troubleshooting

If you have installed Tomcat for the first time, then chances are that the following message will be displayed:

Neither the JAVA_HOME nor the JRE_HOME environment variable is defined

At least one of these environment variables is needed to run this program

In this case, set the JAVA_HOME variable to the directory where Java is installed on your system (and not its bin subdirectory!).

The log produced should be very similar to the one displayed by running Tomcat inside the IDE (as shown in preceding section), apart from the fact that **Apache Portable Runtime** will be available on the classpath and that does not change a thing from the Vaadin point of view.

Using Vaadin applications

Vaadin being a web framework, its output can be displayed inside a browser.

Browsing Vaadin

Whatever way you choose to run our previously created Vaadin project, in order to use it, we just have to open one's favorite browser and navigate to `http://localhost:8080/myfirstvaadinapp/vaadin`. Two things should happen:

1. First, a simple page should be displayed with the message **Hello Vaadin user**

2. Second, the log should output that Vaadin has started

===

Vaadin is running in DEBUG MODE.

Add productionMode=true to web.xml to disable debug features.

To show debug window, add ?debug to your application URL.

===

Troubleshooting

In case nothing shows up on the browser screen and after some initial delay an error pop up opens with the following message:

Failed to load the widgetset: /myfirstvaadinapp/VAADIN/ widgetsets/com.vaadin.terminal.gwt.DefaultWidgetSet/ com.vaadin.terminal.gwt.DefaultWidgetSet.nocache. js?1295099659815

Be sure to add the /VAADIN/* mapping to the web.xml as shown in *Chapter 2* in the section *Declare the servlet mapping* and redeploy the application.

Out-of-the-box helpers

Before going further, there are two things of interest to know, which are precious when developing Vaadin web applications.

The debug mode

Component layout in real-world business-use cases can be a complex thing to say the least. In particular, requirements about fixed and relative positioning are a real nightmare when one goes beyond Hello world applications, as they induce nested layouts and component combinations at some point.

Given the generated code approach, when the code does not produce exactly what is expected on the client side, it may be very difficult to analyze the cause of the problem. Luckily, Vaadin designers have been confronted with them early on and are well aware of this problem.

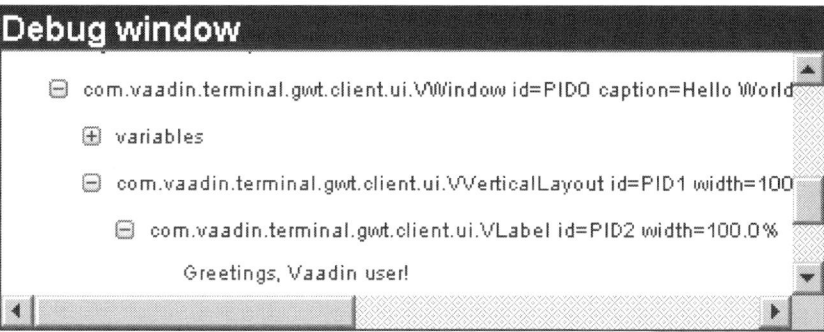

As such, Vaadin provides an interesting built-in debugging feature: if you are ever faced with such a display problem, just append `?debug` to your application URL. This will instantly display a neat window that gives a simplified tree view of your components/layouts with additional information such as the component class, the internal Vaadin id, the caption, and the width.

 Just be aware that this window is not native (it is just an artifact created with the client-side JavaScript). It can be moved with its title bar, which is invaluable if you need to have a look at what is underneath it. Likewise, it can be resized by pressing the *Shift* key while the cursor is over the debug window.

Although it considerably decreases the debugging time during the development phase, such a feature has no added value when in production. It can even be seen as a security risk as the debug windows displays information about the internal state of Vaadin's component tree.

Vaadin provides the means to disable this feature. In order to do so, just add the following snippet to your WEB-INF/web.xml:

```
<context-param>
  <description>Vaadin production mode</description>
  <param-name>productionMode</param-name>
  <param-value>true</param-value>
</context-param>
```

Now, if you try the debug trick, nothing will happen.

Production mode is NOT default

As such, it is a good idea to always set the productionMode context parameter from the start of the project, even if you set it to false. Your build process would then set it to true for release versions. This is much better than forgetting it altogether and having to redeploy the webapp when it becomes apparent.

Restart the application, not the server

We have seen in the *Vaadin's architecture* section that Vaadin's user interface model is sent to the client through UIDL/JSON messages over HTTP. The whole load is sent at the first request/response sequence, when the Application instance is initialized; additional sequences send only DOM updates.

Yet, important changes to the component tree happen often during the development process. As Vaadin stores the UI state in memory on the server side, refreshing the browser does not display such changes.

Of course, restarting the server discards all the states in memory and remedies the problem, but this operation is not free for *heavyweight* application servers. Although recent releases of application servers emphasize better startup time, it is a time waste; even more so if you need to restart 10 or 15 times per hour, which is not an unlikely frequency at the start of a new application development.

As for the debugging feature, Vaadin provides the means to reload the computed UI through an URL parameter: change your server-side code, wait for the changes to take effect on the server, just append ?restartApplication, and watch the magic happen. Alternatively, if you are already in the debug mode, there is a button labeled **Restart app** that has the same effect.

Increase performance

You should remove the `restartApplication` URL parameter as soon as it is not needed anymore. Otherwise, you will re-run the whole initialization/send UI process each time your refresh the browser, which is not welcome.

Behind the surface

Wow, in just a few steps, we created a brand new application! Granted, it does not do much, to say the least. Yet, those simple actions are fundamental to the comprehension of more advanced concepts seen in further chapters. So, let's catch our breath and see what really happened under the hood.

Stream redirection to Vaadin servlet

The URL `http://localhost:8080/myfirstvaadinapp/vaadin` can be decomposed in the following three parts, each part being handled by a more specific part:

1. `http://localhost:8080` is the concatenation of the protocol, the domain, and the port. This URL is handled by the Tomcat server we installed and started previously, whether inside the IDE or normally.

2. `/myfirstvaadinapp` is the context root and references the project we created before. Thus, Tomcat redirects the request to be handled by the webapp.

3. In turn, `/vaadin` is the servlet mapping the Vaadin plugin added to the web deployment descriptor when the project was created. The servlet mapping uses the Vaadin servlet, which is known under the logical name My First Vaadin Application. The latter references the `com.vaadin.terminal.gwt.server.ApplicationServlet` class.

Vaadin request handling

As you can see, there is nothing magical in the whole process: the URL we browsed was translated as a request that is being handled by the `ApplicationServlet.service()` method, just like any Java EE compliant servlet would do.

To be exact, the `service()` method is not coded in `ApplicationServlet` directly, but in its super class, `com.vaadin.terminal.gwt.server.AbstractApplicationServlet`.

Vaadin's servlet directly overrides `service()` instead of the whole group of `doXXX()` methods (such as `doGet()` and `doPost()`). This means that Vaadin is agnostic regarding the HTTP method you use. Purists and REST programmers will probably be horrified at this mere thought, but please remember that we are not manipulating HTTP verbs in request/response sequences and instead using an application.

The following are the rough steps on how the Vaadin servlet services the request response model:

- Finds out which application instance this request is related to; this means either create or locate the instance. It delegates to the effective implementation of the Vaadin servlet. For example, when using Spring or CDI, the code will locate the Spring/CDI bean (see *Chapter 9* for a real-life example).

- If the application is not running, Vaadin launches it. For detailed explanations on the application concept, see the next section.

- Locates the current window and delegates it to the request handling.

- If the need be:
  - Stops the application
  - Or sends initial HTML/JS/CSS to the client that will interact with the server

The initial load time

Be wary of this last step when creating your own applications: an initial screen that is too big in size will generate an important latency followed by a strange update of your client screen. This is generally not wanted: either try to decrease your initial page complexity or use a change manager that will mitigate the user's feelings about it.

What does an application do?

In Vaadin, an application represents the sum of all components organized in windows, layouts, and having a theme applied. The central class representing an application is the `com.vaadin.Application` class.

Application responsibilities

Application responsibilities include the following:

- Managing windows: adding and removing them for the windows registry. Windows are first-level container components, and as such, are of utmost importance to all Vaadin applications.

- Callbacks during the lifecycle of the application: Two such hooks are possible: before starting and after stopping. For example, the following initialization actions are possible:
  - ° Making a connection to a database
  - ° Reading properties file

  These callbacks can replace the Java EE standard — `javax.servlet.Servlet-ContextListener` — which does the same, in a more Vaadin-oriented way.

- Setting themes: Vaadin, being an abstraction layer over HTML/JS/CSS, lets you manage your CSS as a single bundle named a theme. As such, you can change the whole look and feel of your applications by a single server-side command.

> Two themes are provided out-of-the-box by Vaadin (`reindeer` and `runo`). You can also tweak them and reference them under a new theme name or create entirely new themes from scratch. Themes, being very simple to use but much more complex to create, are outside the scope of this book. Readers interested into going further on this road can find documentation at the following link:
>
> `http://vaadin.com/book/-/page/themes.creating.html`

Application configuration

In our first project, having a look at the web deployment descriptor, notice there is an `application` servlet parameter configured for the Vaadin servlet:

```
<servlet>
  <servlet-name>VaadinApplication</servlet-name>
  <servlet-class>
    com.vaadin.terminal.gwt.server.ApplicationServlet
  </servlet-class>
  <init-param>
    <param-name>application</param-name>
    <param-value>
      com.packt.learnvaadin.MyApplication
```

```
        </param-value>
    </init-param>
</servlet>
```

As such, there can be only a single Vaadin application configured for each Vaadin servlet.

Application and session

The most important fact about the `Application` class is that one instance of it is created the first time a user session requests the Vaadin servlet; this instance is stored in the `HttpSession` related to the session from then on.

In reality, the `Application` instances are not stored directly in `HttpSession`, but within a `com.vaadin.terminal.gwt.server.WebApplicationContext` instance that is stored in the session. There is a 1-n relationship from `WebApplicationContext` to `Application` meaning there is a possibility that more than one `Application` could relate to the same session. You should keep in mind that each session stores one and only one application object for each configured Vaadin servlet.

Vaadin's object model encompasses `Application`, `Window`, and `AbstractComponent` as shown in the following diagram:

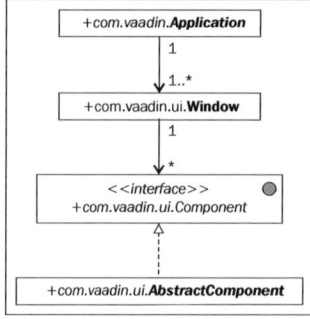

Out of memory

Storing the UI state in the session has a major consequence. Great care must be taken in evaluating the number of users and the average load of each user session because the session is more loaded than in traditional Java EE web applications, thus greater is the risk of `java.lang.OutOfMemoryError`.

Scratching the surface

Having said all that, it is time to have a look at the both the source code that was created by the Vaadin plugin and the code that it generated and pushed on the client.

The source code

The source code was taken care of by Vaadin plugin:

```
import com.vaadin.Application;
import com.vaadin.ui.*;

public class HelloWorldApp extends Application

  public void init() {

    Window mainWindow = new Window("Hello World Application");
    Label label = new Label("Greetings, Vaadin user!");
    mainWindow.addComponent(label);
    setMainWindow(mainWindow);
  }
}
```

Though having no prior experience in Vaadin and only armed with some basic concepts, we can guess what the class does. That is the strength of Vaadin, compared to competitor frameworks, it is self-evident!

- At line 1 of the `init()` method, we create a new window with a title. Windows are first-class components in Vaadin as they can be the top-most elements.

- At line 2, we create a new label. Labels are used to display static messages. They are often found in web forms as description for fields. Our label has a specific text. Notice it is displayed in the final screen.

- At line 3, we add the label to the window. Even when you have no prior experience with component-based development (whether thin or fat client based), it is clear that the label will be displayed in the window.

- Finally, at line 4, we set the window we created as the main window of the screen, displaying it as a root component. We can check that the window's very title takes place in the HTML `<title>` element. With most browsers, it is also shown in the browser window title.

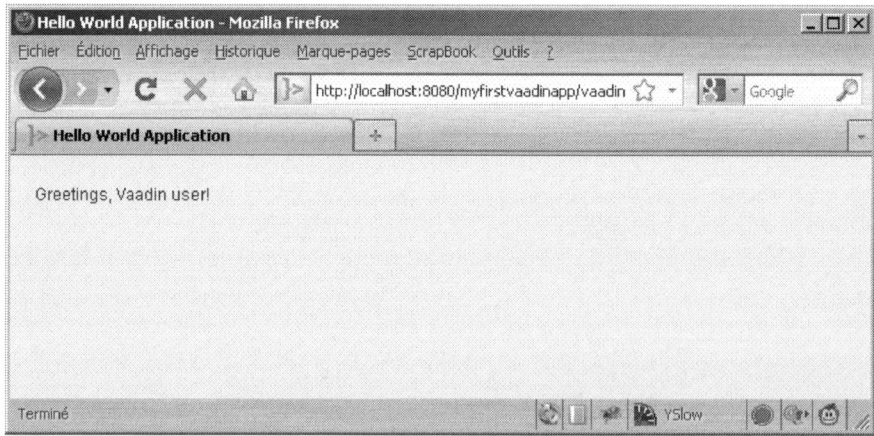

The generated code

In your favorite browser, right-clicking and selecting the menu that shows the source will only display JavaScript—gibberish to the inexperienced eye.

In fact, as the UI is generated with GWT, we don't see anything interesting in the HTML source—only the referenced JavaScript and a single `<noscript>` tag that handles the case where our browser is not JavaScript-enabled (an unlikely occurrence in our time, to say the least).

There is a consensus on the Web that AJAX-powered web applications should degrade gracefully, meaning that if the user deactivates JavaScript, applications should still run, albeit with less user-friendliness. Although a very good practice, most of the time, JavaScript applications will not run at all in this case. GWT and thus Vaadin are no exceptions in this matter.

Of much more interest is the generated HTML/JS/CSS. In order to display it, we will need Google Chrome, Firefox with the Firebug plugin, or an equivalent feature in another browser.

More precisely, locate the following snippet:

```
<div class="v-app v-theme-reindeer v-app-HelloWorldApp"
  id="myfirstvaadinappvaadin-627683907">
  <div class="v-view" tabindex="1" style="">
```

```
<div style="position: absolute; display: none;"
          class="v-loading-indicator"></div>
<div style="overflow: hidden; width: 1680px;
          height: 54px;" class="v-verticallayout">
  <div style="overflow: hidden; margin: 18px;
             width: 1644px; height: 18px;">
    <div style="height: 18px; width: 1644px;
               overflow: hidden; padding-left: 0px;
               padding-top: 0px;">
      <div style="float: left; margin-left: 0px;">
        <div class="v-label" style="width: 1644px;">
                   Greetings, Vaadin user!</div>
      </div>
    </div>
    <div style="width: 0px; height: 0px;
               clear: both; overflow: hidden;"></div>
  </div>
</div>
</div>
</div>
```

Things of interest

First of all, notice that although only a simple message is displayed on the user screen, Vaadin has created an entire DOM tree filled with <div> elements that has both style and class attributes. We will see later in *Chapter 4* that Vaadin (through GWT) creates, at least, such a <div> element for every layout and component. For now, just be aware that:

- The class v-view denotes a window

- The class v-label indicates a label

- The class v-verticallayout represents a vertical layout

 Although we didn't code a vertical layout per se, standard components cannot be the first-level children of windows. By default, the Window class uses a vertical layout and components added to the window are in fact added to the latter.

Moreover, the vertical layout is not the only child div of the view: there is another one that has v-loading-indicator as a class. You probably did not notice as the UI is very simple, but if you refresh the browser window, there should be a circular loading indicator displayed at the left of the page just before the UI finishes loading:

Be aware that it gives no indication on the progress whatsoever, but it at least lets users know that the application is not ready to be used. Such indicators are added, for free, each time a window instance is set as the main window of an application.

Summary

We saw a few things of importance in this chapter.

First, we had an overview of the Vaadin's philosophy. Vaadin creates an abstraction over the classic request/response sequence in order for developers to think in "applications" and no more in "pages".

In order to do that, the Vaadin architecture has three main components:

- The client side: that is JavaScript upon the Google Web Toolkit.
- The server side that generates the client code. One concept of note on the server side is the terminal one: the terminal is in charge of abstracting over the client side. Should the need arise; we could create an abstraction that is not web-oriented.
- Communications between the client and the server are implemented with JSON/UIDL messages over the HTTP protocol.

Then, we deployed the Vaadin application we developed in *Chapter 2*. There is nothing special with Vaadin applications, they are simple web archives and are deployed as such. Two tools bundled with Vaadin will prove useful during the development:

1. The debug window that is very convenient when debugging display and layout-related bugs
2. How to restart the framework without necessarily restarting the application server

Finally, we somewhat scratched the surface of how it all works and most notably:

- The handling of an HTTP request by Vaadin
- The notion of application in the framework
- The code, both the source generated by the plugin and the HTML structure generated by the former

This chapter concludes the introduction to Vaadin. It is a big step on the path to learning Vaadin. If you feel the need to take a pause, then it is the right time to do so. If not, go on to learn about components and layouts in *Chapter 4*!

4

Components and Layouts

In this chapter, we will examine the building blocks of Vaadin applications, namely the components. Technologies such as Swing, SWT, Flex, or JSF all provide components that are composed in order to produce a user interface. It is no mystery then that Vaadin also provides them.

Numerous components are available in Vaadin; even more are available as add-ons and we will see in *Chapter 8, Creating Custom Components*, how to build our own. However, the following which are provided out-of-the-box are fundamental:

- `Window`
- `Label`
- `Field`

Then, we will have a look on how these components can be arranged; this will let us detail the layouts:

- `Layout`
- `Panel`

Starting from this chapter, we will build an application that will be used throughout the rest of this book. The goal of this application will be to interact with Twitter.

Thinking in components

Components are at the core of any rich application framework worth its salt.

Terminology

In Vaadin, the term **widget** refers to the client-side UI component made with GWT, whereas the term **component** refers to the server-side Java-compiled component, as well as the whole GWT + Java class association.

Component class design

Before diving right into concrete components that we will manipulate in order to create our user interface, let's take some time to analyze the component class hierarchy design in Vaadin.

The following is a simplified components class diagram:

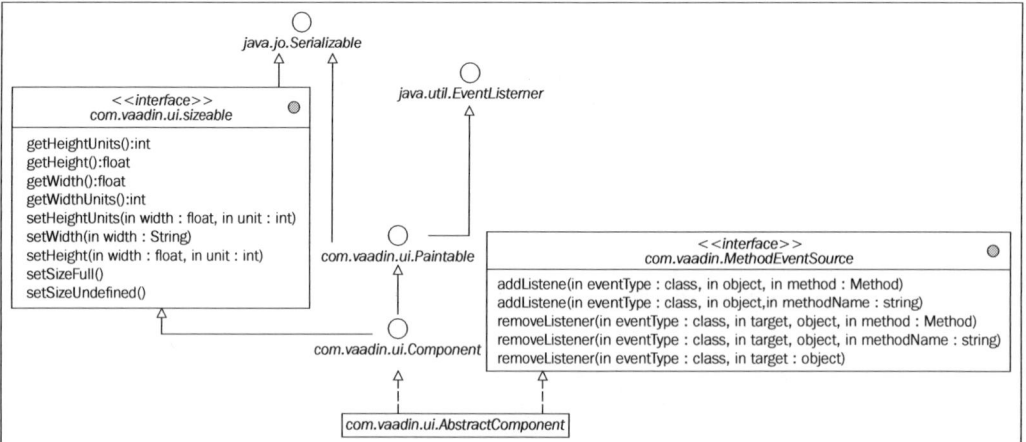

Component

At the root of the Vaadin component hierarchy lies the `Component` interface. This interface inherits, directly or indirectly, from other interfaces, some of which belong to the Java API and others to the Vaadin API:

- `Serializable`: It is critical that Vaadin components be serializable, as we have seen in *Chapter 3, Hello Vaadin!* that `Application` objects are tied to the HTTP session. Were components not serializable, it would still be possible to store `Application` instances in the session, but some application servers would not be able to serialize them between cluster nodes or even when stopping with active sessions. Therefore, Vaadin tackles this problem right from the start and makes all components serializable.

 For example, Apache Tomcat uses serialization to store user sessions before terminating. Also, note the Google App Engine passes user sessions through cluster nodes using serialization.

From a code point of view, this changes nothing as serializable is a marker interface and as such, has no methods. The only thing we have to do when inheriting from Vaadin components is not to forget to add the following serial version unique identifier field:

```
private static final int serialVersionUID = .;
```

This is the sole API requirement for this interface.

- `EventListener`: This interface tags components as being, guess what, an events listener. Like `Serializable`, `EventListener` is a marker interface and changes nothing in the code.

- `Paintable`: The `Paintable` interface is the contract that all objects must adhere to in order for the Vaadin framework to paint them **and** serialize them to UIDL format. This interface is used only by developers who create their own components wrapping GWT widgets, and will be seen in more details in *Chapter 8*.

- `Sizeable`: The `Sizeable` interface is of much more interest as it governs the size the components will have. We will describe it in detail in the section named *Laying out the components* later in this chapter.

MethodEventSource

`MethodEventSource` is an interface that is part of the **Observer** pattern *[GOF:293]*. It represents the subject part of the observer/subject pair. As such, it knows how to register/unregister third-party observers.

This particular interface and its methods will be under intense scrutiny in *Chapter 5, Event Listener Model* where we will detail the event model in Vaadin.

Abstract component

The `AbstractComponent` class implements all the aforementioned interfaces, so that **each and every component in Vaadin will have the same behavior for free**.

This also means that all the custom components we develop, as soon as we inherit from `AbstractComponent`, will be handled just in the way we intend.

 Although this design may seem trivial, it is always a bad surprise when an application does not behave as expected. In Vaadin, all components have the same expected behavior, provided the developer did not implement his/her own, of course.

Immediate mode

`immediate` is a property of `AbstractComponent`. It governs how events are sent from the client to the server (more details on events in *Chapter 5*).

When `immediate` is set to `true`, the event is immediately sent to the server; when set to `false`, it is buffered in a local queue located on the client side and sent along the next immediate event.

As an example, for a form, if we want legacy behavior where the entire form is sent and validated when the user presses a button, we change nothing. However, if we want a more modern behavior where each field is sent and validated separately, we set `immediate` to `true` on each field.

Troubleshooting

The `immediate` mode is the most common source of confusion for Vaadin beginners: if events seem not to be sent to the server, be sure to check the immediate property.

Windows

Windows are every rich application's root component. In fact, the Vaadin plugin, already created a window in our previous "Hello Vaadin" project (see section named *The source code* from *Chapter 3*).

The `Window` class does not inherit directly from `AbstractComponent`; there are some intermediate classes in the hierarchy as seen in the following diagram:

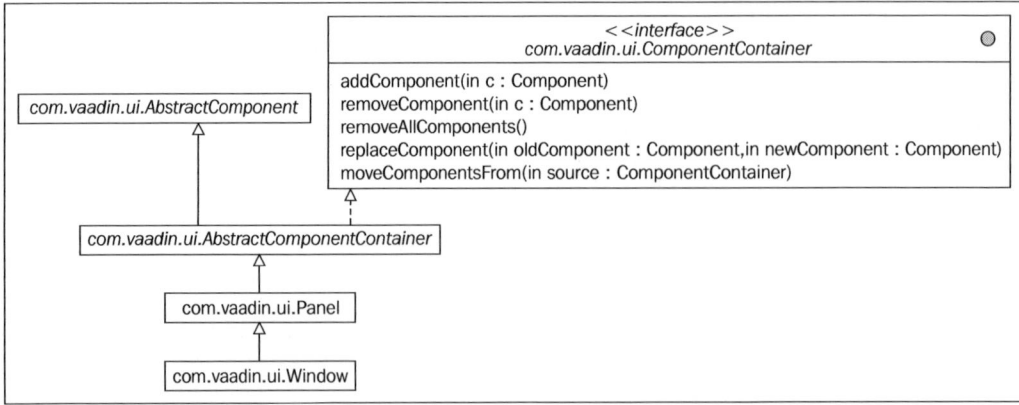

ComponentContainer

The interface named ComponentContainer represents a component that holds other components. As such, it has methods that manage child components and precisely:

- Add a child component
- Remove a child component
- Replace a child component
- Remove all child components
- Move all child components from one component container to another

The abstract class that provides these implementations is AbstractComponentContainer. It also inherits from AbstractComponent and as such, has all features seen earlier.

Panel

Descending the class hierarchy, the next class is a concrete one, Panel. We will use it throughout our application, and as can be guessed, it represents a panel.

Panel adds an interface to the AbstractComponentContainer, Scrollable.

Scrollable lets us programmatically scroll our panel components. Note that the scrolling unit is a pixel.

Panel also adds the content property, of type ComponentContainer. This means that:

- Only a single component can be set as a child element of the panel and it acts as its root
- This component can only be a component container
- Elements added to the panel with the addComponent (Component comp) method are not added to the panel but the root instead

If no content is set prior to adding components, then Vaadin sets a vertical layout as the default window layout.

This means that if a vertical layout is not the intended layout; the latter should be set prior to adding any other component.

Window

Finally, `Window` is the last class in the window class hierarchy. Note that it is not a leaf class, meaning it can be extended should the need arise.

 In **UML** (**Unified Modeling Language**), leaf classes are classes that cannot be extended. In Java, that translates to final classes.

Windows are vital in Vaadin as they form the bridge between the `Application` instance tied to the HTTP session and other components.

Windows are the entry point into some important Vaadin features.

On the client side, and given the web browser terminal, application windows are the outermost component the user sees. As such, the window API is tightly integrated with the browser.

Title

Each window can set its title. This title will be written in the generated HTML output under the `<title>` tag and will be visible in the title bar of most browsers.

Theming

In Vaadin, a combination of CSS, images, and HTML layouts (refer the section named *Layout types* later in this chapter) can be brought together and applied to the application. This combination is called a **theme**.

 Theme creation is a specialized topic and could easily fit a small book in itself. Interested readers can refer to `http://vaadin.com/book/-/page/themes.html` for more information.

Setting a theme can be done application-wide, thus affecting the entire application, but it can also be set on a single window.

In order to do this, call the `setTheme(String theme)` method either on the application or on the window. If set on the window, then we have to set the theme before setting the window as the main window.

Available themes in Vaadin are `reindeer` (the default) and `runo`. Additional themes can be obtained through the Vaadin directory as add-ons (see *Chapter 7* for more information on Vaadin directory and add-ons).

URL fragment

Under normal conditions, Vaadin implements the Single Page Interface, meaning that during the entire application lifecycle and window change, Vaadin does not change the URL of the first request that launched it.

 In order to know more about the Single Page Interface, refer to the following URL:

`https://secure.wikimedia.org/wikipedia/en/wiki/`
`Single-page_application`

This is an acceptable default for standard applications. Yet, for web applications, users are used to bookmark different pages in order to easily find them later: it is the legacy of page-flow applications. Even more, some applications have real need for fine-grained URL, like online stores where each item can be set its own URL. This also lets these different items be referenced separately by search engines such as Google.

In this case, the method `setName(String name)` of the `Window` class is useful in that it lets developers append an URL fragment to the URL application.

As an example, the following snippet will make available `anotherWindow` at the URL `http://localhost:8080/<context>/<vaadin-servlet>/another`:

```
// window is the main window
Window anotherWindow = new Window("Another window");
anotherWindow.setName("another");
```

 Window's name and the main window

In the case of a window that will be set as the main window, the `setName()` method must be called prior to calling `setMainWindow()`; otherwise, Vaadin will throw the following exception: `java.lang.IllegalStateException: Window name can not be changed while the window is in application`.

JavaScript

From a design point of view, the preferred way to add behavior to an application is to create custom reusable components (see *Chapter 8*).

Although Vaadin tries to isolate the developer from the gritty details of the web browser intricacies, there are good reasons to short-circuit everything and execute JavaScript directly. Such reasons include the fact that creating components could be a time-consuming process and project deadlines are sometimes in favor of more direct strategies.

In this case, just use the `executeJavascript(String script)` method and watch the magic happen.

For example, the following snippet will display an alert box when Vaadin sends the response to the client:

```
// window is the main window
window.executeJavaScript("alert('Hello world')");
```

Third-party content

Sometimes, the content sent to the user should not be related to the user interface, but to the third-party content, whether in text or binary format. This is the case when the user requests an image, a PDF, or even a bare HTML document that cannot be served by the Vaadin framework.

In order to cover these cases, Vaadin provides an abstraction: `Resource`.

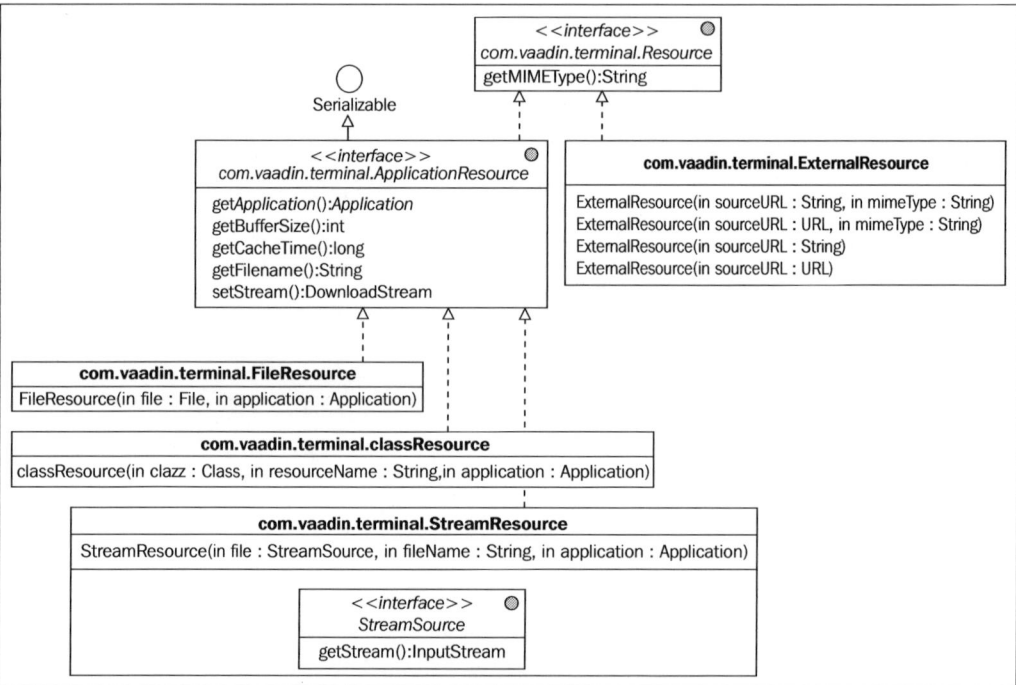

The `Resource` interface represents something provided to the terminal for presentation. How the terminal really handles the display is left to it.

In Vaadin, resources may come from two different locations:

1. From inside the application (or at least from where the application is located, in the case of files):

    ° Resources on the classpath

    ° Resources from streams accessible by the code

    ° File resources located on the server filesystem

2. From outside the application, for example, resources accessible by an URL.

Windows, either main or subwindows, can open resources with the open() method. These resources can be displayed in the same window or in a native pop-up window. In the latter case, Vaadin accepts the new window name (mandatory) and the dimensions (optional).

If a window is already opened with the specified name, then Vaadin replaces its content with the new resource.

Some window names hold a special meaning. Those are the same as in JavaScript's window.open() and are summarized here for ease of reference:

- _blank always opens a new window, even if a previous blank named window is open already

- _self indicates the current window, hence using it is equivalent to not using a window name at all

- _parent and _top reference respectively the frame's parent and the frameset. If frames are not used, then it is the same as _self.

The following snippet creates two pop-up windows displaying the Packt homepage:

```
// window is the main window
try {
  URL url = new URL("http://www.packtpub.com/");
  Resource resource = new ExternalResource(url);
  window.open(resource, "_blank", 640, 480, 2);
  window.open(resource, "_blank", 640, 480, 2);
} catch (MalformedURLException e) {
  throw new RuntimeException(e);
}
```

User messages

Applications generally need to inform users. For example, when a user deletes or updates an entry, it is a good practice to let users know their operation succeeded.

Traditionally, there have been two ways to communicate these facts to the user for web applications:

- Opening an information box through JavaScript. This pop-up is modal, that is, it blocks inputs outside it and forces the user to acknowledge the displayed message.

- A space is reserved for a message on the screen, most of the time a banner at the top of the page. It may also be used for error messages: standard information messages are displayed in a neutral color, errors in red.

Vaadin's notification system employs yet another strategy: the framework displays the message on top of the window.

The notification class

In order to do that, an inner-class from `Window` named `Notification` is used.

From a graphical point of view, a notification displays elements in a horizontal layout in the following order, from left to right: an icon, a caption, and description.

Each one corresponds to a Java property, thus having both a getter and a setter. The following table sums it up:

Property	Type	Constructor argument	Mandatory/ optional	Default value
caption	`String`	yes	mandatory	N/A
description	`String`	yes	optional	`null`
icon	`com.vaadin.terminal. Resource`	no	optional	`null`

A notification is defined by its type. Currently, there are three types denoting different severity level and one special type. The former are, in order of gravity:

- Information, also known as humanized, notifications denote fairly unimportant content, for example, operation acknowledgement such as "Entry deleted". Note that an information message fades as soon as Vaadin detects a keyboard input or a mouse click or move from the user.

  Information notifications are created using the `TYPE_HUMANIZED_MESSAGE` constant in the `Notification` constructor.

- Warning notifications are similar to information messages, except they fade only when a delay has passed or after some user interaction. In this way, they are more noticeable than information messages.

  Warning notifications are created using the TYPE_WARNING_MESSAGE constant in the Notification constructor or leaving it unspecified as it is the default style.

- Error type notifications behave more like modal alert boxes. Their message is shown until the user clicks on the notification (the X in the top right corner is only for show).

  Error notifications are created using the TYPE_ERROR_MESSAGE constant in the Notification constructor.

Finally, tray notifications are used for low-severity messages. However, unlike the other notifications, they will stack in front of one another, always displaying the most recent. Clicking on the visible tray notification will dismiss it and display the underlying notification. This will continue until there are no more notifications to display.

Tray notifications are created using the TYPE_TRAY_NOTIFICATION constant in the Notification constructor.

Beware of humanized notifications

Be aware that if the user interacts in any way with the application while the notification is shown, he/she will likely be unable to read the content of the message. Therefore, it is advised to restrain the use of humanized notifications to information that can be lost without harm. If it is not the case, then it is best to use tray notifications (see below) instead.

Notifications additional properties

Tray notifications are displayed at the bottom left corner; other notifications are centered on the screen. It is however possible to override this position with the `setPosition(int position)` method.

In addition, the delay for the notification can be configured as can the style name. All three, position, delay, and style name are Java properties.

Property	Type	Constructor argument	Mandatory / optional	Default value
position	int	no	optional	Depends on the type
delayMsec	int	no	optional	1500 for TYPE_ WARNING_MESSAGE 3000 for TYPE_ HUMANIZED_MESSAGE
styleName	String	no	mandatory	Depends on the type ("tray", "warning" or "error")

POSITION_TOP_LEFT	POSITION_CENTERED_TOP	POSITION_TOP_RIGHT
	POSITION_CENTERED	
POSITION_BOTTOM_LEFT	POSITION_CENTERED_BOTTOM	POSITION_BOTTOM_RIGHT

Displaying notifications

The standard steps to display notifications are the following:

- Create a new notification instance
- Customize the instance
- Call the `showNotification(Notification notification)` method on the window

As an example, the following snippet displays a welcome message:

```
// window is the main window
Window.Notification notification = new Window.Notification("Welcome
Vaadin", "It's our first application");
window.showNotification(notification);
```

However, we had no need to customize the notification, neither its position nor its display delay. In fact, this is the use-case encountered more frequently: just create a plain notification and display it.

Therefore, Vaadin provides some very productive overrides to the `showNotification()` method:

- `showNotification(String caption)`: Shows a standard warning notification
- `showNotification(String caption, int type)`: Shows a notification, letting us choose the type
- `showNotification(String caption, String description)`: Shows a warning notification complete with description
- `showNotification(String caption, String description, int type)`: Shows a notification, letting us specify description and type

Hence, the previous snippet can be considerably shortened to the following:

```
// window is the main window
window.showNotification("Welcome Vaadin", "It's our first
  application");
```

Use shortcuts when possible

Of course, there is no magic involved: Vaadin creates the notification instance for us. Yet, as creating it ourselves has no interest if we just need standard behavior, it is well advised to use these overridden methods whenever possible. It cleans the code, if only a little, and lets us focus on the real meaningful parts.

Subwindow

Main windows are attached to the application instance and from a user point-of-view are the canvases upon which their child components are displayed.

Subwindows however are attached to a window. There are several limitations on these particular windows:

- They are not accessible through a specific URL
- They cannot attach other subwindows. In effect, this means there is only a single level of subwindowing allowed.

There is no limit to the number of subwindows a window can attach.

Subwindow structure

Subwindows are composed out-of-the-box from the following elements:

- A title bar with:
  - A title located at the top left corner
  - An X icon button located at the top right corner, for closing the pop up
- A handle located at the bottom right corner, for resizing the subwindow
- A canvas, the same as for main windows, where other components can be laid out

Customizing subwindows

Most of the time, the defaults for structure and behavior of a subwindow won't fit our needs. However, the Vaadin framework allows us to customize both.

Basic configuration

Properties are available in order to customize our subwindow. These are summed up in the following table:

Property	Type	Default value
closable	boolean	true
resizable	boolean	true
draggable	boolean	true

- An unclosable subwindow does not display the X icon button in the title bar. Thus, we have to provide another means to close it; or it will stay there indefinitely!

- An unresizable subwindow does not display the handle at the bottom right corner.

- Regular subwindows can be dragged around when the title bar is clicked. However, we can remove this behavior with the `setDraggable(Boolean draggable)` method.

Location

Setting the right location on the user screen is very important from an ergonomic point of view. In order to do this, Vaadin provides a few methods.

Most of the time, centering the subwindow relative to the parent main window fits our needs: just use the `center()` method.

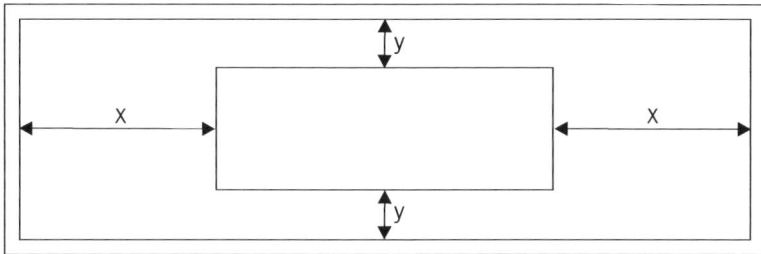

In order to go beyond centering and to set the location of the subwindow relative to the left and the top border of the parent main window, Vaadin respectively provides the `setPositionX(int positionX)` and `setPositionY(int positionY)` methods. The position parameter's unit is the pixel.

Modality

Modality is the capacity for the subwindow to intercept all events from the user to the underlying UI.

In effect, a modal window blocks all relations to the parent application until it is closed, whereas a non-modal window lets the user interact normally with the application.

By default, subwindows are non-modal. However, we can change the modality with the `setModal(boolean modal)` method of the subwindow `Window` instance.

Weak modality

Notice that subwindows are displayed as an HTML `<div>` element on the client-side, not as browser native windows. As a result, modality is enforced, neither by the browser nor the system, but by JavaScript. Hence, we should never rely on this *weak* modality in order to enforce security constraints, as it can easily be bypassed.

In case of a doubt, the `isModal()` method of the `Window` class returns whether the subwindow is indeed modal.

Labels

Labels are widgets used to display **non-editable** text content. In Vaadin, labels are used infrequently as editable fields use captions (refer to section named *Field* in this chapter).

Label class hierarchy

Label is a subclass of `AbstractComponent` but also implements the `Property` interface.

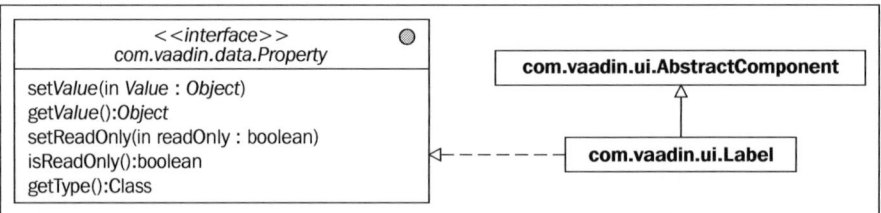

As the `Property` interface is implemented throughout the whole `Component` class hierarchy, it is best to have a look closely at it before going further.

Property

In essence, the `Property` interface simply designates a single value data holder, with accessors.

It is very important to note that Vaadin does not take advantage of Java 5 Generics: values are stored as `Object`. So, don't forget to cast into the right class when needed!

Moreover, there is a read-only property: by contract, calling the `setValue(Object value)` on a read-only instance should throw a `Property.ReadOnlyException`.

Finally, Vaadin provides the `getType()` method to let us query the type stored by the `Property` implementation instance.

Label

As shown in the preceding class diagram, a `Label` is an `AbstractComponent` that implements the `Property` interface.

Formats

However, labels have a distinguishing feature that set them apart from other components: they allow for formatting.

Reminder: In Vaadin, the only provided terminal is the web browser. Therefore, the following formatting explanations are tightly coupled with HTML specifications. Should we use another terminal, either coming from a third-party provider or our own, we would have to be extra careful as to how the terminal really uses these hints.

Available formats are:

- **Text format**: It is not as simple as it sounds since the final output should be valid HTML. Hence, all HTML entity characters are translated into their equivalent HTML alphanumeric code. For example, the < entity is transformed by Vaadin into `&lt;`. This process ensures the user really sees what the developer intended.

  This format is hinted at by the `CONTENT_TEXT` constant.

For the complete entities list, visit the following URL:

`http://www.w3.org/TR/REC-html40/sgml/entities.html`

- **Preformatted**: Browsers conveniently lay out HTML paragraphs depending on the window size. If the size changes, then the paragraph will be laid out differently.

  Yet, it may be required that the paragraph be laid out in a predefined certain way, for example that line breaks occurs at certain places. This is the case for computer code, especially for Python for example. For these use-cases, HTML provides the `<pre>` tag which lays out the paragraph exactly the way it is typed. By using preformatted, Vaadin will also use this tag to render the paragraph.

  This format is governed by the `CONTENT_PREFORMATTED` constant.

- **Raw**: Raw formatting uses the complete set of HTML tags to let us customize the rendering. The written HTML is used as is: if we need a truly XHTML-compliant output, we have to use the format described below.

  This format is used in conjunction with the `CONTENT_RAW` constant.

- **XHTML**: This formatting is similar to the previous one, but also tidies the written HTML, so that the produced output is XML-compliant.

  For example, the following server-code `<ul><li>Hello<li>Vaadin</ul>` will produce this HTML output: `<ul><li>Hello</li><li>Vaadin</li></ul>`.

  This is used with the `CONTENT_XHTML` constant.

- **XML**: This formatting is a legacy from other terminals provided by previous versions of Vaadin. It now behaves the same as XHTML and may possibly be deprecated at the time of reading.

Formatters are either set in the constructor or changed later with the `setContentMode(int contentMode)` method where the `contentMode` parameter is one of the previous constants.

For example, the following code displays a welcome message into our application:

```
// window is the main window
Label label = new LabelWelcomeLabel("WelcomeLabelWelcome to <i
style='color:red' title='Vaadin rules!'>Vaadin", Label.CONTENT_XHTML);
mainWindow.addComponent(label);
```

The following screenshot shows the result:

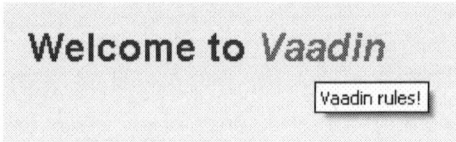

 It should be noted that though label formatting is a feature brought by Vaadin, the proper way to style labels is through themes (and thus CSS).

Text inputs

Text fields are the simplest components available to users in order to send data to an application.

In our case however, they are also a very good entry point into Vaadin field class hierarchy, as they are devoid of more complex features.

Validation

Validation is a major feature of components. As soon as an application needs a user input, there is a need for this input validation. In Vaadin, the validation process is handled by the `Validatable` / `Validator` pair.

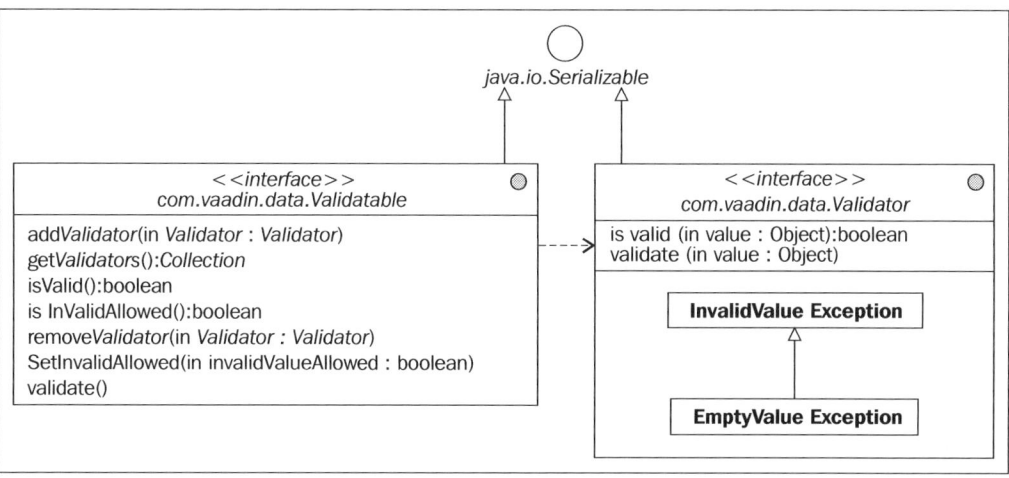

Validator

Validators are specialized objects that fulfill a double purpose:

- Checking if an `Object` is valid
- Validating an `Object`, that is throwing a `Validator.InvalidValueException` if the object is invalid

Validator coherence

It is mandatory, by contract, that the `isValid()` and `validate()` methods be coherent with each other. Vaadin's default implementation respects this rule as `AbstractValidator.validate()` effectively calls `isValid()`. However, when directly implementing `Validator`, we should take care to enforce this in our code.

Validators hierarchy

The validators hierarchy is shown in the following diagram:

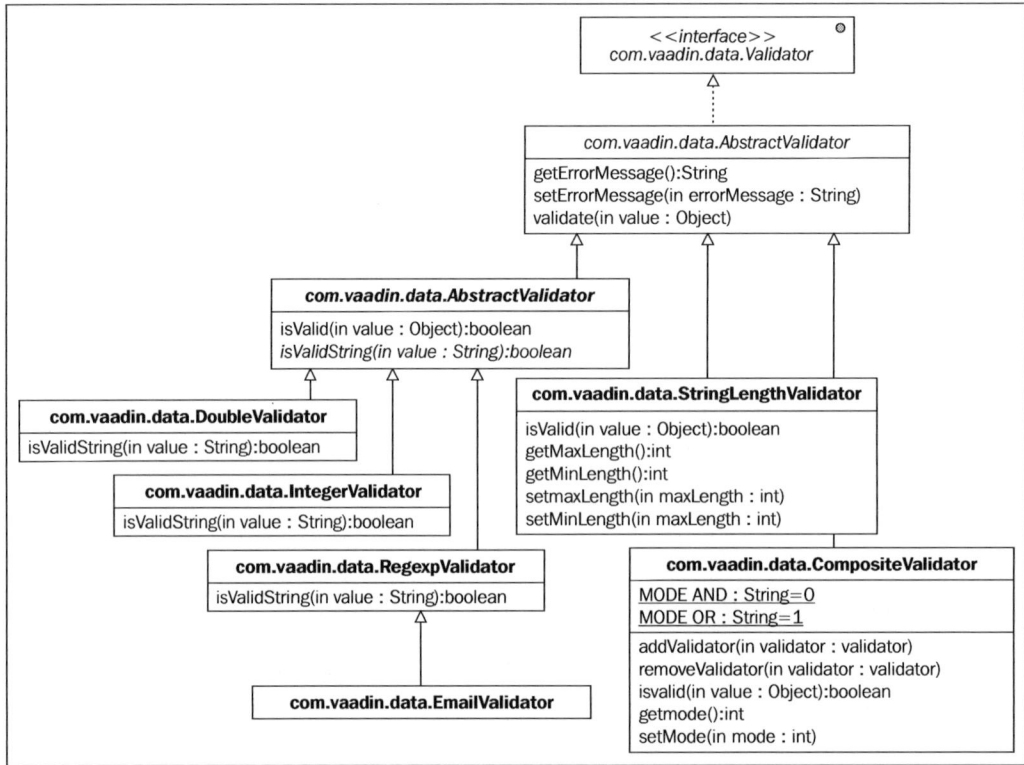

Some concrete validators are available out-of-the-box in Vaadin's API and should fit most of your needs. These are the following:

- `DoubleValidator` and `IntegerValidator` are used for validating `Double` and `Integer` values respectively. Note that although they validate numeric values, they inherit from `AbstractStringValidator` because HTML text input can only hold strings.

- `RegexpValidator` is used for validating regular expressions. This validator is very interesting as it is generic enough to be used for ZIP codes, telephone numbers, and similar objects. The regular expression is passed to the constructor, hence preventing the rule being changed during the validator life.

For more information on regular expressions, visit the following URL:

`http://www.regular-expressions.info/`

For specific patterns and rules used in Java, visit the following URL:

`http://download.oracle.com/javase/6/docs/api/java/util/regex/Pattern.html`

- `EmailValidator` is used for validating e-mails, whereas `StringLengthValidator` is used for string length input.

Regexp, e-mail, and string length validators

Be aware that everything that can be validated with either an `EmailValidator` or a `StringLengthValidator` can also be validated with a `RegexpValidator`. However, the former are much easier to use, are more semantically significant and there is no risk of mistyping regular expressions.

- `CompositeValidator` implements the **Composite** pattern *[GOF:163]*. Each one holds a list of other `Validator` instances. When asking the composite for validation, it will ask each validator in the list for validation.

  Now, the composite may run in two different exclusive modes:

  - In AND mode, validating succeeds if no referenced validators fail validation. **The AND mode is the default one**.
  - In OR mode, validating succeeds if a single referenced validator succeeds.

The order in which the validators are executed has no importance whatsoever as all validators in the list will run, even in OR mode: a failed validation will not stop other validations.

If ours needs go beyond that, and our input cannot be validated with a regular expression, then we should probably use `AbstractStringValidator` as the basis for our brand new validator.

Error message

Validators can be set an error message at the `AbstractValidator` level. `InvalidValueException` instances are initialized using this error message. `InvalidValueException` accepts a single placeholder that is filled with the **field value** should the validation fail, or **null** if the value is `null`.

 The exception handling mechanism itself will be explained in detail in *Chapter 5*.

For example, the following code snippet will display an error message relative to the value when the submit button is pressed:

```
// window is the main window
TextField tf = new TextField();
IntegerValidator validator = new IntegerValidator("{0} is not an
int");
tf.addValidator(validator);
window.addComponent(tf);
Button button = new Button("Submit");
window.addComponent(button);
```

Validatable

A `Validatable` stands for objects that know how to validate their input based on a collection of internal validators.

Like `Validator`, `Validatable` has two main methods that must be kept in synch:

1. `isValid()` that checks if an `Object` is valid
2. `validate()` that throws a `Validator.InvalidValueException` if the object is invalid.

Unlike `Validator`, it delegates this logic to its underlying validators.

Change buffer

In computer software, a buffer is a zone that is used to temporarily store data.

In Vaadin, the `Buffered` interface represents an object that can flush or cancel changes made to its buffer to the real value object, but has the option to override this behavior altogether and ignore the buffer in one or both ways (read and write).

The following schema illustrates this:

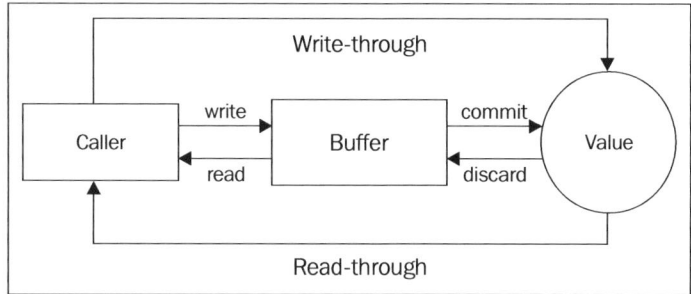

- In a read-through mode, the value read from the buffer is always in sync with the underlying value

- In a write-through mode, the new value is immediately updated

 Note that each behavior is completely independent: A buffered object may be write-buffered but read-through or the opposite, read-buffered but write-through. Beware that those combinations are highly unorthodox, even if sometimes desired, and may result in puzzling behavior at first glance.

The `Buffered` interface is very similar to Relational Databases Management systems as the latter also uses a buffer to handle transactions and isolation levels for SQL Data Manipulation Language (`INSERT`, `DELETE`, and `UPDATE`) statements:

- `commit()` will update the real value with the value held in the buffer

- `discard()` will replace the buffered value with the real one, just like a rollback statement

Buffered and validatable

Input fields can be at the same time buffered and validatable. Vaadin introduces the `BufferedValidatable` to the hierarchy which unsurprisingly inherits from both `Buffered` and `Validatable`.

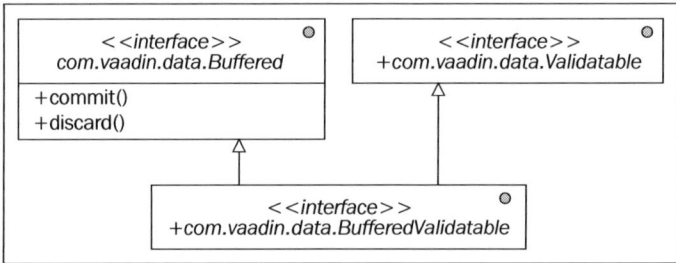

This interface just adds to its superinterfaces how to set/unset that the current buffer invalid value has been committed and query this information through the `invalidCommited` property.

 These methods are used by Vaadin's internals to verify if it needs to send change value events, they can comfortably stay in the dark.

Input

From this point on, Vaadin weaves display features into the data class hierarchy.

Focusable

As inputs are meant to be displayed, they can also receive focus. `Component` describes the `Focusable` interface that has the following three methods:

1. `setTabIndex(int tabIndex)` to set the tabulation order.
2. `getTabIndex()` to get it.
3. Finally, `focus()` to programmatically set focus on a particular component.

A thing worth noticing is that although `Focusable` is declared in `Component`, components are **not intrinsically focusable**, fields are however. That means that labels, which are components but not fields, won't be able to receive focus.

Field

The `Field` interface inherits from `BufferedValidatable`, `Focusable`, and `Component`. Moreover, it adds features that characterize input fields.

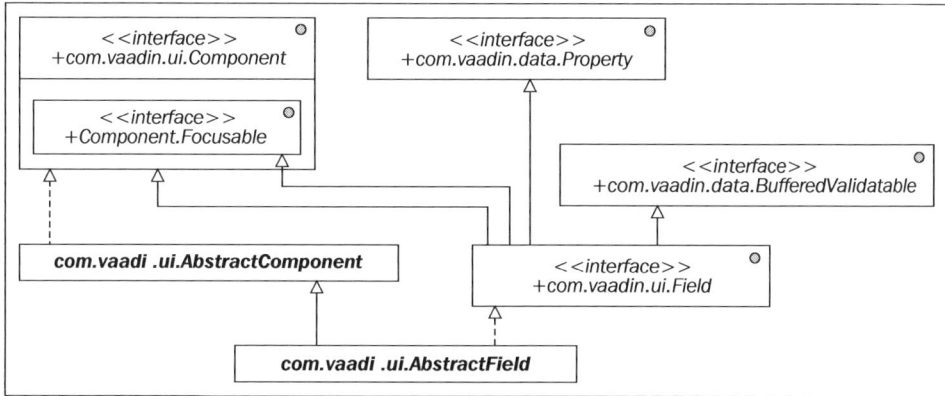

In Vaadin, the following properties are inherent to a field:

Property	Type	Comment
caption	String	Write only
description	String	
required	boolean	
requiredError	String	

- `caption` is the "title" of the field. It is displayed near the field, depending on the layout (see below) while `description` is a detailed explanation about the field. Description is often displayed as a tooltip.

- `required` is an indicator set to `true` if the field should throw an `EmptyValueException` if it is empty, while `requiredError` is the associated message. These are propagated in the same way as `InvalidValueException` seen previously in the above sections.

 As `Field` is an interface, it has no property *per se*, yet getter/setter combinations are handled by properties in the `AbstractField` child class so it is not far-fetched to call them properties even at the interface level

`AbstractField` is a straight abstract class that provides implementation of the `Field` interface. It also inherits from the `AbstractComponent` class, like `Label`, but can hold a value thanks to the `Property` interface.

Also, `AbstractField` provides the `isEmpty()` method to check whether the property managed by the field is empty **or null**.

There is not much more to say about it, except that all input components such as text field, select box, and so on provided by the Vaadin API inherit either directly or transitively from this abstract class. If we need to create our own component, then it is the first class to consider extending.

The text field

The text field class hierarchy in Vaadin begins with `AbstractTextField`, which defines additional features to enhance `AbstractField`.

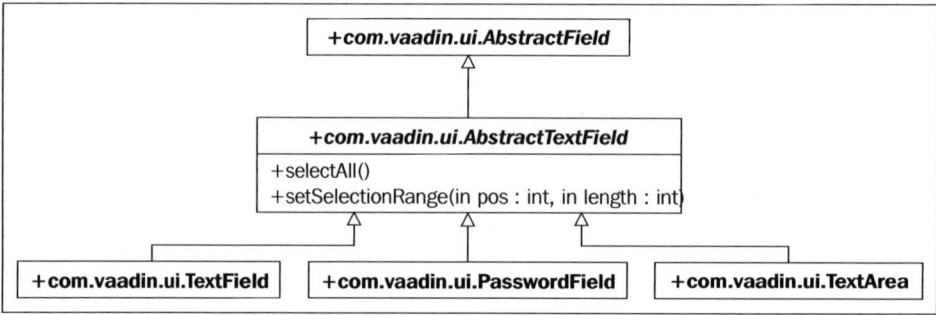

Descending in the hierarchy, there are specialized classes for some use-cases:

- Simple text field when nothing more is needed: this will translate on the browser to an HTML `input` of type `text`
- Password field that hides the characters typed in it which will be displayed with an HTML `input` of type `password`
- Text area that is represented by an HTML `textarea`

However, the real power lies in the `AbstractTextField` that factorizes common behavior and properties. The following table lists those properties that are described below:

Property	Type	Default value	Misc.
columns	int	0	Set to 0 for implicit calculation by the terminal adapter
cursorPosition	int	N/A	
inputPrompt	String	null	

Property	Type	Default value	Misc.
maxLength	int	-1	Set to -1 for unlimited length
nullRepresentation	String	null	
nullSettingsAllowed	boolean	false	

Null

For a computer programmer, null and empty values are not the same thing and may have a very different meaning (or not), both in the code and in the database.

Some software handles the case, others do not. In the former case, the most well known example is when we have to use a GUI to set a NULL value into the database. There is probably a cabalistic keys combination to set the value to null.

The good news is that Vaadin lets us handle null values differently from empty ones. On the other hand, if this is the desired behavior, **the null value must be assigned a string representation**. This means that this string will be interpreted by Vaadin as null, and it won't be available as a real string value anymore. For this reason, it is very important to assign only strings that have no meaning for the user. Examples of such meaningless strings include, but are not limited to: <NULL>, <null>, #null, or an empty string.

Note that this feature may only be used when null values are indeed allowed for the field: it is not the case by default and must be activated if necessary with setNullSettingsAllowed(true) on the text field instance.

Input prompt

An input prompt is the text that is shown in the field itself as a hint for accepted values to the user. As soon as the user starts typing into the field, the prompt is hidden. The prompt font is usually shown with less visibility than the input font itself in order to have a clear discrimination between prompt and input, as shown in the following screenshot:

Setting the input prompt is simply done by calling the setInputPrompt(String inputPrompt) method. We can also query it with getInputPrompt().

The value of the input prompt

Not only is setting an input prompt in your own applications an interesting alternative (as well as a cheaper one) to a carefully documented help, it is also a UI design pattern.

Refer `http://ui-patterns.com/patterns/InputPrompt` for more information.

Cursor

Vaadin lets us programmatically manage the cursor position within the field. This is simple and straightforward. Note that calling the `setCursorPosition(int pos)` will also give focus to the field the method is called on.

Selection

We can select a text field's content with either of the following methods:

- `selectAll()` selects the whole of the text content
- `setSelectionRange(int pos, int length)` selects characters from the `pos` index (included and beginning with 0) to the `pos + length` index (excluded)

For example, the following code snippet will select "23":

```
TextField tf = new TextField();
tf.setValue("123456789");
tf.setSelectionRange(1, 2);
```

A "real-world" text field example

Can you guess what the next code snippet does?

```
TextField tf = new TextField("Age");
tf.setInputPrompt("Please enter age");
CompositeValidator validators = new CompositeValidator();
IntegerValidator intValidator = new IntegerValidator("{0} is not an
age");
validators.addValidator(intValidator);
StringLengthValidator lengthValidator = new StringLengthValidator("Age
must be below 100");
lengthValidator.setMaxLength(2);
validators.addValidator(lengthValidator);
tf.addValidator(validators);
window.addComponent(tf);
```

Here is the answer: It creates a text field, complete with label and input prompt. This field accepts only integer values that have no more than two digits.

Laying out the components

How the UI components are placed on the browser is reliant on the following two factors:

1. The size of the components
2. The layout of the components

Size

Previously, when we stared at the Component interface, we noticed it inherited from Sizeable and we have a look at that now.

Moreover, we have seen in *Chapter 3* that the only terminal concrete implementation provided out-of-the-box with Vaadin is the web browser. As such, size in Vaadin is governed by two properties: unit and value.

Available units are exactly the same as those defined by the W3C CSS1 specifications.

Visit http://www.w3.org/TR/REC-CSS1/#units for detailed information about W3C CSS1 specifications.

As a quick reminder, these are summed up in the following table:

Unit	Type	Symbol	Description	Constant
inch	absolute	in		UNITS_INCH
centimeter	absolute	cm	2.54 cm = 1 inch	UNITS_CM
millimeter	absolute	mm	1000 mm = 1 cm	UNITS_MM
point	absolute	pt	12 pt = 1 pica	UNITS_POINTS
pica	absolute	p	6 picas = 1 inch	UNITS_PICAS
pixel	absolute	px		UNITS_PIXELS
em	relative	em		UNITS_EM
ex	relative	ex		UNITS_EX
percentage	relative	%		UNITS_PERCENTAGE

Setting the length of a component, either the height **or** a width, is done with either of the following two methods:

1. `setHeight`/`setWidth(float length, int unit)`: In this case, both the value and the unit are set. The latter parameter is taken from the constants defined in the `Sizeable` interface, as described in the previous table.

2. `setHeight`/`setWidth(String lengthAndUnit)`: In this case, the Vaadin framework parses the string value in order to compute the desired length and its unit. The string is parsed by following exactly the same rules as followed for CSS 1 length units' specifications.

 Calling `setHeight`/`setWidth()` with either the empty string or `null` as an argument will clear the length value and set the unit to pixel for the desired dimension.

There are also two shortcut methods:

1. `setSizeFull()` is the equivalent to calling `setHeight("100%")` and `setWidth("100%")`.

2. `setSizeUndefined()` clears both the height and width information.

For example, these two lines of code are equivalent:

```
myComponent.setHeight(100, Sizeable.UNITS_PIXEL);
myComponent.setHeight("100px");
```

These two are also equivalent:

```
myComponent.setWidth(20, Sizeable.UNITS_PERCENTAGE);
myComponent.setWidth("20%");
```

Which style to choose?

Using one or the other is more or less a question of taste. Using strings has the disadvantage of mistyping, but you could also use an unwanted unit constant. It is advised to use the style that suits you best but in a consistent manner throughout the project.

Layouts

In Vaadin, layouts are components: they all inherit from
`AbstractComponentContainer`. In this aspect, layouts are full-fledged
components and have an intrinsic size.

About layouts

The web browser terminal translates components into HTML elements. For layouts,
this means each of them generates a `<div>` tag.

Depending on several factors (including user machine performance, web browser
type and version, server performance, and network latency), users may experience
unresponsive behavior when resizing a native window displaying a Vaadin
application, if there are too many nested layouts.

There is already some nesting done by Vaadin, so it is better not to add more than
three extra nested levels. Beyond that, you should take care to know your audience
(intranet, extranet) and to extensively test your UI. Failing all that, the best move is to
migrate from simple nested layouts to a more complex layout, `CustomLayout` being
the ideal candidate (see section *Custom layout* in this chapter for details).

Layout and abstract layout

`Layout` is the base interface for all layouts. It just knows how to use margin or not,
on all four sides or side by side. The space used for the margin is dependent on both
the terminal and the theme used.

`AbstractLayout` is the straightforward implementation of `Layout` and inherits from
`AbstractComponentContainer`.

Layout types

Vaadin provides many different layouts out-of-the-box; there will always be one that
will fit your needs. If you are really stuck with a particularly complex graphic design,
then just take a look at `CssLayout` which is described in this section. The following
are the types of layout:

- **Simple layouts**: Simple layouts are efficient and let you forget about HTML
  and CSS.

- **Horizontal and vertical layouts**: Horizontal and vertical layouts position child components respectively in a horizontal and vertical way. Those layouts are the simplest we can use: they just put components next to one another in a single neat row/column, regardless of the user screen's dimensions. It is the responsibility of the web browser to provide the means to display UI parts that are out of view, usually with the help of scrollbars.

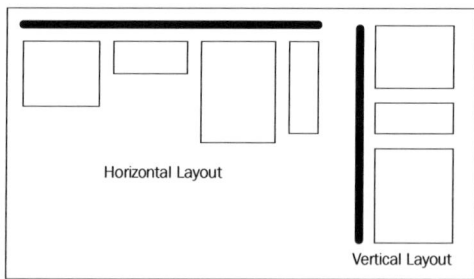

- **Grid layout**: Of more interest is the GridLayout. As its name implies, Vaadin will lay out the child components in a grid-like fashion.

  GridLayout's constructor needs both the number of columns and the number of rows.

- **Form layout**: Fields captions are usually displayed on the top of the relevant field; it is the default location. However, forms are usually label-field pairs where the label is displayed left of the field and each pair stacked vertically. Vaadin emulates this presentation when using the form layout. This is shown in the following screenshot:

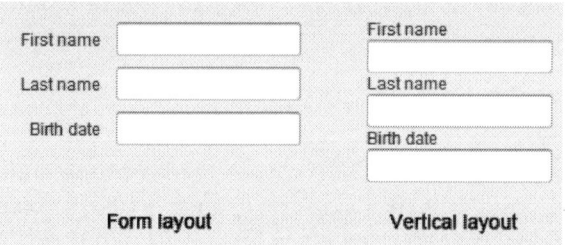

- **Advanced layouts**: When our needs are more elaborate than the preceding simple cases, Vaadin still has the answer. In fact, HTML and CSS let you have a more precise hand over the overall design of your screens.

Leaky abstractions

Using these layouts is a case of leaky abstraction: In most cases, Vaadin shields us from the mechanics and the technology of lower layers. On the contrary, absolute, CSS, and custom layouts force us to dirty our hands with gritty details. Do not overuse them (or at least, be aware), for their use defeats the abstraction the frameworks bring.

- **Absolute layout**: The Absolute layout translates to absolute CSS positioning. As a reminder, it has four possible attributes: `top`, `bottom`, `left`, and `right`. Each attribute can be affected by a length, containing both a value and a unit as seen in the section named *Size* earlier in this chapter, and the browser will draw the component at the exact position relative to the screen.

It may seem counterintuitive but "absolute positioning" means "relative to the layout area edges".

In order to make that work, `AbsoluteLayout` adds the `addComponent(Component c, String cssPosition)` where `cssPosition` is the absolute position written respecting the CSS specifications.

For example, the following code will display the label in the bottom left corner:

```
layout.addComponent(new Label("Made with Vaadin"),
  "left:10px;bottom:10px");
```

Made with Vaadin

- **CSS layout**: The CSS layout goes even further than the previous absolute layout in that it renders its children components in the same HTML `<div>` and lets the CSS position them on the final page. Obviously, it is only to be used for the web browser's terminal.

A whole book could be devoted to CSS specifications and Vaadin theming and targeted at designers. For developers like us, the only thing to know is that each Vaadin component is affected a CSS class in the generated HTML. In order to effectively use CSS, we have to tell the designer how the class name is computed.

The rule is very simple: the class name is "v-" concatenated with the name of the Java component **in lowercase**. The following table shows some examples of this rule:

Java component	CSS class name
TextField	v-textfield
Button	v-button
CssLayout	v-csslayout

 Remember that layouts are components too!

- **Custom layout**: Vaadin can also be used as a templating engine with the help of the CustomLayout. In order to do this, carry out the following steps:

    ° First, find the desired HTML template to feed the layout, whether on the fly by loading the desired resource from an input stream or through a theme template.

 With theme templates, the template is fetched either from the web application's root or from an accessible JAR. In both cases, the layout is referenced under VAADIN/themes/<CURRENT_THEME>/ layouts/<LAYOUT_NAME>.html.

    ° Then, set the placeholders. Placeholders must be div elements and should be set a unique location attribute.

    ° Finally, add components to the CustomLayout by using addComponent(Component c, String location). Vaadin will replace the previously defined div with the corresponding component using location as the key.

As an example, the following snippet of code warmly welcomes Vaadin:

```
// window is main window
CustomLayout layout = new CustomLayout
  (new ByteArrayInputStream("<body><h1>Hello</h1>
    <div location='who' />".getBytes()));
layout.addComponent(new TextField("name", "Vaadin!"), "who");
window.setContent(layout);
```

Choosing the right layout

It may seem a banal, but the right layout is the one that fits your needs. However, there are some general guidelines:

- It is a good practice to begin with a simple layout, that lets you forget HTML and CSS specifications, and then progress to advanced ones if there is a real added-value
- If you come from a client-server background (Swing, SWT, or something else), then realize there is a performance penalty when nesting too many levels of layout
- If only a small part of the screen is complex, then prefer a top-level simple layout that nests an advanced one over a single advanced one

Of course, these principles are too broad to be one-size-fits-all. Nonetheless, they should be useful most of the time: don't have any scruples in adapting them to each specific situation though.

Split panels

In Vaadin, split panels are designed as specialized layouts. They behave as their client-server counterpart though: they contain two components separated by a split bar.

Available properties are as follows:

Property	Type	Default value
firstComponent	Component	null
secondComponent	Component	null
locked	boolean	false

Regardless of the locked indicator, we can programmatically set the position of the split bar with the setSplitPosition() method. It accepts the following parameters:

- The position value as an int, required.

- The position unit as an int (optional and defaults to UNITS_PERCENTAGE). See the section named *Size* for a refresher on available units.

- A reverse indicator as a boolean, optional. If not specified or if set to false, then the position is measured by the first region, else it is by the second.

For example, the following code fragment displays a locked vertical split panel where the first pane takes 100 pixels and the second the rest of the screen:

```
AbstractSplitPanel panel = new HorizontalSplitPanel();
panel.setFirstComponent(new Label("Hello"));
panel.setSecondComponent(new Label("Vaadin!"));
panel.setLocked(true);
panel.setSplitPosition(100, Sizeable.UNITS_PIXELS);
```

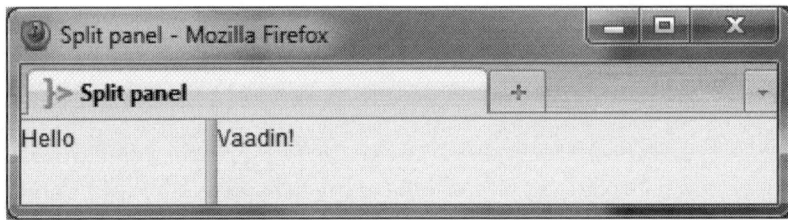

Bringing it all together

Before jumping into the next chapter, in order to learn from a real world example, we will begin creating an application in Vaadin. This application will be our main thread in bringing together all we learned of the framework.

Introducing Twaattin

Our application's focus will be to provide an interface to Twitter. As it will be developed with the Vaadin framework, it is only natural to name this brand new application Twaattin.

The Twaattin design

In this chapter, we will focus our design on what we learned here. From a window point of view, there will be the following two windows:

1. Twaattin won't let us connect to Twitter without first requesting a login and a password. The first window is thus the login window.

2. The Twitter timeline is shown as the second window.

The login window

The login window contains a login field, a password field, and a submit button.

If the login process fails, for whatever reason, then Twaattin does nothing but display an error message. If the login is successful, then Twaattin displays the Twitter timeline and shows a confirmation message.

The main window

The main window aggregates tweets, stacked from the more recent to the more ancient vertically.

Let's code!

OK, the design is done; now we will begin the real work.

Project setup

Create another project like the one we did in *Chapter 2, Environment Setup*, although there are some changes:

-   `Twaattin` should be the project name
-   Use `com.packtpub.learnvaadin.twaattin` for the base package name
-   The application class name is `TwaattinApp`
-   Finally, the context-root is better changed to `twaattin`

Project sources

The sources consist of files updated or created by hand.

Application

```
package com.packtpub.learnvaadin.twaattin;

import com.packtpub.learnvaadin.twaattin.ui.LoginWindow;
import com.packtpub.learnvaadin.twaattin.ui.TimelineWindow;
import com.vaadin.Application;
import com.vaadin.ui.Window;

public class TwaattinApp extends Application {

  private Window loginWindow;
  private Window timelineWindow;

  @Override
  public void init() {

    loginWindow = new LoginWindow();

    timelineWindow = new TimelineWindow();

    setMainWindow(loginWindow);
  }

  public void applicationUserChanged(UserChangeEvent event) {

    setMainWindow(timelineWindow);

    removeWindow(loginWindow);

    timelineWindow.showNotification("You're authentified");
  }
}
```

The application class of Twaattin has not much more than the one generated by the plugin apart from the following:

* Private attributes for windows. Although the parent class has references to windows, there is a need for a distinction between them in order to show/ hide them.

- The `applicationUserChanged()` method. This method is called nowhere in the code right now, but all will be explained in *Chapter 5*.

For now, just bear in mind how to change the main window: first set another main window, and then remove the previous window. Notice the user is also notified that he has currently been logged as per the specs and that the notification is to occur on the new window.

The login window

```
package com.packtpub.learnvaadin.twaattin.ui;

import static com.vaadin.ui.Window.Notification.TYPE_ERROR_MESSAGE;

import com.vaadin.ui.Button;
import com.vaadin.ui.Button.ClickEvent;
import com.vaadin.ui.FormLayout;
import com.vaadin.ui.PasswordField;
import com.vaadin.ui.TextField;
import com.vaadin.ui.Window;

public class LoginWindow extends Window {

  private TextField loginField;
  private PasswordField passwordField;
  private Button submitButton;

  public LoginWindow() {

    loginField = new TextField("Login", "packtpub");
    passwordField = new PasswordField("Password");
    submitButton = new Button("Submit");

    setCaption("Twaattin Login");

    FormLayout formLayout = new FormLayout();

    formLayout.setMargin(true);

    formLayout.addComponent(loginField);
    formLayout.addComponent(passwordField);
    formLayout.addComponent(submitButton);

    addComponent(formLayout);
  }

  public void authenticate(ClickEvent event) {
```

```
    String login = (String) loginField.getValue();

    if ("packtpub".equals(login)) {

      getApplication().setUser(login);

    } else {

      showNotification("You couldn't be authenticated","",
        TYPE_ERROR_MESSAGE);
    }
  }
}
```

Wow, that is our first real window! There are a few occurrences worth noticing:

- First, like our application references windows, the login window in turn references each widget as private attributes.

- Instantiating the objects is the first thing done in the constructor. Doing it here or in each attribute declaration is largely a matter of taste.

- Finally, like in the application, there is a mysterious method that does not seem to be called anywhere. It seems to check the user input, and then either sets the application's user (uh?) or warns the user that his login has been rejected.

The timeline window

```
package com.packtpub.learnvaadin.twaattin.ui;

import static com.vaadin.ui.Label.CONTENT_XHTML;

import com.vaadin.ui.Label;
import com.vaadin.ui.VerticalLayout;
import com.vaadin.ui.Window;

public class TimelineWindow extends Window {

  public TimelineWindow() {

    VerticalLayout vLayout = new VerticalLayout();

    vLayout.setMargin(true);
    vLayout.setWidth(300, UNITS_PIXELS);

    setContent(vLayout);
```

```
        fillTweets();
    }

    public void fillTweets() {

        for (int i = 0; i < 10; i++) {

            Label label = new Label();

            label.setValue("Lorem ipsum dolor sit amet, consectetur " +
                "adipisicing elit, sed do eiusmod tempor incididunt " +
                "ut labore et dolore magna aliqua. Ut enim ad minim " +
                "veniam, quis nostrud exercitation ullamco laboris " +
                "nisi ut aliquip ex ea commodo consequat.");

            label.setContentMode(CONTENT_XHTML);

            addComponent(label);
        }
    }
}
```

For now, the timeline window is just a placeholder: a bunch of labels stacked vertically. In all cases, there is no way it can be displayed at the time.

Summary

In the first section of this chapter, we have seen the building blocks of the Vaadin framework, namely widgets. This was a good reason to detail the Component class hierarchy, which was an excuse to have a look at the following classes and interfaces:

- Component is the root interface for widgets, and has important ancestors
    - MethodEventSource to add listeners to the widget
    - Paintable to make the component displayable on the terminal
    - Sizeable to let the widget be resized

- Window is the base class for screens. It introduced us to:
    - ComponentContainer, a component that can hold other widgets
    - The concept of both "main window" and "subwindow"

- `Label` is the simplest widget in Vaadin. It showed the `Property` interface, a way to decouple the widget itself from its value.
- Text field is a plain input field. Yet, we discovered several features not present in plain labels, brought by its hierarchy:
  - ° Validation with the Validator/Validatable pair
  - ° Change buffering with the Buffered interface
  - ° Focus feature brought by Focusable
  - ° Finally, the Field interface and its properties

Although we only brushed the surface of the variety of components Vaadin offers, looking at each node in the class hierarchy allows us to easily understand future as-yet-unseen widgets.

Components are interesting intrinsically, but each UI worth its salt needs them to be laid out the way we want. The second section lets us browse the many layouts, which also are components, provided by Vaadin:

- Simple layouts such as vertical/horizontal layouts, grids, or even forms
- More advanced ones, such as absolute, CSS, or custom layouts. These are much more powerful, but at the cost of a tighter coupling with the web browser terminal.

Finally, we examined split panels, which are handled by Vaadin as specialized layouts.

We finished this chapter with the first Java classes of our Twaattin killer application!

As yet, components and layouts are next to useless because there is no interaction between them and the server. The next chapter is the answer to this lack, as we will dive into the event-listener model in Vaadin.

5
Event listener model

In this chapter, we will see how Vaadin widgets communicate with each other.

Widgets have to work together in order to achieve a common goal. Like ants, they cannot do so without a means to pass information. In Vaadin and other software, this is done through events and listeners.

In the first section of this chapter, we will explain this whole event and listener thing. We will have a look at the famous observer pattern and the way it is used in Java EE applications.

Then, we will get a grasp on how it is implemented in Vaadin and the different ways one can wire widgets together so one can be the subject and the other observers. A discussion will follow in order to determine which components category is the more suitable to serve as observers.

Finally, we will go further into Twaattin and wire some event listener behaviors into it.

Event-driven model

Most of the time, web developers are blissfully ignorant of what is known as **event-driven software**. It is however, the bread and butter of the client server application developers. We will have a detailed look at this model.

The observer pattern

The event-driven model is based on a design pattern described in detail in *Design Patterns: Elements of Reusable Object-Oriented Software* by Gamma, Helm, Johnson, and Vlissides.

In this computer software book, the authors present answers to common software challenges. Each problem-solution pair is known as a design pattern and constitutes a design library one can draw upon when facing a particular quandary. The **observer** pattern is such a pattern. Here is the problem and its associated solution:

Suppose we have an object that is subject to changes throughout the application lifecycle. Now, this object has to tell other objects about these updates. For example, when a user clicks on a button (the main object) and until the server responds, the button has to be disabled, the menu has to be grayed, and a waiting cursor should be displayed.

We could of course handle the button click from the user and, having references to the other widgets call the adequate methods on them. Then again, the separation of concerns principle encourages us to decouple the button's code from other widgets.

That is where the Observer pattern comes into play. Using it, we will register widgets that are interested in being informed that a click occurred. At the time of the click, a single generic method (for example `notify()`) will be called in each of the observers. What the method really does is up to the implementation of each observer.

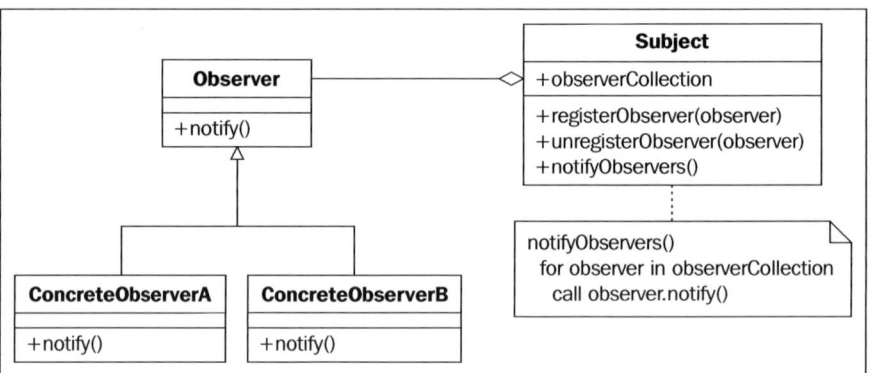

Enhancements to the pattern

The observer pattern is very general and has nothing to do with user interfaces. In order to manage the complexity of the latter, there are some necessary enhancements.

Event

An **event** is an action that is initiated outside the flow of the software:

- The code may or may not handle an event
- **Event-handling** may be either synchronous or asynchronous
- Those events can in turn fire other events

Event details

In the plain observer pattern, the `notify()` method has no parameters. In order to pass information from the subject to the observers, we can introduce one in the form of a detail object.

Detail attributes may include the timestamp of the event, the event's source, and other attributes depending on the event type (see below).

Event types

Passing information through a parameter somewhat enhances the starting pattern, but lacks handling granularity. This means that an observer that is registered to two or more subjects is unable to distinguish between them when notified of an event.

Therefore, an area of improvement is the creation of different event types. The granularity of types is of course dependent on the considered system, no differentiation between types to a type per real event (click, value selection, key type, and so on).

Events in Java EE

Interestingly enough, events and the observer pattern are not widespread throughout Java EE. There are some notable exceptions though:

- Java Messenger Service listeners are objects that connect to a JMS queue. As soon as a message is posted in the queue, the `onMessage()` method of the listener is called.
- Message Driven Beans are specialized Enterprise Java Beans that integrate a JMS listener in the EJB architecture, adding transactional and security features.

- In web application specifications, there are also some listener interfaces available since version 2.3. As a reminder, they correspond to events regarding:
  - ° Request: creation/destruction and attributes binding/unbinding in request scope
  - ° Session: creation/destruction, activation/passivation, and attributes binding/unbinding in session scope
  - ° Application: start/stop and attributes binding/unbinding in application scope

Now, readers probably noticed Java EE does not provide any event-listener pair that is both related to user interface and generic: Java Server Faces specifications has its own event handling, provided of course that we use the whole stack, which is not our goal.

UI events

Thus, event handling in JSF-free Java web applications has to use another path. This path is not specific to Java, but can also be used in PHP, ASP, or other web applications technologies.

Client-server events

One type of event that has to be addressed is the sending of messages from the client tier to the server tier, which can be referred to as "HTTP events".

For example:

- When the user clicks on a submit button, the client asks an URL resource from the server, the server sends the whole page, and the browser displays it
- When the user needs to open a pop-up window, it is the same

In traditional web pages, you can navigate URLs by clicking on hyperlinks and submitting forms whether in straight HTML or through JavaScript.

Different interactions maybe represented by different URLs or a single URL can interpret HTML parameters, so as to have different actions depending on those parameters and their respective values.

Client events

Likewise, client events—events that are limited to the client—are implemented in JavaScript. Examples of such events include the following:

- Changing values of a particular drop-down list depending on the selected value of another: when sex is *Male*, selectable title values should be set to *Mr*

- Clicking on a submit button disables all buttons on a page so as to prevent multiple submissions
- On the contrary, checking a checkbox labeled as "Accept general terms and conditions" enables the submit button

Limitations of URL and JS for events

In addition, there are several limitations to these particular client event implementations:

- First, they are as low-level as can be. This directly translates into a lack of abstractions and therefore, a lack of productivity. In modern computer software, you don't have to think about bits.

- Then, both the client and server code have to be kept synchronized. Changing one end can have side effects on the other one. Unit testing is thus impossible; one has to rely on integration tests that are more complex, more heavyweight, and more fragile.

- Finally, as was said earlier in *Chapter 1*, JavaScript is somewhat browser-dependent and code that goes beyond "Hello world" has to take the differences between browsers, versions, and platforms into account. Not only does it vastly increase the code complexity and decrease readability, but also makes bugs more probable. All these factors have a direct impact on costs.

Event model in Vaadin

The event model in Vaadin is twofold:

1. Implement the Observer pattern
2. Add an abstraction layer to the HTML/JavaScript event

In Vaadin, there are two different ways to add event routing to our objects.

 Note that Vaadin handles the sending of client-side browser events and firing its own events on the server side.

Standard event implementation

The first way for Vaadin to offer event routing capabilities is with an implementation based on typed event-listener pairs. Each event has a corresponding pair.

For example, in order to act on focus and blur events, Vaadin provides the following pairs:

- `BlurListener` / `BlurEvent`
- `FocusListener` / `FocusEvent`

 This design is very similar to what is done in AWT. However, there is a subtle difference in the implementation: the pairs are specialized and are related to a single occurrence type. For example, whereas in AWT there is a single event-listener for both focus and blur event, with the listener having to implement two methods even if it needs only one of the two, in Vaadin there is one for focus and one for blur events, leading to a decrease in useless code.

Event class hierarchy

At the root of Vaadin event class hierarchy lies a core Java library class, namely `java.util.EventObject`. As a reminder, event object is just a thin wrapper around the event source (and it has access to it).

Event

The first class that Vaadin introduces, and that inherits from the former is `Event`. The only contribution of event is to narrow the return type of `Event.getSource()`: it provides the `getComponent()` method that, guess what, surprisingly returns a `Component` instance, which is just a way not to cast yourself.

Typed events

Subclasses of `Event` are of much more interest to us. In fact, each of the widgets seen in *Chapter 4* holds at least one event inner class of its own.

 The design of these event classes shows a good use of inner classes as the event type is only pertaining to its outer class. For example, `CloseEvent` defined in `Window`, has no sense for labels.

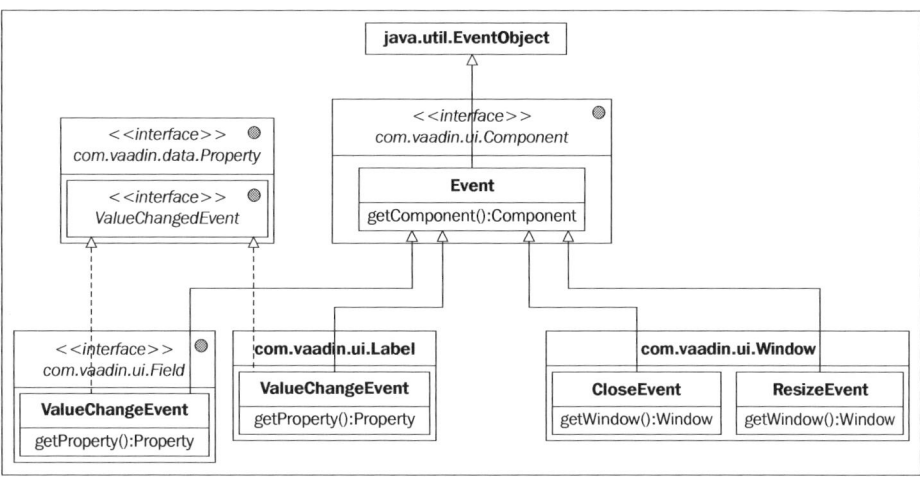

See how subclasses of Event add a getter method with the narrowest return type possible in order to avoid casting the event source? Should you extend the hierarchy further, it is advised to do so, even if nothing enforces it. It is one of those nice comfortable features that makes Vaadin so comfortable to code with.

Listener interfaces

There are many listeners available in Vaadin, and they all share some common features:

- There is one listener for each event type; events and listeners go in pairs.
- There is no inheritance hierarchy between them.
- They extend Serializable so as to be serialized during the session serialization
- They are designed as inner interfaces of the relevant class; for example, ClickListener which waits for click events on buttons is defined in the Button class
- Also, they are defined as being static
- They have a semantic significance, meaning one can understand what it does without looking at the documentation
- They are single method interfaces and the latter:
    ° has a name pertaining to the listener
    ° has a single parameter which is an event coupled to the listener

In order to continue with the ClickListener, the only method's signature is buttonClick(ClickEvent event).

Window

Now, remember our old friend the Window widget from *Chapter 4*? At the time, nothing was said about it, but it contains the following two listeners (as well as two events, but let's focus on the former):

1. CloseListener: that triggers when a window is closed, whether it is a main window or a subwindow.

2. ResizeListener: that is called when the user resizes it.

The following code will display a notification when the subwindow is closed:

```
public class MyWindow extends Window implements CloseListener {

    private Window subwindow = new Window();

    public MyWindow() {

        addWindow(subwindow);

        subwindow.addListener((CloseListener) this);
    }

    public void windowClose(CloseEvent e) {

        showNotification("Just closed the window");
    }
}
```

Note that we have to cast this to the right listener type, otherwise, the compiler complains about the ambiguous type.

Managing listeners

Each widget that may be an event source has two methods for each event-listener pair:

1. A method to add a specific listener, addListener(XXXListener listener).

2. The inverse method to remove it, removeListener(XXXListener listener).

This leads us to the following schema, inner classes' structure notwithstanding:

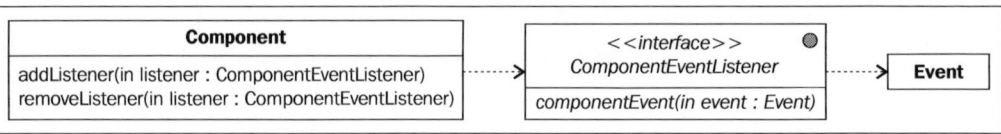

This design is used throughout Vaadin, so it is better to keep it in mind as it is very helpful when using a component-listener-event triplet we don't know. In addition, if we implement our own, it is better to copy this design.

Multi-implementations listeners

Note that listeners adding and removing methods are all called respectively `addListener()` and `removeListener()` with no regard to the listener type. If a widget needs to be the subject for different listener types, we need different methods whose only difference comes from the listener type parameter. It is not a problem for Java, as it comes bundled with a method-overloading feature.

 For more information about the method overloading, refer to the following URL:

`http://en.wikipedia.org/wiki/Function_overloading`

However, troubles arise when the listener passed in a parameter has more than one listener implementation and when the widget is able to add (or remove) these alternative implementations.

We will take an example: our good friend `Window` can have listeners for both close and resize events. If we add a listener that is both a close and a resize listener, which method should be called? Since there is no deterministic answer, the compiler loudly complains:

```
The method addListener() is ambiguous for the type Window
```

This means that we have to cast the parameter into the wanted type parameter to let the compiler know which method will have to be called:

```
window.addListener((ResizeListener) myMultiListener);
```

Alternative event implementation

The standard listener implementation has a "clean" design from an architectural point of view. Nonetheless, it carries the limitation that the listener has to implement an interface. While this may be only undesirable in some cases, it may also be downright impossible when integrating classes from a third party API.

In order to address this problem, Vaadin also provides an untyped listener implementation. Although very powerful, be aware that its versatility comes at a price. It enforces no contract on the listener, thus making it very hard to analyze what objects are listeners in the end.

Method event source details

In Vaadin, this type of flexibility is achieved through the use of reflection. The framework introduces the MethodEventSource interface, which is an implementation of the Observer pattern mentioned earlier in this chapter.

 For detailed information about Java reflection, visit the following URL:
http://download.oracle.com/javase/tutorial/reflect/index.html

It has the following methods:

- addListener(Class<?> eventType, Object object, String methodName) will add a single listener where:
    - eventType is the event class the listener will respond to
    - object is **the listener object itself**
    - methodName is the method that will be called when the event type is received. Other event types won't trigger anything

For example, the following code extract will invoke the "sayHello" method of the current object when it receives a ResizeEvent:

```
Window window = new Window();
window.addListener(ResizeEvent.class, this, "sayHello");
```

 Note: an overloaded method exists that accepts java.lang.reflect.Method instead of a string. It is advised not to use it unless the Method object is already available: code to obtain the latter has to be cluttered with an exception handling logic and it is the same code that Vaadin executes in the method with the String parameter method anyway.

- removeListener(Class<?> eventType, Object object, String methodName) where the parameters are the same as above; it will remove the previously added listener.

Additionally, not using the third argument will remove **all** listeners for the event type on the target object.

Note that Vaadin's implementation has both pros and cons regarding the former typed listener approach:

- Using a `String` as the method name's parameter, whether directly or through a `Method`, is very unfriendly toward refactoring. This means that if we refactor a method's name, we run the risk of that method being called in the code through reflection: it will still compile all right but will cause a runtime exception when running.

- However, this strategy lets us use any object as a listener (or observer). Of course, these can be Vaadin widgets, but also our service layer or even third-party classes that can be used as-is since **there is no contract to be enforced on their part**!

  This is a very powerful tool that Vaadin puts at our disposal. However, remember, with great powers come great responsibilities!

- As a corollary, using strings also means that advanced programming techniques such as **Aspect-Oriented Programming** (visit `http://en.wikipedia.org/wiki/Aspect-oriented_programming` for more information on **AOP**) will be very difficult to implement, if at all since there is no common transversal interface to capture in our pointcuts.

  Of course, one could use marker interfaces, but that would not solve which method to advise, and would raise other problems such as keeping referenced listeners and interfaces in synch.

Listener methods

Although we can use any method of any object as a listener model in the Vaadin model, there are some subtle limitations one should be aware of in order to prevent nasty surprises at runtime.

Return value discard

First, return values are ignored by the event listener mechanism. This does not mean that the method signature cannot have a return value, just that it won't be handled anywhere.

For example, the following snippet will execute flawlessly, but there won't be any sign of it as `toString()` only returns the `String` representation of the object:

```
Object object = new Object();
Window window = new Window();
window.addListener(ResizeEvent.class, this, "toString");
```

 Functional programming gurus, take heed: listener methods should not use functional programming style (that is with no side-effects) as return values are discarded.

Parameter types

Listener methods can either have:

- No arguments: method will be called as expected.
- A **single** argument: in this case, the parameter type should be of the type of the listened event **or** a more general super type.

In order to illustrate these interactions, consider the following event class hierarchy: the fictional `ChildEvent` class inherits from also fictional `ParentEvent`. The following table describes what happens when a certain event interacts with a given parameter type.

Sent type →	ChildEvent	ParentEvent
Parameter type		
↓		
No parameter	Method is called	Method is called
ChildEvent	Method is called	Throws `IllegalArgumentException` when adding listener
ParentEvent	Method is called	Method is called
Object	Method is called	Method is called

> Notice that Vaadin does not enforce any bound for the event type `Class` parameter. However, it is a good idea to limit yourself to subtypes of `EventObject` (see below), since it makes sense. In addition, future implementations of Vaadin may not be so lenient.

Overloaded method bug

At the time of the writing of this book, there is a nasty bug in the way reflection is used. As it can only use a single method as a listener, it uses the last it finds based on the string passed as a parameter.

This means that using overloaded methods, methods with the same name but different signatures (read parameters) may work or not depending on the order of said methods in your source files. **It is a good idea not to use overloaded methods as listeners until this bug is closed.**

Abstract component and event router

Now, the contract is for every abstract component to also be a method event source. In order to achieve this, Vaadin introduces an implementation of the method event source, the `EventRouter`.

This class has the following two important advantages:

1. Abstract components can delegate the event routing logic to the router, thus decoupling event and widget concerns.

2. Additionally, it lets us, if the need be, encapsulate an event router in our own widgets, should we choose not to inherit from `AbstractComponent` but rather use our own implementation.

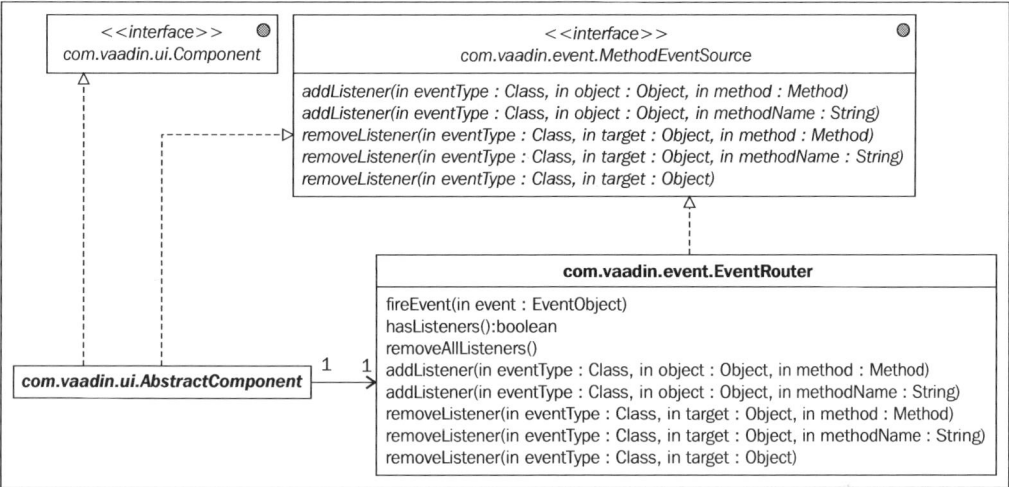

Expanding our view

The respective class and listener classes described earlier are by no means extensive. As for the widgets, it makes no sense to plainly list them, it has no benefit, and such is not the scope of this book. It would only paraphrase the Javadocs anyway.

However, a concrete example will show us that there is no need for it as Vaadin implementation is uniform throughout the class hierarchy: what we learned here can be extended to **any** provided widget.

 If you want to challenge my claim, feel free to do so. Take a widget and verify it is designed as it should be, you will be pleasantly surprised: that is what makes Vaadin such an enjoyable framework to work with.

Button

Buttons are such standard widgets that Vaadin of course provides them.

The most important thing that can happen on a button is the click. From what we have learned, Button should provide an inner class ClickEvent or something similar. This event should have a single method, getButton() that returns a Button, the latter being the button the user clicked on.

Also, Button should encompass a static inner interface ClickListener that has a single method with the following signature buttonClick(ClickEvent e).

Finally, there has to be an addListener(ClickListener listener) method on the Button class itself.

Looking at http://vaadin.com/api/com/vaadin/ui/Button.ClickEvent.html, we can challenge our theory. It appears completely in line with what we have just guessed before!

com.vaadin.ui
Class Button

```
java.lang.Object
  └ com.vaadin.ui.AbstractComponent
      └ com.vaadin.ui.AbstractField
          └ com.vaadin.ui.Button
```

Nested Class Summary

class	**Button.ClickEvent** Click event.
static interface	**Button.ClickListener** Interface for listening for a Button.ClickEvent fired by a Component.
static class	**Button.ClickShortcut** A ShortcutListener specifically made to define a keyboard shortcut that in

Method Summary

void	**addListener**(Button.ClickListener listener) Adds the button click listener.
void	**addListener**(FieldEvents.BlurListener listener) Adds a BlurListener to the Component which gets fired when a Field loses keyb·

Events outside UI

In general, but also in Vaadin, events are not limited to interactions with user interface.

User changed event

In fact, there is one event that is of particular interest to us not only because it is used in Twaattin, but also because there are good chances it will be used throughout your future Vaadin applications. It is the "user changed" event; its structure follows the guidelines we saw earlier in this chapter.

In most applications, once a user logs in, its name, login, or whatever is displayed on the screen. Vaadin takes that into account and provides the following:

- A way to store an object representing the user in the application. As every widget knows its window, and the window in turn has a reference to the application, every widget can access and use the user object.

> Note that Vaadin makes no assumption on the particular object type used. It can be a principal, a Spring Security user details, a plain string, or your own custom implementation.
>
> For more details on Java security, JAAS, and Principal, visit `http://java.sun.com/developer/technicalArticles/Security/jaasv2/`
>
> Fore more details on Spring Security and `UserDetails`, visit `http://static.springsource.org/spring-security/site/docs/3.0.x/reference/springsecurity-single.html#d0e1588`

- An event model centered about changes made to the user stored in the application.

- A user change event that holds both the previous user and the new user. This design lets us manage both login events (when old user is `null` and new user is not) and logout events (when old user is not `null` but new user is) and react accordingly.

The only limitation is that even if listeners can be registered to user changed events, we have to call the `setUser()` method explicitly: such a call usually is made when the actual user successfully passed the authentication process, whatever it is.

Architectural considerations

Until then, we described the event model in Vaadin but we didn't map these listeners to any component (in the conceptual sense) or objects belonging to a particular layer in our architecture.

In fact, there are so few constraints enforced on listener classes (and even fewer when using the alternative implementation) that any object is a candidate for being a listener in its own right, isn't it?

Yet, it is not because something is possible that it is the right thing to do. Here, we stray from the pure Vaadin learning path to something that is more conceptual and thus, more subject to debate. Some architectural choices are in order for listeners.

Anonymous inner classes as listeners

As Swing developers know, the vast majority of Swing examples found on the Web, and even some Sun code, use a vast amount of anonymous inner classes.

This Java language feature lets developers implement an interface or override a class while creating a new instance like in the following example:

```
window.addListener(new ResizeListener() {

  public void windowResized(ResizeEvent e) {

    showNotification("Window resized");
  }
});
```

Anonymous inner classes have both pros and cons:

- Inner classes have access to their wrapping class final attributes
- Overuse of them renders the code confused and decreases readability

Overall, beyond simple "Hello world" applications or prototypes, it is discouraged to use them in applications.

Widgets as listeners

"Widgets as listeners" is the simplest option possible. In fact, there is nothing that prevents us to make them so, as it is legal to do so. Twaattin is constructed this way (see the section named *Twaattin is back*) and it works just fine.

However, this model has some limits that are worth mentioning:

- When going beyond simple "Hello world" applications, the sheer number of event listening methods just clutters the code and dreadfully impairs its readability.

- From a design point of view, this grouping denies the single responsibility principle that forms the basis of good object-oriented software: widget responsibilities should be limited to displaying and event **firing**, not event handling.

- As a corollary, this coupling also prevents us from reusing separately both widgets and event handling behaviors, which is a shame since it should be a feature of OO design.

Nonetheless, this design lets us create quickly simple applications that just work. If used only within this restricted perimeter, or for prototypes, then it is the right choice as it follows the KISS principle.

 For more details on the KISS principle, visit the following URL:
`http://en.wikipedia.org/wiki/KISS_principle`

Presenters as listeners

In "standard" web applications, the Model View Controller design pattern is a common occurrence. In Java, this pattern is implemented like so:

- The view is represented by a Java Server Page. It has only presentation logic and the data is set by the controller.

- The controller is a servlet that:
    - Requests data from the model
    - Feeds the data to the view
    - Redirects the control flow to the latter

- Finally, the model is implemented either as Session Enterprise Java Beans or as Plain Old Java Objects, depending on each application's architecture.

 In order to know more about Plain Old Java Objects, refer to the following URL:
`http://en.wikipedia.org/wiki/Plain_Old_Java_Object`

In rich client applications, the MVC model is often replaced with the Model-View-Presenter design pattern. There are some slight differences between them, but the most important is that the view is in charge for managing UI events, whereas it is the controller's responsibility in MVC.

In such architecture, presenters are listeners *par excellence*.

Services as listeners

Most applications are also designed as layered: the first is the presentation, the second the service (also known as business), finally the data access. Such designs let us change a layer and affect only the calling layer.

One could think about services being called through an event handling mechanism; for example, in order to populate a widget's data in response to a button click.

However, this does not work well in Vaadin, in either event model implementation for the classic one has no return values in listener methods, and the reflection one discards them if they exist.

Conclusion on architecture

In regards to architecture, there is no universal good or bad design. As in construction, architecture in software is contextual and should always be thought of from this point of view. A whole book could be entirely devoted to this subject, and it won't even begin to cover all the cases, as architectural considerations are somewhat empirical and somewhat based on personal experiences.

However, the following points represent some of the factors that can influence architectural decisions:

- **Application size**: A small application is more lenient towards cluttering. In this case, we can probably use anonymous inner classes without too many side effects. On the contrary, a big application will require a more structured way in order to be manageable.

- **Expected lifespan**: For a constant ROI, the lesser the lifespan of an application, the lesser the cost. As such, an application that is a temporary solution has not to be designed as a software jewel. For example, a Proof of Concept application is just that, it probably will be discarded after the proof has been made. Don't waste time on architecture!

- **Team experience**: In this regard, experience is not only quantitative, but also qualitative. While it is true that more experienced developers are naturally inclined to use more structured solutions, you should also consider how developers actually code. If your team already practices MVP daily, then maybe it is a good thing not to change things to much.

- **QA**: Of course, QA is the biggest reason of all to adopt a specific architecture. If the norm is to use widgets as listeners, then don't hurt your head too much and do as you are told.

The previous sections are some examples of possible architectures: there is nothing that prevents you to design other solutions. In fact, you are encouraged to do so if none fit your particular needs for an application.

Twaattin is back

We will put what we have seen in this chapter regarding events and listeners to good use: Twaattin awaits us!

We have left it in a state where only the login window could be displayed, although we provided a timeline window, because we did not know how to manage login. As now we can, let's continue our coding to conform to the following sequence diagram:

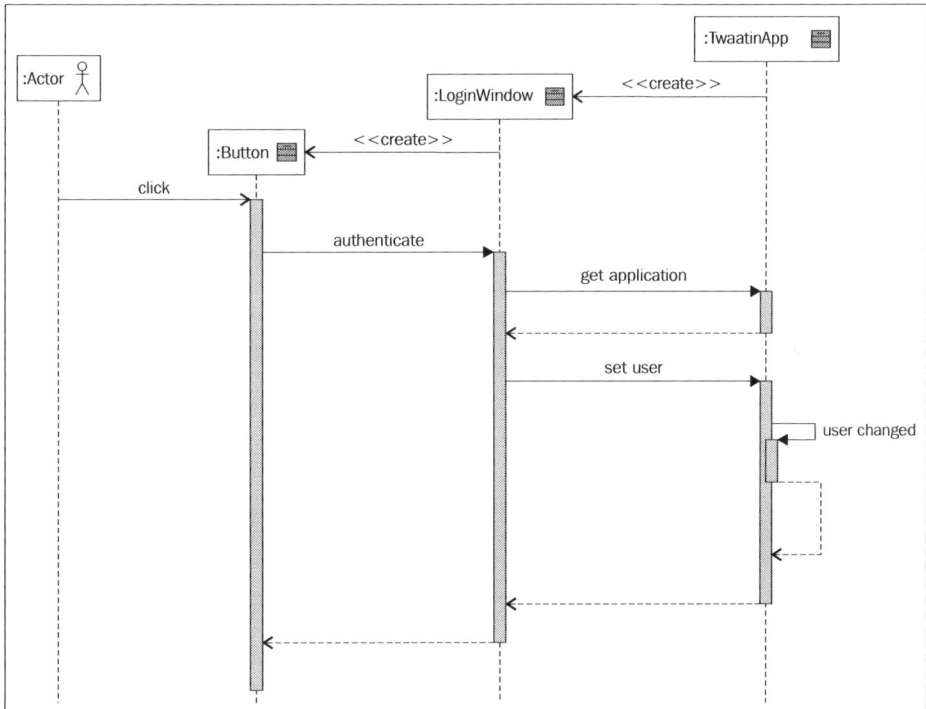

Project sources

These are the complete files. Differences with *Chapter 4* are outlined.

The login window

```
package com.packtpub.learnvaadin.twaattin.ui;

import static com.vaadin.ui.Window.Notification.TYPE_ERROR_MESSAGE;

import com.vaadin.ui.Button;
import com.vaadin.ui.Button.ClickEvent;
import com.vaadin.ui.FormLayout;
import com.vaadin.ui.PasswordField;
import com.vaadin.ui.TextField;
import com.vaadin.ui.Window;

public class LoginWindow extends Window {

  private static final long serialVersionUID = 1L;

  private TextField loginField;

  private PasswordField passwordField;

  private Button submitButton;

  public LoginWindow() {

    loginField = new TextField("Login", "packtpub");
    passwordField = new PasswordField("Password");
    submitButton = new Button("Submit");

    submitButton.addListener(ClickEvent.class, this, "authenticate");

    setCaption("Twaattin Login");

    FormLayout formLayout = new FormLayout();

    formLayout.setMargin(true);

    formLayout.addComponent(loginField);
    formLayout.addComponent(passwordField);
    formLayout.addComponent(submitButton);

    addComponent(formLayout);
  }

  public void authenticate(ClickEvent event) {

    String login = (String) loginField.getValue();
```

```
    if ("packtpub".equals(login)) {

      getApplication().setUser(login);

    } else {

      showNotification("You couldn't be authentified",
        TYPE_ERROR_MESSAGE);
    }
  }
}
```

In the login window, we just add a single line in order for the authenticate method to act as a listener when the button is clicked.

Now, on the button click, the authenticate method is called: if the authentication succeeds, it sets the application user as the login; if not, it displays a failure message.

Note that the `ClickEvent` parameter is not used in the method, and it would be legal to remove it as we have seen in the section named *Parameter types* earlier in this chapter. However, it has the following two advantages:

1. It marks the method as being used as a listener in Vaadin. It is arguably a benefit, but if used in a consistent manner throughout the application, it lets us analyze which methods are listeners, as well as use advanced programming techniques such as AOP.

2. It lets us use the parameter if the need arises and has no side effect whatsoever.

Application

```
package com.packtpub.learnvaadin.twaattin;

import com.packtpub.learnvaadin.twaattin.ui.LoginWindow;
import com.packtpub.learnvaadin.twaattin.ui.TimelineWindow;
import com.vaadin.Application;
import com.vaadin.Application.UserChangeListener;
import com.vaadin.ui.Window;

public class TwaattinApp extends Application implements
UserChangeListener {

  private static final long serialVersionUID = 1196719916711333325L;

  private Window loginWindow;

  private Window timelineWindow;

  @Override
```

```
public void init() {

  loginWindow = new LoginWindow();

  timelineWindow = new TimelineWindow();

  setMainWindow(loginWindow);

  addListener(this);
}

public void applicationUserChanged(UserChangeEvent event) {

  setMainWindow(timelineWindow);

  removeWindow(loginWindow);

  timelineWindow.showNotification("You're authentified");
}
}
```

For the application class, we have to implement the user changed listener and add the application itself as the listener.

 We cannot use reflection event handling because `Application` is not a `Component` and as such, does not have the right method. Alternatively, we could have encapsulated `MethodEventSource` and added the right delegate method to it. Yet, what is done is much simpler.

Now step back and have a look: with two and half lines of code, we introduced event handling. However, it is impressive, even if listener methods were already present.

Additional features

However, now we can log in, two more features would be nice to have:

1. Since we could log in to more than one user, the ability for the application to display the user log in is necessary.
2. Additionally, being able to log out without closing the browser and deleting the cookie is a good thing.

Some small changes are in order to implement these new features.

The timeline window

```
package com.packtpub.learnvaadin.twaattin.ui;

import static com.vaadin.ui.Label.CONTENT_XHTML;

import com.vaadin.Application.UserChangeEvent;
import com.vaadin.Application.UserChangeListener;
import com.vaadin.ui.Button;
import com.vaadin.ui.HorizontalLayout;
import com.vaadin.ui.Label;
import com.vaadin.ui.Layout;
import com.vaadin.ui.VerticalLayout;
import com.vaadin.ui.Window;
import com.vaadin.ui.Button.ClickEvent;

public class TimelineWindow extends Window implements
UserChangeListener {

  private static final long serialVersionUID = 1L;

  private Label user;

  private Button logout;

  public TimelineWindow() {

    VerticalLayout mainLayout = new VerticalLayout();

    mainLayout.setSpacing(true);
    mainLayout.setMargin(true);

    setContent(mainLayout);

    HorizontalLayout hLayout = new HorizontalLayout();

    hLayout.setSpacing(true);

    addComponent(hLayout);

    user = new Label();

    hLayout.addComponent(user);

    logout = new Button("Logout");

    logout.addListener(ClickEvent.class, this, "logout");

    hLayout.addComponent(logout);

    VerticalLayout vLayout = new VerticalLayout();

    vLayout.setWidth(300, UNITS_PIXELS);

    addComponent(vLayout);
```

```
    fillTweets(vLayout);
  }

  public void logout() {

    getApplication().setUser(null);
  }

  public void fillTweets(Layout layout) {

    for (int i = 0; i < 10; i++) {

      Label label = new Label();

      label.setValue("Lorem ipsum dolor sit amet, consectetur "
            + "adipisicing elit, sed do eiusmod tempor incididunt "
            + "ut labore et dolore magna aliqua. Ut enim ad minim "
            + "veniam, quis nostrud exercitation ullamco laboris "
            + "nisi ut aliquip ex ea commodo consequat.");

      label.setContentMode(CONTENT_XHTML);

      layout.addComponent(label);
    }
  }

  public void applicationUserChanged(UserChangeEvent event) {

    user.setValue(event.getNewUser());
  }
}
```

Of course, we need a label to display the user and a logout button that listens to click events, just as we have seen previously.

More interesting is the way the logout method is implemented: it just sets the new user as `null`, which is semantically equivalent as unsetting the current user.

Moreover, this version is now a user changed listener, with the implementation method changing the user label; it is necessary but not enough as will be seen in the `TwaattinApp` code.

TwaattinApp

```
package com.packtpub.learnvaadin.twaattin;

import com.packtpub.learnvaadin.twaattin.ui.LoginWindow;
import com.packtpub.learnvaadin.twaattin.ui.TimelineWindow;
import com.vaadin.Application;
import com.vaadin.Application.UserChangeListener;
import com.vaadin.ui.Window;
```

```java
public class TwaattinApp extends Application implements
UserChangeListener    private static final long serialVersionUID = 1L;

  private Window loginWindow;

  private TimelineWindow timelineWindow;

  @Override
  public void init() {

    loginWindow = new LoginWindow();

    timelineWindow = new TimelineWindow();

    setMainWindow(loginWindow);

    addListener(this);

    addListener(timelineWindow);
  }

  public void applicationUserChanged(UserChangeEvent event) {

    if (event.getNewUser() == null) {

      setMainWindow(loginWindow);

      removeWindow(timelineWindow);

      loginWindow.showNotification("You're logged out");

    } else if (event.getNewUser() != null) {

      setMainWindow(timelineWindow);

      removeWindow(loginWindow);

      timelineWindow.showNotification("You're authentified");
    }
  }
}
```

In the application, there are two things of note:

1. The timeline window is added as a listener for user changed events. Thus, when the new user is set, the appropriate method will be called and the label changed as well.

2. The user changed method is updated to take into account that it will be called in two different contexts: when a user logs in and when he logs out. The logout behavior is symmetric to the login one: set the new main window, remove the old one, and show a notification with the latter.

Summary

In this chapter, we tackled the concept of events and listeners. Both form the basis for the observer design pattern implementation. The latter can be summed up as: when objects want to be notified of certain occurrences in another object, they register as observers and a certain behavior is called, depending on each object's implementation.

Then, we learned that this pattern is used throughout fat client software's user interfaces, but web developers are seldom aware of it: there are some event model implementations in Java EE, but they are unrelated to UI.

In Vaadin, however, we can keep our event-listener related knowledge (or acquire it) because it is fully observer-compliant. There are two ways to register an observer:

1. The old-fashioned way with the implementation of an interface.
2. With a powerful reflection-based API.

The latter has the advantage of making any method a listener method, thus easily integrating the third-party code.

Then, we discussed architectural considerations: the thing to remember here is that the architecture is based on each project's own features. There is no right or wrong answer, but this section hinted at some factors one has to take into account to determine which components are the best for listeners.

Finally, we went further into building Twaattin. Now we have the entire login-logout behavior fully implemented.

In the next chapter, we will connect objects and collections to UI widgets.

6
Containers and Related Widgets

In previous chapters, we have learned about Vaadin's widget-based approach and how it is implemented and how those widgets send events to each other in a nicely decoupled way. This chapter is about the second important part of the framework, data binding.

This chapter is separated into two sections. In the first section, after a general view on data binding, we will have a thorough look at the three types available in Vaadin: property, item, and container.

In the second section, we will discover two new widgets that are able to display containers, tables, and trees. As tables are present in so many applications, Vaadin provides a great deal of features which we will take some time to describe in detail.

Data binding

Data binding is the ability of an application to link the value displayed by a widget with the underlying data. However, it is not a monolithic feature but has the following properties, which can be implemented or not depending on the technology:

- Accessing the data either in the read mode, that is, displaying the data through the widget, or in the write mode, that is, updating the data through the widget

- Storing changes made to the widget's value in a buffer so they could be committed.

- Binding the data to the widget, so that changes to the underlying data value change the value displayed to the user.

Data binding properties

Properties of data binding are as follows: renderer and editor, buffering, and value-widget binding.

Renderer and editor

The important aspect is that there is a transformation necessary between the data, which is an object in its own right and its graphical representation.

For example, one can ask how a date should be shown to the end user. Most solid frameworks create the following two abstractions in order to standardize this process:

1. A renderer component that is able to display data items on the screen, thereby creating a string representation of the data.

   In our example, the date can be processed by the renderer that will probably format it in some way, based on either a standard locale or even the user's locale.

2. An editor component that allows us to change objects; this can be done either from a string representation or from a specialized widget.

   Again, with our date example, the editor could let us change the date from its string representation, and take the risk that days and month are not at the same place depending on which region of the globe you come from, or display a nice calendar.

Buffering

Buffering is a way for widgets to discard changes made to it concerning the underlying data. In this regard, the widget also provides a way to commit the buffered value to the underlying data, or to reset the buffer from the latter.

Note that it is different from an HTML text field that holds a value as the widget could disappear from a view and still hold the buffered value as long as it is the same object.

Data binding

Data binding comes in two flavors: the easiest is when updating the UI component's displayed value really changes the underlying data.

The other flavor is very addictive once tasted: imagine the ability for a value to send change events to widgets to which it is bound. For example, when changing the person's first name variable in the code, the value is magically changed for the user in the GUI.

In order to achieve this, data is to be wrapped by a custom component that adds a whole event-listener model around it.

Data in Vaadin

The good news is that Vaadin brings renderers, editors, and buffering to the table. The bad news is that data is not supported out-of-the-box.

Entity abstraction

Regarding the entity abstraction problem, Vaadin provides a clean design with three interfaces corresponding to a different grouping level:

- A property level
- An item level, the item here being the entity
- A container, representing a collection of related items

Property

We have seen in *Chapter 4*, *Components and Layouts* the `Property` interface. As a reminder, it represents a single isolated value, with accessors available for value, read only indicator and data type (only getter available). In *Chapter 5*, *Event Listener Model* we have seen that it also provides a change event listener.

Now is a good time to learn that `Property` also provides two interfaces: `Viewer` and `Editor`, which `Field` extends.

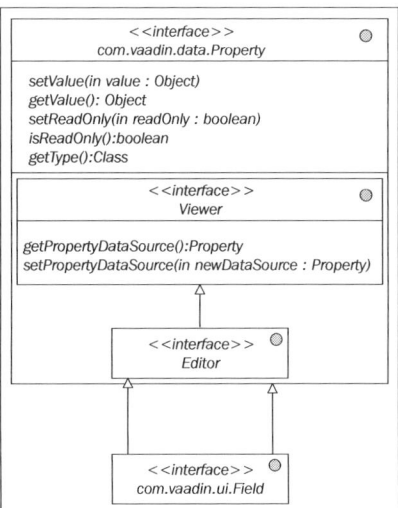

The following two facts are worth noticing:

1. First, viewer and editor have a slightly different meaning than above:

    ○ A viewer represents a class able to use a property as a data source.

    ○ Editor is only a marker interface. It means that the property can be changed through the editor. If not implemented, then the property can still be set, but only in the code with the setValue() method. Likewise, even if implemented, we still cannot call the previous method if the property is in read-only mode.

2. Second, for a property to be and editor, it has to be a viewer, which makes sense: ever tried to edit a value you couldn't see?

Finally, as we have seen before, Property's single subinterface is Field, which is implemented by all widgets in the class hierarchy (with the notable exception of widgets that do not wrap around an editable value such as labels, menu bars, layouts, and so on).

Object property

ObjectProperty is a straight implementation of Property and ValueChangeNotifier.

It also forms the basis of a wrapper around values connected to widgets. The following code snippet connects a date object to a label:

```
Property property = new ObjectProperty<Date>(new Date());

Label label = new Label();

label.setPropertyDataSource(property);
```

It will display the current date as follows:

```
Thu Mar 10 23:23:56 CET 2011
```

Note that Vaadin core components automatically listen to the change events of their respective data sources: changes to the underlying property will be propagated to the label widget.

Property formatter

Astute readers may have some questions regarding the previous example: we have seen previously that a viewer component should bridge the object world and their string representation. The date displayed earlier is just a straightforward result of toString().

Of course, Vaadin provides a way to display our date the way we want in the form of the abstract `PropertyFormatter` class, which is a `Property` in its own right, but adds formatting and parsing features.

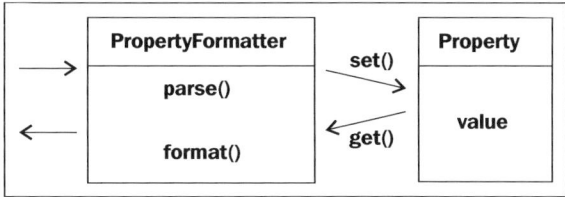

Given this ancestry, `PropertyFormatter` can act as a wrapping proxy around the "real" property. Let's change our previous example somewhat, starting by creating a date formatter:

```
public class DateFormatter extends PropertyFormatter {

    private static final String PATTERN = "MM/dd/yy";

    public DateFormatter(Property propertyDataSource) {

        super(propertyDataSource);
    }

    @Override
    public String format(Object value) {

        if (value instanceof Date) {

            return new SimpleDateFormat(PATTERN).format((Date) value);
        }

        throw new RuntimeException(value + " is not a Date");
    }

    @Override
    public Object parse(String formattedValue) throws Exception {

        return new SimpleDateFormat(PATTERN).parse(formattedValue);
    }
}
```

Now, just wrap the object property inside the formatter as follows:

```
label.setPropertyDataSource(new DateFormatter(property));
```

The same can be done with an editable widget, with the expected result. We just have to replace the label with a text field and it yields the correct result as follows:

03/10/11

Real-world date field

The previous example is just that, an example. If you need a text field that holds the date value, then just pick a Vaadin widget made just for this case: `com.vaadin.uiDateField`, or even better, `com.vaadin.ui.PopupDateField` that comes bundled with a nice calendar editor, you will love it.

Just remember that common use-cases have a high probability of having been dealt with by Vaadin developers.

Handling changes

As seen in *Chapter 4*, all Vaadin widgets are buffered regarding the data they hold and as such, have two important operations: `commit()` and `discard()`. Now that we have seen properties and events, it is the right time to put it all together.

Consider the following use-case: we have a text-field. Once updated, its changes can either be saved or cancelled. The next window code does exactly that:

```
import static com.vaadin.ui.Window.Notification.TYPE_TRAY_
NOTIFICATION;

import com.vaadin.data.Property;
import com.vaadin.data.util.ObjectProperty;
import com.vaadin.event.FieldEvents.TextChangeEvent;
import com.vaadin.event.FieldEvents.TextChangeListener;
import com.vaadin.ui.Button;
import com.vaadin.ui.HorizontalLayout;
import com.vaadin.ui.TextField;
import com.vaadin.ui.Window;
import com.vaadin.ui.Button.ClickEvent;
import com.vaadin.ui.Button.ClickListener;

public class CommitDiscardWindow extends Window {

    private TextField tf;

    public CommitDiscardWindow() {

        setContent(new HorizontalLayout());
```

```
Property property = new ObjectProperty<String>("ABC");

tf = new TextField();

tf.setImmediate(true);

tf.setWriteThrough(false);

tf.setPropertyDataSource(property);

tf.addListener(new TextChangeListener() {

  public void textChange(TextChangeEvent event) {

    showNotification("Change : " + event.getText(),
        TYPE_TRAY_NOTIFICATION);
  }
});

addComponent(tf);

Button commit = new Button("Save");

commit.addListener(new ClickListener() {

  public void buttonClick(ClickEvent event) {

    showNotification("Before commit (property) : " +
      tf.getPropertyDataSource().getValue(),
        TYPE_TRAY_NOTIFICATION);

    tf.commit();

    showNotification("After commit (property) : " +
      tf.getPropertyDataSource().getValue(),
        TYPE_TRAY_NOTIFICATION);
  }
});

addComponent(commit);

Button discard = new Button("Cancel");

discard.addListener(new ClickListener() {

  public void buttonClick(ClickEvent event) {

    showNotification("Before discard (buffer) : " +
        tf.getValue(), TYPE_TRAY_NOTIFICATION);

    tf.discard();

    showNotification("After discard : (buffer) " +
        tf.getValue(), TYPE_TRAY_NOTIFICATION);
  }
});

addComponent(discard);
  }
}
```

The graphical result is as follows:

From this point on, try the following sequential interactions:

1. Change the text: changes are immediately sent to the server with the `setImmediate(true)` call on the text field.

2. Click on Cancel. Prior to the click, `tf.getValue()` returns the previously entered value, stored in the buffer. In essence `tf.getValue() != datasource.getValue()`. After the click, the buffer is reset to `"ABC"` which is the value of the data source.

3. Change the value again, and click on **Commit**. As the field is in a read-through mode, prior to the click, `tf.getValue()` delegates to `datasource.getValue()` and returns `"ABC"`; after the click, `tf.setValue()` calls `datasource.setValue()`.

Item

The previous section taught us about formatting, parsing, and buffering on individual fields. We did not address the unrelated fields syndrome described earlier.

Method property

When faced with the challenge of displaying a structured object, the first solution to our quandary would be to get a reference to each single attribute, wrap it inside an `ObjectProperty`; and then connect it to the right field. That would be too cumbersome and against Vaadin's philosophy.

There is a shortcut to this whole thing, in the form of the `MethodProperty` class. Whereas `ObjectProperty` envelops a single object, `MethodProperty` encapsulates an **accessor** method.

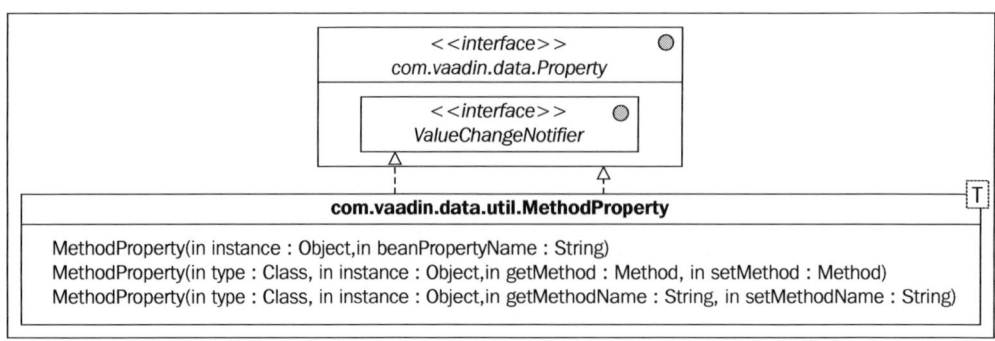

For example, let's consider our previous `Person`, which has properties for first name, last name, and birthdate and a read-only ID. In order to display a person, we would have to do the following:

```
MethodProperty<Person> firstName = new MethodProperty<Person>(person,
"firstName");
```

It is understood that it would have to be done for each single field we would want to display. It is better than the previous solution, but still not satisfactory.

The right level of abstraction

The right thing to do is to use one of Vaadin's most important interfaces, `Item`.

Just as `ObjectProperty` wraps a simple object and `MethodProperty` wraps a structured object's methods, `Item` wraps a bag of properties. Even better, wrapping a `BeanItem`, `Item`'s standard implementation around such an object will automatically enclose each of its property inside `MethodProperty`!

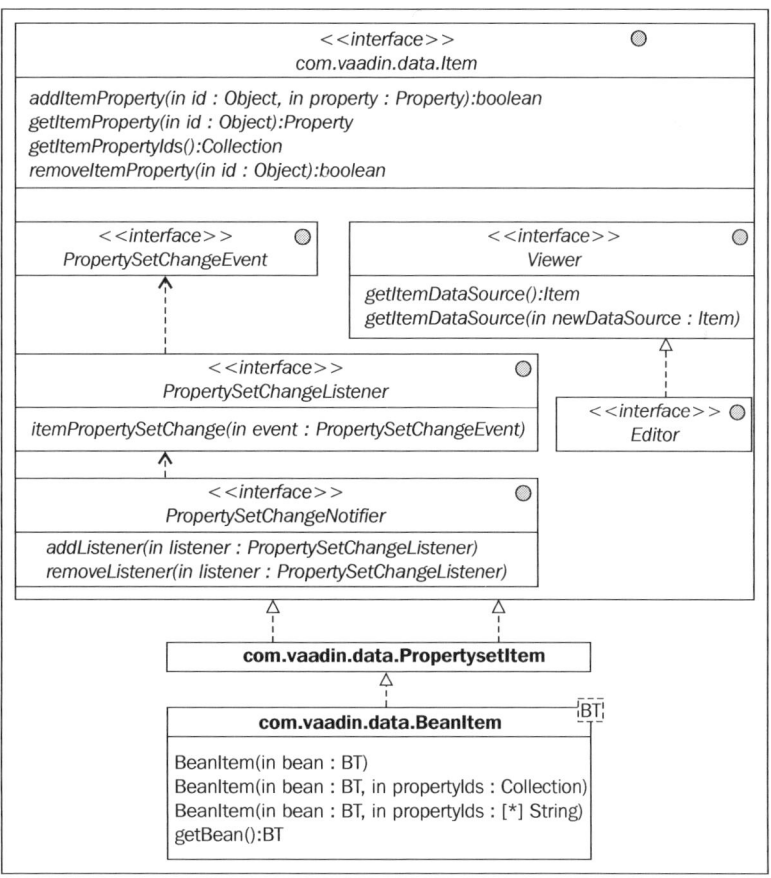

Notice that the previous class diagram represents every aspect of Vaadin seen previously in the same class diagram: event model and viewer/editor pair.

Also, note that in order to see the big picture, I did not represent that all interfaces and classes are serializable. Just keep it in mind for future development.

This wrapping may be done in different ways, but the reference to the enclosed object is immutable, that is, it cannot be changed after the item instantiation. The constructor has different available signatures:

- When only the wrapped bean is specified, automatic wrapping occurs based on reflection. Vaadin will try to find the appropriate bean descriptor (see http://download.oracle.com/javase/6/docs/api/java/beans/BeanDescriptor.html for more information) and if not found will default to listing methods and finding those, which begin with get/set.

- In addition to the wrapped bean, properties to be wrapped can also be specified as a collection of strings or as a string array.

Reflection and valid properties

In all three cases, Vaadin will wrap a Property only if a valid getter/setter pair can be found (actually, a property with no setter is equally valid from a Vaadin point of view, but enforces the property to be read only). In the first case, this is easy as the framework will provide only valid ones. For the last two, extra-care has to be taken in order to synchronize the string parameter values with real properties.

Remember, reflection, and string mean painful refactoring.

Once wrapped inside BeanItem, we can query for the right Property and set it as a field data source very easily.

The following window uses a Person instance and wraps it inside BeanItem, ready to be used in our application:

```
import java.util.Date;

import com.vaadin.data.util.BeanItem;
import com.vaadin.ui.Label;
import com.vaadin.ui.TextField;
import com.vaadin.ui.Window;
```

```
public class PersonWindow extends Window {

  private TextField firstName;
  private TextField lastName;
  private TextField birthdate;

  public PersonWindow() {

    Person person = new Person(1L);

    person.setFirstName("John");
    person.setLastName("Doe");
    person.setBirthdate(new Date(0));

    BeanItem<Person> item = new BeanItem<Person>(person);

    Label id = new Label(item.getItemProperty("id"));
    firstName = new TextField("First name",
        item.getItemProperty("firstName"));
    lastName = new TextField("Last name",
        item.getItemProperty("lastName"));
    birthdate = new TextField("Birthdate", new
        DateFormatter(item.getItemProperty("birthdate")));

    addComponent(id);
    addComponent(firstName);
    addComponent(lastName);
    addComponent(birthdate);
  }
}
```

The following screenshot shows the final result:

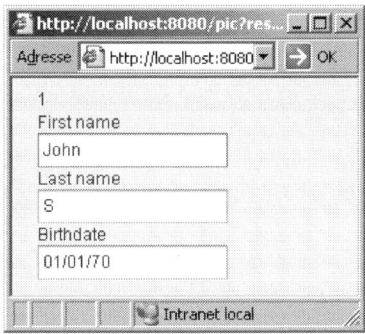

Easy commit with forms

Our screen is nice and good, but probably misses a commit and a cancel button, as shown for the single date field previously.

If we try to do it, we are going to run into some hardship. Which one? Well, in our previous date example, committing or discarding involved a single field. Now, with three fields, are we going to commit/discard each field individually? That wouldn't be very productive; surely, there must be a way to make it easier.

In fact, there is one, in the form of the Form class. We talked about Form when describing available layouts in *Chapter 4*. Forms have another nice feature: they can have an Item as their data source, but they also have both global commit() and discard() operations that will **commit/discard all wrapped item properties globally**.

 Form's default layout is FormLayout which displays fields on the same "line" as their respective label but it can have any layout.

Just replace the individual component addition in the previous snippet with the following code:

```
Form form = new Form();
form.setItemDataSource(item);
addComponent(form);
```

We get the following result, without any further configuration:

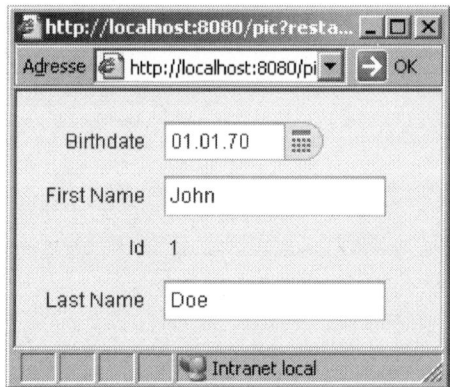

This approach has both pros and cons. Among the advantages, we can list the following:

- It is both simpler and more concise
- We get a date field input for free, with calendar included
- When there is no setter, Vaadin is smart enough to only display a label
- Labels are given for free

However, field formatting and field ordering defaults may not suit our needs. The good news is that all these defaults are fully configurable!

Configuring field types

By default, Vaadin creates fields for each of the following types:

Type	Field	Graphical representation
java.util.Date	PopupDateField	
boolean	CheckBox	
Any other type	TextField	

Nonetheless, it is always possible to override this behavior with a little effort.

Above, we presented the Item interface: it has methods for managing properties, so it is feasible to remove the one we don't like and add what we prefer. Restoring the previous date field is just a matter of doing it:

```
Property property = new MethodProperty<Person>(person, "birthdate");
item.removeItemProperty("birthdate");
item.addItemProperty("birthdate", new DateFormatter(property));
```

As a word of warning, be aware that adding an already present property to an item will change nothing, but return `false` to hint at this behavior; in this regard, it is very similar to the Collections API. It is also why we have to remove the property first before adding a new one under the same key.

Ordering fields

Default field ordering is unspecified, so it has to be configured in most cases.

Ordering fields is as simple as passing the rightly ordered array to the `BeanItem` constructor along with the object to wrap. It also has the side effect of allowing us to remove the fields we don't want to be shown.

In our case, this code orders the fields as in our original person example.

```
BeanItem<Person> item = new BeanItem<Person>(person, new String[]
{"id", "firstName", "lastName", "birthdate"});
```

Changing captions

Default captions use the property name and convert it to upper cased spaced text.

If the caption is not desired, `Form` has a field getter method, `getField(Object propertyId)`. Changing a caption is just a matter of getting a reference on the right field and changing its caption property. The following code removes the caption of the ID and sets the caption for `firstName` and `lastName`:

```
form.getField("id").setCaption(null);
form.getField("firstName").setCaption("First name");
form.getField("lastName").setCaption("Last name");
```

Updating our code to reflect these changes gives us the following appearance:

Overall form configuration

In most cases, `Form` default display behavior is enough and the remaining configuration is small potatoes compared to creating all fields from scratch.

In other cases, however, the configuration effort nears the amount of scratch code required. Think about the single case of dates: in Vaadin, date fields use the JVM locale for formatting and parsing dates. This may be a desirable default, but some companies store such preferences elsewhere, requiring us to access and use that preference. Thus, we would need to access the latter and the formatting to the desired value.

We could of course manage to configure each date throughout our applications, but that doesn't sound like a very interesting task to do (not to mention the probability of oversights). It is fortunate indeed that Vaadin provides the right way to do it, which works as follows.

In fact, fields provided by forms do not come out of thin air. Forms delegate their creation to a factory, and Vaadin provides one that, for example, creates pop-up date fields from `Date` properties.

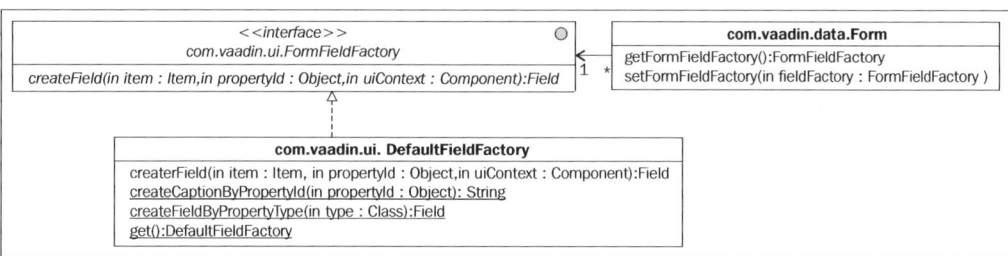

We have several options in order to create our own factory:

- Create one from scratch
- Inherit from the default and override the `createField()` method
- Compose one from encapsulating the default and delegate appropriate calls to it

As composition is preferable over inheritance and the default factory is a singleton, we will implement the last solution. It is a two-step process.

First, create a text field class that knows how to display dates as strings and strings as dates. It reuses the former date formatter;

```
public class CustomDateField extends TextField {

  @Override
  public void setPropertyDataSource(Property newDataSource) {

    super.setPropertyDataSource(new DateFormatter(newDataSource));
  }
}
```

Second, create the factory. It creates a custom date field if the property is of the type Date, otherwise delegate to the default field factory:

```
public class CustomFieldFactory implements FormFieldFactory {

  private FormFieldFactory delegate = DefaultFieldFactory.get();

  @Override
  public Field createField(Item item, Object propertyId,
    Component uiContext) {

    Class<?> type = item.getItemProperty(propertyId).getType();

    if (Date.class.isAssignableFrom(type)) {

      CustomDateField cdf = new CustomDateField();

      cdf.setCaption(
        DefaultFieldFactory.createCaptionByPropertyId(propertyId));

      return cdf;
    }

    return delegate.createField(item, propertyId, uiContext);
  }
}
```

Now, setting the custom field factory to the form **before** setting the data source will yield the expected result, as shown in the following screenshot:

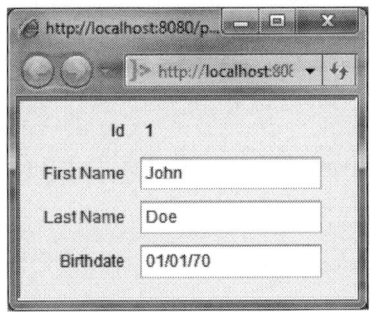

Container

In the previous section, we made the step from displaying a single object to a structured object. The next step is to learn how to display a list of structured objects, and that is the realm of Vaadin's `Container` interface.

Containers bring a completely new dimension to data binding.

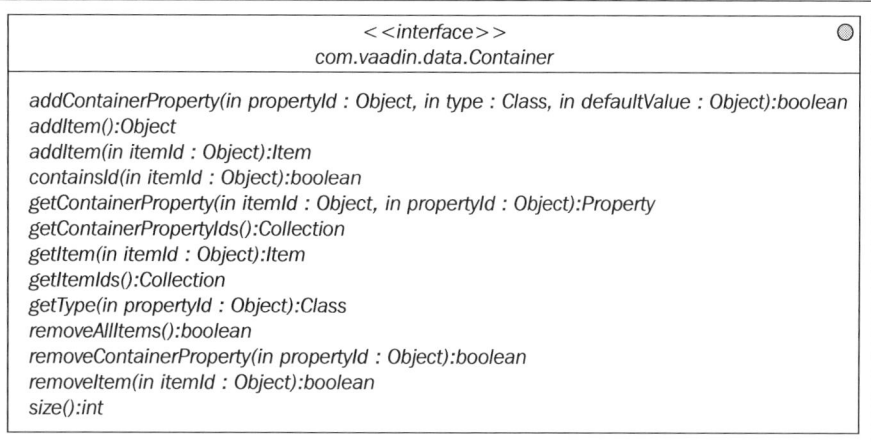

```
<<interface>>
com.vaadin.data.Container

addContainerProperty(in propertyId : Object, in type : Class, in defaultValue : Object):boolean
addItem():Object
addItem(in itemId : Object):Item
containsId(in itemId : Object):boolean
getContainerProperty(in itemId : Object, in propertyId : Object):Property
getContainerPropertyIds():Collection
getItem(in itemId : Object):Item
getItemIds():Collection
getType(in propertyId : Object):Class
removeAllItems():boolean
removeContainerProperty(in propertyId : Object):boolean
removeItem(in itemId : Object):boolean
size():int
```

The best way to picture a container is to think of a 2D matrix: lines are items and columns are properties or a SQL table where a single property is a column, items are rows and the container the table itself.

However, there are some constraints on items put in a container:

- All items in a container must have the same properties, meaning:
  - Properties must have the same ID
  - Properties must have the same data type
- Each item must be identified by a unique non-null identifier. `Container` enforces no particular condition on this ID, though children classes can. In essence, the ID is a key to access the corresponding item.

Filtering and sorting

Containers may also have additional capabilities.

Filterable

Filterable containers may display only some of its contained items, based on declared filters.

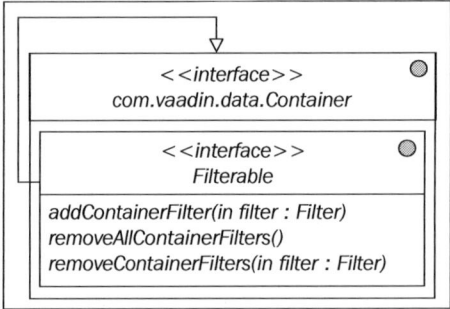

Filters can be either added or removed, and they are **additive**.

Filter

API change

Filters are the single are of incompatibility between Vaadin 6.5 and 6.6. In version 6.5, only filters based on string representations could be added. Version 6.6 filters are described below: when migrating, take care of filters.

Filters are based on the `Filter` interface, which has two simple methods:

1. `appliesToProperty(Object propertyId)` checks whether this filter applies to a specific property and returns a boolean accordingly. It's used as a first step, in order to avoid possible algorithm overheads by the second method.

2. `passesFilter(Object itemId, Item item)` applies the real filter to the object and also returns a boolean whether this object passes the filter and should be displayed.

Ordered

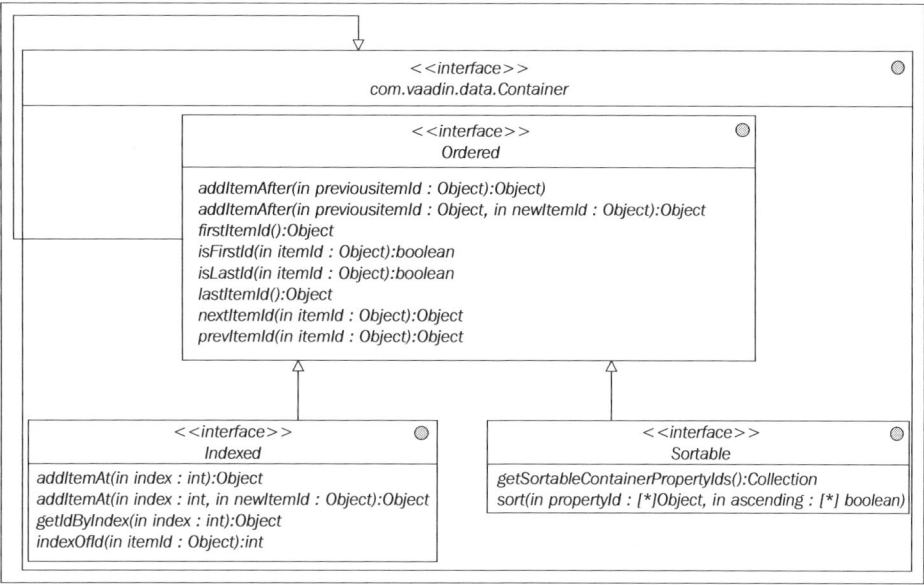

An ordered container lets us:

- Insert an item after an already present item
- Get the first/last present item
- Get the next/previous item given a present item ID

That is it, it stops there. However, it has two more interesting child interfaces.

Containers that are also `Indexed` let us add items based on an index, as well as get the index of an object from its ID and vice versa. These features are seldom used; of much more interest is the `Sortable` interface.

As its name implies, it allows us to sort the items found in the container. The `sort()` method accepts the following two parameters:

1. An array of property IDs. The sort is executed on the first property. If there is equality, sort continues with the second property, and so on.
2. An array of boolean values that refer to the sort order; `true` meaning ascending, `false` descending.

Note that both arrays must have the same length. Moreover, we have to explicitly tell which properties are sortable with the `getSortableContainerPropertyIds()` method.

Before playing with ordering, we will need some data. We will use the `Person` class defined earlier

ID	First name	Last name	Birth date
1	John	DOE	01/01/1970
2	Jane	doe	01/01/1970
3	jules	winnfield	12/21/1948
4	vincent	Vega	02/17/1954

If we try to sort combinations on the sample data, here are the results:

Property	Ascending	Lines order
firstName	true	2, 1, 3, 4 ("Jane", "John", "jules", "vincent")
firstName	false	4, 3, 1, 2 ("vincent", "jules", "John", "Jane")
lastName	true	1, 4, 2, 3 ("DOE", "Vega", "doe", "winnfield")
birthdate	true	3, 4, 1, 2

The first and the second sort seem to display the expected result. However, the third sort seems to be case-sensitive. However, with the fourth sort, it gets right again: sort is based on underlying the date value, which is desirable.

Item sorter

The fact is, concrete sortable container classes (which we will see later in this chapter, have patience) delegate sorting to an item sorter.

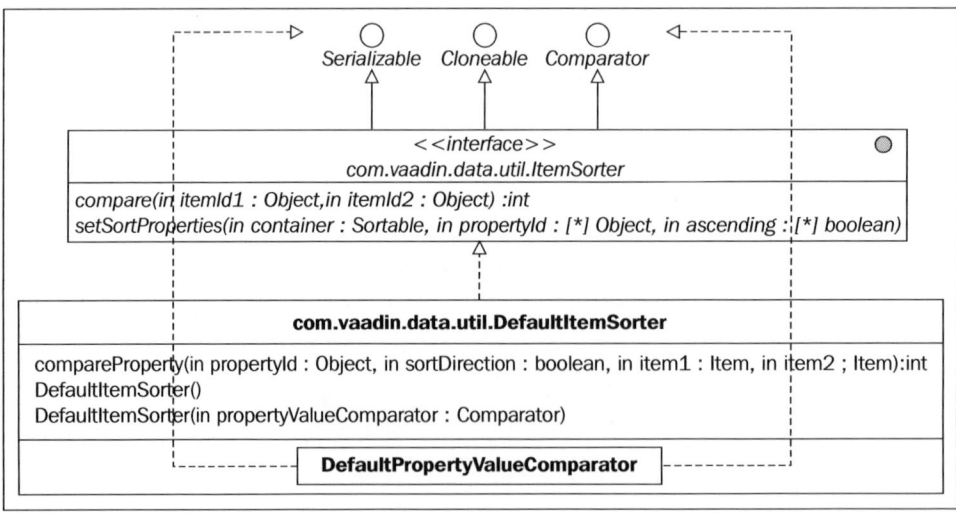

`DefaultItemSorter` is, guess what, the item sorter that is used if no other is set. In turn, it uses a `DefaultPropertyValueComparator` in order to compare each property. Note that the latter implementation infers compares properties using `Comparable`.

 If properties are not `Comparable`, Vaadin will throw a `ClassCastException`.

Therefore, dates being `Comparable` are sorted in the right order. Yet, last names being strings are compared using the `compareTo()` method which is case-sensitive manner by default. In order to be case-insensitive, we should use `compareToIgnoreCase()`.

As an example, we will create a property value comparator that will sort persons by names, either first or last, with no regard to case:

```java
public class CaseInsensitivePropertyValueComparator
  implements Comparator<Object> {

  private Comparator<Object> delegate = new
    DefaultPropertyValueComparator();

  @Override
  public int compare(Object prop1, Object prop2) {

    if (prop1 instanceof String && prop2 instanceof String) {

      String string1 = (String) prop1;
      String string2 = (String) prop2;

      return string1.compareToIgnoreCase(string2);
    }

    return delegate.compare(prop1, prop2);
  }
}
```

This new comparator does the same as the default one (in fact, it delegates to it if compared properties are not strings), but compares strings with the right method.

Then, it is just a matter of passing the comparator as a constructor argument to the sorter, and then the sorter to the container implementation. Now, the third sort becomes 1, 2, 4, and 3 ("DOE", "doe", "vega", "winnfield") which is the expected result.

Concrete indexed containers

Though container properties (filterable, sortable, and ordered) are designed so as to be independent, the vital `AbstractBeanContainer` implements all three. This suits our needs just fine nonetheless.

`AbstractBeanContainer` also introduces two important concepts:

1. Item sorter, that we just talked about above
2. Bean ID resolver. When we described container previously, we saw that an ID was just a key to a glorified hash map. Now, there must be some way to get the key: either pass it when adding an item or provide a way to compute the key from the bean. The latter is the responsibility of the bean ID resolver.

From there, the framework provides two simple implementations, which both use introspection on items to define what the container properties will be:

- `BeanItemContainer` which uses the bean itself as the identifier. In order to do this, it redefines a very simple bean ID resolver `IdentityBeanResolver`
- `BeanContainer` which either enforces:
    - Passing an identifier along with the item to be added with the `addItem()` method
    - Using a bean ID resolver which computes an ID when adding a bean with the `addBean()` method

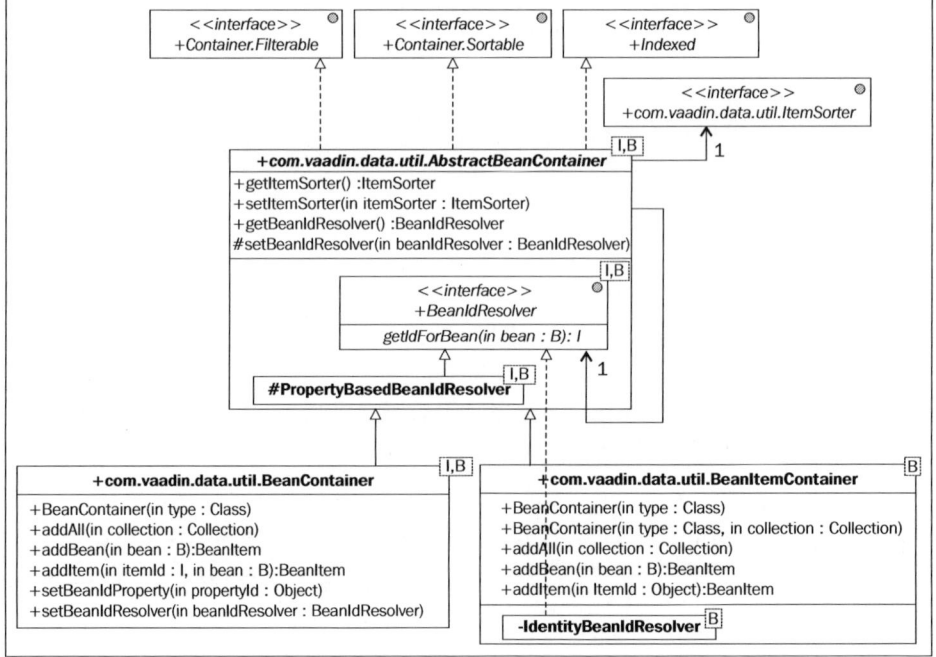

 In order not to add even more complexity to the diagram, which is already dense enough, methods coming from `Ordered` and `Indexed` are not shown. Just remember they exist.

As an example, let's create a bean container for our persons. This container will use the person's `id` as the key to the person itself.

The first step consists of creating the bean ID resolver. It is simple enough:

```
public class PersonIdResolver implements BeanIdResolver<Long, Person>
{

  @Override
  public Long getIdForBean(Person person) {

    return person.getId();

  }

}
```

Then, we can use our bean container as expected:

```
BeanContainer<Long, Person> container =
  new BeanContainer<Long, Person>(Person.class);

container.setBeanIdResolver(new PersonIdResolver());

container.addAll(persons);

Person person1 = container.getItem(1L);
```

This example is trivial, however, how many times will we need an ID resolver that is not based on an identifier present in the bean? In order to prevent creating a bean ID resolver each time, Vaadin also provides a bean ID resolver based on a property. The previous code therefore becomes:

```
BeanContainer<Long, Person> container =
  new BeanContainer<Long, Person>(Person.class);

container.setBeanIdProperty("id");

container.addAll(persons);
```

Now, we can forget about our custom bean ID resolver. Note that Vaadin uses the `PropertyBasedBeanIdResolver` under the covers.

Hierarchical

Simple tabular data management is addressed by the previous features and `AbstractBeanContainer` implementations; hierarchized data management, however, is not.

Vaadin provides another abstraction to manage it however, with the `Hierarchical` interface.

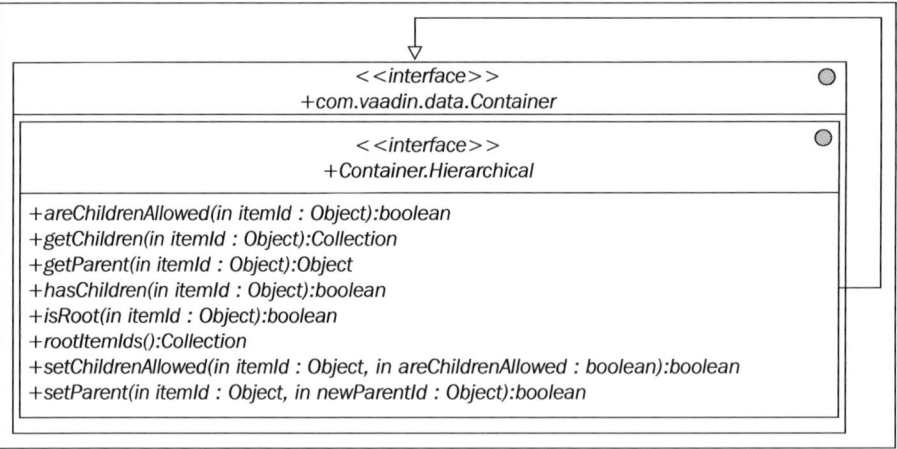

It provides some ways to organize data in a tree-like way:

- Get/set leaf status of a node
- Get root status of a node
- Query for root nodes, note that multiple roots are possible
- Get the parent/children of a node
- Set a new parent for a node, thereby moving it around

Containers and the GUI

When we talked about `Property` earlier, it was a no-brainer to set it as a text field data source in order to display it.

Container data source

In order to use `Container` as a widget data source, there are still some details about it we have to understand:

- First, `Container` mimics the structure of `Property` insofar as it encloses both a `Viewer` and an `Editor` interface.
- Second, there is a parallel between `AbstractField` and `AbstractSelect`, the parent class for all widgets able to display a `Container`.

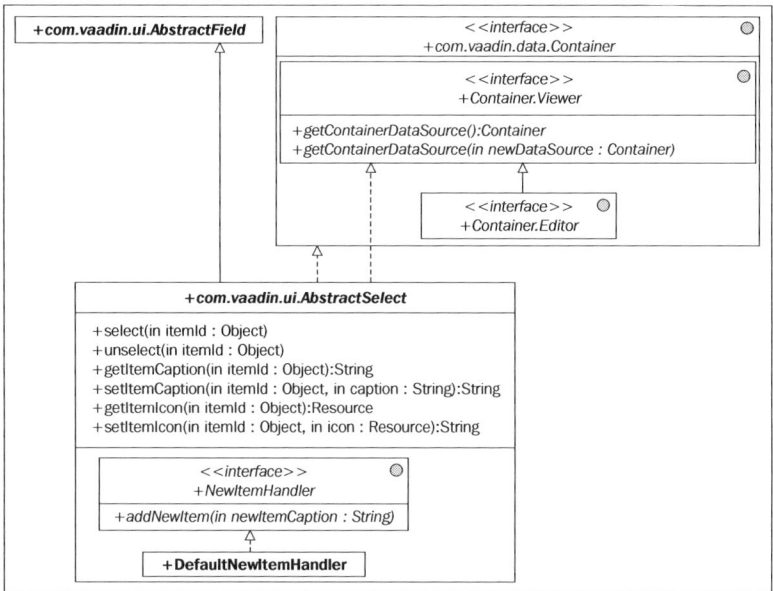

In addition to the previous methods, `AbstractSelect` also has some properties. These are summarized in the following table:

Property	Type	Default value
itemCaptionMode	int	ITEM_CAPTION_MODE_EXPLICIT_DEFAULTS_ID
itemCaptionPropertyId	Object	null
itemIconPropertyId	Object	null
multiSelect	boolean	false
newItemHandler	NewItemHandler	DefaultNewItemHandler
newItemsAllowed	boolean	false
nullSelectionAllowed	boolean	true
nullSelectionItemId	Object	null

Displaying items

Items may be represented both by caption and by icon.

The simplest way to do that is to assign a specific item a caption and/or an icon with the `setItemCaption()` and `setItemIcon()` respectively:

```
// select is an abstract select
select.addItem(person);
select.setItemCaption(person, person.getFirstName() + " " + person.
getLastName());
```

However, in this case, we have to add items one by one and lose the ability to initialize the widget with a container data source which is the whole point.

Abstract select has a mode property that lets us manage it as such. Available values for this property are:

Constant	Computed caption value
`ITEM_CAPTION_MODE_EXPLICIT`	None: we have to set it for each item explicitly, like in the previous example
`ITEM_CAPTION_MODE_ICON_ONLY`	None: only an icon is shown. Icon must be set explicitly for each item
`ITEM_CAPTION_MODE_ID`	Item's id `toString()`
`ITEM_CAPTION_MODE_ITEM`	Item `toString()`
`ITEM_CAPTION_MODE_INDEX`	Item's index in the container
`ITEM_CAPTION_MODE_EXPLICIT_DEFAULTS_ID`	By default Item's id `toString()`, but individual items can be set a caption, thus overriding the default value
`ITEM_CAPTION_MODE_PROPERTY`	An item property is used, which is specified with `setItemCaptionPropertyId()`

Note that setting the caption item by item or using a general strategy is mutually exclusive, save in the case of `ITEM_CAPTION_MODE_EXPLICIT_DEFAULTS_ID`, which is the default. Also, be aware that:

- The defined strategy will take precedence over manually set caption
- The framework won't say anything about it if we try to set it anyway

As an example, let's display our persons. We would like to show both the first and the last name, and nothing really suits our needs: item IDs have a whole different purpose and redefining `toString()` seems a bad option. However, we could surely create a computed property from scratch as follows:

```
public String getDisplayName() {
  return firstName + " " + lastName;
}
```

Then, using this property is just a matter of configuring the abstract select:

```
select.setItemCaptionMode(AbstractSelect.ITEM_CAPTION_MODE_PROPERTY);
select.setItemCaptionPropertyId("displayName");
```

 From a design point of view, it would have been cleaner to create a view object but for clarity's sake, it is simpler this way.

Handling new items

New items may be added to the abstract select. The exact behavior is delegated to a `NewItemHandler`. The default one just checks whether the select is read-only and throws a `Property.ReadOnlyException` in this case.

Typical use-cases of new item handlers include:

- Inserting the new item as a row in the data tier (read database)
- Tracing the identity of the connected user and so on

Null items

Use-cases may allow (or not) selecting `null` values. Such configuration can easily be done through the `nullSelectionAllowed()` method.

`null` values cannot be added to containers as such, but `AbstractSelect` can have items that contain `null` value. Just create a specific item ID (or object depending on the bean item container implementation) and call `setNullSelectionItemId()` with it as a parameter.

Now querying the value of the widget when the dummy is selected will return `null` and not the real object.

Container widgets

Beyond `AbstractSelect`, there are some concrete widgets that all may display a container in the GUI.

Depending on the properties described earlier and the type of implementation, we can get virtually any result we need.

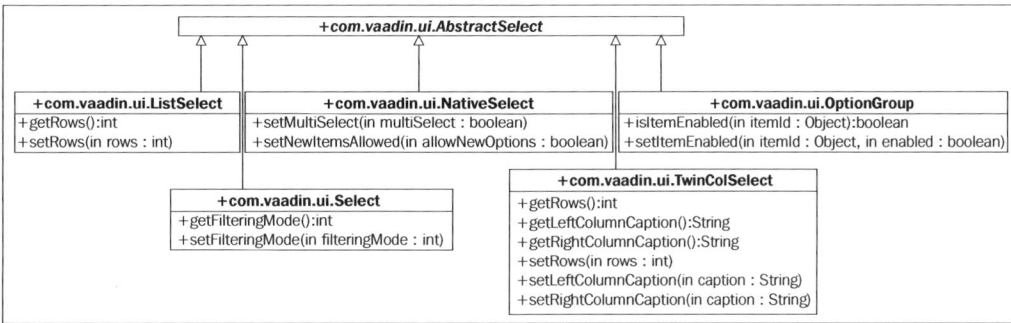

Note that all subclasses of `AbstractSelect` have the following constructors:

- A constructor with no parameters that comes in handy when we have no idea of the content at the instantiation time.

- A constructor with a `String` parameter. It is the same as the previous constructor, only with a caption.

- A constructor with both `String` and `Container` parameters. The `String` references the widget's caption and the `Container` the items to be displayed in the widget.

Moreover, widgets in this section (but excluding tables and trees) have a fourth constructor that accepts both a caption and a `Collection` parameter.

Since a picture is worth a thousand words, here are samples of different configurations of the preceding widget, all set a person's bean item container as a data source:

Code	Representation
`ListSelect select = new` `ListSelect();`	Person@9d9edd Person@15b2043 Person@1a33662 Person@476914
`NativeSelect select = new` `NativeSelect();`	Person@1e481c1 Person@102d81c Person@1ba4806 Person@ce82cc
`OptionGroup select = new` `OptionGroup ();`	○ Person@9576fd ○ Person@b6e385 ○ Person@1136da6 ○ Person@83df14

`OptionGroup select = new`
`OptionGroup ();`
`Select.setMultiSelect(true);`
	☐ Person@106d4ea
	☐ Person@1847a42
	☐ Person@769d7a
	☐ Person@15cd49f

Code	Representation
`Select select = new Select();`	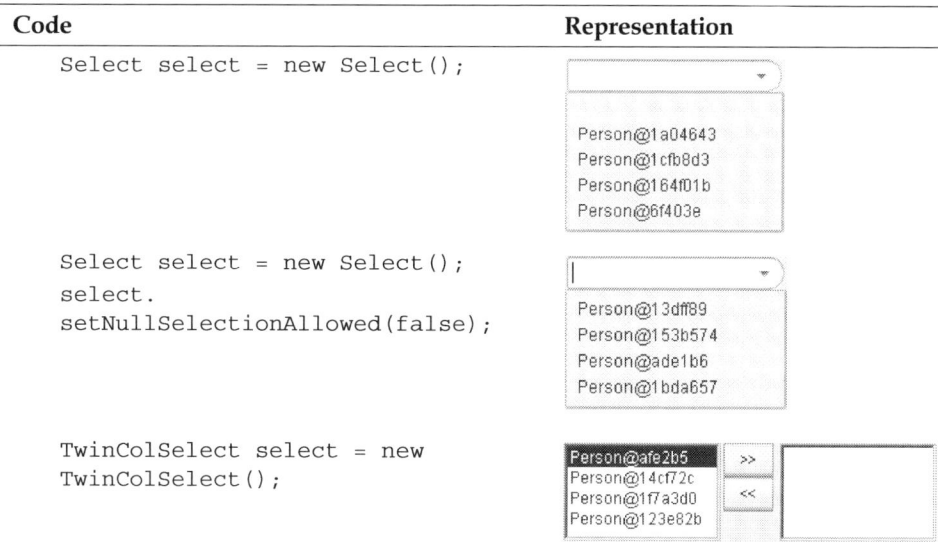

`Select select = new Select();`
`select.`
`setNullSelectionAllowed(false);`	

`TwinColSelect select = new` `TwinColSelect();`	

Notice that in the previous snippets, configuring the same widget in different ways gets us a different graphical representation.

For a practical example, consider we want the user to select a single person. Space requirement constrains us to use the smallest space possible. Moreover, there maybe many persons available: it would be a good idea to let the user type some characters in order to filter out choices. In this case, our widget of choice is `Select`, as it does not use much space and lets us filter options:

```
public class SelectPersonWindow extends Window {

  public SelectPersonWindow() {

    Select select = new Select();

    select.setImmediate(true);

    select.setNullSelectionAllowed(false);

    select.setItemCaptionPropertyId("firstName");

    Person person = new Person();

    BeanItemContainer<Person> bic = new
      BeanItemContainer<Person>(Person.class, ...
      person collection...);

    select.setContainerDataSource(bic);

    addComponent(select);

    select.addListener(new ValueChangeListener() {
```

```
public void valueChange(ValueChangeEvent event) {
    Person selected = (Person) ((Select)
      event.getProperty()).getValue();

    getWindow().showNotification(selected.getId() +
      " (" + selected.getFirstName() + ")");
    }
  });
 }
}
```

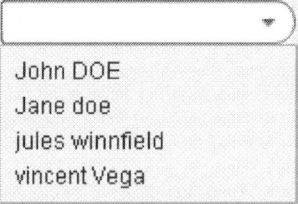

Three points are important in the previous code:

- `setBeanIdProperty("id")` lets us use the `id` property of the person item as its ID. We could have used any other property, but it is the only one that guarantees uniqueness, as per the contract.

- We use the computed `displayName` property in order to display a user-friendly value to the user. If the probability to have duplicates were higher, then we should also have included unique data such as the ID.

- In `Select`, filtering is enabled by default in the "starts with" pattern. There is nothing more to code to make it work.

- Last but not least, getting the select's value returns the item itself! This means that getting the selected value is a breeze.

Value type

The return type in the signature of the `getValue()` method is `Object`. We can easily cast it to the item type, in our example `Person`. Be aware however, that when multi selection is enabled, the returned value is a set of all selected item IDs. When multi selection can be enabled or disabled take extra-care when casting the return value.

Tables

Tables merit their own section as they display multiple columns, something the widgets in the previous section are not meant to handle.

Besides specific event-listener pairs, tables add important features to a simple select:

- Computed columns, that is, columns not found in the underlying container. Does the display name property ring any bells?
- Configurable columns, in order to display exactly what we want; it includes displaying date values with the right format but also using checkboxes for `boolean` values, and so on
- Drag-and-drop; tables are both eligible source and target
- A viewpoint to a very high number of items

Consistence of table hierarchy

In essence, tables are abstract selects, of sorts. This means that they add methods and behaviors of their own, but some defined in their parent class have no meaning: for example, for `Table` instances, the `itemCaptionMode` property makes no sense.

Table structure

The first thing to understand for Vaadin tables is how they are structured.

	Prop.$_1$ header	Prop.$_2$ header	Prop.$_n$ header	Gen. col.$_1$ header
item$_1$.row header	item$_1$.property$_1$	item$_1$.property$_2$	item$_1$.property$_n$	item$_1$.gencol$_1$
Item$_2$.row header	item$_2$.property$_1$	item$_2$.property$_2$	item$_2$.property$_n$	Item$_2$.gencol$_1$
Item$_n$.row header	Item$_n$.property$_1$	item$_n$.property$_2$	item$_n$.property$_n$	Item$_n$.gencol$_1$
	Prop.$_1$ footer	Prop.$_2$ footer	Prop.$_n$ footer	Gen. col.$_1$ footer

Columns

Each column of a table is referenced by a property ID. Those IDs are either explicitly set, but in most cases, it is the property's name of the bean item type stored in the underlying container. For our `Person` type, they are `firstName`, `lastName`, and so on.

Column properties can either be set or get:

- Globally, the method expects an array of the right types as parameter
- Column by column, parameters are respectively the property ID and the right type

For example, should we want to set column headers in one line, we could do the following:

```
table.setColumnHeaders(new String[] {"First Name", "Last Name", "Birth
date", "ID", "Display name"});
```

Alternatively, the same result could be achieved with the following:

```
table.setColumnHeader("firstName", "First Name");
table.setColumnHeader("lastName", "Last Name");
table.setColumnHeader("birthdate", "Birth date");
table.setColumnHeader("id", "ID");
table.setColumnHeader("displayName", "Display name");
```

Global column properties are summed up in the following table:

Property	Type	Default value
columnAlignments	String[]	
columnHeaders	String[]	
columnIcons	Resource[]	

The following table recaps single column "properties":

Property	Type	Default value
columnAlignment	String	ALIGN_LEFT
columnCollapse	boolean	
columnExpandRatio	float	
columnFooter	String	null
columnHeader	String	
columnIcon	Resource	null
columnWidth	int	-1

Most are self-describing, however, a little explanation on how table width works in Vaadin would be in order.

As the web terminal is the sole terminal available, it boils down to how the framework integrates with HTML: when the column width is set to -1, no width is set in it and thus, it bases its real width on both CSS and available space in the page. If not, it uses the width set.

Collapsing

Vaadin allows us to hide some columns at first, but provides us with the means to display them later. This is known as **collapsing column**. First, we have to call `setCol umnCollapsingAllowed(true)` in order to enable the feature.

Then, individual columns may be collapsed with the `setColumnCollapse()` method. This code collapses unnecessary columns:

```
table.setColumnCollapsed("firstName", true);
```

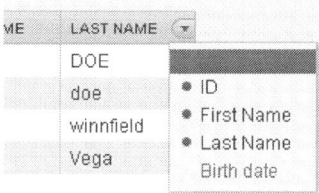

In the previous screenshot, see how Vaadin displays a selector to choose columns to be shown.

Table width and collapsing

Beware that collapsed columns are not used when computing total table width. It is advised to explicitly set the table's width in order to ensure un-collapsed columns will get enough place to be put in view.

Header and footer

Headers and footers are structuring elements of tables.

The former code snippet showed us how to set headers explicitly, even if most of the time, the strategy used for creating headers (which is the same as the one for creating captions, see the section *Changing captions* in this chapter) from item properties is good enough.

Like captions, we can change the strategy used with the `setColumnHeaderMode()` and these constants:

Constant	Computed row header value
COLUMN_HEADER_MODE_HIDDEN	No column header is shown
COLUMN_HEADER_MODE_EXPLICIT	None: we have to set it for each column explicitly
COLUMN_HEADER_MODE_EXPLICIT_DEFAULTS_ID	Default: spaced uppercased property is used, but individual columns can be set a header, thus overriding the computed value
COLUMN_HEADER_MODE_ID	Spaced uppercased property

Footers however **must be set independently** as they are empty by default. Moreover, we have to call `setFooterVisible(true)` to display the entire footer bar as it is hidden otherwise.

Row header column

The row header column is a special column hidden by default. Think of it as a summary of the row item, made comprehensible for mere humans. In fact, it works exactly the same as the caption mode of `AbstractSelect` only the method is `setRowHeaderMode()` and the constants are the following:

Constant	Computed row header value
ROW_HEADER_MODE_HIDDEN	Default value: no header column is shown
ROW_HEADER_MODE_EXPLICIT	None: we have to set it for each item explicitly
ROW_HEADER_MODE_ICON_ONLY	None: only an icon is shown. Icon must be set explicitly for each item
ROW_HEADER_MODE_ID	Item's ID `toString()`
ROW_HEADER_MODE_ITEM	Item `toString()`
ROW_HEADER_MODE_INDEX	Item's index in the container
ROW_HEADER_MODE_EXPLICIT_DEFAULTS_ID	By default item's ID `toString()`, but individual items can be set a header, thus overriding the default value
ROW_HEADER_MODE_PROPERTY	An item property is used, which is specified with `setItemCaptionPropertyId()`

In our `Person` table, we could use the display name property as the row header:

```
table.setRowHeaderMode(Table.ROW_HEADER_MODE_PROPERTY);
table.setItemCaptionPropertyId("displayName");
```

Ordering and reordering

By default, column ordering is incomprehensible to say the least. In all cases, it is better to explicitly set column ordering with the `setVisibleColumns(String[] visibleColumns)` method which takes an array of item properties as an argument.

By default, users cannot change column ordering. By calling `setColumnReordering Allowed(true)`, this behavior can be enabled. Note that both of these changes do not affect the row header column.

For our example, the following order suits our need just fine. Notice that the `displayName` property is not used (but is as the row header in a previous snippet):

```
table.setVisibleColumns(new String[] {"id", "firstName", "lastName",
"birthdate"});
```

Formatting properties and generated columns

Formatting table properties can be achieved through three different means:

1. Using a property formatter (see section *Property formatter* in this chapter). It is particularly unwieldy since it would require wrapping the to-be-formatted-property of each item individually.

2. Overriding the protected `formatPropertyValue(Object itemId, Object propertyId, Property property)` method.

   For example, let's format the birth date value in our `Person` table as follows:

   ```
   @Override
   protected String formatPropertyValue(Object itemId,
     Object propId,
       Property property) {

     Object value = property.getValue();

     if (value instanceof Date) {

       Date date = (Date) value;

       return new SimpleDateFormat("MM/dd/yyyy").format(date);
     }

     return super.formatPropertyValue(itemId, propId, property);
   }
   ```

Alternatively, we could have checked on the property's ID. Our choice is better since if other date attributes are added to the JavaBean, they will benefit from the formatting.

3. Finally, creating a generated column that overrides the wanted property's name is a definite possibility. Generated columns offer something more though.

In abstract selects, we had to explicitly create the display name computed property on `Person`. It was bad design but alternatives were either complex or unsatisfying.

`Table` offers a feature that `AbstractSelect` does not: computed columns. These columns are the answer to the previous quandary and implement it in a clean way. In order to achieve this, Vaadin introduces the `ColumnGenerator` interface.

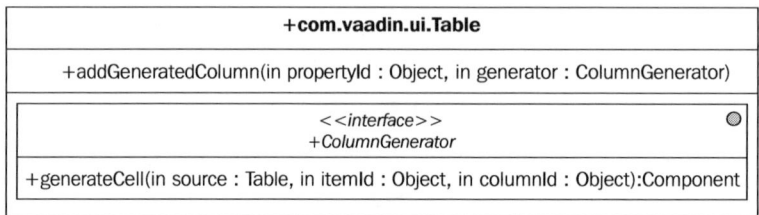

Once implemented, it can be added to the table under a property id. Let's remove the display name property on the `Person` and create it as a generated column.

```
public class DisplayNameColumn implements ColumnGenerator {

  @Override
  public Component generateCell(Table source, Object itemId,
    Object columnId) {

    Item item = source.getItem(itemId);

    String firstName = (String)
      item.getItemProperty("firstName").getValue();
    String lastName = (String)
      item.getItemProperty("lastName").getValue();

    return new Label(firstName + " " + lastName);
  }
}
```

Now, it's just a matter of using the generated column:

```
table.addGeneratedColumn("displayName", new
    DisplayNameColumn());
table.setColumnHeader("displayName", "Display name");
table.setVisibleColumns(new String[] { "id", "displayName",
    "birthdate" });
```

 Notice that generated columns cannot be sorted (see below) as there is no underlying property the container may be aware of.

Sorting

By default, Vaadin tables are sortable: users can choose a column to sort from, by clicking on the column header.

 Note that sorting is executed on the underlying property value, and not on its string representation.

User sorting

In order to prevent the user sorting, there are two solutions:

1. Calling the `setSortDisabled(true)` method
2. Hiding column headers with `setColumnHeaderMode(COLUMN_HEADER_MODE_HIDDEN)` seen previously

Programmatic sorting

Alternatively, developers can use sorting on the server side, based on the two properties: the property's ID and an indicator on whether the sort is ascending (which is the default).

For example, the following snippet sorts the table from the last name, descending:

```
table.setSortContainerPropertyId("lastName");
table.setSortAscending(false);
```

This approach has a strong limitation; it can only be used for sorting on a single column. In order to overcome this, remember that `Container.Sortable` provides the `sort(Object[] propertyId, boolean[] ascending)` method. Thus, the following snippet is equivalent to the former:

```
table.sort(new String[] {"lastName"}, new boolean[] {false});
```

Viewpoint

Tables can be set a container with a very high number of items and still be efficient since not all are displayed to the user. In order to achieve this, tables use the concept of viewpoint when the number of items is greater than the number of rows shown.

First, we can set the number of visible rows with the `setPageLength(int pageLength)` method, which is 15 by default. Notice that in combination to row height, it sets the default table height. If set to zero, the table will adjust its height to display all the items in the container: be sure that it is the desired behavior, since it can have a great impact on both performance and ease of use. Also, setting the page length to zero means that the table will adhere to the `setHeight()` contact; otherwise it won't. This is important when trying to fit the table in a specific place, for example, when `setSizeFull()` must scale the table accordingly.

Additionally, we can programmatically scroll to the first item in the list, either by item's ID or by index. This is done with the methods `setCurrentPageFirstItemId(Object currentPageFirstItemId)` and `setCurrentPageFirstItemIndex(int newIndex)` respectively.

Viewpoint change event

`Table` does not come with an event model around scrolling visible items. Out-of-the-box, the framework displays the range of visible items when the user scrolls at the top of the table, just below the column headers. If we need to be informed about scrolling, we would have to override the protected `refreshRenderedCells()` method, in order to implement the desired behavior (and still call the parent method, of course).

Improving responsiveness

Scrolling the viewpoint in order to show different items will make the table fetch newly visible items from the underlying container. As such, there would be a noticeable waiting time for the user if not for a nifty feature of the framework.

Indeed, the table fetches more items than need to be displayed and caches the superfluous items in-memory. The number of such items is `pageLength` times the value of a property named `cacheRate`, above and below the table. Therefore, if users complain about response time, increasing the cache rate could be a good idea.

Of course, if the user scrolls too fast, it won't do anything. In most cases, however, it just increases the responsiveness with no side effect.

Editing

Until now, we have learned how to configure data to display the way we want and that is no mean feat. Nonetheless, displaying is one thing but editing is another.

In Vaadin, making a table editable is as simple as calling `setEditable(true)` on it. Behold the result: in just one line, we have a fully editable table.

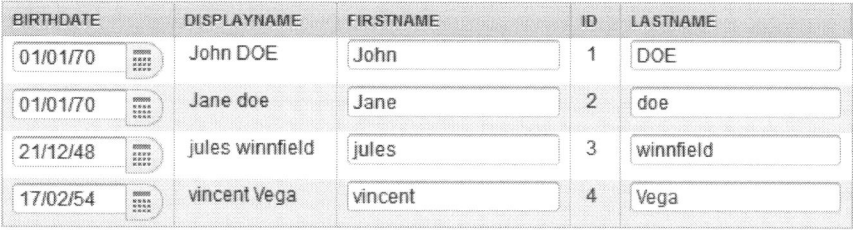

The following two things are worth noticing:

1. Editable fields are specifically tailored to the property type and in exactly the same way as for single fields (see section *Configuring field types* in this chapter).

2. Properties with no setter such as the computed display name property are still shown as simple read-only labels and not as a field.

In fact, like forms, tables delegate field generation to a factory: a `TableFieldFactory` interface and `DefaultFieldFactory` also implements it, as presented in the following diagram:

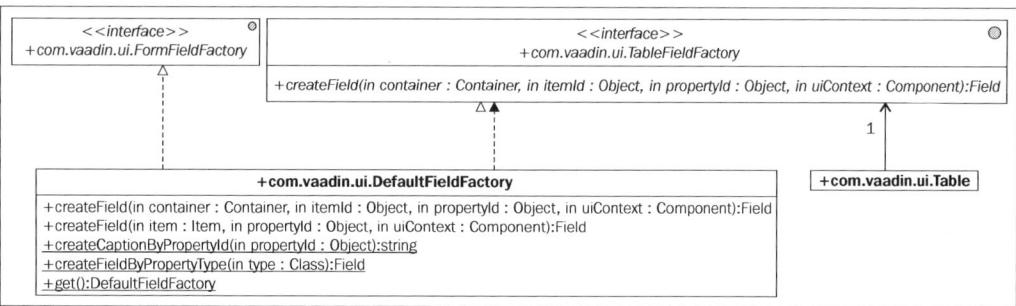

Configuring our editable table is just a matter of creating the right table field factory. If we want not to display calendars but old-fashioned fields for dates, then it is just a matter of creating the implementation:

```
public class CustomTableFieldFactory implements TableFieldFactory {

    private TableFieldFactory delegate = DefaultFieldFactory.get();

    @Override
    public Field createField(Container container, Object itemId,
      Object propertyId, Component uiContext) {
```

```
    Class<?> type = container.getType(propertyId);

    if (Date.class.isAssignableFrom(type)) {

      return new CustomDateField();
    }

    return delegate.createField(container, itemId,
      propertyId, uiContext);
  }
}
```

Notice that it is very similar to our previous custom form field factory. Well, it is even simpler since column header is not handled (and should not be).

Selection

On the client side, items in standard tables are just a bunch of characters put one next to another.

Just calling the `setSelectable(true)` on the table will make each row appear as a single object to the user and selectable as such.

By default, only a single row can be selected at a time. In order to select multiple rows, we need to invoke `setMultipleSelect(true)` on the table. When multiple selections is enabled, users can select a range of rows with the *SHIFT* key and individual rows can be added or removed from the selection with the *CTRL* key.

Drag-and-drop

Tables are a good entry point into Vaadin's drag-and-drop capabilities.

The framework uses the following abstractions in order to accomplish drag-and-drop:

* `Transferable` represents the data transferred
* `DragSource` stands for the source component
* `DropTarget` denotes the target component

Transferable

`Transferable` wraps the data to be dragged and dropped between components.

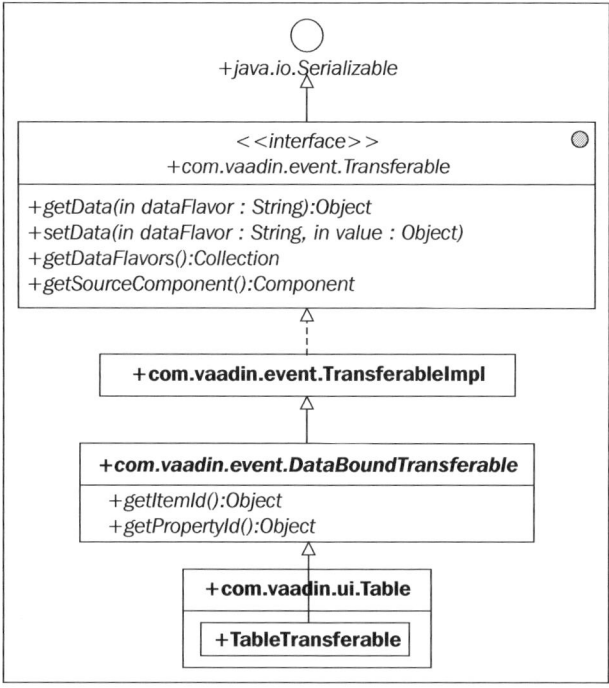

`TransferableImpl` is just a straightforward implementation of `Transferable`. As `Transferable` may apply to a great number of differently structured data, it is built around a hash map.

Keys are called data flavors and vary depending on the concrete type of transferable. We can query for all data flavors of a particular transferable with the `getDataFlavors()` method. Then, `DataBoundTransferable` is a specialized transferable designed for containers.

Finally, at the table level, drag sources are cells, so `TableTransferable` is an implementation that you can get both the cell's item ID and its property ID from.

Drag source

`DragSource` knows how to create a transferable object. Concrete classes shall implement the single method `getTransferable(Map<String, Object> rawVariables)` that return a `Transferable` instance to do just that.

Drop target

Drop target model design is somewhat more complex than the drag source. Some classes need to collaborate to provide the wanted behavior.

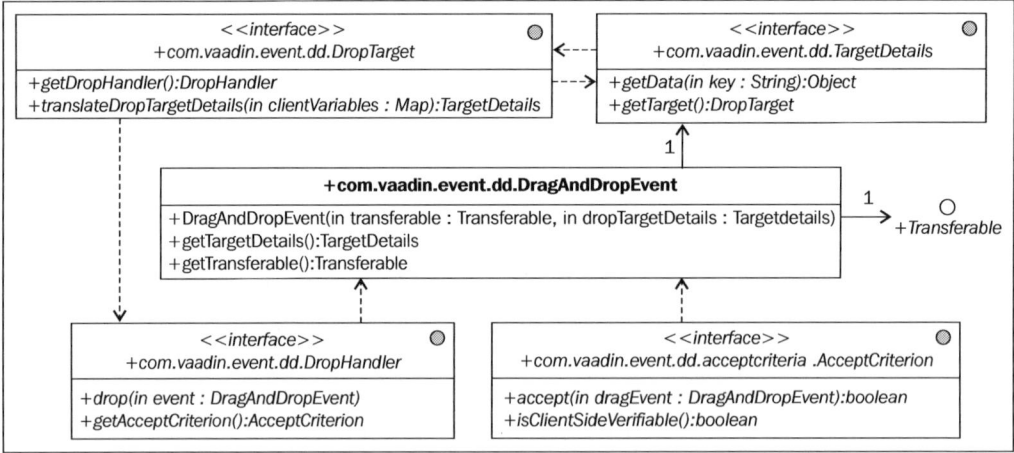

- At the heart of the model lies `DragAndDropEvent`, which is not a real event *per se* (it does not inherit from `EventObject`) but is still sent by the framework. It encapsulates both a transferable and a `TargetDetails` instance.

- `TargetDetails` in turn wraps the drop target, as well as all information contained in the aforementioned transferable. Concrete target details classes are provided throughout Vaadin by components, including tables (and trees).

- `DropTarget` represents the target of the drag-and-drop operation. It delegates the drop itself to a `DropHandler`.

- `DropHandler` is the class responsible for managing what really happens in the drop through the `drop()` method. However, in order to improve performance, drop handlers have to detail under what conditions the drop is valid.

- `AcceptCriterion` wraps possibly many criteria in order to determine whether to drop the transferable on the target or to abort the operation.

Accept criterion

Accept criterion can be rescinded into two main groups: criteria that can work solely on the client side and criteria that need server-side validation.

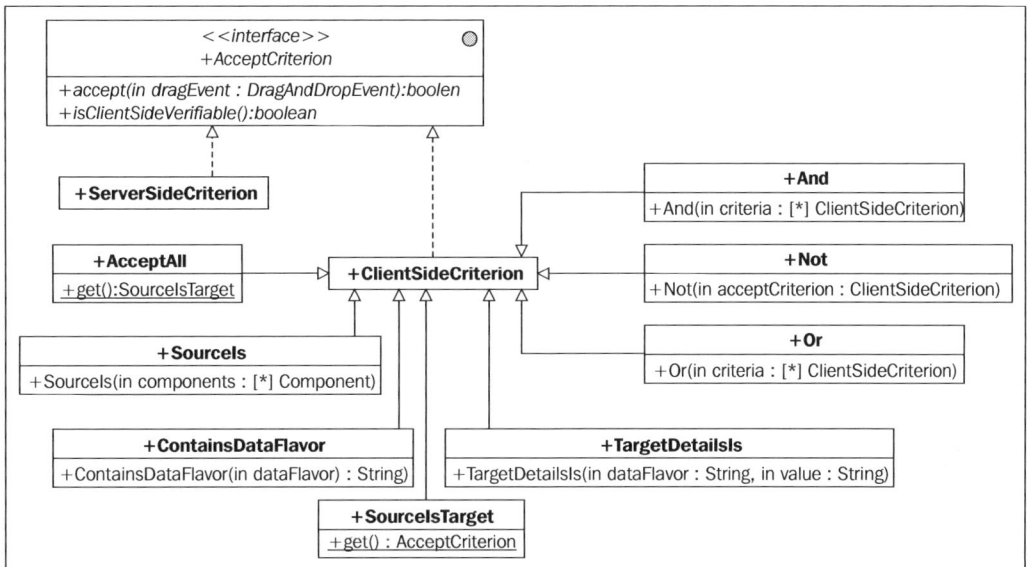

 In order to ease the understanding of the diagram, package was not represented. It is `com.vaadin.event.dd.acceptcriteria`.

From this point, the different types of criteria are fairly self-explanatory.

Table drag-and-drop

Table is a component which is drag-and-drop ready, having implementations on all previous interfaces, save `DropHandler`, which is application-specific anyway.

In order to enable dragging from the table, we just have to call `setDragMode(TableDragMode dragMode)` with the right value: either `ROW` or `MULTIROW`. It is `NONE` by default, meaning the drag is disabled. Note that in order for multirow to work, table must be set as selectable and multi select.

Now, in order to enable dropping to a table, we just have to create a new `DropHandler` and set it on the table.

The following example duplicates the dragged person in the table:

```
table.setDragMode(ROW);

table.setDropHandler(new DropHandler() {
  public void drop(DragAndDropEvent event) {
    TableTransferable transferable = (TableTransferable) event
        .getTransferable();

    Object itemId = transferable.getItemId();

    BeanItem<Person> item = (BeanItem) table.getItem(itemId);

    Person originalPerson = item.getBean();

    Collection<?> itemIds = table.getItemIds();

    Long maxId = getMax(itemIds) + 1;

    Person newPerson = new Person(maxId);

    newPerson.setFirstName(originalPerson.getFirstName());
    newPerson.setLastName(originalPerson.getLastName());
    newPerson.setBirthdate(originalPerson.getBirthdate());

    table.addItem(newPerson);

    table.requestRepaint();
  }
  private long getMax(Collection<?> itemIds) {
    long max = 0;
    for (Object itemId : itemIds) {
      BeanItem<Person> item = (BeanItem) table.getItem(itemId);
      Person person = item.getBean();
      max = Math.max(max, person.getId());
    }
    return max;
  }
  public AcceptCriterion getAcceptCriterion() {
    return SourceIsTarget.get();
  }
});
```

Some noteworthy facts are as follows:

- We set the drag mode to row, in order for the table to be a drag source
- We created a drop handler and set it on the table, so as to make the latter a drag source too
- Finally, the accept criterion constrains the drop source, so that it can only be the table itself

Trees

Trees are another widget that has the capability to use a container data source, whereas tables are meant to display items of flat containers, trees are meant to do the same for hierarchical ones (see the section named *Hierarchical* for a small reminder in this chapter).

From a UI point of view, trees are about nodes and parent-child relationships between them.

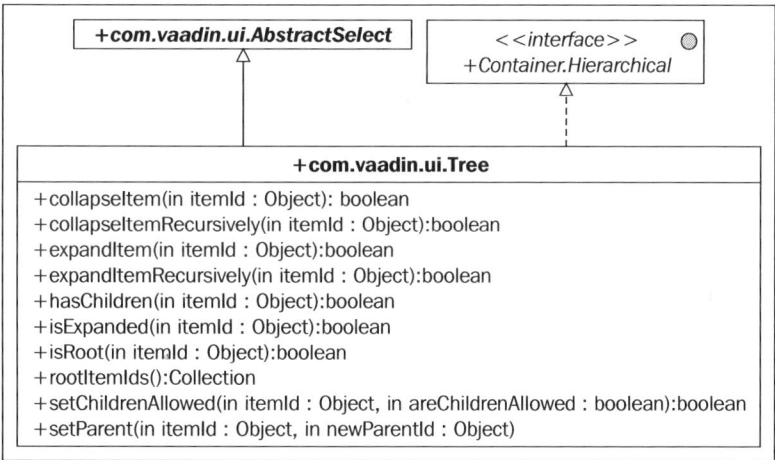

The Tree class is much simpler than Table as there are no columns: only nodes are displayed, albeit in a hierarchical fashion.

Collapse and expand

A feature of Tree is its ability to let us either collapse a node (hide its children) or expand it (show its children) programmatically.

Two method flavors are available:

1. One that just acts upon the node and its direct children
2. The other proceeds recursively from the node parameter

One can also query for expanded status of a particular node with the `isExpanded(Object itemId)` method.

Parent and child

As trees are all about parent and child nodes, Vaadin provides the following methods in order to manage relationships:

* With the `rootItemIds()` method, we can get the root item IDs
* For a particular item, `isRoot()` returns the root status and `hasChildren(Object itemId)` whether it has children (that would be pretty self-explanatory)

Then, leaf status of a node can be set with the help of the `setChildrenAllowed()` method.

Finally, one can change the entire node structure by using `setParent()`. For example, the following snippet simply rearranges the second and the fourth items respectively under the first and third items for a 4-items tree:

```
Tree tree = new Tree("", container);

Iterator<?> iterator = tree.getVisibleItemIds().iterator();

tree.setParent(iterator.next(), iterator.next());
tree.setParent(iterator.next(), iterator.next());
```

Item labels

Labels are handled the same way for trees as for selects, meaning we should use the same solutions as seen in the section *Displaying items*, earlier in this chapter.

Refining Twaattin

Finally, we are ready to connect Twaattin to the Twitter API. For that, we will use Twitter4j, available at `http://twitter4j.org/`. Twitter4j is open source, free, and well designed so it just fits our needs. As this book is not about it, detailed information can be found on the website.

Requisites

In order to use Twitter for authentication, the first thing to do is to register a client application using the following form: `https://dev.twitter.com/apps/new`. This will get us a consumer key and a consumer secret that will have to be passed to Twitter4j, then to Twitter to prove who we are.

Adaptations

The biggest adaptation to our application is that since the Twitter API uses OAuth for authentication, we don't need to log in in Twaattin but in Twitter.

 OAuth is an open protocol that delegates authentication to so-called OAuth providers. More information is available at `http://oauth.net/`.

When authenticated, the latter will return us a PIN that will be used to verify our credentials in later calls.

Thus, the login window will have to be changed in order to provide a link to Twitter's authentication window and a PIN field.

Sources

Here are the new Twaattin sources.

The login window

```
package com.packtpub.learnvaadin.twaattin.ui;

import static com.vaadin.ui.Window.Notification.TYPE_ERROR_MESSAGE;
import twitter4j.TwitterException;
import twitter4j.User;

import com.packtpub.learnvaadin.twaattin.TwaattinApp;
import com.packtpub.learnvaadin.twaattin.service.TwitterService;
import com.vaadin.terminal.ClassResource;
import com.vaadin.terminal.ExternalResource;
import com.vaadin.ui.Button;
import com.vaadin.ui.Embedded;
import com.vaadin.ui.Link;
import com.vaadin.ui.TextField;
import com.vaadin.ui.VerticalLayout;
```

```java
import com.vaadin.ui.Window;
import com.vaadin.ui.Button.ClickEvent;

public class LoginWindow extends Window {
  private static final long serialVersionUID = 1L;

  private TextField pinField;
  private Button submitButton;
  private Link link;

  public LoginWindow() {
    VerticalLayout layout = new VerticalLayout();

    layout.setMargin(true);

    setContent(layout);

    link = new Link();

    link.setCaption("1. Get PIN");

    link.setTargetName("twitter");

    addComponent(link);

    pinField = new TextField("2. Enter PIN");

    addComponent(pinField);

    submitButton = new Button("3. Submit");

    submitButton.addListener(ClickEvent.class, this, "authenticate");

    addComponent(submitButton);
  }

  public void initialize() {
    TwitterService twitterService = ((TwaattinApp) getApplication()).
      getTwitterService();

    try {
      String authUrl = twitterService.getAuthenticationUrl();

      link.setResource(new ExternalResource(authUrl));

    } catch (TwitterException e) {
      e.printStackTrace();

      showNotification("Initialization error: " + e.getMessage(),
        TYPE_ERROR_MESSAGE);
    }
  }
```

```
public void authenticate(ClickEvent event) {

  TwitterService twitterService = ((TwaattinApp)
    getApplication()).getTwitterService();

  try {

    User user = twitterService.authenticate((String)
      pinField.getValue());

    getApplication().setUser(user);

    pinField.setValue("");

  } catch (TwitterException e) {

    e.printStackTrace();

    showNotification("Authentication error: " + e.getMessage(),
      TYPE_ERROR_MESSAGE);
  }
 }
}
```

Noteworthy parts are as follows:

- The declaration of a `Link` object: Links render as HTML links to a wrapped `Resource`. In our case, it is wrapped around Twitter's authentication page URL.

- The target's name property for `Link` lets us create a new pop-up window. When not specified, the URL is opened in the current window.

- The creation of the `initialize()` method. It is a common mistake found in beginners Vaadin code: remember that the `ExternalResource` constructor takes the application as a parameter. It is possible for a window to query its application, but **it will return** `null` **if it has not been set as the main window**. Thus, it is impossible to initialize the resource in the constructor; it has to be delayed until the window has been set.

- Finally, we use a stateful Twitter service to use the Twitter4j API for us. The former is a facade over the latter that allows us to conveniently ignore the API itself.

The Twaattin application

```
package com.packtpub.learnvaadin.twaattin;

import com.packtpub.learnvaadin.twaattin.service.TwitterService;
import com.packtpub.learnvaadin.twaattin.ui.LoginWindow;
import com.packtpub.learnvaadin.twaattin.ui.TimelineWindow;
```

```java
import com.vaadin.Application;
import com.vaadin.Application.UserChangeListener;

public class TwaattinApp extends Application implements
UserChangeListener {

  private static final long serialVersionUID = 1L;

  private LoginWindow loginWindow;
  private TimelineWindow timelineWindow;
  private transient TwitterService twitterService;

  @Override
  public void init() {

    loginWindow = new LoginWindow();

    timelineWindow = new TimelineWindow();

    setMainWindow(loginWindow);

    loginWindow.initialize();

    addListener(this);

    addListener(timelineWindow);

  }

  public void applicationUserChanged(UserChangeEvent event) {

    if (event.getNewUser() == null) {

      setMainWindow(loginWindow);

      loginWindow.initialize();

      removeWindow(timelineWindow);

      loginWindow.showNotification("You're logged out");

    } else if (event.getNewUser() != null) {

      setMainWindow(timelineWindow);

      removeWindow(loginWindow);

      timelineWindow.showNotification("You're authentified");

    }

  }

  public TwitterService getTwitterService() {

    if (twitterService == null) {

      twitterService = new TwitterService();

    }

    return twitterService;

  }

}
```

The application class is changed in order to first create the login window, and then initialize it, as said previously.

The timeline window

```
package com.packtpub.learnvaadin.twaattin.ui;

import java.util.Iterator;

import twitter4j.ResponseList;
import twitter4j.Status;
import twitter4j.TwitterException;
import twitter4j.User;

import com.packtpub.learnvaadin.twaattin.TwaattinApp;
import com.packtpub.learnvaadin.twaattin.service.TwitterService;
import com.vaadin.Application.UserChangeEvent;
import com.vaadin.Application.UserChangeListener;
import com.vaadin.data.util.BeanContainer;
import com.vaadin.ui.Button;
import com.vaadin.ui.HorizontalLayout;
import com.vaadin.ui.Label;
import com.vaadin.ui.Table;
import com.vaadin.ui.VerticalLayout;
import com.vaadin.ui.Window;
import com.vaadin.ui.Button.ClickEvent;

public class TimelineWindow extends Window implements
    UserChangeListener {

  private static final long serialVersionUID = 1L;
  private Label user;
  private BeanContainer<Long, Status> container;

  public TimelineWindow() {

    VerticalLayout mainLayout = new VerticalLayout();

    mainLayout.setSpacing(true);

    mainLayout.setMargin(true);

    setContent(mainLayout);

    HorizontalLayout menuBar = new HorizontalLayout();

    menuBar.setSpacing(true);

    addComponent(menuBar);

    user = new Label();

    menuBar.addComponent(user);

    Button logout = new Button("Logout");
```

```
logout.addListener(ClickEvent.class, this, "logout");

menuBar.addComponent(logout);

Button timelineButton = new Button("Timeline");

timelineButton.addListener(ClickEvent.class, this, "fill");

addComponent(timelineButton);

container = new BeanContainer<Long, Status>(Status.class);

container.setBeanIdResolver(new BeanIdResolver<Long, Status>() {

  public Long getIdForBean(Status status) {

    return status.getId();

  }

});

Table table = new Table("", container);

addComponent(table);

customizeTable(table);

}

public void logout() {

  getApplication().setUser(null);

}

public void fill() {

  TwitterService twitterService = ((TwaattinApp)
    getApplication())
      .getTwitterService();

  container.removeAllItems();

  try {

    ResponseList<Status> statuses =
      twitterService.getTimeline();

    Iterator<Status> iterator = statuses.iterator();

    while (iterator.hasNext()) {

      Status status = iterator.next();

      container.addBean(status);

    }

  } catch (TwitterException e) {

    throw new RuntimeException(e);

  }
```

```
  }

  public void applicationUserChanged(UserChangeEvent event) {

    User newUser = (User) event.getNewUser();

    if (newUser != null) {

      user.setValue(newUser.getScreenName());

    }

  }

  private void customizeTable(Table table) {

    table.addGeneratedColumn("when", new WhenColumnGenerator());

    table.addGeneratedColumn("user", new NameColumnGenerator());

    table.setVisibleColumns(new String[] { "user", "text", "when" });

  }

}
```

The three important pieces of code that take place in the new timeline window are as follows:

1. The first noticeable lines use a bean container and the status ID property as its key with the help of a custom bean resolver. Using the status ID for the status goes a long way towards making our life easier for manipulating the items in the container. Alternatively, we also could have used `container.setBeanIdProperty("id")` instead of a bean resolver and then added items with the status key (not beans) to our container. It is cleaner this way though.

2. Second, as what we get is a response list, we have to add each item in the container manually and specify the item's ID.

3. Finally, we define which columns are meant to be shown, as well as assign column generators to two of them in order to tweak the display. Beware that adding a column generator under a new label must take place before using the aforementioned label or Vaadin will loudly complain.

The name column generator

```
package com.packtpub.learnvaadin.twaattin.ui;

import twitter4j.Status;
import twitter4j.User;

import com.vaadin.data.util.BeanItem;
import com.vaadin.ui.Component;
import com.vaadin.ui.Label;
import com.vaadin.ui.Table;
```

```
import com.vaadin.ui.Table.ColumnGenerator;

class NameColumnGenerator implements ColumnGenerator {

  public Component generateCell(Table source, Object itemId,
      Object columnId) {

    BeanItem<Status> item = (BeanItem<Status>)
        source.getItem(itemId);

    Status status = (Status) item.getBean();

    Label label = new Label();

    User user =  status.isRetweet() ? status.getRetweetedStatus().
      getUser() : status.getUser();

    label.setValue(user.getScreenName());

    return label;
  }
}
```

We need a name column generator as the `getUser()` method of the `Status` object
returns a structured `User` object and not an easily displayed `String`. Moreover, this
lets us choose to display the original message sender over the retweeter when the
former is indeed a retweet.

> At present, `Table`'s `setVisibleColumns()` only accept
> properties of the container's bean type such as `job` for a `Person`
> but not subproperties, such as `job.label`. Watch out for this
> feature in the future, or even better, implement it yourself! Until
> that point, use column generators.

The date column generator

```
package com.packtpub.learnvaadin.twaattin.ui;

import java.text.DateFormat;
import java.text.SimpleDateFormat;
import java.util.Calendar;

import twitter4j.Status;

import com.vaadin.data.util.BeanItem;
import com.vaadin.ui.Component;
import com.vaadin.ui.Label;
import com.vaadin.ui.Table;
import com.vaadin.ui.Table.ColumnGenerator;
```

```java
class WhenColumnGenerator implements ColumnGenerator {
  public Component generateCell(Table source, Object itemId,
      Object columnId) {
    Label label = new Label();
    BeanItem<Status> item = (BeanItem<Status>)
      source.getItem(itemId);
    Status status = item.getBean();
    Calendar oneDayAgo = Calendar.getInstance();
    oneDayAgo.add(Calendar.DAY_OF_MONTH, -1);
    Calendar tweetTime = Calendar.getInstance();
    tweetTime.setTime(status.getCreatedAt());
    String value;
    if (tweetTime.after(oneDayAgo)) {
      value = getLabel(tweetTime, Calendar.HOUR_OF_DAY, "hour");
      if (value == null) {
        value = getLabel(tweetTime, Calendar.MINUTE, "minute");
      }
      if (value == null) {
        value = "right now";
      }
    } else {
      DateFormat format = new SimpleDateFormat("d MMM yy");

      value = format.format(tweetTime.getTime());
    }

    label.setValue(value);
    return label;
  }
  private String getLabel(Calendar then, int field, String label) {
    Calendar now = Calendar.getInstance();
    int diff = 0;
    while (then.before(now)) {
      now.add(field, -1);
      diff++;
    }
    switch (diff) {
```

```
        case 0: return null;
        case 1: return diff + " " + label + " ago";
        default: return diff + " " + label + "s ago";
      }
    }
  }
```

Column generators are not limited to trivial display: In this case, we show the tweet's date only if it is older than one day ago. Otherwise, we compute the time from now and display it in either hours or minutes. Finally, the timeline window looks similar to the one shown in the following screenshot:

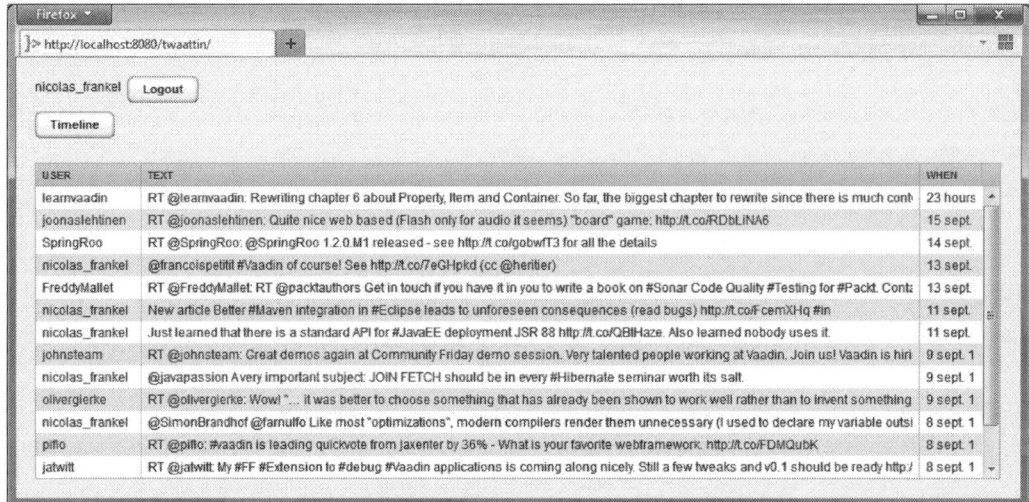

Summary

In this chapter, we have learned two great parts of many Vaadin applications.

The first part described the three levels of data wrapping in Vaadin:

1. `Property`: It represents a simple object such as a `String` or a `Date`. Properties can be tweaked in order to display the encapsulated data the way we really want.

2. `Item`: It wraps around a single structured object. We used our `Person` class to show how it could be encapsulated in `Item`, and finally displayed in a form. Forms are a nice façade over a single item, whether in a read-only or read-write mode.

3. `Container`: It is the final level and lets us wrap around a collection of items. Containers may have additional properties such as filterable, sortable, and hierarchical, each one bringing features to the container.

Then, we saw two important widgets that are able to be set container data sources: tables and trees. Where trees are hierarchical containers, tables can be filterable and sortable at the same time. As tables are such important widgets of many applications, Vaadin provides many configuration features around them and we spent some time looking at those capabilities:

- Column features such as collapsing, ordering, and headers and footers
- Sorting, both from a user point of view and a developer point of view
- Table viewpoint
- Selection and editing of tables
- Finally, the drag-and-drop feature was a good entry point into the more general drag-and-drop model in Vaadin

At this point, we have seen all the basics of the framework. You should now be able to create simple applications from scratch. The next chapter is about advanced features of the framework, both out-of-the-box and third party.

7
Advanced Features

In this chapter, we will go beyond simple features to tackle what will make our applications well thought out and professional.

The first section of this chapter will be devoted to features provided out-of-the-box by the framework that we have not seen until now. These include:

- Accessing request and response objects from Vaadin
- Bookmarking windows state
- Embedding Vaadin applications in third-party applications
- Default error handling and how to override it
- Application lifecycle

As the Vaadin team wants to keep the framework as cohesive as possible, some very interesting capabilities are not integrated into the core, but are available as add-ons.

In the second section, we will describe the Vaadin add-ons portal then detail some add-ons that bring new features or just make our life easier. Those will be:

- Embedding Vaadin applications in third-party sites
- SQL container to connect our tables to, so as to directly display tables to Vaadin
- Push capabilities!

Core features

Core features are capabilities provided by the Vaadin JAR.

Accessing with the request-response model

In some cases, we will want to get a handle on the underlying request-response model. This could be motivated by the following needs:

- Access some web application context where the entry-point is the request, including:
    - ° The servlet context in order to integrate with some third-party framework: Spring comes to mind but other frameworks also store information in this context.
    - ° The session context, to get data stored there by a legacy part of the application.
- Managing cookies, either to read or write them, for example to pass cookie-based authentication reverse-proxies

The possibilities are virtually endless! The problem is that in the previous chapters, no method signature provided a handle to either our good old `HttpServletRequest` or `HttpServletResponse`.

Do not send redirect!

Never ever send redirects response streams outside the current Vaadin application (even to another Vaadin application in the same web application). The client part is waiting for some server sent information and will complain rather loudly if it does not get them.

If you really need to escape the application, then use the `open(ExternalResource)` method of the `Window` class.

The brute force approach

The first approach is to get a reference on the Vaadin application object from outside the framework and then communicate with it, for example setting it objects.

This is done with the help of a simple utility class. This class is `WebApplicationContext`.

Application contexts store individual applications and information about them. For web applications, the web application context stores the context under the user session. The most important thing is that we can get the application context with the static `getApplicationContext(HttpSession session)` method.

 Notice the plural about applications. Even if it is a very rare occurrence, we might need to serve to different subcontexts with one single Vaadin servlet for each: they will all be grouped under the same `WebApplicationContext` and that is stored in the user's HTTP session.

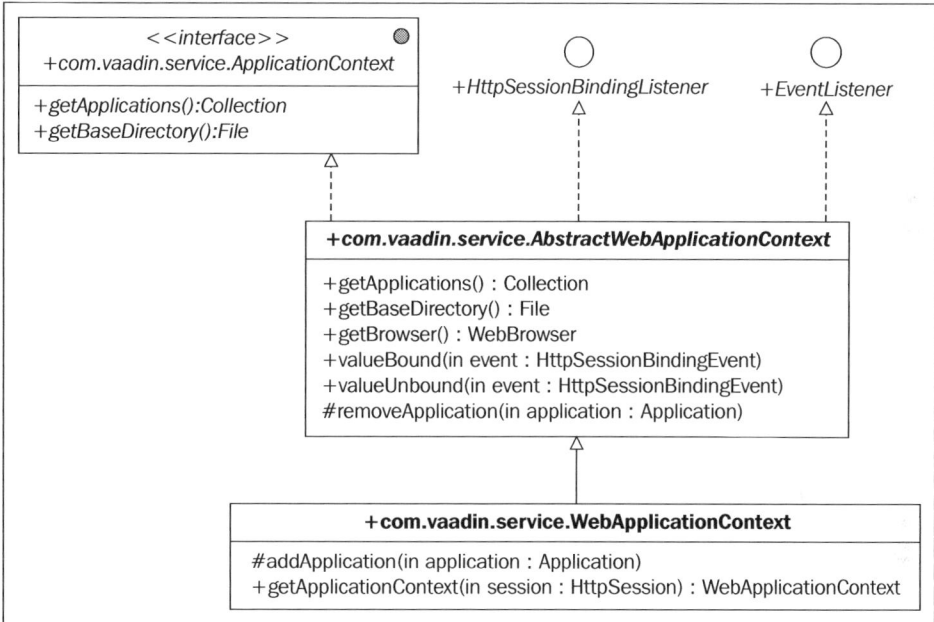

As an example, we could make use of a servlet filter to get a handle on the application itself.

```
public void doFilter(ServletRequest req, ServletResponse resp,
  FilterChain chain) throws IOException, ServletException {

  HttpServletRequest request = (HttpServletRequest) req;

  WebApplicationContext ctx =
WebApplicationContext.getApplicationContext(request.getSession(true));
```

```
    Collection<Application> apps = ctx.getApplications();

    Application app = null;

    if (!apps.isEmpty()) {

      Application app = apps.iterator().next();

      // Set a cookie here
    }

    chain.doFilter(req, resp);

    if (app == null) {

      // Read a cookie there
    }
}
```

The integrated approach

The previous approach works well but put the responsibility of the integration outside the Vaadin application, meaning external components have to know the internals of Vaadin, which is not particularly desirable.

In order to provide a solution, Vaadin comes up with the HttpServletRequestListener interface.

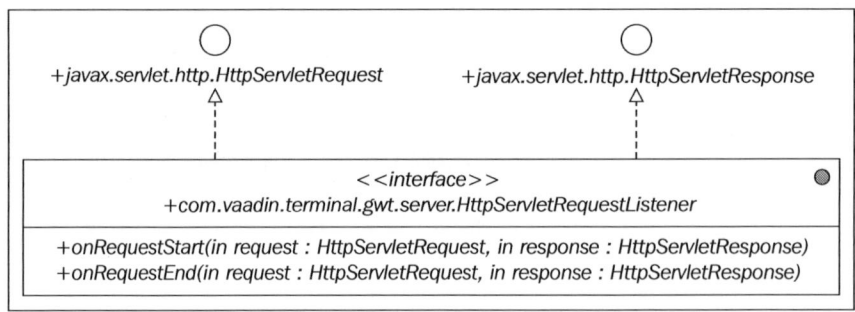

When implemented by an application, Vaadin will call onRequestStart(HttpServletRequest request, HttpServletResponse response) and onRequestEnd(HttpServletRequest request, HttpServletResponse response) respectively at the start and end of each request-response sequence.

 Vaadin will call the methods **only when implemented by an application**. This will have no effect whatsoever when implemented by components, windows or anything else.

The previous code could advantageously be replaced with the following snippet:

```
import javax.servlet.http.HttpServletRequest;
import javax.servlet.http.HttpServletResponse;

import com.vaadin.Application;
import com.vaadin.terminal.gwt.server.HttpServletRequestListener;
import com.vaadin.ui.Window;

public class MyApplication extends Application implements
  HttpServletRequestListener {

  @Override
  public void init() {

    setMainWindow(new Window());
  }

  @Override
  public void onRequestStart(HttpServletRequest request,
    HttpServletResponse response) {

    // Set cookie here
  }

  @Override
  public void onRequestEnd(HttpServletRequest request,
    HttpServletResponse response) {

    // Read cookie there
  }
}
```

 Other use-cases such as making the application accessible to unrelated classes are possible: in this case, the use of the ThreadLocal pattern is advised, as discussed at the following URL:

https://vaadin.com/wiki/-/wiki/Main/ThreadLocal%20 Pattern.

Bookmarks

We discussed in *Chapter 1* about Vaadin's approach opposite to traditional page flow paradigm and how it is a good thing since applications are about windows and not pages.

However, this single URL thing is precisely what prevents us from bookmarking individual pages. We have seen in *Chapter 4* that windows can be set a name that translates to a subcontext in the URL bar but this subcontext property only captures a specific window, completely disregarding its exact state.

In some cases, however, this is highly desirable. Consider for example the following use-cases:

- A large bookstore application offers many features dispatched in different screens. A single screen displays details about the book, and the publisher really wants customers to bookmark a precise book. In fact, any such catalogue application would probably have the same requirements.

- In the same vein, a forum application could probably host many different subjects. It would be a real asset to this application to let users bookmark a specific subject or even a particular thread.

URL fragment

HTML provides a nice feature in the form of the URL fragment. Quoting the W3C:

> *Some URIs refer to a location within a resource. This kind of URI ends with "#" followed by an anchor identifier (called the fragment identifier).*

Refer the following URL for more details:
`http://www.w3.org/TR/html401/intro/intro.html#h-2.1.2`

Therefore, this enables us to stay in the same "page", and yet reference different states, that can be read or written on the server side. Be aware that it is up to the application developer to bridge between the string fragment and the whole state. Taking our previous use-cases as examples, the fragment can be the book's, forum's, or thread's ID. Let's do this with Vaadin!

URI fragment utility

First, we have to understand that Vaadin widgets may have a graphical representation but it is not mandatory. The non-graphical part is just as important as it adds the behavioral code.

In Vaadin, URI fragments are managed in the form of the `UriFragmentUtility` component.

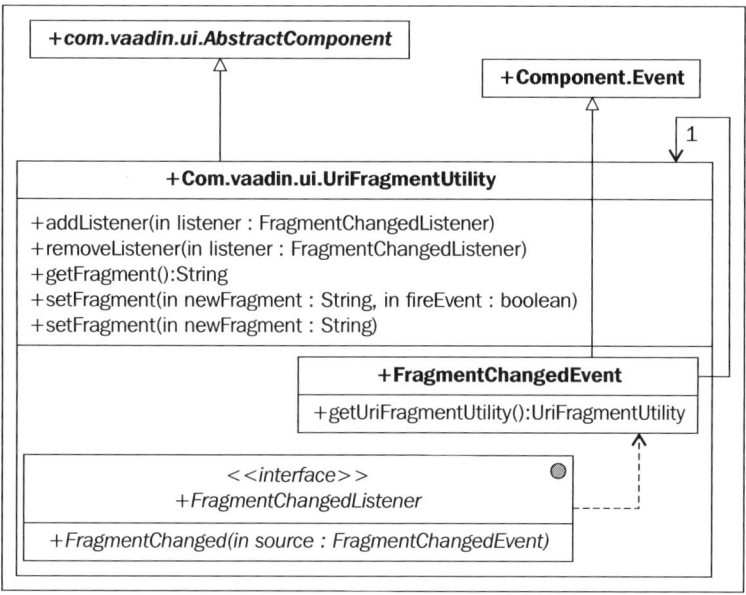

The widget comes bundled with a whole event-listener model wrapped around changing fragments.

The following code displays the fragment to the user when it is changed on the address bar:

```
import com.vaadin.Application;
import com.vaadin.ui.Label;
import com.vaadin.ui.UriFragmentUtility;
import com.vaadin.ui.UriFragmentUtility.FragmentChangedEvent;
import com.vaadin.ui.UriFragmentUtility.FragmentChangedListener;
import com.vaadin.ui.Window;

public class FragmentApplication extends Application {

  private UriFragmentUtility ufu = new UriFragmentUtility();

  private Label label = new Label();

  @Override
  public void init() {

    Window window = new Window();

    ufu.addListener(new FragmentChangedListener() {
```

```
        @Override
        public void fragmentChanged(FragmentChangedEvent source) {

            label.setValue(ufu.getFragment());
        }
    });

    window.addComponent(ufu);
    window.addComponent(label);

    setMainWindow(window);
    }
}
```

This will provide us with the following display:

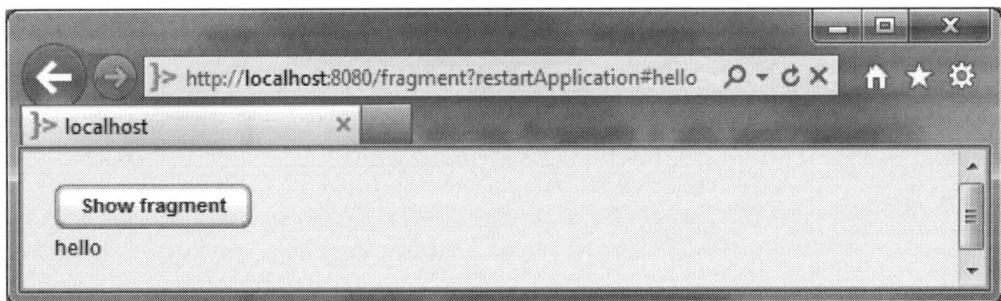

 Of course, more realistic examples could load the corresponding entity. Using the entity's ID directly is good enough for catalogue applications. Depending on the required level of security, it may be a bad idea to expose it: in this case, symmetric encoding may be the solution.

Note that there is no point to add more than one URI fragment utility to a single window as they will all share the same fragment (their state).

Embedding Vaadin

In our previous examples, the whole application was a Vaadin-based web application. This may not be desirable for a variety of reasons:

- Legacy applications may have to be upgraded one part at a time, thus having one part managed by the old application and the other part by the Vaadin framework.

- Even though Vaadin-based applications can easily be integrated with other frameworks, some may be unsuitable for such integration, thus creating the need for embedding either the Vaadin or the other application.

- Finally, we may need to display more than one Vaadin application at the same time in the same page.

In addition, sometimes there is a need to use the Vaadin application as a small part of a larger, static web page. Sometimes, the static content is better made with something else than Vaadin. That is why it is great that it is so easy to embed Vaadin.

Basic embedding

At the simplest level, Vaadin can be embedded using a simple HTML `iframe`. In this case, the embedding page and the iframe Vaadin servlet have to come from the same domain.

 More information on iframes can be found at the following URL:
`http://www.w3.org/TR/html4/present/frames.html#h-16.5`

In this case, we need a dedicated servlet mapping in the web application deployment descriptor to serve Vaadin and use it as the iframe `src`'s attribute. The servlet mapping would look something akin to the following:

```
<servlet-mapping>
  <servlet-name>VaadinServlet</servlet-name>
  <url-pattern>/vaadin/*</url-pattern>
</servlet-mapping>
```

On the HTML page, the iframe is referenced as follows:

```
<iframe src="/vaadin/">[Cannot display Vaadin]</iframe>
```

This technique is very easy to use and requires no specific knowledge at all. Nonetheless, using iframes brings some disadvantages, including:

- Making the bookmarking feature discussed earlier impossible

- Increasing complexity of page-iframe communications

- Decreasing accessibility of pages as screen readers have two different structures to analyze

Nominal embedding

The next embedding approach uses Vaadin directly in a `div` on the desired page, without the need for further artifacts. However, whereas Vaadin took care of loading the client-side engine when used in non-embedded mode, this method requires us to go into the detail of doing it ourselves.

The following is the whole HTML page, each following section details a part:

```html
<html>
<head>
<!-- Configuration -->
<script type="text/javascript">
  var vaadin = {
    vaadinConfigurations : {
      twaattin : {
        appUri : '/<CONTEXT_ROOT>/<SERVLET_MAPPING>',
        versionInfo : {
          vaadinVersion : "<VERSION>",
          applicationVersion : "NONVERSIONED"
        }
      }
    }
  };
</script>
<!-- End configuration -->
<!-- Loading -->
<script type="text/javascript"
  src='/<CONTEXT_ROOT> /VAADIN/widgetsets/com.vaadin.terminal.gwt.
DefaultWidgetSet/com.vaadin.terminal.gwt.DefaultWidgetSet.nocache.
js'></script>
<!-- End loading -->
<!-- Stylesheet -->
<link rel="stylesheet" type="text/css"
  href="/<CONTEXT_ROOT>/VAADIN/themes/<THEME_NAME>/styles.css">
<!—End stylesheet -->
</head>
<body>
  <!-- Here will be shown the Vaadin app -->
  <div id="<APP_NAME>" class="v-app"></div>
</body>
</html>
```

Configuration

The first step is to configure the framework, so that the loader can do its job. This is done through JavaScript with JSON structure. It has to be included in a `script` tag in the HTML page's head.

Replace the following values, as shown above, with your real values:

- `APP_NAME` is the application's name in Vaadin internal repository. Different Vaadin applications can be used in the same page using different entries.

- `CONTEXT_ROOT` is the web application's context root since Vaadin uses links relative to the server root. When possible, it is better to use either scriptlets or JSTL to read it dynamically and not to hard-code it.

- `SERVLET_MAPPING` is the mapping of the application mapping (as more than one is possible).

- `THEME_NAME` is the desired theme's name. If unsure, just use "reindeer", which is the default.

- `VERSION` is the framework's version. Just look at the version of the JAR.

Loading

Loading the client-side engine is just a matter of writing the second script (after the configuration): Aside from the context root, everything else is static.

Style sheet

As Vaadin does not serve the whole page, a link has to be manually added to reference the correct CSS.

Div

Finally, in the HTML page, we must insert a `div` element that has exactly the same `id` attribute as the aforementioned `APP_NAME` in the preceding section named *Configuration*.

 There might be a slight difference in appearance about a full Vaadin application. If we want the same output, then we should set the "v-app" value to the `class` attribute of the `div`.

The final way of embedding Vaadin applications is to use an application deployed on another server altogether. It is not as simple as it seems because browser security models tend to view AJAX requests made across third-party domains as security breaches.

As complying with security rules and still providing the feature is not trivial, this is proposed as a third-party capability under the form of an add-on (see section *Cross-site embedding* in this chapter for more details).

Custom error handling

Until now, two different error types are apparent in Vaadin.

- Caught exceptions: these are managed in the way the developer wants. Most of the time, they are printed as a stack in the `System.err` and the user is displayed an error notification, with more or less detail.

- Uncaught exceptions: such exceptions are uncaught, either because they are runtime exceptions that are left to propagate upwards, or because they are outside the developers reach. In those cases, it falls to the `ApplicationServlet` to handle it.

- The component at the cause of the exception is decorated with a little error icon and when the user hovers over it, a pop up displaying the stack trace is shown.

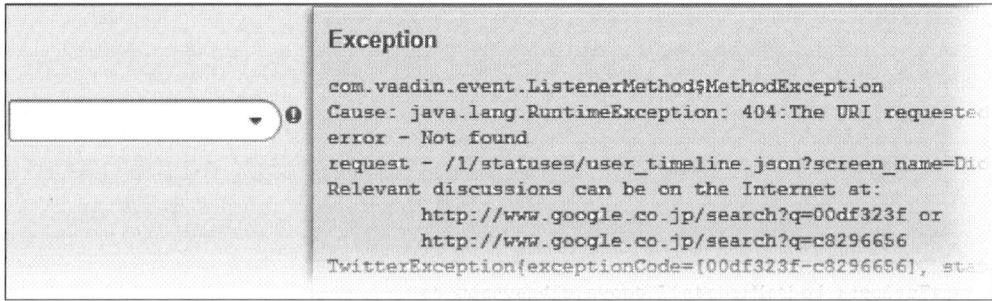

This behavior exposes the user to the inner intricacies of the technology that is not something desirable most of the time. The section *Error listener example* in this chapter proposes an alternative.

Design

The main elements in the error handling chains are the following:

- The upper component in the exception handling chain, the one tasked to manage the behavior, is the servlet like in most other web applications.

- The next item in the chain is the application instance itself, which contains an error listener.

- The real magic is done in the `Application` which inherits from `ErrorListener` and an application is its own listener if another is not set. By default, the application-listener does some interesting things:
    - Locate the component at the root of the exception-causing event
    - Set the object in error, that is displaying the icon and the stack trace in a hover pop up
    - Finally, log the stack in the `System.err`

The following diagram shows the collaborating classes in the default exception handling mechanism:

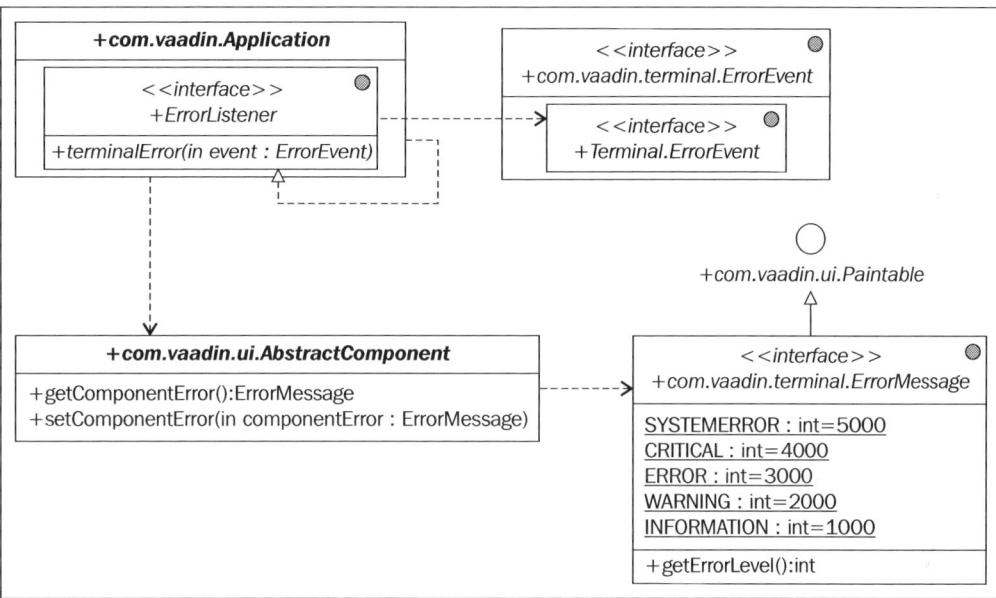

Another look at the system can be from a dynamic point of view.

Note that on one hand, the `terminalError()` method takes an `ErrorEvent` as a single parameter, which is only a simple Vaadin wrapper around a `Throwable` instance.

On the other hand, the `setComponentError()` takes an `ErrorMessage`. An error message is a `Paintable`, which means it can be displayed on the client side.

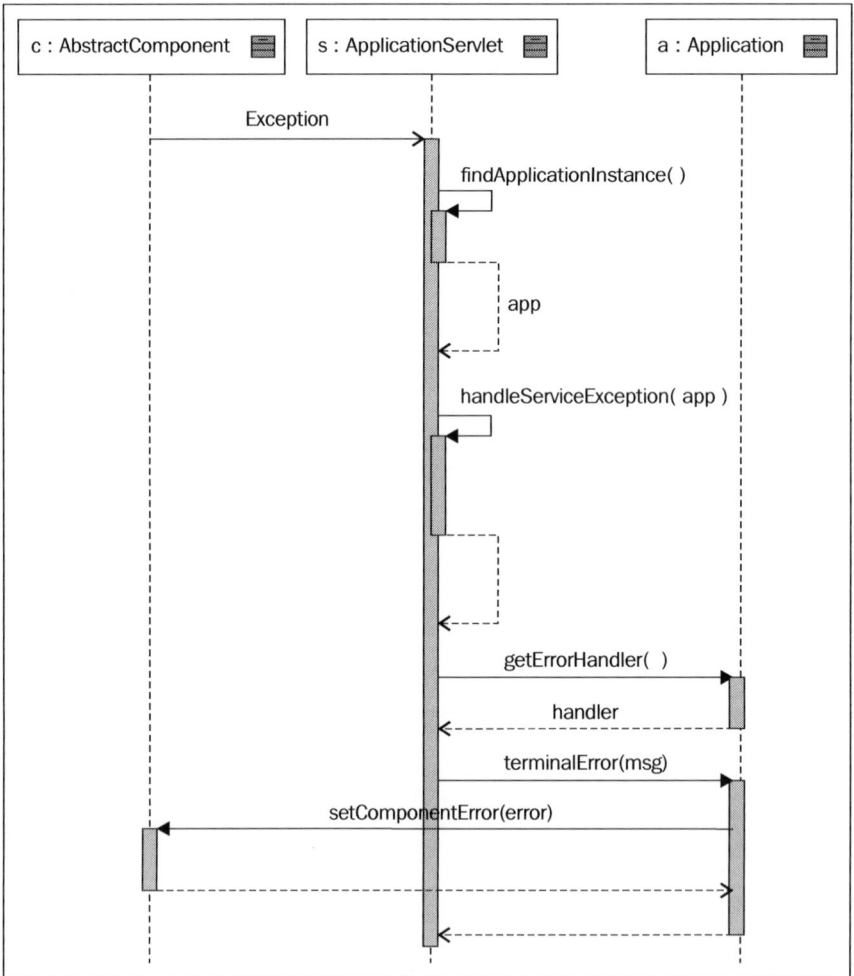

Error messages

Different flavors of error messages are available out-of-the-box in Vaadin. The most important of those are:

- User errors that represent errors provoked by the user. They are expected during the course of the application, and are intended as a guide to the user.

- System errors, on the other hand, are unexpected errors. It inherits from `RuntimeException` in order to convey contextual information about these abnormal conditions.

Another group of error messages is formed by messages that are internal to Vaadin behavior and components. Most of the time, we won't have to interact with them, and in that case, it is enough to know the `ErrorMessage` API.

Finally, the `CompositeErrorMessage` class allows us to encapsulate one or more error messages should the need arise.

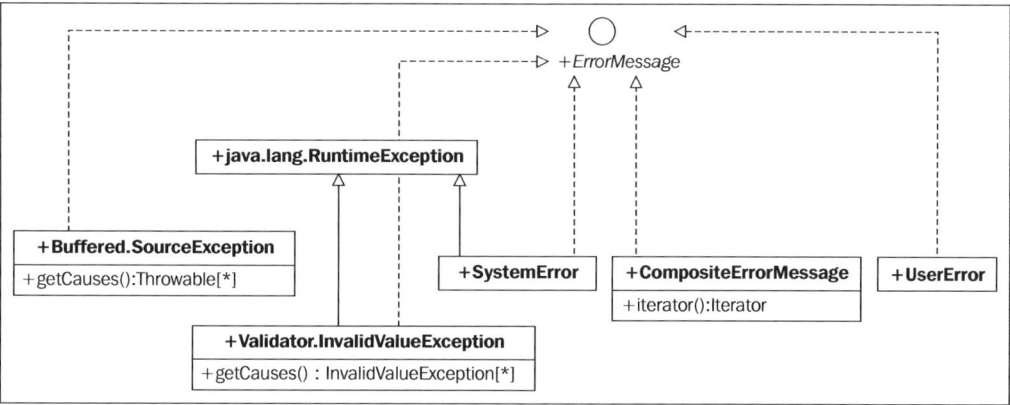

Error listener example

Suppose the default behavior does not suit us: the error should be displayed in a more visible manner and the user should not be shown the stack.

As a trivial example, window tray notifications seen in *Chapter 4* could do the trick. Let's create such a listener.

Application

The following initialization code creates a simple application with a button that provokes an exception:

```
public void init() {

  Window mainWindow = new Window("Error Listener example");

  Button button = new Button("Create an exception");

  button.addListener(new ClickListener() {

    @Override
    public void buttonClick(ClickEvent event) {

      Exception first = new Exception();
```

```
        IllegalArgumentException second = new
          IllegalArgumentException(first);

        RuntimeException third = new RuntimeException(second);

        throw third;
      }
    });
    mainWindow.addComponent(button);

    setMainWindow(mainWindow);
  }
```

Clicking on the button logs the exception stack in the error log and shows an exclamation mark icon right next to the text on the button.

The listener

The next code just does what is expected; displays a tray notification for each exception.

```
    public class TrayNotificationListener implements ErrorListener {

      private Application application;

      public TrayNotificationListener(Application application) {

        this.application = application;
      }
      @Override
      public void terminalError(ErrorEvent event) {

        Window window = application.getWindows().iterator().next();

        DateFormat format = DateFormat.getTimeInstance();

        String msg = format.format(new Date()) + ":
          an unexpected error occured";

        window.showNotification(msg, TYPE_TRAY_NOTIFICATION);

        Throwable e = event.getThrowable();

        // Logs Throwable with the desired API
      }
    }
```

Note that the listener constructor has to be passed the reference to the application since the `ErrorEvent` parameter cannot access it.

We just have to instantiate a listener object and set it as the error handler in the application `init()` method as follows:

```
    setErrorHandler(new TrayNotificationListener(this));
```

Lifecycles

In *Chapter 3*, we saw about the application's `init()` method and how we could not only build the GUI, but also initialize resources. However, Vaadin's objects lifecycle is much richer than that.

Application lifecycle

Regarding the application, there is a counterpart to the initialization phase, the closing phase implemented by the `close()` method. By default, the following actions take place in this method:

- The application stops returning windows

- Vaadin's servlet removes the application from the user session

- From there, two things can happen:

  ° By default, the user is redirected to the root of the application, thus starting the application initialization again.

  ° Alternatively, we can set an URL through the application's `setLogoutURL()` method and we will be redirected to it. Note that Vaadin uses the `sendRedirect()` method from the `HttpServletResponse` and as such, the set URL can be either relative to the context root or absolute.

Even the name might be slightly misleading; most of the time closing the application will be done when the user logs out.

Avoid serving Vaadin from the context root

Mapping Vaadin at the context root will cause every closing action to restart the whole start sequence again, including creating a new application and storing it in the user session. That is why it is advised to create a simple welcome page and serve Vaadin from the context root rather than from a subcontext.

Third-party additional features

Vaadin's design is made around a restricted core of features. In order not to bloat this core, additional capabilities are added by third-party modules.

Therefore, beside the preceding elements, there are many more available or that can be developed. In conclusion, it is not because Vaadin does not offer a required feature that it is the end of the road.

Vaadin add-ons

In Vaadin, third-party modules are called add-ons. Some are supplied by Vaadin Ltd, but the most part is by others (either individuals or companies).

Add-ons directory

Vaadin provides an add-on store available online at `http://vaadin.com/directory`. Anyone, including you, can publish on this directory.

Add-ons search

The store provides categorization in order to search for certain specific features. Those categorizations are available in different flavors.

Results obtained using the following criteria, either alone or in conjunction, can then be sorted. Sorting is possible by release date, number of downloads and grade.

Typology

Available categories are:

- **UI components**: these add-ons have graphical representations that are displayed to users when added to a window.
- **Data components**: this category groups add-ons containers that can connect to data tiers, such as SQL databases. These connectors provide a way to manage data (direct SQL, JPA, Hibernate, and so on).
- **Themes**: theme add-ons offer a quick route to change an application look and feel.
- **Miscellaneous**: add-ons that are no part of another category are put in there.

Stability

Add-ons are classified into different stability levels:

- Certified add-ons are provided by Vaadin Ltd, the company behind the framework, and as such guarantee the best level of reliability and integration. Third-party add-ons can also be certified by the company, against a set fee.

- Stable add-ons have been subject to at least one whole release lifecycle. They can usually be trusted to function in an expected way.

- Beta add-ons are just that. It is advised not to use them in a production environment because they do not guarantee to be completely bug-free.

- Experimental add-ons should not be used: they are here just to give you a preview of what is to come. If interested, you should probably contact the publisher to help!

Add-ons presentation

Add-on presentation is handled by the directory and thus highly standardized. Each add-on has two views: a summarized view, displayed in search results, and a detailed view.

Summarized view

Displayed information in the summarized view includes:

- Name
- Category
- Provider
- A short description
- Version
- Maturity
- Grade, rated from 1 to 5
- Number of downloads

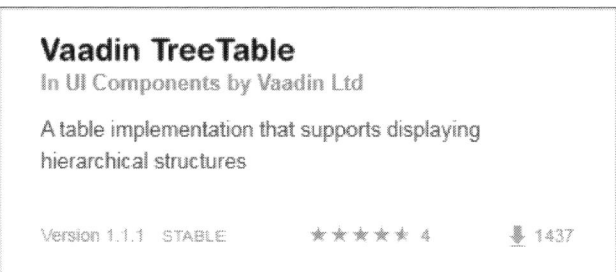

Detailed view

Clicking on the add-on's name opens the detailed view. In addition to the previous information, it displays:

- The version: it is selectable so we can see the data related to previous versions
- The license information
- A table of browsers' compatibility (including versions)
- A detailed description
- One or more pop-up windows providing either code example or screenshot
- The release notes for the current version
- A download link
- The Maven snippet to include in the POM
- A list of links; commons links include (but are not limited to):
  - Demo application
  - Source Control Manager repository
  - Afferent documentation
  - Discussion forum
  - Issue tracker
- A "like it" bar, for sharing the add-on on a variety of social networks
- Finally, the page's permalink

These are depicted in the following screenshot:

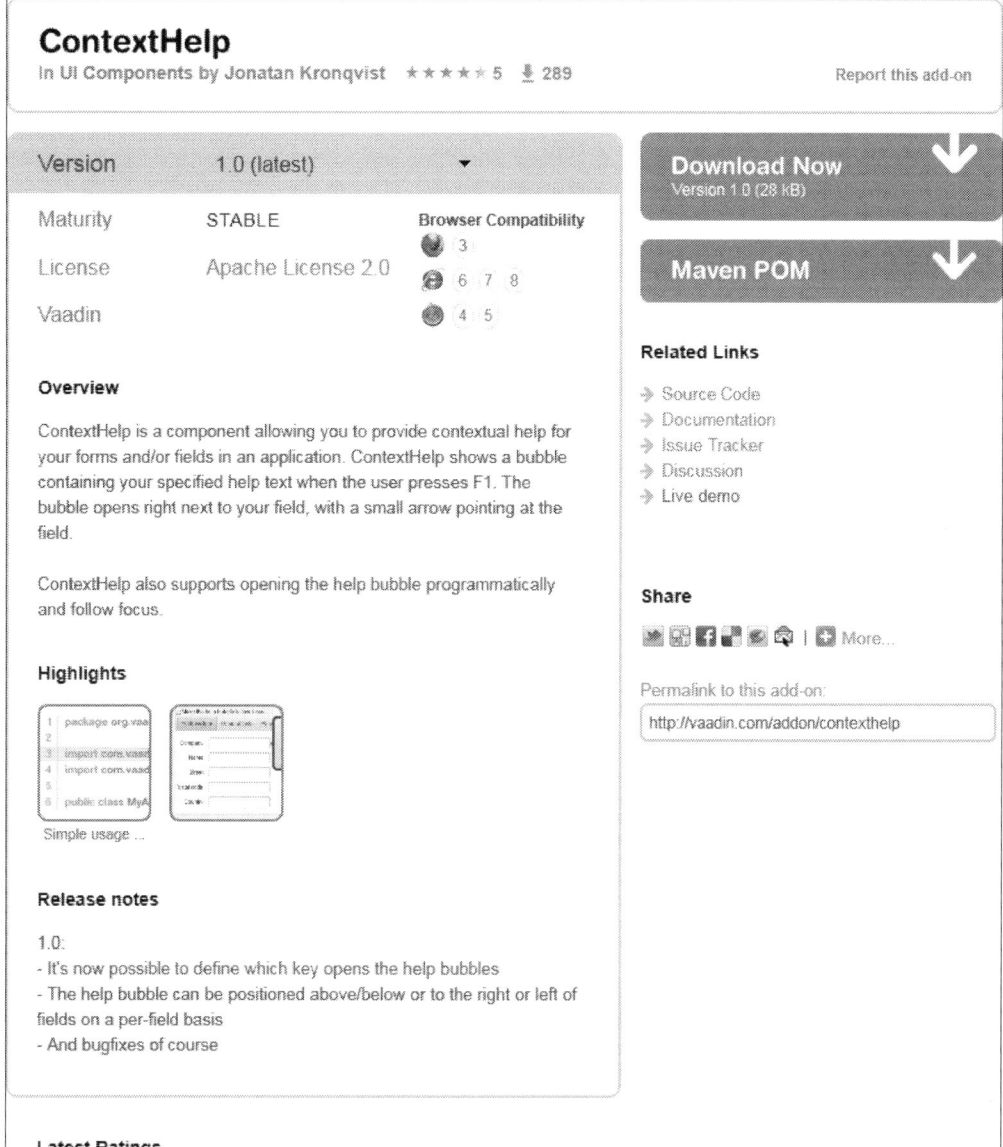

Noteworthy add-ons

At the date of the writing of this book, the Vaadin directory contains 51 add-ons, stable or certified on a total of 198 (at the time of writing). It is well beyond the scope of this book to see them all in detail. However, a few are worth describing, as they really set Vaadin on another level.

Cross-site embedding

Earlier we looked at different ways to embed Vaadin applications. Those are provided out-of-the-box, but there is another method provided by the Vaadin XS plugin, available at `http://vaadin.com/directory#addon/vaadin-xs`.

Stability risk

Note that at the moment of the writing of this book, the XS add-on is only available in **beta** because of some possible incompatibilities with third-party libraries and/or JavaScript. Things may change quickly depending on its popularity, which may uncover those mismatches (and the solutions).

Use-case

Vaadin XS provides a different way of application embedding from the previous ones. Both former methods are intended to be used in the same context or at least in the same domain.

Vaadin XS enables us to reuse applications cross-domain. Suppose we have designed a nice application available online at `http://packtpub.com`. We want to embed this application in our site `http://frankel.ch` by reusing the available instance instead of deploying another one.

Tweaks

Vaadin XS provides three differences to the standard Vaadin behavior:

- First, whereas in standard mode Vaadin creates and stores an application instance per user session, Vaadin XS does it per authorized external domain.

- Second, as domains access the Vaadin application using GET, payloads would easily be accessible in logs or simple HTTP listeners. In order to prevent this, Vaadin XS encrypts the payload using 128-bits based Advanced Encryption Standard (AES).

- Finally, the communication "method" is changed from `XmlHttpRequest` to JSON with Padding (or JSONP). For an overview of JSONP, see `http://en.wikipedia.org/wiki/JSONP`.

Installation

Like any other add-on, in order to use it, just add the right dependency snippet in your Maven POM or drop the JAR in the WEB-INF/lib of your application.

 In the latter case however, don't forget to also drop the commons-codec JAR along, as the add-on has a dependency on it (if using Maven, it does it for you).

Compilation

The following steps will have to be carried out in order for the add-on to function. The Eclipse plugin will take care of them; if not using it, you will have to execute them manually which goes well beyond the scope of this book. See GWT's documentation at the following URL:

http://code.google.com/webtoolkit/gettingstarted.html#compile

 Note that some add-ons do not have a client-side component: those don't need compilation.

- Creation of a widget set XML file in the source folder. If generated by the plugin, the name of the file and its content are dependent on the dropped JAR itself. The extension should be gwt.xml. For the XS add-on, it should include the following line:

  ```
  <inherits name="com.vaadin.addons.xs.gwt.XSWidgetSet" />
  ```

- Compilation of the Java GWT code into JavaScript in order for the GWT framework to be able to use it. The Vaadin Eclipse plugin will take care of that for us: a warning will appear. Click on **Yes** and wait for the compilation to finish, as shown in the following screenshot:

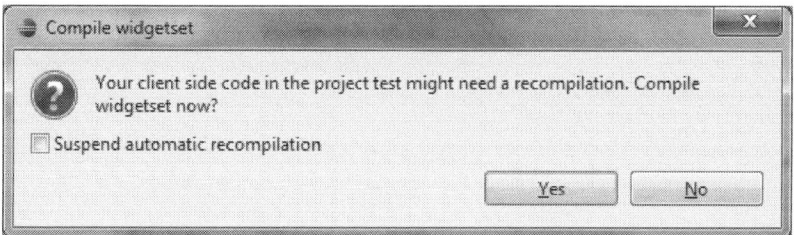

Shortening widgetset compilation time

During development, we can drastically shorten the widgetset compilation time by compiling only for the browser used. Go to the `gwt.xml` widgetset file and follow instructions in the comment.

Compiled files are located in the web content under the `VAADIN/widgetsets` folder.

Note that this compilation step has to be executed each time a new different JAR is embarking Vaadin add-ons that have a client-side presence (not necessarily a graphical representation).

- Last but not least, the web deployment descriptor has to be updated:
  - ° The Vaadin servlet should point to the `com.vaadin.addons.xs.server.XSApplicationServlet`. Note that is not necessary for all add-ons: most are usable as-is with Vaadin's default `ApplicationServlet`.
  - ° The widgetset `init-param` should reference the previous widget set XML file.

```
<servlet>
  <servlet-name>EmbeddedVaadinApplication</servlet-name>
  <servlet-class>
    com.vaadin.addons.xs.server.XSApplicationServlet
  </servlet-class>
  <init-param>
    <param-name>application</param-name>
    <param-value>
      com.packtpub.learnvaadin.EmbeddedApplication
    </param-value>
  </init-param>
  <init-param>
    <param-name>widgetset</param-name>
    <param-value>
com.packtpub.learnvaadin.widgetset.EmbeddedvaadinexampleWidgetset
    </param-value>
  </init-param>
</servlet>
```

Use

Having done all the previous steps, using the application from another domain is just a matter of creating a `div` in the calling page with the exact subcontext `getEmbedJs`.

This would look like the following code:

```
<div>
  <script src="path/to/Vaadin/app/getEmbedJs"
    type="text/javascript">
  </script>
</div>
```

Add-on configuration

By default, all external domains are allowed to reference our application. Nonetheless, it seldom should be the case, as we probably don't want any domain to access it, but only our own.

This is done through the `allowedReferrers` init parameter of the Vaadin XS servlet in the web deployment descriptor. Different domains are separated by carriage returns, like so:

```
<init-param>
  <param-name>allowedReferrers</param-name>
  <param-value>http://portal.packtpub.com/
    http://packtpub.com/</param-value>
</init-param>
```

SQL adapter

In *Chapter 6*, when we looked into the table widget, we left how to fill the container with data aside. Were we in a standard layered architecture, we would explicitly call the service layer in order to call the persistence layer which would itself query the database.

If our needs are just to manage CRUD operations, this is simply overkill. In order to manage these, the add-ons directory provides many database-oriented containers. Those are able to directly connect to a database using an API depending on the kind of add-on.

Facts

At present, we will have a look at the SQLContainer add-on, which lets us directly connect to a SQL database and present the data in a tabular manner. It is available at `http://vaadin.com/directory#addon/vaadin-sqlcontainer`.

SQLContainer is provided by Vaadin Limited, is released under the friendly Apache 2.0 license, and is tagged as stable. Considering the general high quality of the framework in general, the add-on can be taken as an optional feature, not a separate module.

The latest version available at the time of the writing of this book is 1.0.0 and provides compatibility with HSQLDB, MySQL, Microsoft SQL Server, and Oracle.

Architecture

The Vaadin SQLContainer add-on is built around the SQLContainer class, which has all the nice properties we expect from a container: it is indexed, sortable, and filterable.

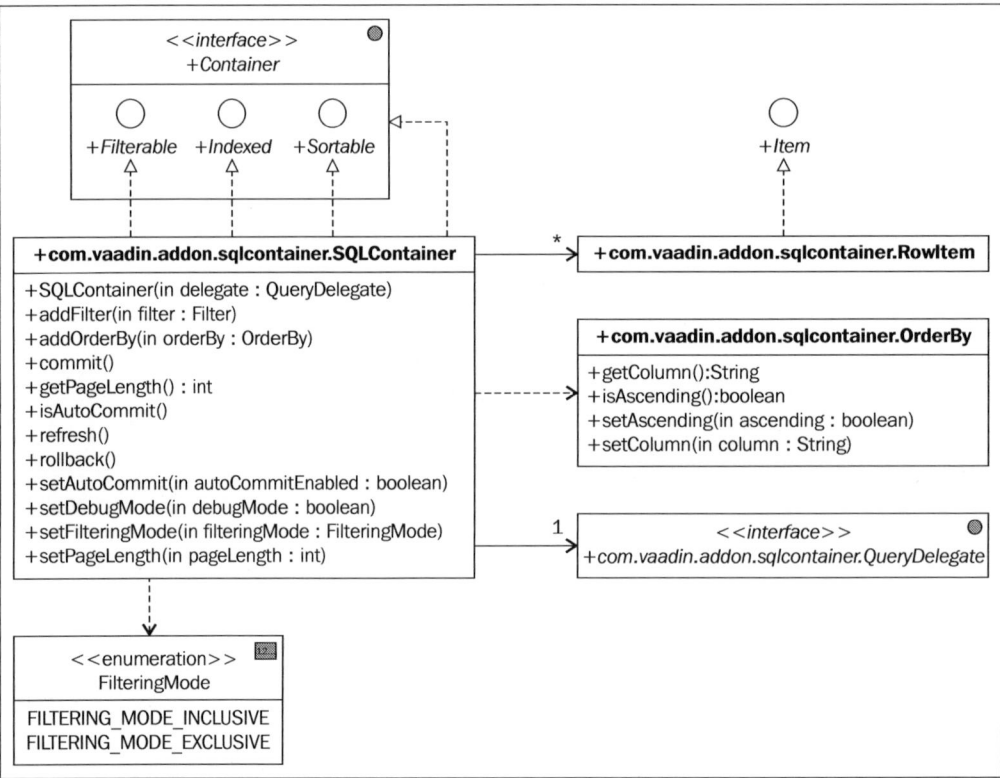

Items in the container are specialized instances, namely RowItem. This type is encapsulated and not to be manipulated directly by the developer, even though it is part of the API (it has public visibility).

Features

Features of SQL container include:

- Transaction management: Changes made to the container can be either committed or rollbacked to the data tier. Alternatively, we can set each operation to the container to be autocommited. Note that **the default behavior doesn't use autocommit**.

- Programmatic filtering: Uses Vaadin's filter API already seen in section *Filter* of *Chapter 6*.

- Programmatic ordering: An `OrderBy` instance is as simple as a column name and whether it is ascending or descending.

- Initialization: The container can be initialized with data from the underlying data tier with the `refresh()` method.

- Paging: The container uses a page length attribute in order to optimize performance. Like in tables (see section *Viewpoint* in *Chapter 6*), SQL containers use a page length, as well as a cache ratio. Unlike table, cache ratio is set to 2 and cannot be changed, at least not without serious hacking. This means that requests made through the query delegate (see below) limit the number of occurrences to 2 times the page length.

Query delegate

SQL container's responsibilities are those of a container. Real interaction with the database is delegated to an instance of `QueryDelegate`, which in turn delegates connection management to an instance of `JDBCConnectionPool`.

JDBC connection pool can either wrap a direct connection to the database, driver manager style or a data source retrieved from the application server, depending on the type of the concrete class. Note that in the former case, the class creates a **pseudo-shareable**. For more information on driver manager, visit the following URL:

`http://download.oracle.com/javase/6/docs/api/java/sql/DriverManager.html`

For more information on data source, visit the following URL:

`http://download.oracle.com/javase/6/docs/api/javax/sql/DataSource.html`

Query delegates come in two flavors:

- For simple table display, just use a `TableQuery`, passing the table's name and the JDBC connection pool to use. The delegate will retrieve all occurrences from the database. The only thing left to do is to customize the appearance of the table as was done in *Chapter 6*.

- Alternatively, when we need to go beyond only getting all occurrences from a single table, we can use `FreeformQuery`. It allows us pass the query, as well as the JDBC connection pool, and all primary key columns.

Note that without the last parameter, only SELECT orders can be executed, thus rendering the wrapping table read-only.

In both cases, programmatic order bys and filters can be added in order to go even further.

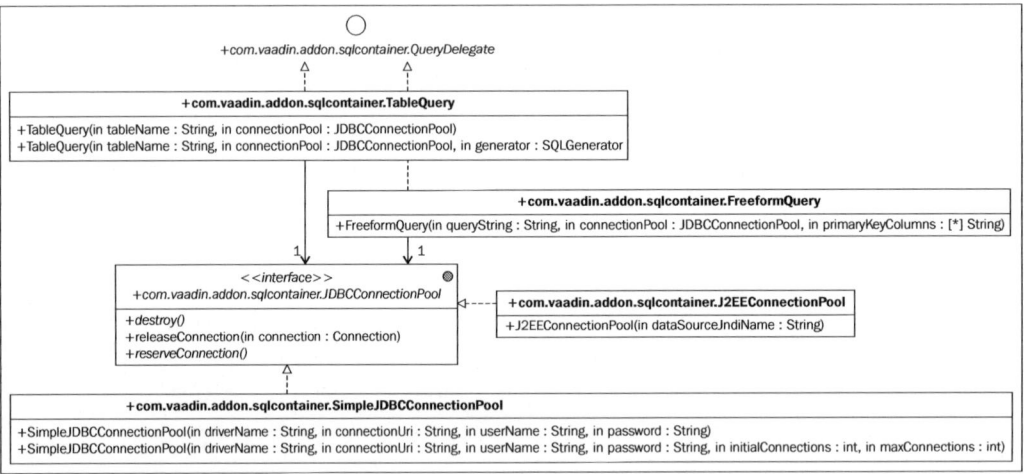

Not that table query is relatively straightforward, and does not require much effort in order to create an editable table widget backed by a database table.

In fact, we could in theory create adapters for other relational data base management systems.

 NoSQL backends are incompatible with the SQL container add-on

As table query delegates much of the SQL generation to a `SQLGenerator`, using another RDBMS is just a matter of creating the right implementation (inheriting from `DefaultSQLGenerator` seems a good starting point).

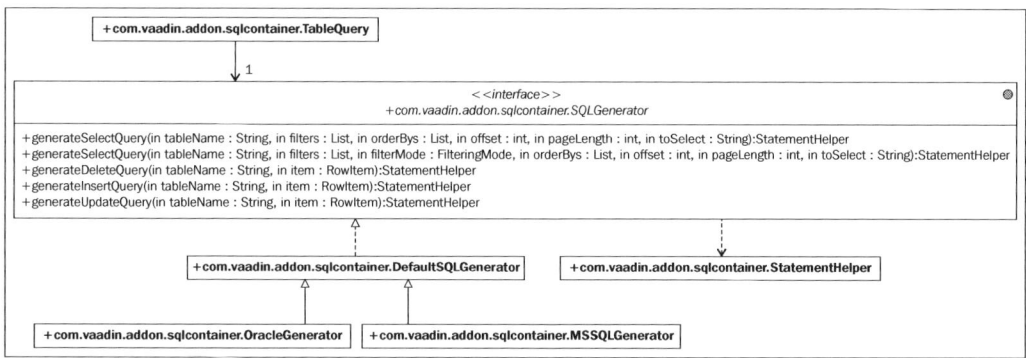

 Note that `SQLGenerator` represents an abstraction over the RDBMS product whereas `StatementHelper`, as its name implies, is a helper whose responsibility is to help creating SQL statements; it should generally not be used directly.

From there, it is easy to create a generic window meant to display any data table (with a Primary Key constraint) within a table widget, along with two global commit/rollback buttons. Each row also shows a delete button:

```java
package com.packtpub.learnvaadin;

import java.sql.SQLException;

import com.vaadin.addon.sqlcontainer.SQLContainer;
import com.vaadin.addon.sqlcontainer.query.QueryDelegate;
import com.vaadin.addon.sqlcontainer.query.TableQuery;
import com.vaadin.ui.Button;
import com.vaadin.ui.Button.ClickEvent;
import com.vaadin.ui.Component;
import com.vaadin.ui.HorizontalLayout;
import com.vaadin.ui.Table;
import com.vaadin.ui.Table.ColumnGenerator;
import com.vaadin.ui.VerticalLayout;
import com.vaadin.ui.Window;

public class MainWindow extends Window {

    private static final long serialVersionUID = 1L;

    private final String tableName;

    private SQLContainer container;

    private Table table;
```

```
@SuppressWarnings("serial")
public MainWindow(String tableName) {

  this.tableName = tableName;

  VerticalLayout vLayout = new VerticalLayout();

  vLayout.setMargin(true);

  setContent(vLayout);

  table = new Table();

  table.setPageLength(10);
  table.setEditable(true);
  table.setSizeFull();

  table.addGeneratedColumn("delete", new ColumnGenerator() {

    @Override
    public Component generateCell(Table source, Object itemId,
    Object columnId) {

      Button button = new Button("Delete");

      button.setData(itemId);

      button.addListener(ClickEvent.class, MainWindow.this,
        "delete");

      return button;
    }
  });

  addComponent(table);

  HorizontalLayout hLayout = new HorizontalLayout();

  hLayout.setMargin(true);
  hLayout.setSpacing(true);

  Button commit = new Button("Commit");
  commit.addListener(ClickEvent.class, this, "commit");
  hLayout.addComponent(commit);

  Button rollback = new Button("Rollback");
  rollback.addListener(ClickEvent.class, this, "rollback");
  hLayout.addComponent(rollback);

  addComponent(hLayout);
}

public void initialize() throws SQLException {

  // Provide the JDBC pool instance here
  QueryDelegate query = new TableQuery(tableName, ...);

  container = new SQLContainer(query);
```

```
    table.setContainerDataSource(container);
  }
  public void commit() throws SQLException {

    container.commit();

    showNotification("Changes committed");
  }
  public void rollback() throws SQLException {

    container.rollback();

    showNotification("Changes rolled back");
  }
  public void delete(ClickEvent event) {

    Object itemId = event.getButton().getData();

    container.removeItem(itemId);
  }
}
```

In order to use this window, we just have to provide a JDBC pool instance, for example by tasking the application to create it during initialization as follows:

```
public class SqlContainerApplication extends Application {

  private JDBCConnectionPool jdbcPool;

  @Override
  public void init() {

    MainWindow window = new MainWindow();

    setMainWindow(window);

    try {

      jdbcPool = new
        SimpleJDBCConnectionPool("org.hsqldb.jdbc.JDBCDriver",
        "jdbc:hsqldb:mem:learnvaadin", "SA", "");

      window.initialize();
    } catch (SQLException e) {

      e.printStackTrace();

      throw new RuntimeException(e);
    }
  }

  JDBCConnectionPool getJdbcPool() {

    return jdbcPool;
  }
}
```

Notice that we use the data property from AbstractComponent to pass the row item's ID from the button to the delete() method through the event.

> The initialize() method could have been coded in the constructor. Yet, separating the code in two as it is done lets us get the JDBC pool instance from the application. Remember the application cannot be retrieved from a window until the window has been set as the application's main window.

Let's take as an example, a table that maps our Person entity from *Chapter 6*.

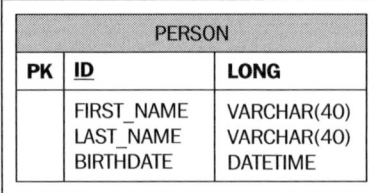

If we use the previous window on a table that maps, we get the following display:

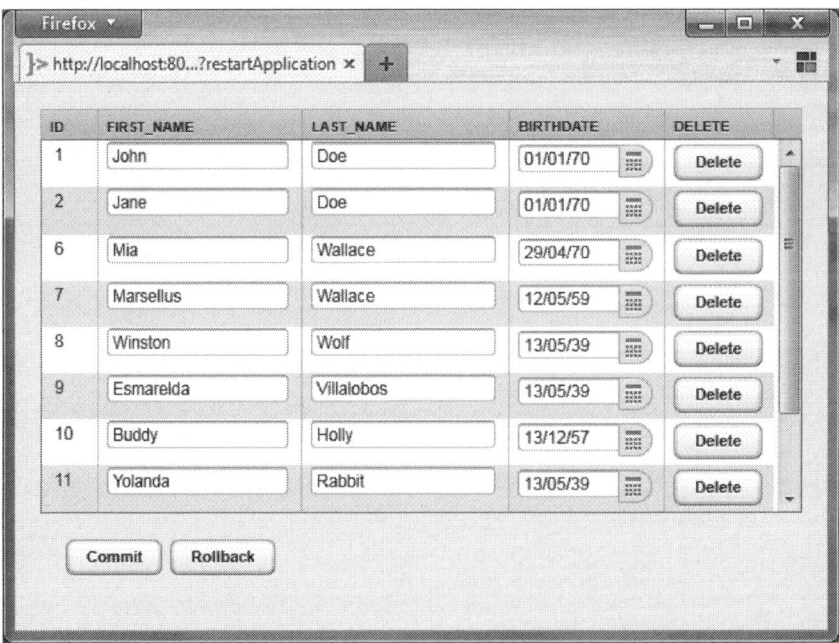

Notice that the `ID` column is automatically set as read-only, and shown as a label and not a field, since it represents the Primary Key!

References

Table queries are enough when viewing/updating data from a single table. However, most of the time, data is scattered through more than one table.

In truth, SQL containers know how to reference other SQL containers so Vaadin can create relationships of sort without using a single line of SQL. In order to do that, the add-on uses `Reference` instances internally. Such references are relationships between a referencing container and its referencing column and a referenced container and its referenced column.

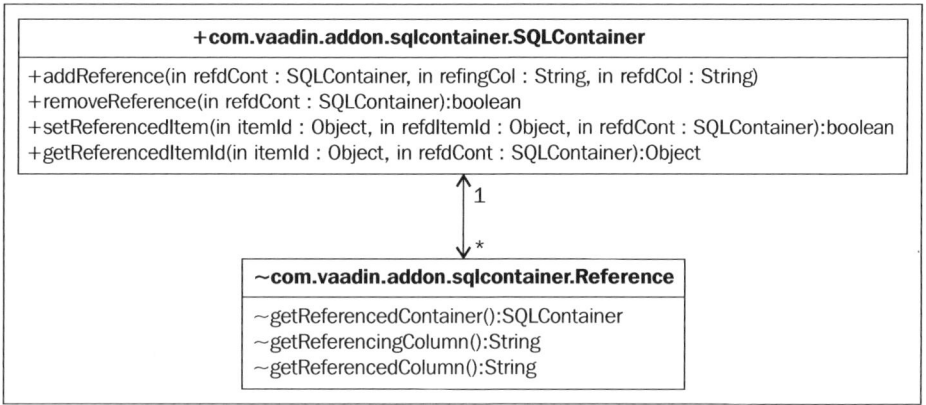

As an example, let's change our former table diagram to create n-to-1 job relationships for each person.

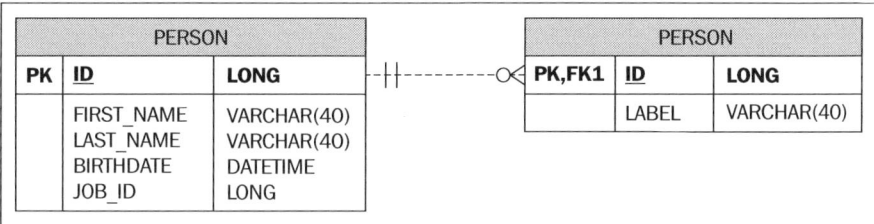

Changes to the previous window's code let us view this new data. Notice that in this case, it is hard to be generic so it is better to just display what we want:

```java
@SuppressWarnings("serial")
public void initialize() throws SQLException {

  SqlContainerApplication app = (SqlContainerApplication)
    getApplication();

  QueryDelegate personsQuery = new TableQuery("PERSON",
    app.getJdbcPool());
  QueryDelegate jobsQuery = new TableQuery("JOB", app.getJdbcPool());

  personsContainer = new SQLContainer(personsQuery);
  // jobsContainer is declared as a window attribute
  jobsContainer = new SQLContainer(jobsQuery);

  personsContainer.addReference(jobsContainer, "JOB_ID", "ID");

  table.setContainerDataSource(personsContainer);

  table.addGeneratedColumn("Job", new ColumnGenerator() {

    @Override
    public Component generateCell(Table source, Object itemId,
      Object columnId) {

      Label label = new Label();

      Item job = personsContainer.getReferencedItem(itemId,
        jobsContainer);

      Property property = job.getItemProperty("LABEL");

      label.setValue(property.getValue());

      return label;
    }
  });
  table.setVisibleColumns(new String[] {"ID", "FIRST_NAME",
    "LAST_NAME", "BIRTHDATE", "Job", "delete"});
}
```

The most important lines above are:

- Create the relationship between the person's job ID in the persons container and the job's ID in the jobs container
- Retrieve the job as an item without coding a single line of SQL

Free form query

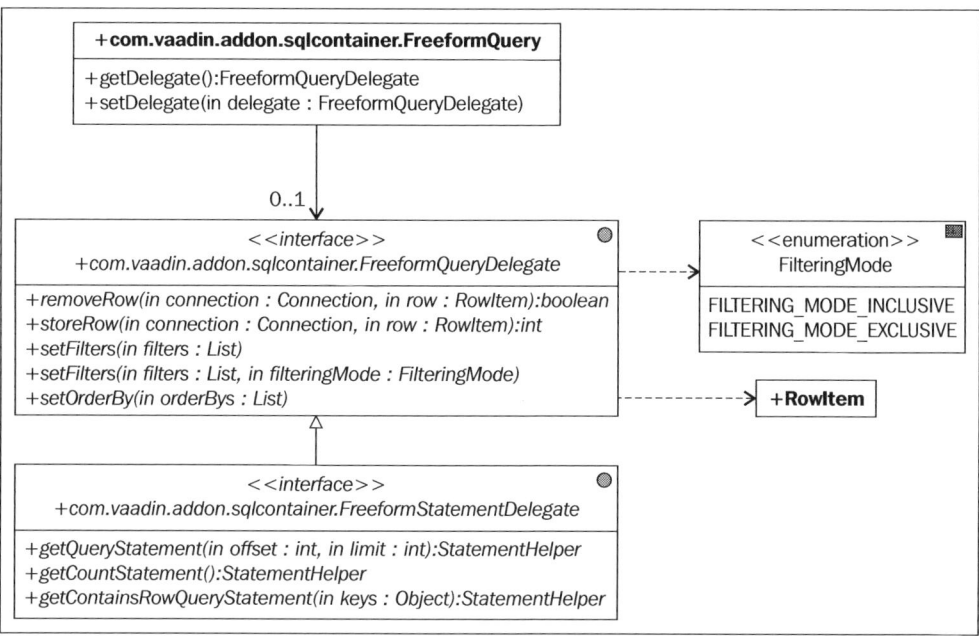

Free form queries offer much more flexibility than table queries, but we need to write SQL code. Moreover, they also require more effort, at least when executing CUD statements.

 CRUD without read: INSERT, UPDATE, and DELETE

As was seen in section *Query delegate*, we have to pass both the SQL select statement and the IDs collection to the `FreeformQuery` constructor. If we reuse our previous persons/jobs example, then the window's code has to be changed as follows:

```
public void initialize() throws SQLException {

  SqlContainerApplication app = (SqlContainerApplication)
    getApplication();

  QueryDelegate personsQuery = new FreeformQuery(
    "SELECT ID, FIRST_NAME, LAST_NAME, BIRTHDATE,
      LABEL AS JOB FROM PERSON, JOB WHERE PERSON.JOB_ID = JOB.ID",
    app.getJdbcPool());

  personsContainer = new SQLContainer(personsQuery);
```

```
table.setContainerDataSource(personsContainer);

table.setVisibleColumns(new String[] {"ID", "FIRST_NAME",
  "LAST_NAME", "BIRTHDATE", "JOB", "delete"});
}
```

Pros and cons are readily visible: the code as a whole is much shorter but in exchange, we need to code the SQL select statement, which may be more or less easy depending on the relationships between tables.

Troubleshooting

Always be careful to use the right column name: when Vaadin complains about `Ids must exist in the Container or as a generated column`, `missing id: xxx`, the first thing to check is the visible column names case. As a first measure, it is advised to always use upper case when referencing column names from the database.

The preceding code produces the following output:

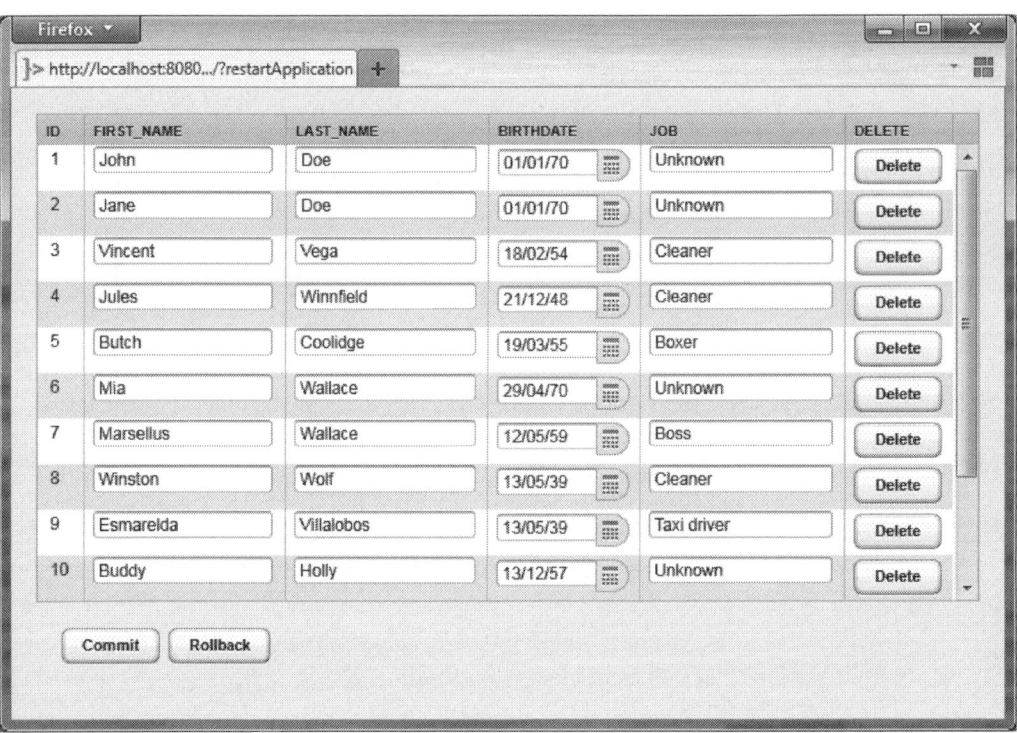

The only difference between using referenced containers and free form queries is that in the former case, referenced column IDs are displayed as labels by default, thus read-only whereas in the latter, all non-identity columns are displayed as fields, thus read-write.

This minor update is enough to display data, but as soon as we need to make updates, we have to go beyond that.

Using table queries, Vaadin can infer from the table metadata. When using free form queries, it is impossible. As such, any CUD operation delegates to a free form statement query delegate that has to be set in order to execute such operations.

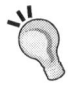

Troubleshooting

If Vaadin complains about `java.lang.`
`UnsupportedOperationException: FreeFormQueryDelegate`
`not set`, it is because setting a delegate to handle updates to the underlying data was forgotten.

Developing a free form query delegate may be done at two different levels:

1. For simple implementations, `FreeformQueryDelegate` is enough to fit our needs.

2. If we want to use `PreparedStatement` instead of regular statements, we need to implement `FreeformStatementDelegate`.

The add-on's code is smart enough to adapt what is used to the implemented interface.

Considering `PreparedStatement` is compiled once to the native RDBMS internal language and then reused over and over, and the decreased possibility of SQL injection, it is advised to always use it.

Similar add-ons

Should SQL be a little too old-fashioned (or if your developers cannot code SQL), some add-ons may be of interest:

- A container over a Hibernate backend, HbnContainer, provided by Matti Tahvonen of the Vaadin team. It is provided in Version 1.0 under the friendly Apache 2.0 license and is considered stable.

- EclipseLink Container is similar to the previous, but with EclipseLink in mind instead of Hibernate. However, beware that it is considered beta, and has seen no update since late 2009.

- Finally, JPAContainer is a commercial add-on, also available under an AGPL license that provides a nice way for widgets to use a JPA backend.

All of those can be downloaded from the directory.

Server push

Traditional HTML-based applications use the request-response model. Requests are initiated by the client, sent to the server, and the latter sends the response back to the client.

Nonetheless, some use-cases require the server to notify the client without the client initiating the sequence. Such use-cases would include chat applications and real-time trading platforms.

At present, push is not provided by Vaadin as-is but by two add-ons: ICEPush and DontPush. The following table sums up some key information about them:

	ICEPush	DontPush
Underlying technology	ICEPush	WebSocket, a part of HTML5
Version browser compatibility	Firefox 3	Firefox 3
	Chrome 5→7	Chrome 7
	Internet Explorer 6à8	Internet Explorer 8
	Opera 10	Opera 10
	Safari 3à5	Safari 5
Server compatibility	Servlet API 2.5	Jetty 7
	Otherwise, server agnostic	
Approach	Invisible widget on window	Use of the event-listener model
	Calls to push() method	

Both add-ons are experimental and provided by members of the Vaadin team. DontPush, however, is highly coupled to the Jetty API, especially the WebSocket part and as such only presented as a *proof of concept*.

Even if ICEPush is also experimental, it has more usages in its current form: let's look at it in detail.

Installation

In order to use ICEPush, we need to add the dependency snippet in our Maven POM or drop the JAR in the `WEB-INF/lib` of our application. In the latter case, the JAR add-on is distributed with the ICEPush JAR itself and an adapter for GWT.

Once done, the compilation step takes place, either automatically or manually (see section Compilation of Vaadin XS above, it's the same).

How-to

For the push to take place, some specific steps are necessary:

- First, the Vaadin servlet in the web application deployment descriptor should be updated with the `org.vaadin.artur.icepush.ICEPushServlet` class.
- From there, we have to add a single `org.vaadin.artur.icepush.ICEPush` widget to our window. It does not appear to the user as the client side is just JavaScript making heavy use of AJAX.
- Finally, once the need for pushing data to the client arises, call the `push()` method on the ICEPush widget. Done!

 Note that like in many matters in Vaadin, the gritty details are completely abstracted under some very simple steps. We don't have to understand ICEPush (although you can browse through its documentation).

Example

As an example, we want to start a client-side clock upon user interaction and stop it upon another one.

```
package com.packtpub.learnvaadin;

import java.text.DateFormat;
import java.text.SimpleDateFormat;
import java.util.Date;

import org.vaadin.artur.icepush.ICEPush;

import com.vaadin.Application;
import com.vaadin.data.Property.ValueChangeEvent;
import com.vaadin.data.Property.ValueChangeListener;
import com.vaadin.ui.CheckBox;
import com.vaadin.ui.Label;
import com.vaadin.ui.Window;
```

```java
@SuppressWarnings("serial")
public class PushApplication extends Application {

  private Thread thread = new Thread(new TimeRunnable());

  private Label label = new Label();

  private ICEPush icepush = new ICEPush();

  private CheckBox checkbox;

  @Override
  public void init() {

    Window window = new Window("Push Application");

    window.addComponent(icepush);

    checkbox = new CheckBox("Check to start");

    checkbox.addListener(new ValueChangeListener() {

      @Override
      public void valueChange(ValueChangeEvent event) {

        boolean checked = (Boolean) event.getProperty().getValue();

        if (checked && !thread.isAlive()) {

          thread.start();
        }
      }
    });

    checkbox.setImmediate(true);

    window.addComponent(checkbox);

    window.addComponent(label);

    setMainWindow(window);

    changeLabel();
  }

  private class TimeRunnable implements Runnable {

    @Override
    public void run() {

      try {

        while (true) {

          if ((Boolean) checkbox.getValue()) {

            changeLabel();
```

```
            icepush.push();
          }
          Thread.sleep(1000);
        }
      } catch (InterruptedException e) {
      } catch (Exception e) {
        e.printStackTrace();
      }
    }
  }
  private void changeLabel() {
    DateFormat format = new SimpleDateFormat("hh:mm:ss");
    String date = format.format(new Date());
    label.setValue(date);
  }
}
```

Important snippets above create the ICEPush widget and add it to the window.

The rest starts the thread the first time the checkbox is checked: once started, it periodically checks for the checked state to update the label and send it to the client if it is "on".

Threads in web application

The preceding code should not be taken at face value and used in a production environment as spawning new threads is frowned upon in a Java EE application. Threads should not be started unless you really know what you are doing. Real-world applications should probably use an event-based stack, such as JMS, an EJB timer or a third-party framework like Quartz.

Twaattin improves!

Given the current state of Twaattin and our current knowledge, some improvements automatically come to mind:

- Change the way a user logs out in order to use the application's close feature
- Provide an ability to browse other users' timelines, as well as to store previously browsed timelines. We will use the SQL container add-on to do this.

From a GUI point-of-view, the screen name field has to be changed to a combo. Values in the combo are previously entered screen names.

- Automatically refresh timelines when displayed, thus push changes to the client, with the help of the ICEPush add-on.

 Two additional third-party components will be needed: a database to be connected to the SQL container and a scheduling framework to manage threads. We will use HSQL DB for the former and Quartz for the latter.

In order to get more information about HSQL DB, visit http://hsqldb.org/ and to know further about Quartz, visit http://www.quartz-scheduler.org/.

Twaattin application

```
package com.packtpub.learnvaadin.twaattin;

import static org.quartz.JobBuilder.newJob;
import static org.quartz.TriggerBuilder.newTrigger;

import java.sql.SQLException;

import org.quartz.JobDetail;
import org.quartz.Scheduler;
import org.quartz.SchedulerException;
import org.quartz.SimpleScheduleBuilder;
import org.quartz.Trigger;
import org.quartz.impl.StdSchedulerFactory;

import com.packtpub.learnvaadin.twaattin.service.TwitterJob;
import com.packtpub.learnvaadin.twaattin.service.TwitterService;
import com.packtpub.learnvaadin.twaattin.ui.LoginWindow;
import com.packtpub.learnvaadin.twaattin.ui.TimelineWindow;
import com.vaadin.Application;
import com.vaadin.Application.UserChangeListener;
import com.vaadin.addon.sqlcontainer.connection.JDBCConnectionPool;
import com.vaadin.addon.sqlcontainer.connection.
SimpleJDBCConnectionPool;

public class TwaattinApp extends Application implements
UserChangeListener {

    private static final long serialVersionUID = 1L;
```

```
private LoginWindow loginWindow;

private TimelineWindow timelineWindow;

private JDBCConnectionPool jdbcPool;

private transient TwitterService twitterService;

@Override
public void init() {
  try {
    jdbcPool = new
      SimpleJDBCConnectionPool("org.hsqldb.jdbc.JDBCDriver",
      "jdbc:hsqldb:file:" + PathUtils.getDbDataPath() +
      "/data", "SA", "");
    loginWindow = new LoginWindow();

    timelineWindow = new TimelineWindow();

    setMainWindow(loginWindow);

    loginWindow.initialize();

    addListener(this);

    addListener(timelineWindow);
  } catch (SQLException e) {
    throw new RuntimeException(e);
  }
}

public void applicationUserChanged(UserChangeEvent event) {
  setMainWindow(timelineWindow);

  removeWindow(loginWindow);

  timelineWindow.showNotification("You're authentified");

  try {
    timelineWindow.initialize();

    Scheduler scheduler =
      StdSchedulerFactory.getDefaultScheduler();

    scheduler.getContext().put("window", timelineWindow);

    JobDetail details =
      newJob(TwitterJob.class).withIdentity("twitter").build();

    SimpleScheduleBuilder ssb =
      SimpleScheduleBuilder.repeatSecondlyForever(30);

    Trigger trigger =
      newTrigger().withSchedule(ssb).startNow().build();

    scheduler.scheduleJob(details, trigger);
```

```
      scheduler.start();
    } catch (SQLException e) {
      throw new RuntimeException(e);
    } catch (SchedulerException e) {
      throw new RuntimeException(e);
    }
  }
  public TwitterService getTwitterService() {
    if (twitterService == null) {
      twitterService = new TwitterService();
    }
    return twitterService;
  }
  public JDBCConnectionPool getJdbcPool() {
    return jdbcPool;
  }
  public void close() {
    try {
      Scheduler scheduler =
        StdSchedulerFactory.getDefaultScheduler();
      scheduler.shutdown();
    } catch (SchedulerException e) {
      e.printStackTrace();
    }
    super.close();
  }
}
```

Updates made to the application class are of two types:

- Creation of the JDBC connection pool for the SQL container and the code that lets the timeline window use it.

- Starting and stopping the scheduler to launch the job that will update the timeline regularly.

   Describing the Quartz code in detail, however, is outside the scope of this book. Just know that the init() method starts the refreshing thread and the close() method stops it.

Timeline window

```
package com.packtpub.learnvaadin.twaattin.ui;

import java.sql.SQLException;
import java.util.ArrayList;
import java.util.Collection;
import java.util.Iterator;

import org.quartz.SchedulerException;
import org.vaadin.artur.icepush.ICEPush;

import twitter4j.ResponseList;
import twitter4j.Status;
import twitter4j.TwitterException;
import twitter4j.User;

import com.packtpub.learnvaadin.twaattin.TwaattinApp;
import com.packtpub.learnvaadin.twaattin.persistence.
NewNameItemHandler;
import com.packtpub.learnvaadin.twaattin.service.TwitterService;
import com.vaadin.Application.UserChangeEvent;
import com.vaadin.Application.UserChangeListener;
import com.vaadin.addon.sqlcontainer.RowId;
import com.vaadin.addon.sqlcontainer.SQLContainer;
import com.vaadin.addon.sqlcontainer.connection.JDBCConnectionPool;
import com.vaadin.addon.sqlcontainer.query.TableQuery;
import com.vaadin.data.Item;
import com.vaadin.data.util.BeanContainer;
import com.vaadin.ui.Button;
import com.vaadin.ui.Button.ClickEvent;
import com.vaadin.ui.ComboBox;
import com.vaadin.ui.Field.ValueChangeEvent;
import com.vaadin.ui.HorizontalLayout;
import com.vaadin.ui.Label;
import com.vaadin.ui.Table;
import com.vaadin.ui.VerticalLayout;
import com.vaadin.ui.Window;
public class TimelineWindow extends Window implements
UserChangeListener {
  private static final long serialVersionUID = 1L;
  private Label userLabel = new Label();
```

```java
private BeanContainer<Long, Status> tweetsContainer = new
  BeanContainer<Long, Status>(Status.class);
private SQLContainer namesContainer;
private ComboBox namesCombo = new ComboBox();
private ICEPush pusher = new ICEPush();
public TimelineWindow() {
  VerticalLayout mainLayout = new VerticalLayout();
  mainLayout.setSpacing(true);
  mainLayout.setMargin(true);
  setContent(mainLayout);
  HorizontalLayout menuBar = new HorizontalLayout();
  menuBar.setSpacing(true);
  addComponent(menuBar);
  menuBar.addComponent(userLabel);
  Button logout = new Button("Logout");
  logout.addListener(ClickEvent.class, this, "logout");
  menuBar.addComponent(logout);
  addComponent(namesCombo);
  namesCombo.setNewItemsAllowed(true);
  namesCombo.setNullSelectionAllowed(false);
  namesCombo.setImmediate(true);
  namesCombo.setItemCaptionPropertyId("SCREEN_NAME");
  namesCombo.addListener(ValueChangeEvent.class, this, "fill");
  tweetsContainer.setBeanIdProperty("id");
  Table table = new Table("", tweetsContainer);
  table.setSizeFull();
  addComponent(table);
  customizeTable(table);
}
public void logout() throws SchedulerException {
  getApplication().close();
}
public void fill() {
  TwitterService twitterService = ((TwaattinApp)
    getApplication()).getTwitterService();
  tweetsContainer.removeAllItems();
  Item item = namesContainer.getItem(namesCombo.getValue());
```

```
    try {
      String screenName = (String)
        item.getItemProperty("SCREEN_NAME").getValue();

      ResponseList<Status> statuses =
        twitterService.getTimeline(screenName);

      Iterator<Status> iterator = statuses.iterator();

      while (iterator.hasNext()) {

        Status status = iterator.next();

        tweetsContainer.addItem(status.getId(), status);
      }
    } catch (TwitterException e) {
      throw new RuntimeException(e);
    }
}
public void applicationUserChanged(UserChangeEvent event) {
User newUser = (User) event.getNewUser();
  String screenName = newUser.getScreenName();
  userLabel.setValue(screenName);
  Collection<RowId> eligibleIds = new ArrayList<RowId>();
  Collection<?> ids = namesContainer.getItemIds();
  for (Object id : ids) {
    Item item = namesContainer.getItem(id);
    Object value = (String)
      item.getItemProperty("SCREEN_NAME").getValue();
    if (screenName.equals(value)) {
      eligibleIds.add((RowId) id);
      break;
    }
  }

  if (!ids.isEmpty()) {
    namesCombo.select(ids.iterator().next());
  }
}
private void customizeTable(Table table) {
  table.addGeneratedColumn("when", new WhenColumnGenerator());
  table.addGeneratedColumn("user", new NameColumnGenerator());
  table.setVisibleColumns(new String[] { "user", "text", "when" });
}
```

```
public void initialize() throws SQLException {
  TwaattinApp TwaattinApp = (TwaattinApp) getApplication();
  JDBCConnectionPool jdbcPool = TwaattinApp.getJdbcPool();
  TableQuery tableQuery = new TableQuery("TWITTER", jdbcPool);
  namesContainer = new SQLContainer(tableQuery);
  namesCombo.setContainerDataSource(namesContainer);
  NewNameItemHandler newItemHandler = new
    NewNameItemHandler(TwaattinApp.getTwitterService(),
    namesContainer);
  namesCombo.setNewItemHandler(newItemHandler);
  addComponent(pusher);
}
public void fillAndPush() {
  fill();
  pusher.push();
}
}
```

Important lines of preceding code are the following:

- Declaration, instantiation, and initialization of the SQL container, the ICEPush widget and the new item handler (see the following section)
- Declaration of a method to be called by the polling job that will get new tweets, fill the table, and push the result to the client
- Automatically select the logged in user in the combo

New item handler

In *Chapter 6*, we have learned about new item handlers. Those are used when new values are entered in an abstract select: it is exactly what we need, so that those values are persisted in the database.

```
package com.packtpub.learnvaadin.twaattin.persistence;

import java.sql.SQLException;

import twitter4j.TwitterException;
import twitter4j.User;

import com.packtpub.learnvaadin.twaattin.service.TwitterService;
import com.vaadin.addon.sqlcontainer.RowId;
import com.vaadin.addon.sqlcontainer.RowItem;
import com.vaadin.addon.sqlcontainer.SQLContainer;
import com.vaadin.ui.AbstractSelect.NewItemHandler;
```

```java
public class NewNameItemHandler implements NewItemHandler {
  private static final long serialVersionUID = 1L;
  private final TwitterService twitterService;
  private final SQLContainer nameContainer;
  public NewNameItemHandler(TwitterService twitterService,
    SQLContainer nameContainer) {
    this.twitterService = twitterService;
    this.nameContainer = nameContainer;
  }
  public void addNewItem(String userName) {
    try {
      User user = twitterService.getUser(userName);
      RowId id = (RowId) nameContainer.addItem();
      RowItem item = (RowItem) nameContainer.getItem(id);
      item.getItemProperty("TWITTER_ID").setValue(user.getId());
      item.getItemProperty("SCREEN_NAME").setValue
        (user.getScreenName());
      nameContainer.commit();
    } catch (TwitterException e) {
      throw new RuntimeException(e);
    } catch (SQLException e) {
      throw new RuntimeException(e);
    }
  }
}
```

Summary

In this chapter, we learned about some advanced features of Vaadin that span a large perimeter. In the first section, we saw the following use-cases and the way Vaadin could meet our needs out-of-the-box:

- Should we need to go deeper in order to access any of the available web contexts (servlet, application and session), we just have to make our application implement HttpServletRequestListener.

- With the help of Vaadin's bookmarking capabilities, we can capture the state of a window, and set it as an URL fragment on the address bar while staying on the same screen. Also, the reverse can be done: taking the fragment and using it to set information on the window, all thanks to the UriFragmentUtility widget.

- Moreover, we learned how legacy applications and/or sites can be integrated with Vaadin application and how more than one Vaadin application can run in the same context, with just a touch of HTML and JavaScript configuration.

- If the default error handler mechanism does not suit us, we know how to override it to do exactly what we want with the `ErrorListener` interface.

- Also, we found out how to stop Vaadin the proper way and eventually redirect the user to an URL outside (to prevent it from starting again) with the `setLogoutURL()` method.

In the second section, we detailed how Vaadin can be enriched with an add-on coming from the Vaadin directory and how we could search the latter.

In particular, other features are brought by third-party add-ons:

- Safely embedding Vaadin applications in third-party sites from another domain. The add-on manages the security, so as to configure domains permitted to access the application.

- Most applications need a data backend and Vaadin ones are not different. The SQL Container add-on is an easily configurable adapter between the GUI and the database.

- Finally, when the application needs to send updates to clients, we can count on the ICEPush add-on that draws on the power of the ICEPush product. It is only a matter of adding the right widget to the window and calling the push method when we need to.

At this point, we understand Vaadin fairly well. Features that are not part of the core framework, such as additional widgets, persistence features, themes and others, should be searched in the directory.

In the next chapter, we will get on the next step to develop top-notch Vaadin applications, creating custom components.

8
Creating Custom Components

Although Vaadin provides many great components out-of-the-box, you may have a need to create a widget of your own. Also, enterprises as well as individual developers are bound to propose some, either free of charge or commercially.

Allowing the creation of custom components is a feature designed into Vaadin itself. In this chapter, we'll have a look at doing it in two different ways:

- The first method to create a custom component in Vaadin is to compose it from other widgets
- The second way is to wrap a GWT widget in a Vaadin envelope

Learning both these techniques will get you a long way toward getting the best out of the framework.

Widget composition

Composing other widgets can either be very simple or be a daunting task depending on the number of widgets involved.

Widget composition is by far the easiest way (compared to wrapping GWT components) to create custom widgets. However, it fits only limited use-cases, for example, when we need to reuse some graphical part of an application, the keyword here being reusable component. Examples of such components include:

- An address component, with address lines, state, zip code, and city.
- A yes/no/cancel options dialog, similar to the ones found in Swing.
- A window template, including a top menu and a left bar.
- A reusable menu among all the windows of an application.

The following screenshot is an example of a reusable dialog box.

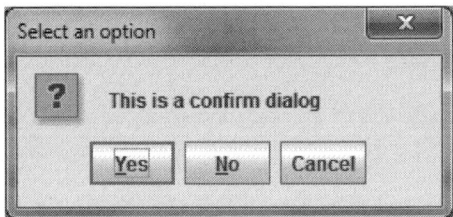

Manual composition

The basis of custom widget composition in Vaadin is the `CustomComponent` class, which is inherited from `AbstractComponentContainer`.

As far as components are considered, custom components are very straightforward since they just inherit from the abstract component container, as seen in *Chapter 4*, along with windows and panels.

The only twist is that the `addComponent()` method doesn't work (it throws an `UnsupportedOperationException`) and it should be replaced with the `setCompositionRoot()` method. Adding components is just a matter of adding them to the parameter of the latter method—the root, which probably is a layout.

Limitation

An important limitation of this approach is that we have to basically create at least two classes: one being the custom component, playing the role of the content, and the other being the topmost widget, the content container. Such containers can be windows, panels, or whatever, so long as we reuse them.

This is it! There's no fancy API: we just add the child widgets to our custom component's root and we are good to go.

As an example, let's create a reusable custom confirm dialog, just like the one seen above. It would look something along these lines:

```
public class CustomDialog extends Window {
  private static final long serialVersionUID = 1L;
  private String clickedValue;
  public CustomDialog() {
    addComponent(new CustomComponentDialogContent());
  }
```

```java
public String getClickedValue() {
  return clickedValue;
}

private class CustomComponentDialogContent extends CustomComponent {
  private static final long serialVersionUID = 1L;

  private Label message = new Label("This is a confirm dialog.");

  private Button yesButton = new Button("Yes");
  private Button cancelButton = new Button("Cancel");
  private Button noButton = new Button("No");

  public CustomComponentDialogContent() {
    VerticalLayout mainLayout = new VerticalLayout();

    mainLayout.setMargin(true);
    mainLayout.setSpacing(true);

    setCompositionRoot(mainLayout);

    HorizontalLayout upperLayout = new HorizontalLayout();

    mainLayout.addComponent(upperLayout);

    upperLayout.addComponent(message);

    HorizontalLayout buttonLayout = new HorizontalLayout();

    mainLayout.addComponent(buttonLayout);

    Button[] buttons = new Button[] { yesButton, noButton,
      cancelButton };

    for (Button button : buttons) {

      buttonLayout.addComponent(button);
      button.addListener(new StoreLabelListener());
    }
  }
}

private class StoreLabelListener implements ClickListener {
  private static final long serialVersionUID = 1L;

  @Override
  public void buttonClick(ClickEvent event) {

    Button button = (Button) event.getSource();

    clickedValue = (String) button.getCaption();

    Window popup = button.getWindow();

    popup.getParent().removeWindow(popup);
  }
}
}
```

As explained before, we have two widget classes: `CustomComponentDialogContent` for the content and `CustomDialog` for the window. The `StoreLabelListener` is just common behavior for all three buttons.

Strategy for custom components

The reason behind using custom components is reuse. As such, a well thought out design is a must have in those cases.

In the preceding code, this is very straightforward: we provided the `getClickedValue()` method to return the button clicked. And yet, we should ask ourselves some questions:

- Is `String` the right return type? Or should we provide an `enum` to carry the return type?
- Neither the text for the buttons nor the message can be customized. For the buttons, it prevents internationalization, but a static message prevents reuse!
- Shouldn't the cancel button be optional?

In practice, reusable component design should be constrained by two major concerns: providing sensible defaults, but enabling parameterization so that the component can really be reused in a variety of contexts (but not too much!).

Apart from that, only experience will tell you how much you should expose in your personal context.

Graphic composition

Previous sections explained about manual coding of custom components to meet our needs.

Nonetheless, the fastest way to create a custom component by assembling widgets is to do it graphically. It's a nice thing then that the Vaadin Eclipse plugin provides a graphical editor, named the Visual Editor (or VE for short).

Visual editor setup

Vaadin's graphical editor is bundled within the plugin. To check that it is installed, go to **Help | Install New Software** and select the Vaadin update site.

The update site URL is `http://vaadin.com/eclipse`. Go back to *Chapter 2* if you need more information.

Vaadin graphical editor is experimental at the time of writing. If anything unexpected happens, fill a bug in Vaadin's Trac at `http://dev.vaadin.com/` because, well... it's expected.

We'll also need XUL Runner from the Mozilla Foundation, in version 1.9+. For Windows users, download it from `SourceForge.net` at `http://sourceforge.net/projects/xulrunnerinstal/` and install it. For Linux users, download it from the Mozilla Foundation at the following URL:

`http://releases.mozilla.org/pub/mozilla.org/xulrunner/releases/`

Troubleshooting

If at any point a dialog appears with the message "Could not start XULRunner (version 1.9 or higher required)", you should install XUL Runner from the Sourceforge link provided and not from the Mozilla Foundation download site.

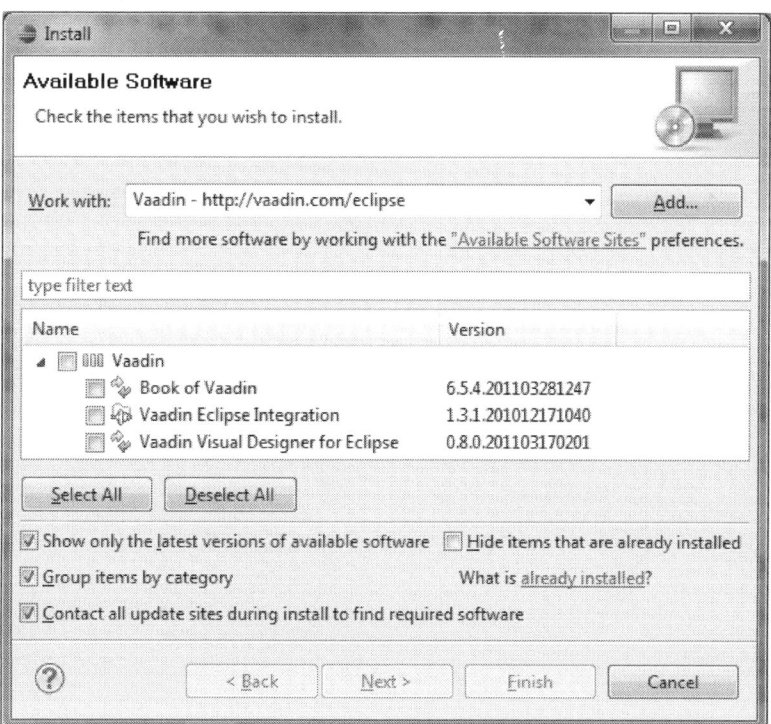

Visual editor use

Once the graphical editor is installed, just go the **File** menu and click on **New**.

Then choose **Vaadin | Vaadin Composite**. It immediately opens the standard Java code viewpoint where there are two tabs underneath, a code one that is shown, and a design one.

Selecting the design tab will display the graphical editor. It is separated into two main parts:

- A canvas with a gridline occupies the main space.
- A vertical bar at the left displays the following three sections:
  - A component palette that shows all available widgets. Remember that in *Chapter 4* we learned that layouts are components too (albeit special ones).
  - The custom widget component hierarchy.
  - The properties of the currently selected widget.

Components from the palette can be dragged-and-dropped either to the canvas or to the component hierarchy.

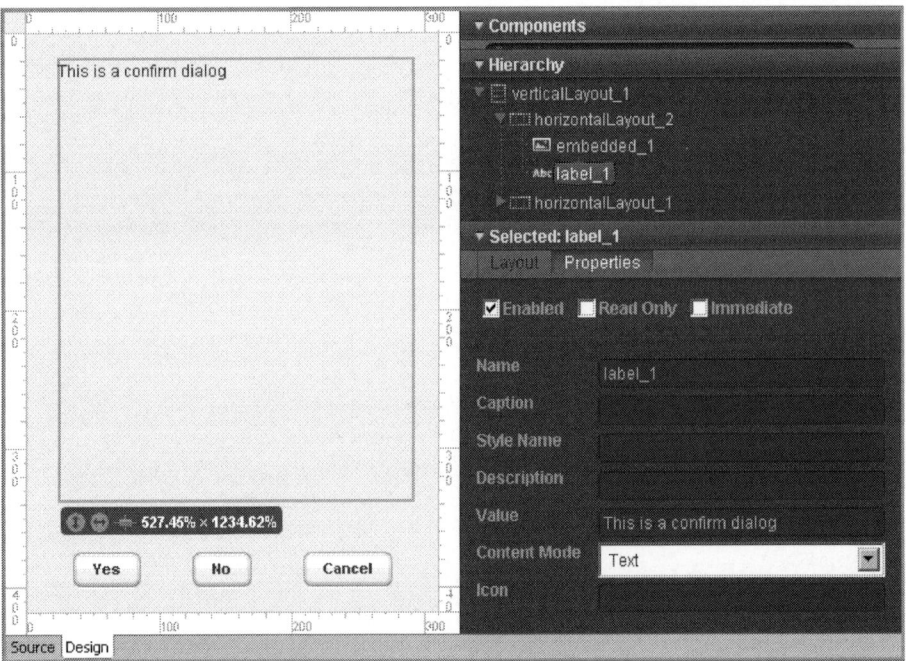

A full guide to the Visual Editor is beyond the scope of this book, but there are nonetheless some guidelines that will save us a considerable amount of time.

Position and size

The first tab for a selected component is the layout one. It represents properties that manage position and size.

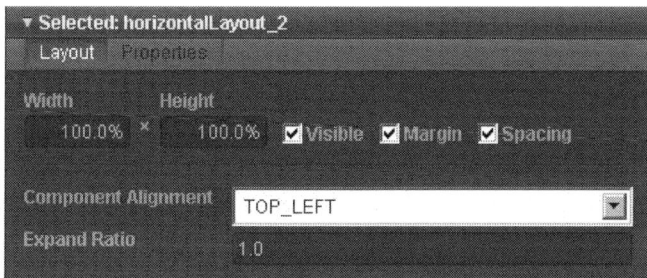

Available properties are:

- Width and height. Those correspond respectively to the `setWidth()` and `setHeight()` methods of the Paintable interface, and accept the same values. In order to use `setXXXUndefined()`, the value to enter is "auto".

- Visible, margin and spacing are standard properties seen in *Chapter 4*. Note that setting the margin independently on the four borders is not possible with the VE.

- Component alignment manages the position of the element in its available space.

- Expand ratio refers to the space provided to the component when space has to be shared.

On the design canvas, we can also see a small rectangle when selecting a component. It's a shortcut to changing size and position.

The second tab displays every property not shown on the first tab.

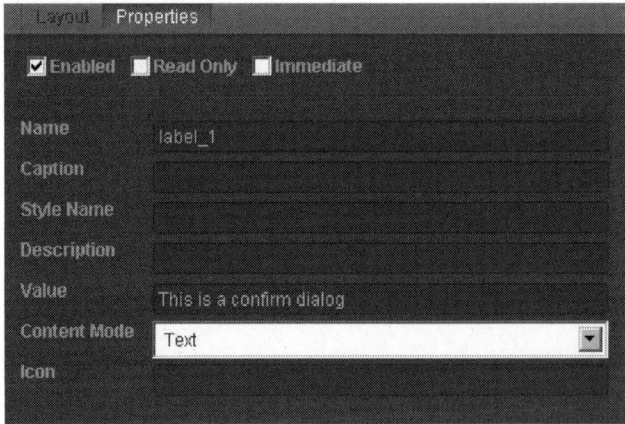

The preceding screenshot presents the available properties for a label.

Limitations

Note that the editor is an important tool for designing Vaadin applications and is deemed as such by Vaadin's team. Therefore, at the time of writing, a new version of the editor called the Visual Designer is being developed and will overcome some of the following limitations.

Restricted compatibility

The most important limitation of the Visual Editor in its current state is its inability to display existing components, whether windows or applications, or any component that was not initially designed with the VE.

Top level element

Moreover, the top level element designed in the VE can only be a layout. By default, it's an `AbsoluteLayout`. If we need to change this, we cannot graphically update the type: we have to go to the code tab and modify the code itself.

This prevents us from creating reusable windows, complete with title. The biggest reusable unit is the window's **content**.

Rigid structure

The generated code is set to some pattern that the editor expects. This has three important consequences:

- Every component is declared as an attribute and assigned an `AutoGenerated` annotation.

- It is instantiated and configured in its own private builder method that is called in the constructor.

- Custom non-generated code, if it exists, has to take place after those calls in the constructor.

Any change to these will likely prevent Vaadin from opening the Visual Editor.

Limited embed capability

The `Embedded` component lets us display a `Resource`, which was seen in *Chapter 4*. However, some resources need a reference to the application instance, which is only set when the parent window is set as the application window.

Thus, legal resources can only be those which do not need a reference to the application: `ExternalResource` (available online from HTTP) and `ThemeResource` (available under a theme). Other types (file system, class and stream resources) won't work.

GWT widget wrapping

The second way to create custom components in Vaadin is to wrap an available GWT widget under a Vaadin layer. This is the way that out-of-the-box Vaadin components are themselves provided.

Before diving into widget wrapping, we have to understand somewhat how Vaadin uses GWT under the cover.

 This book is not about GWT, but since Vaadin uses GWT, we need some basic comprehension about how it works. For more information, see `http://code.google.com/webtoolkit/`.

Vaadin GWT architecture

Vaadin GWT architecture is based on two foundations: the client side and the server side.

 In this section, we'll use the GWT incubator as a source for new and interesting widgets. Nevertheless, it's only an example since we can use every available GWT widget! See `http://code.google.com/p/google-web-toolkit-incubator/`

Client side

On the client side, we have to inherit from the desired widget with a class implementing `com.vaadin.terminal.gwt.client.Paintable`. Be aware that **it's not the same** `Paintable` we've seen in *Chapter 4*, as this one is on the client side!

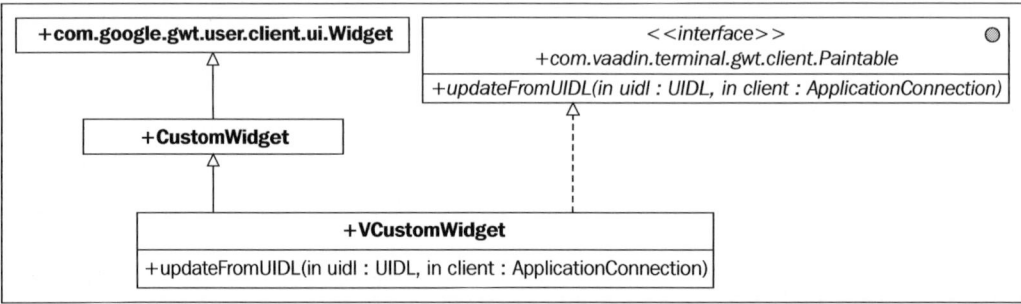

We tackled the UIDL in *Chapter 3*, when talking about Vaadin architecture. As a short reminder, UIDL is the way the user interface is sent to the client by Vaadin.

The `updateFromUIDL()` method from `Paintable` is responsible for reading the UIDL stream sent from the server, and updating the client component accordingly. If that sounds daunting, rejoice since the `ApplicationConnection` parameter does just that with its `updateComponent()` method. It takes three parameters:

- The widget to update, in our context, `this`.
- The UIDL sent, which is the other parameter in the calling method.
- Finally, a `boolean` value that indicates whether to delegate caption, icon, description, and error messages management to the parent component. In most cases, captions and icons are handled by layouts by placing them next to the component.

It also returns `true` if no further action is necessary. This method is tasked with synching the different graphical attributes of the component with the state sent from the server. Such attributes include:

- `disabled`
- `readonly`
- `invisible`
- `style` (for the CSS)

Thus, a typical implementation of the method is the following:

```
public void updateFromUIDL(UIDL uidl,
    ApplicationConnection client) {
  if(client.updateComponent(this, uidl, true)) {
    return;
  }
  // Do more here, if needed
}
```

Some possible additional actions include storing data from parameters, for example:

- The UIDL unique ID in order to send back information to the server, mostly upon user interaction.

- The immediate attribute so that future events are sent immediately.

GWT and compilation

In *Chapter 7*, when using add-ons from the directory, Vaadin always asked us about compiling the widget set. It's exactly the same when creating our own widgets.

Before going further, we have to understand some things about the Google Web Toolkit. Google's approach to web applications is that the development is made in Java then a compiler translates the code into JavaScript and HTML to be executed on the client side by the browser.

In order to create the client-side Vaadin widget, we have to do a little more:

- First things first, we have to create the client-side code, as seen in the previous section. It should be under a `ui.client` sub-package, relative to the `widgetset` file (see the following code).

- Then, we have to create this `widgetset` file. It's an XML file that should have the `gwt.xml` suffix and be present in a package ending with `widgetset`. It should list all widget sets used by the Vaadin code.

  ```
  <?xml version="1.0" encoding="UTF-8"?>
  <!DOCTYPE module PUBLIC "-//Google Inc.//DTD Google Web Toolkit
  1.7.0//EN" "http://google-web-toolkit.googlecode.com/svn/
  tags/1.7.0/distro-source/core/src/gwt-module.dtd">
  ```

```
<module>
  <inherits name="com.vaadin.terminal.gwt.DefaultWidgetSet" />
  <!-- Just an example of a third-party widgetset -->
  <inherits name="com.google.gwt.widgetideas.WidgetIdeas" /></
module>
```

- Finally, the path to this file must be referenced in the web deployment descriptor in an `init` parameter of the Vaadin servlet, just like so:

```
<init-param>
  <param-name>widgetset</param-name>
  <param-value>com.packtpub.vaadin.widgetset.GwtWrapperWidgetset</
param-value>
</init-param>
```

The whole setup should present the following structure:

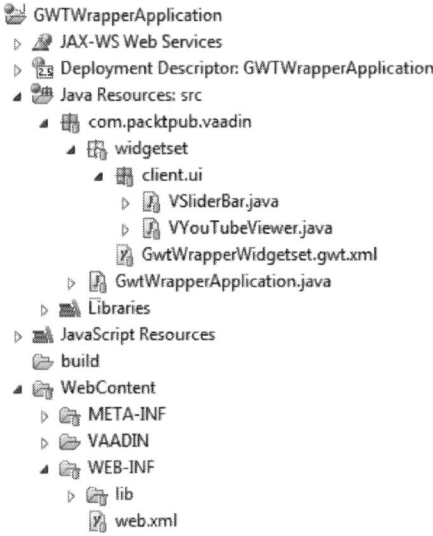

Notice the whole `widgeset` and `client.ui` packages and their hierarchy.

The good news is that the Vaadin Eclipse plugin takes care of the creation of the `gwt.xml` file and its use in the `web.xml`. However, we have to manually include GWT XML modules in it. Moreover, each time Vaadin detects a change that has an effect on the generated JavaScript, it will ask to compile.

Optimizing compilation

The compilation is a very lengthy process, since the compiler creates compatible JavaScript files for every supported browser. In order to speed it, it's advised to only compile for the browser used during development. This is done in the main widget set file, through the `user.agent` property. This is the documentation found in the template file, reproduced here for simplicity's sake:

"Multiple browsers can be specified for GWT as a comma separated list. The supported user agents at the moment of writing were:

```
ie6,ie8,gecko,gecko1_8,safari,opera
```

The value `gecko1_8` is used for Firefox 3 and later and Safari is used for webkit-based browsers including Google Chrome."

A limitation of the client class is that it has to have a zero-argument constructor.

Even if we provide a constructor with arguments along the zero-argument one, Vaadin will use the latter through reflection.

Widget styling

Application and custom widgets style are different: we need some notions about the latter when wrapping GWT widgets since Vaadin doesn't provide a CSS style for them.

The stylesheet can be named however we like, but has to be present in a `public` directory and referenced in the `widgetset gwt.xml` file like so:

```
<stylesheet src="<CSS_NAME>.css" />
```

Troubleshooting

If nothing shows in the browser, first check the DOM with your browser (Google Chrome or Firefox with the Firebug plugin) to see if the widget is here. In most cases, it's the case but it has no CSS attached.

Example

As an example, let's create a simple Vaadin client wrapper around one of the simplest GWT Incubator widgets, the `YouTubeViewer`.

```
public class VYouTubeViewer extends YouTubeViewer implements Paintable
  public VYouTubeViewer() {

    super("5P-29p7-Knc");// The string is just the video's id
  }

  @Override
  public void updateFromUIDL(UIDL uidl, ApplicationConnection client)
  {

    if(client.updateComponent(this, uidl, true)) {
      return;
    }
  }
}
```

Notice there's nothing fancy apart from a no-argument constructor that calls the one-argument super constructor.

> As a convention, it's recommended that custom client-side widget names are prefixed with V (like Vaadin). Not only is it done in the core framework, it also prevents us from confusing the client and server classes as well as using fully-qualified class names to distinguish between them in the same file.

Server side

The server side widget is the object we will manipulate when developing our standard applications.

First, it has to inherit from a Vaadin component: the hardest thing will be to determine which component to inherit from. This choice will be driven by common sense, depending on the client widget's type. As a rule of thumb, most of the time, extend `AbstractComponent`.

Second, it has to be bound to the client side widget: it's done with the `@ClientWidget` annotation on the type, which takes the client class as the value.

In order to create the server side for the YouTube viewer, we just have to write the following lines:

```
@ClientWidget(VYouTubeViewer.class)
public class YouTubeViewer extends AbstractComponent {

  private static final long serialVersionUID = 1L;
}
```

Now, if we use this newly created widget in a window, we have a mighty surprise!

Note that since the GWT widget is just a thin wrapper around a Flash object, it's all right to inherit from `AbstractComponent` as we don't need to draw the widget on the browser, the Flash Player will manage it on its own.

Server client communication

Having a widget on each side is nice, but it feels a little useless. It would be a great asset to pass information from the server to the client.

In the *Client side* section, we learned about `updateFromUIDL()`. Changes sent from the server to the client are found in the `uidl` parameter of this method.

As was seen in *Chapter 3*, UIDL is the serialized form of the user interface (or GUI change fragments).

UIDL characteristics

UIDL is characterized by some properties:

- The paintable identifier (or PID), a unique identifier for each component.
- The tag name, which is also unique but for each **component type** and not per instance. For example, for `Button` objects, it is "button".
- **Attributes**, which are those usually found in JSON (remember UIDL is JSON). There's an attribute for each widget's property. For example, there are `disabled` and `readonly` attributes for fields.
- Finally, there are **variables** that are more like stored values.

Object serialization

Objects are serialized in UIDL format with the help of two methods, `paint()` which writes the start and the end tags, and `paintContent()` which writes the content, as you can guess. Both methods use a `PaintTarget` as a parameter.

 The previous versions of Vaadin used XML serialization. The writing of end tags has endured in newer versions, albeit in JSON, it's a no-brainer.

The latter is an interface, with a single concrete implementation, `JsonPaintTarget` used by Vaadin to serialize widget instances into UIDL format.

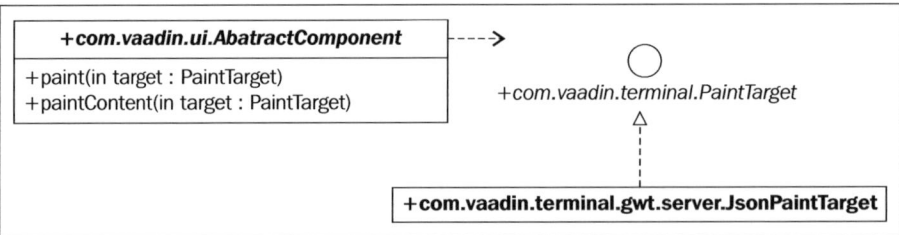

Descending communication

Apart from the preceding methods, paint targets have a bunch of methods of the form `addVariable(VariableOwner owner, String name, <TYPE> value)` where:

- The `owner` parameter is the component itself.

- `name` is the key to store the variable under.

- And `TYPE` can be `boolean`, `int`, `long`, `float`, `double`, `String`, `string arrays` and `com.vaadin.terminal.Paintable`.

These methods are used to pass information from the server component to the client component.

On the client side, it's in the `updateFromUIDL()` that the reading takes place, as the UIDL is the first parameter.

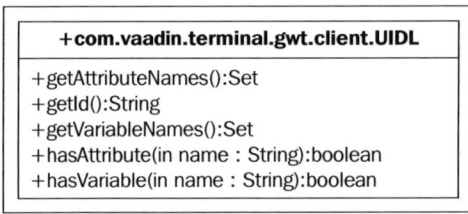

Also, UIDL has methods of the form `get<TYPE>Variable(String name)` where `TYPE` can be the same as in the previous `addVariable()` method. Thus, the server widget can set variables and the client component can read them (without the need for casting).

Do not forget super.paintContent()

Adding variables takes place in the `paintContent()` method. However, each component type has code on its own to manage content serialization. Thus, we have to call `super.paintContent()` or the widget's content will not be sent to the client side and it will be invisible to the user.

YouTube viewer example

Creating a component that can display a single video is nice, but we would like to be able to have a component that can display any video: that's the point of reuse, after all and the current one doesn't fit this need as the video key is initialized in the constructor.

Astute readers may have noticed that the binding between the server and the client components is achieved through an annotation that takes a class: it prevents us from using constructors that have arguments. The only way left is through standard Vaadin server-to-client communication.

Let's update our previous viewer with the way to pass the movie ID from the server to the client. The client component's code now looks like this:

```
public class VYouTubeViewer extends YouTubeViewer implements Paintable
{

  public VYouTubeViewer() {

    super("");
  }

  @Override
  public void updateFromUIDL(UIDL uidl, ApplicationConnection client)
  {

    if(client.updateComponent(this, uidl, true)) {
      return;
    }

    String movieId = uidl.getStringVariable("movie-id");

    setMovieID(movieId);
  }
}
```

Important parts show that no movie ID is initialized at first, but that it's extracted from the UIDL in the update method as a string.

 The `setMovieID()` is part of the YouTubeViewer GWT widget API and plays no part in our understanding of Vaadin

On the server side, the changes are slightly more important:

```
public class YouTubeViewer extends AbstractComponent {

  private static final long serialVersionUID = 1L;

  public String movieId;

  public YouTubeViewer(String movieId) {

    this.movieId = movieId;
  }

  @Override
  public void paintContent(PaintTarget target) throws PaintException {

    target.addVariable(this, "movie-id", movieId);

    super.paintContent(target);
  }

  public void setMovieId(String movieId) {

    this.movieId = movieId;
  }
}
```

Important stuff takes place in the `paintContent()` method: it just adds the movie ID as a string variable. The rest of the changes are just there to pass the movie ID between the setter or the constructor and the paint method.

 The viewer doesn't need any CSS to be displayed, so we can easily forget the theming part.

Client server communication

Server-client communication is not enough: in most cases, we'll want to listen to user events, and now it's the other way around, from client to server.

The sending on the client part is achieved through the `ApplicationConnection` parameter available in the `updateFromUIDL()` method. It has `updateVariable(String paintableId, String variableName, <TYPE> newValue, boolean immediate)` methods. TYPE is the same as those from the previous section variables.

On the server part, the component's method `changeVariables(Object source, Map<String, Object> variables)` is called when the framework is made aware of a change on the client side: immediately if the `immediate` flag is set to `true` or `false` during the next event when not. As for the paint target's `paintComponent()` method, **we have to call the parent method in order for the Vaadin framework to function properly**.

Slider example

The GWT incubator has an appropriate example for client-server communication in the form of the slider widget. Let's create a Vaadin component around it so as to use it in our applications.

Client wrapper

Like for the YouTube viewer previously, the client component inherits from the GWT widget and implements `Paintable`.

```
public class VSliderBar extends SliderBar implements Paintable {

    private ApplicationConnection client;

    private  String uidlId;

    public VSliderBar() {
        super(0, 100);
        setTitle("Percentage");
        setNumLabels(10);
        setNumTicks(20);
        setStepSize(5);
        setCurrentValue(50);

        addChangeListener(new ChangeListener() {

            @Override
            public void onChange(Widget sender) {

                client.updateVariable(uidlId, "value", VSliderBar.this.
                 getCurrentValue(), true);
            }
        });
    }
```

```
@Override
public void updateFromUIDL(UIDL uidl, ApplicationConnection client)
{

  if(client.updateComponent(this, uidl, true)) {

    return;
  }

  this.client = client;

  uidlId = uidl.getId();
}
}
```

Two things are worth noticing:

- The update method stores the `ApplicationConnection` and the UIDL identifier for later use.
- We have to add a change listener using GWT's API which calls the `updateVariable()` with the help of the attributes we stored. This depends on the widget used, so be aware that you'll have to read its documentation (in the case it exists!).

Style

Luckily, there's a supplied CSS for the slidebar at `http://code.google.com/docreader/#p=google-web-toolkit-incubator&s=google-web-toolkit-incubator&t=SliderBar`. We just have to copy its content into a new CSS under the `widgetset/public` folder and reference it in `GwtWrapperWidgetset.gwt.xml`.

Server component

Plenty of options are possible but just displaying the new value as a notification is a good example.

```
@ClientWidget(VSliderBar.class)
public class SliderBar extends Label {

  private static final long serialVersionUID = 1L;

  @Override
  public void changeVariables(Object source, Map<String, Object>
   variables) {

    super.changeVariables(source, variables);

    double value = (Double) variables.get("value");

    getWindow().showNotification("Value changed: " + value);
  }
}
```

This snippet is self-explanatory. Just don't forget to call the method of the parent class to prevent strange behavior!

Componentized Twaattin

The table we used to display our tweets in *Chapter 7* displayed the data, but it was lacking in design.

Moreover, Twitter itself has another way of showing the tweets: looking at the site, we can easily see there's potential for a reusable component in the form of a tweet widget!

Designing the component

On the Twitter site, a tweet looks something like this:

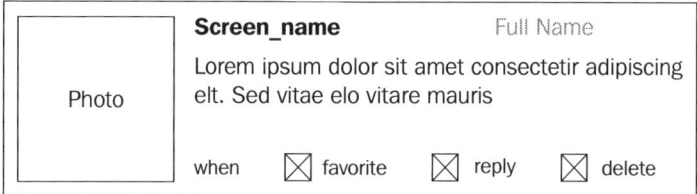

There's not much chance a GWT widget is available. So, we are going to go for the composition approach we learned about in the first section.

Laying out the component would look something like this:

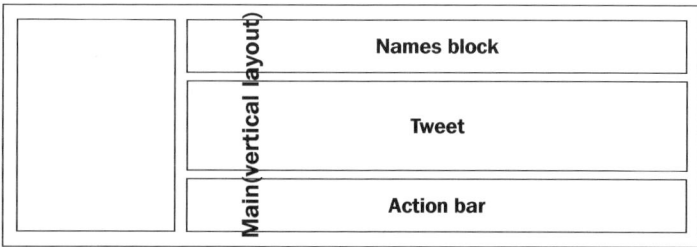

Updating Twaattin's code

The most important Twaattin change is the new component.

Tweet component

In the component, we only use base widgets seen before: layouts, labels, links, and embedded.

```
package com.packtpub.learnvaadin.twaattin.ui;

import java.net.URL;
import java.util.Date;

import com.vaadin.terminal.ExternalResource;
import com.vaadin.ui.CustomComponent;
import com.vaadin.ui.Embedded;
import com.vaadin.ui.HorizontalLayout;
import com.vaadin.ui.Label;
import com.vaadin.ui.Link;
import com.vaadin.ui.VerticalLayout;

@SuppressWarnings("serial")
public class TweetComponent extends CustomComponent {

  public TweetComponent(URL picture, String screenName, String
    fullName, String text, Date when, long tweetId) {

    setStyleName("v-tweet-component");

    HorizontalLayout root = new HorizontalLayout();

    root.setSizeFull();
    root.setSpacing(true);
    root.setMargin(true, false, true, false);

    setCompositionRoot(root);

    Embedded pictureEmbed = new Embedded("", new
      ExternalResource(picture));

    root.addComponent(pictureEmbed);

    VerticalLayout main = new VerticalLayout();

    main.setWidth("100%");

    root.addComponent(main);
    root.setExpandRatio(main, 1);
```

```
    HorizontalLayout namesBlock = new HorizontalLayout();

    namesBlock.setSpacing(true);

    main.addComponent(namesBlock);

    Link screenNameLink = new Link(screenName, new
        ExternalResource("http://twitter.com/#!/" + screenName));

    screenNameLink.setStyleName("v-tweet-screen-name");

    namesBlock.addComponent(screenNameLink);

    Label fullNameLabel = new Label(fullName);

    fullNameLabel.setStyleName("v-tweet-full-name");

    namesBlock.addComponent(fullNameLabel);

    TweetLabel tweet = new TweetLabel(text);

    tweet.setWidth("100%");

    main.addComponent(tweet);

    HorizontalLayout actionsBar = new HorizontalLayout();

    main.addComponent(actionsBar);

    actionsBar.addComponent(new WhenLink(when, screenName, tweetId));
  }
}
```

Apart from the whole layout code, two important things are worthy of notice:

- The first is the component constructor. It has parameters for all data needed for the component creation. We don't provide setters so that this data is used for initialization only, the component is immutable.

>  We could have used the `Status` Twitter4J object directly as a single parameter: it would have rendered the signature more readable at the cost of the component coupling with the Twitter4J API.

- Also, we remembered to use the `setCompositionRoot()` method and not to add components directly to the component but to the root instead.

Of less importance, the `setStyleName()` calls are here so we can customize the design with theming. They should be used in any composite component worth reusing.

Tweet label

The previous component used an unknown class, the TweetLabel. Such a specialized label changes the displayed text so as to display HTML hyperlinks on specific characters or groups thereof: URL of course but also @ and #.

This process is done at instantiation time with the help of three recursive methods, one for each group.

 Note that the next code could be further refined: at present, it will sometimes include the trailing punctuation character in the URL.

```
package com.packtpub.learnvaadin.twaattin.ui;

import com.vaadin.ui.Label;

@SuppressWarnings("serial")
public class TweetLabel extends Label {

  private static final String PROFILE_URL = "http://twitter.com/";

  private static final String SEARCH_URL = "http://twitter.com/#!/
    search?q=";

  public TweetLabel(String text) {

    setContentMode(CONTENT_XML);

    String enrichedText = enrichUrlRecursive(text, 0);

    enrichedText = enrichProfilesRecursive(enrichedText, 0);

    enrichedText = enrichSearchRecursive(enrichedText, 0);

    setValue(enrichedText);

    setStyleName("v-tweet-text");
  }

  private String enrichUrlRecursive(String text, int start) {

    StringBuilder builder = new StringBuilder(text);

    int http = text.indexOf("http", start);

    if (http > -1) {

      int space = text.indexOf(' ', http);

      if (space == -1) {
```

```
        space = text.length();
      }

    String url = text.substring(http, space);

    builder.insert(http, "<a href='" + url + "'>");

    int length = http + 2 * url.length() + 11;

    builder.insert(length, "</a>");

    return enrichUrlRecursive(builder.toString(), length + 4);
  }

  return builder.toString();
}

private String enrichProfilesRecursive(String text, int start) {

  StringBuilder builder = new StringBuilder(text);

  int at = text.indexOf('@', start);

  if (at > -1) {

    int space = text.indexOf(' ', at);
    int colon = text.indexOf(':', at);

    int end = colon == space - 1 ? colon : space;

    if (end == -1) {

      end = text.length();
    }

    String profile = text.substring(at + 1, end);

    String profileUrl = "<a href='" + PROFILE_URL + profile + "'>";

    builder.insert(at + 1, profileUrl);

    int length = end + profileUrl.length();

    builder.insert(length, "</a>");

    return enrichProfilesRecursive(builder.toString(), length + 4);
  }

  return builder.toString();
}

private String enrichSearchRecursive(String text, int start) {

  StringBuilder builder = new StringBuilder(text);
```

```
     int hash = text.indexOf('#', start);

     if (hash > -1) {

       int space = text.indexOf(' ', hash);
       int semicolon = text.indexOf(',', hash);

       int end = semicolon == space - 1 ? semicolon : space;

       if (end == -1) {

         end = text.length();
       }

       String term = text.substring(hash, end).replace("#", "%23");

       String searchUrl = "<a href='" + SEARCH_URL + term + "'>";

       builder.insert(hash, searchUrl);

       int length = hash + searchUrl.length() + term.length() - 2;

       builder.insert(length, "</a>");

       return enrichSearchRecursive(builder.toString(), length + 4);
     }

     return builder.toString();
   }
}
```

When label

Also, the Tweet component uses another custom class, the WhenLink. It's just a
simple port of our previous WhenColumnGenerator (see *Chapter 6* if you forgot
about it) that generates the tweet's creation date and adds a hyperlink to the tweet
on Twitter.

```
package com.packtpub.learnvaadin.twaattin.ui;

import static java.util.Calendar.DAY_OF_MONTH;
import static java.util.Calendar.HOUR_OF_DAY;
import static java.util.Calendar.MINUTE;

import java.text.DateFormat;
import java.text.SimpleDateFormat;
import java.util.Calendar;
import java.util.Date;

import com.vaadin.terminal.ExternalResource;
import com.vaadin.ui.Link;
```

```java
@SuppressWarnings("serial")
public class WhenLink extends Link {
  public WhenLink(Date when, String screenName, long tweetId) {
    Calendar oneDayAgo = Calendar.getInstance();
    oneDayAgo.add(DAY_OF_MONTH, -1);
    Calendar tweetTime = Calendar.getInstance();
    tweetTime.setTime(when);
    String value;
    if (tweetTime.after(oneDayAgo)) {
      value = getText(tweetTime, HOUR_OF_DAY, "hour");
      if (value == null) {
        value = getText(tweetTime, MINUTE, "minute");      }
      if (value == null) {
        value = "right now";
      }
    } else {
      DateFormat format = new SimpleDateFormat("d MMM yy");
      value = format.format(tweetTime.getTime());
    }
    String tweetUrl = "http://twitter.com/" + screenName + "/status/"
      + tweetId;
    setResource(new ExternalResource(tweetUrl));
    setCaption(value);
    setStyleName("v-tweet-date");
  }
  private String getText(Calendar then, int field, String label) {
    Calendar now = Calendar.getInstance();
    int diff = 0;
    while (then.before(now)) {
      now.add(field, -1);
      diff++;
    }
    switch (diff) {
```

```
    case 0:
      return null;

    case 1:
      return diff + " " + label + " ago";

    default:
      return diff + " " + label + "s ago";
    }
  }
}
```

As custom components go, we treat it in the same way: provide all needed data in the constructor and set a style name for possible CSS customization.

Timeline window

The timeline window has to be changed to remove the table and add a panel to stack the tweet components. You can download this code from the Packt site.

In the code itself, changes are few and involve replacing the table with a panel. The most important thing is to use a `Panel` instead of a layout: it has the ability to show a scrollbar to let the user display the entirety of its content.

Final touch

The final touch consists of setting a theme during the application's initialization:

```
setTheme("twaattin");
```

Also, we have to create a `styles.css` file under the `WebContent/VAADIN/themes/twaattin` folder. This CSS inherits from the reindeer theme and is used in order for Twaattin to look like the Twitter application.

This file is printed below for reference:

```css
@import "../reindeer/styles.css";

.v-link-v-tweet-screen-name {

  font-weight: bold;
  font-size: 11pt;
}

.v-link-v-tweet-screen-name a:link span,
.v-link-v-tweet-screen-name a:visited span {

  color: #333333;
  text-decoration: none;
}

.v-tweet-text a:link,
.v-tweet-text a:visited {

  color: #2970a6;
  text-decoration: none;
}

.v-link-v-tweet-screen-name a:hover span,
.v-tweet-text a:hover {

  color: #2970a6;
  text-decoration: underline;
}

.v-tweet-component {

  border-bottom: 1px solid #ebebeb;
}

.v-tweet-component:hover {

  background-color: #e9f0f6;
}
```

```css
.v-tweet-full-name {

  color: #999999;
}

.v-tweet-date a:link span,
.v-tweet-date a:visited span {

  font-size: 8pt;
  color: #999999;
  text-decoration: none;
}

.v-tweet-date a:hover span {

  color: #2970a6;
  text-decoration: underline;
}
```

Summary

In this chapter, we learned the two ways to create custom components to extend our palette of existing widgets.

The first section told us about component composition. Composition is all about inheriting from `CustomComponent`. This can be done manually or graphically through the Visual Editor available in the Eclipse Vaadin plugin.

In the second section, we saw that the way Vaadin wraps GWT widgets is also available to us as developers. We just have to provide:

- A client class that inherits from the GWT widget and has to implement `Paintable`. It will be compiled into JavaScript and managed by GWT.
- A server class that binds the client class through an annotation. It will be this one we will use in our code.

Communication between the two components is possible, in a bidirectional route. From the server to the client, changes are sent through the standard UIDL serialization process. For the other way, they are managed by GWT event handlers. In both cases, they are stored in the variables attached to each widget.

9
Integration with Third-party Products

At this point, we are fairly proficient with the Vaadin framework as all its concepts have been seen in the previous chapter. However, just the presentation layer is not enough in most applications.

In those cases, we will need to go beyond even advanced notions and integrate Vaadin with other third-party APIs and products, which have other responsibilities. In this chapter, we will look at some widespread or rising products which we will have to integrate with at one point or another. These are as follows:

- Spring, on the service layer. Spring is a great and widely used framework that allows us to decouple classes in applications. Using Spring in Vaadin will produce components that can be assembled through configuration.

- Java EE 6, and more precisely Context and Dependency Injection, as well as Servlet 3.0. The former is highly similar to Spring, and the latter will let us create a Java EE 6-compatible servlet.

- Hibernate, on the data access layer. Hibernate was the bootstrap for persistence layer standards such as JPA and is still widely used. We will use it to connect tables to databases.

However, note that beyond a general presentation, the goal of this chapter is not to explain those different products in detail (which is well beyond the scope of a single book anyway). You are welcome to browse through Packt available books for detailed books on the subject at hand at `http://www.packtpub.com/`

Spring

Spring is a proprietary framework made available by SpringSource (http://www.springsource.org/about) that provides Inversion of Control through Dependency Injection.

Inversion of Control and Dependency Injection

Inversion of Control and Dependency Injection are notions that are often used interchangeably, but there is a slight difference between them.

Inversion of Control

Inversion of Control, or IoC, is the principle by which a component can get a reference on another component without first instantiating it so there is low coupling between the two.

In Java and Java EE, there are several ways to achieve IoC:

- The first way is through the **Abstract Factory** *[GOF:87]* pattern which is possible in pure Java.

- Another implementation in Java EE only, is through the **Service Locator** pattern. In this pattern, the application server instantiates services and make them available, whereas applications look up for them in order to use them.

- The final possibility is Dependency Injection.

 For more information on Service Locator, visit the following URL:
http://java.sun.com/blueprints/corej2eepatterns/Patterns/ServiceLocator.html

Dependency Injection

Dependency Injection, or DI, is a specific form of IoC. In DI, both object creation and injection of its dependencies are delegated to a specific part of the system.

IoC comes in different flavors:

- **Interface injection** is the most intrusive. In this case, we have to implement an interface to benefit from injection.

- **Constructor injection** needs constructors where all needed dependencies are passed as parameters. This is a one-time initialization.

- Finally, in **setter injection**, the class has to provide a setter for each dependency. The injector then has to call the setter associated with each configured dependency.

Spring use-cases

Spring is used to decouple the building blocks of our application from one another, be they classes, packages, or JARs. Spring lets us abstract our dependencies, so we can inject a class in an environment such as an integration test, and another class in the standard running environment.

This also allows us to stub our dependencies with mock objects to test our class in isolation, for unit testing.

As an example, the Twitter service used in Twaattin is a good use case of using Spring. The current code has flaws: the application is tightly coupled to the service, thus preventing unit testing: it is not possible to test the UI without using Twitter, which makes testing difficult.

Prerequisites

Once the Vaadin project is developed in our favorite IDE, we need to do a few things first.

Downloading Spring

Our first action is to download Spring itself. It is available on the SpringSource website, at `http://www.springsource.com/download/community`. Just grab the latest distribution, which is 3.0.6 at the time of writing.

Open the archive and copy from the `dist` folder to the `WebContent/WEB-INF/lib` directory the following modules: asm, beans, context, core, expressions, and web.

Also, note that Spring has dependencies on some third-party frameworks. For non-Maven users, we will need to download them manually:

JAR	Download URL	Description
Commons Logging 1.1.1	`http://commons.apache.org/ logging/download_logging.cgi`	Facade over other logging tools such as Log4j or JDK 1.4 log
CGLIB 2.2	`http://sourceforge.net/ projects/cglib/files/`	Bytecode manipulation

JAR	Download URL	Description
AOP Alliance 1.0	`http://sourceforge.net/ projects/aopalliance/files/ aopalliance/`	Cross-cutting concerns management through an abstraction over raw bytecode manipulation

 Maven is an open source build tool brought by the Apache Foundation. If you don't already use Maven, then you are welcome to browse through `http://maven.apache.org/`

IDE enhancements

In order to ease Spring application development, there are a few options:

- The easiest way is to use the **Spring Tools Suite (STS)**, which was discussed in *Chapter 2. Environment Setup*. STS is the IDE to use when heavily developing with the Spring framework.

- Alternatively, we could also use the Spring IDE Eclipse plugin. It is available as an update site at `http://springide.org/updatesite`. See *Chapter 2* for reminders on how to configure an update site in Eclipse.

- Finally, there is partial Spring support in NetBeans. Detailed feature matrix is available at `http://wiki.netbeans.org/SpringSupport`.

Whatever the choice you make, be sure that you are comfortable with it.

Design

Before developing the integration glue between Vaadin and Spring, we have to understand how both work in more detail.

Bean factory and application context

In Spring, every object is a bean and the bean factory's responsibility is to instantiate them. Moreover, the latter also configures the beans and wires them together to fill the dependencies when needed. This wiring can either be done explicitly or detected automatically.

Spring applications use a refined bean factory, the application context, that provides additional features such as internationalization (i18n), event handling and lifecycle management, such as stopping the context.

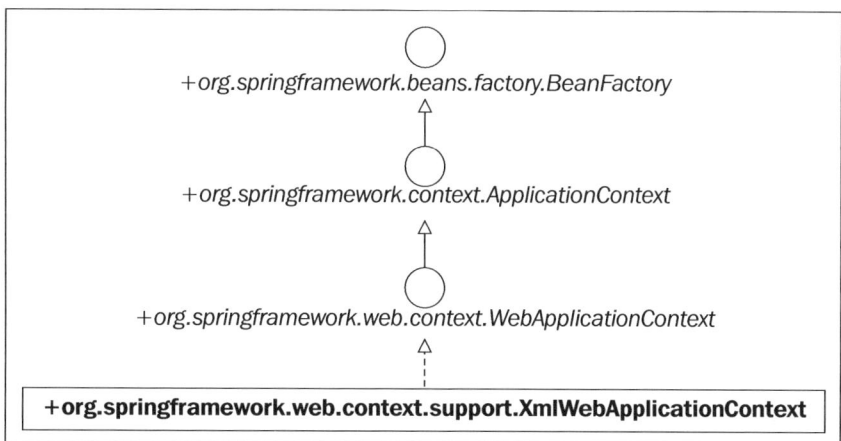

Finally, Spring web applications use a special application context that the framework binds to the servlet context of the web application.

Vaadin application and servlet

In Chapter 3, *Hello Vaadin*, we learned that one of the servlet's responsibilities is to create (and subsequently locate) the application instance relative to the user's session.

Integrating Spring would change this default behavior in order to configure the application instance in the Spring's application context and connect to the latter to retrieve it. That is what we are going to do.

Requirements and specifications

In order to be the most generic and be used in as many applications as possible, it is best to have some requirements and specifications:

- Code should not have additional dependencies but Vaadin, Spring, and Spring's own transitive dependencies.

- Configuration should not need custom files. It should only be done in the web deployment descriptor, or in Spring bean definition files.

- The code should fit seamlessly into the existing Vaadin framework.

- Finally, the code should not impose limitations or inheritance requirements, so that legacy applications could be migrated without changes.

Code

The code is very straightforward and takes a single servlet to implement:

Servlet code

The following is the servlet code:

```java
package com.packtpub.vaadin;

import javax.servlet.ServletConfig;
import javax.servlet.ServletContext;
import javax.servlet.ServletException;
import javax.servlet.http.HttpServletRequest;

import org.springframework.web.context.WebApplicationContext;
import org.springframework.web.context.support.
WebApplicationContextUtils;

import com.vaadin.Application;
import com.vaadin.terminal.gwt.server.AbstractApplicationServlet;

@SuppressWarnings("serial")
public class SpringApplicationServlet extends
  AbstractApplicationServlet {

  private static final String DEFAULT_APP_BEAN_NAME = "application";

  private String name;

  private WebApplicationContext wac;

  @Override
  public void init(ServletConfig config) throws ServletException {

    super.init(config);

    String name = config.getInitParameter("applicationBeanName");

    this.name = name == null ? DEFAULT_APP_BEAN_NAME : name;

    ServletContext servletContext = config.getServletContext();

    wac = WebApplicationContextUtils.getWebApplicationContext
      (servletContext);

    if (wac == null) {

      throw new ServletException("Cannot
        initializeWebApplicationContext");
    }
  }
```

```
    @Override
    protected Application getNewApplication
      (HttpServletRequest request) throws ServletException {

      Object bean = wac.getBean(name);

      if (!(bean instanceof Application)) {

        throw new ServletException("Bean " + name + " is not of
          expected class Application");
      }

      return (Application) bean;
    }

    @SuppressWarnings({ "unchecked", "rawtypes" })
    @Override
    protected Class<? extends Application> getApplicationClass() throws
      ClassNotFoundException {

      Object bean = wac.getBean(name);

      if (bean == null) {

        throw new ClassNotFoundException("No application bean found
          under name " + name);
      }

      return (Class) bean.getClass();
    }
  }
```

The Spring integration servlet is just a simple servlet that inherits from
AbstractApplicationServlet. Thus, we have to implement two methods,
respectively getApplicationClass () and getNewApplication().

- The first one is also the first one called. It is mainly used to get the CSS class
  name of the application, as well as get internationalized messages templates.
  In our case, we just read the bean from the context and get its class.

- The second method is used to get the application instance itself. As
  previously, we get it from the Spring context.

The servlet itself is pretty straightforward and not cause for many questions. The
only thing to take care of is error management (if the bean is not present in the
context or not of the right class).

Additionally, we supply a way to configure the expected bean name in the Spring context. By default, it is "application" but it can also be parameterized in the `web.xml`:

```
<servlet>
  <servlet-name>Spring Integration</servlet-name>
  <servlet-class>
    com.packtpub.vaadin.SpringApplicationServlet
  </servlet-class>
  <init-param>
    <param-name>applicationBeanName</param-name>
    <param-value>app</param-value>
  </init-param>
</servlet>
```

This way, we can work with more than one Vaadin servlet, each having its own bean.

Spring configuration

The Spring configuration however, is a little bit more complex.

Scope

Application instances are stored in the session scope. Spring "standard" scopes are singleton, meaning there is only a single instance for the entire application, and prototype, which means a new instance is returned for each get.

Spring, and more particularly the web module, provides more scope than these two. In particular, there is a session scope. However, its use requires some explanations.

When working with session-scoped dependencies, Spring fills them with proxies. It is only when there is enough information that those proxies are replaced with the real dependency. This has some important consequences:

- First, we need to use Aspect-Oriented Programming in order to change the bytecode. Don't worry, Spring will take care of most tasks.
    - We have to add the namespace "`http://www.springframework.org/schema/aop`" to our Spring bean configuration file under the `aop` prefix.
    - In order for the dependency to be temporarily replaced by a proxy, the bean should use a subtag `<aop:scoped-proxy />`.

The following is an example of such a configuration file:

```xml
<?xml version="1.0" encoding="UTF-8"?>
<beans xmlns="http://www.springframework.org/schema/beans"
  xmlns:xsi="http://www.w3.org/2001/XMLSchema-instance"
  xmlns:aop="http://www.springframework.org/schema/aop"
  xsi:schemaLocation="http://www.springframework.org/schema/beans
    http://www.springframework.org/schema/beans/spring-beans-
      3.0.xsd
    http://www.springframework.org/schema/aop
    http://www.springframework.org/schema/aop/spring-aop-3.0.xsd">
  <bean name="application" scope="session"
    class="com.packtpub.vaadin.SpringVaadinApplication">
    <aop:scoped-proxy />
    <property name="message" value="Hello World!" />
  </bean>
</beans>
```

- Second, we need the proxied application to be replaced with the real session-scoped application when the request is received (and thus, when the session becomes available). This is done in the web deployment descriptor through Spring's `RequestContextListener`.

An example of such web.xml would look like so:

```xml
<?xml version="1.0" encoding="UTF-8"?>
<web-app xmlns:xsi="http://www.w3.org/2001/XMLSchema-instance"
  xmlns="http://java.sun.com/xml/ns/javaee" xmlns:web="http://
java.sun.com/xml/ns/javaee/web-app_2_5.xsd"
  xsi:schemaLocation="http://java.sun.com/xml/ns/javaee
    http://java.sun.com/xml/ns/javaee/web-app_2_5.xsd"
  id="WebApp_ID" version="2.5">
  <display-name>SpringVaadinApplication</display-name>
  <context-param>
    <param-name>productionMode</param-name>
    <param-value>false</param-value>
  </context-param>
  <servlet>
    <servlet-name>Spring Integration</servlet-name>
    <servlet-class>
      com.packtpub.vaadin.SpringApplicationServlet
    </servlet-class>
  </servlet>
  <servlet-mapping>
    <servlet-name>Spring Integration</servlet-name>
    <url-pattern>/*</url-pattern>
```

```
    </servlet-mapping>
    <listener>
      <listener-class>
    org.springframework.web.context.ContextLoaderListener
      </listener-class>
    </listener>
    <listener>
      <listener-class>
  org.springframework.web.context.request.RequestContextListener
      </listener-class>
    </listener>
  </web-app>
```

In addition, notice the Spring framework bootstrapping listener is configured to start Spring automatically.

Additional thoughts

This very simple servlet lets us use Spring transparently in our applications. We can create injected Spring—managed instances fairly simply.

Moreover, this lets us use more than one Vaadin application in our application: each is configured as a Vaadin servlet and can be configured its own application bean in the Spring context. For more details on how to configure more than one application on the same page client side, see the section named *Nominal embedding* of *Chapter 7, Advanced Features*.

Finally, there is one drawback to this approach: the serialized application has to reattach itself to the Spring context when being deserialized. This behavior is left as an exercise to the reader.

Java EE 6

Java EE 6 is the latest version in the line of available standard platforms for Java Enterprise applications. In our case, two stacks are of particular interest to us: Java Servlet 3.0 (also known as JSR 315) and Context and Dependency Injection (also known as JSR 299).

Introduction

Before going further, we will need to quickly browse through Java EE 6 101.

Profiles

Java EE 6 comes with the concept of profiles. A profile is a combination of different stacks, oriented toward specific use-cases. This strategy let suppliers provide less than the full stacks implemented, yet fulfill customer needs and be recognized as Java EE 6-compliant.

The smallest support that encompasses both Servlet 3 and CDI is called the **Web Profile**, which is intended for applications not needing the whole package of enterprise-grade features.

 For a complete description of all stacks included in the Web Profile, refer to the following URL:

```
http://java.sun.com/developer/technicalArticles/
JavaEE/JavaEE6Overview_Part3.html#webprof
```

Tomcat and the web profile

Unfortunately, even the latest version of Tomcat does not implement the Web Profile. It only provides JSP 2.2, EL 2.2, and Servlet 3.0. As such, Tomcat is not suitable for illustrating our Vaadin Java EE 6 integration.

Prerequisites

As Tomcat does not meet our needs, we need to use a compliant application server.

Glassfish 3.1

Glassfish is a fully compliant Java EE 6 open source application server supplied by Oracle and completely free. As it fits all our requirements, let's see how we can use it.

Glassfish download

Glassfish can be downloaded on java.net at `http://glassfish.java.net/downloads/3.1-final.html`. Choose the full platform or the web profile distribution: the latter is enough for our usage.

Glassfish installation

Once downloaded, launch the executable. As the Glassfish installation is beyond the scope of this book and there is a fairly complete guide, refer to it at `http://glassfish.java.net/docs/3.1/installation-guide.pdf`.

Eclipse integration

Prior to creating the managed server under Eclipse, we have to install the Glassfish plugin available at `http://dlc.sun.com.edgesuite.net/glassfish/eclipse/helios/`. Please refer to *Adding WTP to Eclipse* in *Chapter 2* for instructions in how to use or install a plugin. You will have to restart Eclipse at the end of the installation.

In the Server view (where we already created the Tomcat server), right click: **New | Server**. It will open a dialog window, as shown in the following screenshot: select Glassfish 3.1 and click on **Next**:

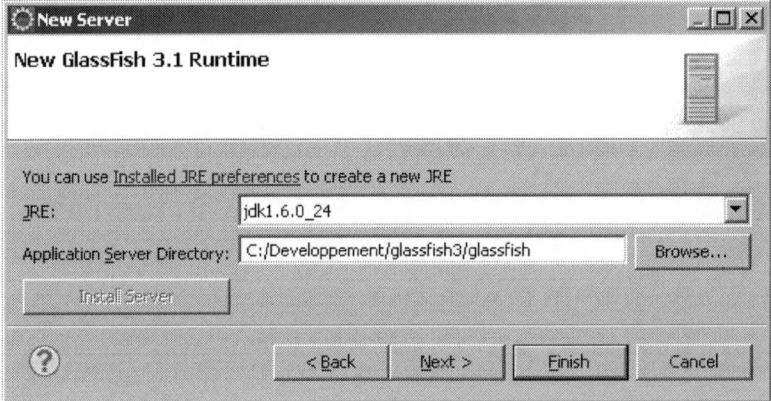

Fill in the chosen JDK (must be at least Java 6) and the path to the folder you installed Glassfish in and click on **Next**.

> If Eclipse complains that "The specified directory is not a valid GlassFish installation, but contains a glassfish subdirectory which might be valid", be sure to choose the `glassfish` subdirectory.

Fill the values according to the values entered during the Glassfish installation.

Click on **Finish** and we are ready to go!

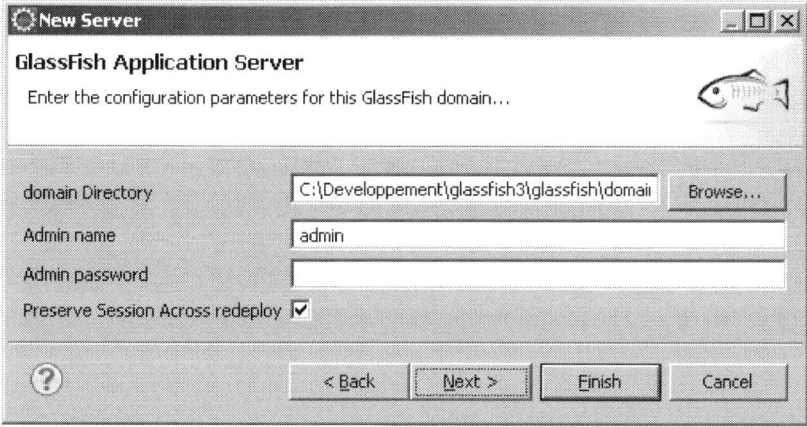

From this point on, we just have to deploy Java EE applications to Glassfish just as we did for Tomcat under Eclipse.

Code

Like in Spring, the main focus of Java EE 6 integration lies in the dependency injection through CDI. Like in Spring, this is done in the servlet; unlike in Spring, it is a no-brainer.

Servlet

The CDI-Vaadin integration servlet looks like this:

```
package com.packtpub.vaadin;

import javax.enterprise.context.SessionScoped;
import javax.inject.Inject;
import javax.servlet.ServletException;
import javax.servlet.annotation.WebServlet;
import javax.servlet.http.HttpServletRequest;

import com.vaadin.Application;
import com.vaadin.terminal.gwt.server.AbstractApplicationServlet;

@SuppressWarnings("serial")
```

```
@WebServlet(urlPatterns = "/*")
public class CdiIntegrationServlet extends AbstractApplicationServlet
{

    @Inject
    private CdiIntegrationApplication application;

    @Override
    protected Application getNewApplication(HttpServletRequest
      request) throws ServletException {

  return application;
    }

    @Override
    protected Class<? extends Application> getApplicationClass()
      throws ClassNotFoundException {

  return application.getClass();
    }
}
```

For dependency injection, we just use the `@Inject` annotation. As the application instance is stored in the session, don't forget to annotate it with `@SessionScoped` (see below). That is all!

Additionally, we can map the servlet to an URL pattern in the code itself.

 In this case, note that this decreases the portability of your code in third-party applications as annotations belong to the code. Alternatively, we could let end-developers map the servlet in their webapps own deployment descriptor.

Application

The following is the Vaadin application's code:

```
package com.packtpub.vaadin;

import javax.enterprise.context.SessionScoped;
import javax.inject.Inject;
import javax.servlet.http.HttpServletRequest;
import javax.servlet.http.HttpServletResponse;

import com.vaadin.Application;
import com.vaadin.terminal.gwt.server.HttpServletRequestListener;
```

```
@SuppressWarnings("serial")
@SessionScoped
public class CdiIntegrationApplication extends Application implements
HttpServletRequestListener {

    @Inject
    private CdiWindow window;

    @Override
    public void init() {

    setMainWindow(window);
    }

    public void onRequestStart(HttpServletRequest request,
      HttpServletResponse response) {

    window.setSessionId(request.getSession().getId());
    }

    public void onRequestEnd(HttpServletRequest request,
      HttpServletResponse response) {}
}
```

The application has a single requirement: it has to be annotated with @SessionScoped in order for the CDI component to store it in the session, just like in the standard behavior.

From there, we can configure attributes to be injected in application instances.

This particular application implementation reads jessionid, so that we can test two different instances to really be in two separate sessions.

Window

A window example looks like the following:

```
package com.packtpub.vaadin;

import javax.annotation.PostConstruct;

import com.vaadin.ui.Button.ClickEvent;
import com.vaadin.ui.Button.ClickListener;
import com.vaadin.ui.CheckBox;
import com.vaadin.ui.Label;
import com.vaadin.ui.Window;
```

```
@SuppressWarnings("serial")
public class CdiWindow extends Window {

    private Label label;

    public CdiWindow() {

    super("CDI Integration");
    }
    @PostConstruct
    protected void initialize() {

    label = new Label("Hello");

    addComponent(label);

    CheckBox check = new CheckBox();

    check.setImmediate(true);

        check.addListener(new ClickListener() {

      public void buttonClick(ClickEvent event) {

        CdiWindow.this.showNotification(event.getSource().toString());
        }
    });

    addComponent(check);
    }

    public void setSessionId(String id) {

    label.setValue("Hello " + id);
    }
}
```

Finally, windows are nothing special. However, in our code, we used the `@PostConstruct` annotation to nicely decouple the constructor code and initialization code.

Our specific implementation displays both the session identifier and a message stating whether the checkbox is checked or not. These let us make sure that the application and its associated window is bound to the session.

Hibernate

Hibernate, along with EclipseLink (formerly TopLink), is one of the most used Object Relational Mapping in the Java world. Chances are you are already using it and in this case, you will probably want to keep it, this time in conjunction with Vaadin.

Hibernate mappings

Hibernate being an ORM tool, basically maps between a Java class and a table, and their respective attributes and columns.

Seeing is believing

Throughout this section, we will take a simple example. In order to simplify things, we will use the Person/Job example already used in *Chapter 7* and update it to use Hibernate.

Job

The following is the source of the Job entity:

```
package com.packtpub.learnvaadin;

import javax.persistence.Entity;
import javax.persistence.Id;

@Entity
public class Job {

  @Id
  private Long id;
  private String label;

  ... // Trivial getters and setters
```

The Job class is as straightforward as can be. In order for the class to become an entity, we use JPA annotations: specifically @Entity and @Id from the javax.persistence package.

Person

The following is the source of the Person entity, which has an association to a single Job:

```
package com.packtpub.learnvaadin;

import java.util.Date;

import javax.persistence.Entity;
import javax.persistence.Id;
import javax.persistence.ManyToOne;
```

```
@Entity
public class Person {

    @Id
    private Long id;
    private String firstName;
    private String lastName;
    private Date birthdate;
    @ManyToOne
    private Job job;

    ... // Trivial getters and setters
```

A person can have a job, which can be the same for two or more persons. As such, we introduce the @ManyToOne annotation to qualify such an association.

 Both sources use simple JPA annotations. For the complete reference documentation on the JSR, visit the following URL:

```
https://cds.sun.com/is-bin/INTERSHOP.
enfinity/WFS/CDS-CDS_JCP-Site/en_US/-/USD/
ViewProductDetail-Start?ProductRef=ejb-3_0-fr-
eval-oth-JSpec@CDS-CDS_JCP
```

Hibernate container

We learned in *Chapter 7* about the SQL Container add-on. There is also a Hibernate add-on available, which suits our needs just fine.

Container architecture

The container's architecture is very simple. It is a single class, the container itself, with an associated session manager that handles Hibernate sessions.

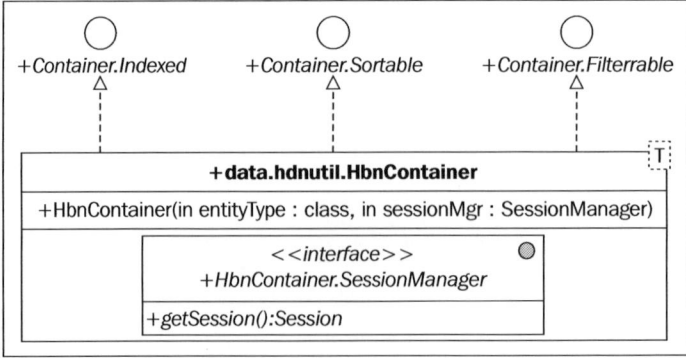

The Hibernate container has all the properties from a container used for tables.

HbnContainer maturity

The Hibernate container add-on was developed from a proof-of-concept. As such, and although it is fully functional, it also has some flaws. First, it packages examples in the production JAR. Second, the update method uses `save()` instead of `update()` or `merge()`: you should not use it but rely on `Session` methods directly.

The container needs a session manager. The latter is an interface whose sole responsibility is to supply Hibernate sessions.

In web applications, this is done with the `getCurrentSession()` method of the `SessionFactory` instance. This method either opens a connection to the database and stores it in a specific context or it retrieves it from the same context. This context can be configured when creating the session factory. In prototyping use-cases, it is the thread with the help of the `ThreadLocal` class.

More information on contextual sessions is available at the following URL:

`http://docs.jboss.org/hibernate/core/3.6/reference/`
`en-US/html_single/#architecture-current-session`

Managing transactions

The real challenge in using Hibernate in a Vaadin context lies in the transaction manager. For example, Hibernate will vehemently complain if it does not find an active transaction before creating a criterion. This is exactly what the Hibernate container does.

org.hibernate.HibernateException: createCriteria is not valid without active transaction

Thus, a transaction is necessary, meaning we have to demarcate the transaction that is both a start point and a commit/rollback to end it.

Starting transaction

Starting the transaction is very straightforward: basically, it can be done when asking the session manager for a session.

In this case, do not forget to check to see whether there is a transaction already started (a possible occurrence) on the session:

```
public Session getSession() {

  Session session = factory.getCurrentSession();

  if (!session.getTransaction().isActive()) {

    session.beginTransaction();
  }

  return session;
}
```

Committing/rollbacking

Rollbacking is never a problem: when there is an exception, check if there is an active transaction and then rollback changes.

On the contrary, committing should only be called if everything ran fine and should be executed at the very end. The question is how can we find this "very end" spot?

This is a complex question with multiple answers.

Committing filter

The first solution is to use a standard Java EE filter. Filters are the solution when one wants to change either or both the request and/or the response.

In this case, the filter is used to "clean" our transaction. Although not really among standard filters' use-cases, it works.

```
package com.packtpub.learnvaadin;

import java.io.IOException;
import java.util.Iterator;

import javax.servlet.Filter;
import javax.servlet.FilterChain;
import javax.servlet.FilterConfig;
import javax.servlet.ServletException;
import javax.servlet.ServletRequest;
import javax.servlet.ServletResponse;
```

```
import javax.servlet.http.HttpServletRequest;
import javax.servlet.http.HttpSession;

import org.hibernate.Session;

import com.vaadin.Application;
import com.vaadin.terminal.gwt.server.WebApplicationContext;

public class CommitFilter implements Filter {

  @Override
  public void destroy() {}

  @Override
  public void doFilter(ServletRequest req, ServletResponse res,
    FilterChain chain) throws IOException, ServletException {

    chain.doFilter(req, res);

    HttpServletRequest request = (HttpServletRequest) req;

    HttpSession httpSession = request.getSession();

    WebApplicationContext context =
      WebApplicationContext.getApplicationContext(httpSession);

    Iterator<Application> apps =
      context.getApplications().iterator();

    if (apps.hasNext()) {

      SqlContainerApplication app = (SqlContainerApplication)
        apps.next();

      Session session = app.getSessionManager().getSession();

      Transaction transaction = session.getTransaction();

      if (transaction.isActive()) {

        transaction.commit();

      }
    }
  }

  @Override
  public void init(FilterConfig config) throws ServletException {}
}
```

Application contexts were seen in *Chapter 7*. If you need a quick reminder, please refer to the section *Accessing with the request-response model* in *Chapter 7*.

In essence, the filter passes the request to the servlet and then:

- Gets the application from the session
- Gets the session from the application; we assume it is one of its responsibilities: it's valid for the rest of this section
- Gets the transaction from the session and commits it **if it is active**

Note that the filter is applied for every request, even if there are no changes to commit. As such, it is not very efficient.

Committing aspect

Committing here has to be executed just before sending the response; it is a potential subject of an **Aspect Oriented Programming (AOP)**. In this regard, an aspect that runs just after the `service()` method of the Vaadin servlet(s) would suit our needs just fine.

As AOP is well beyond the scope of this book, readers interested in this approach are encouraged to create an aspect using their preferred framework: the preceding filter code is basically the same.

Committing servlet

Another solution, albeit a bit brutal, would be to inherit from Vaadin's `com.vaadin.terminal.gwt.server.ApplicationServlet` and override the `service()` method to add the commit code.

```
package com.packtpub.learnvaadin;

import java.io.IOException;
import java.util.Iterator;

import javax.servlet.ServletException;
import javax.servlet.http.HttpServletRequest;
import javax.servlet.http.HttpServletResponse;
import javax.servlet.http.HttpSession;

import org.hibernate.Session;
import org.hibernate.Transaction;

import com.vaadin.Application;
import com.vaadin.terminal.gwt.server.ApplicationServlet;
import com.vaadin.terminal.gwt.server.WebApplicationContext;

@SuppressWarnings("serial")
public class CommitServlet extends ApplicationServlet {
```

```
@Override
protected void service(HttpServletRequest request,
  HttpServletResponse response) throws ServletException, IOException
{

    super.service(request, response);

    HttpSession httpSession = request.getSession();

    WebApplicationContext context =
      WebApplicationContext.getApplicationContext(httpSession);

    Iterator<Application> apps =
      context.getApplications().iterator();

    if (apps.hasNext()) {

      SqlContainerApplication app =
        (SqlContainerApplication) apps.next();

      Session session = app.getSessionManager().getSession();

      Transaction transaction = session.getTransaction();

      if (transaction.isActive()) {

        transaction.commit();
      }
    }
  }
}
```

The main drawback of this strategy is that it is highly dependent on the servlet, thus preventing us to reuse it with either our Spring or CDI servlets (or at least needing a certain amount of copy-pasted code).

Vaadin native approach

The application context is designed to add/remove transaction listeners.

These listeners are called before each communication between the server and client (what is called a transaction).

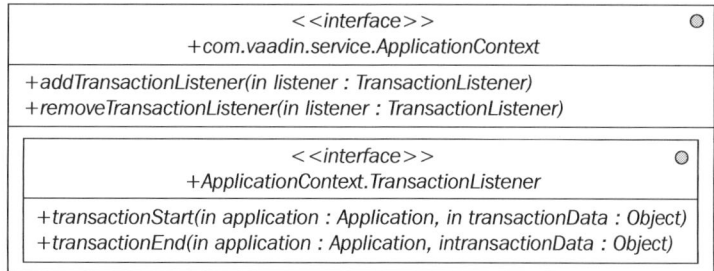

In essence, we keep the database transaction start when we get the session and we commit it when the communication is sent to the client (and only if active).

Such a transaction listener would look like this:

```
package com.packtpub.learnvaadin;

import org.hibernate.Session;
import org.hibernate.Transaction;

import com.vaadin.Application;
import com.vaadin.service.ApplicationContext.TransactionListener;

@SuppressWarnings("serial")
class CommitTransactionListener implements TransactionListener {

  @Override
  public void transactionStart(Application application, Object
    transactionData) {}

  @Override
  public void transactionEnd(Application application, Object
    transactionData) {

    SqlContainerApplication sqlContainerApplication =
      (SqlContainerApplication) application;

    Session session =
      sqlContainerApplication.getSessionManager().getSession();

    Transaction transaction = session.getTransaction();

    if (transaction.isActive()) {

      transaction.commit();
    }
  }
}
```

We reuse the same code as before, but in a "Vaadin way". Note that both methods are called for every communication. Thus, it is added for every UI change. For example, when displaying the content of a list box for which there is no reason for a transaction.

As such, as for filters, the preceding code may not be very efficient.

Example session manager

Now that the commit strategy is chosen, we need a session manager implementation. As said previously, it's best to rely on the `getCurrentSession()` that either creates the session or gets it from a context.

```
package com.packtpub.learnvaadin;

import org.hibernate.Session;
```

```
import org.hibernate.SessionFactory;
import org.hibernate.cfg.Configuration;

import com.vaadin.data.hbnutil.HbnContainer.SessionManager;

final class CurrentSessionManager implements SessionManager {

  private final SessionFactory factory;

  CurrentSessionManager() {

    Configuration cfg = new Configuration().addAnnotatedClass
      (Person.class).addAnnotatedClass(Job.class);

    factory = cfg.buildSessionFactory();
  }

  @Override
  public Session getSession() {

    Session session = factory.getCurrentSession();

    if (!session.getTransaction().isActive()) {

      session.beginTransaction();
    }

    return session;
  }
}
```

Note we also start the transaction if it wasn't already active.

The application

The application is tasked with making sessions available, and delegates to the session manager.

```
package com.packtpub.learnvaadin;

import java.sql.Date;

import org.hibernate.Session;

import com.vaadin.Application;
import com.vaadin.data.hbnutil.HbnContainer.SessionManager;

public class SqlContainerApplication extends Application {

  private static final long serialVersionUID = 1L;

  private transient SessionManager sessionManager;

  @Override
  public void init() {
```

```
  getContext().addTransactionListener
    (new CommitTransactionListener());

  // GUI code here
}

public synchronized SessionManager getSessionManager() {

  if (sessionManager == null) {

    sessionManager = new CurrentSessionManager();
  }

  return sessionManager;
}
}
```

Important facts about the previous code are:

- As the session manager should not be serialized, it is marked as `transient`.

- In order to retrieve the session manager when it has not already been instantiated (either because it is the first call or because the application has just been deserialized), we use the singleton pattern with a lazy initialization. Notice the method is synchronized to have only a single instance at any time. Besides, it may be seen as overkill since two different instances would return the same session anyway.

At last, the window

The last piece in our application is the window itself. It displays persons in a table, with text fields for simple attributes, a select widget for the job and a delete button for removing the entity from the table.

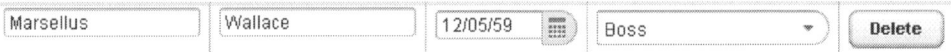

Delete button

The delete button is a basic implementation and is not tied to the underlying container, Hibernate or whatever.

```
package com.packtpub.learnvaadin;

import com.vaadin.ui.Button;
import com.vaadin.ui.Button.ClickEvent;
import com.vaadin.ui.Button.ClickListener;
import com.vaadin.ui.Component;
import com.vaadin.ui.Table;
import com.vaadin.ui.Table.ColumnGenerator;
```

```java
@SuppressWarnings("serial")
class DeleteColumnGenerator implements ColumnGenerator {

  @Override
  public Component generateCell(final Table source, Object itemId,
    Object columnId) {

    Button button = new Button("Delete");

    button.setData(itemId);

    button.addListener(new ClickListener() {

      @Override
      public void buttonClick(ClickEvent event) {

        Object itemId = event.getButton().getData();

        source.removeItem(itemId);
      }
    });

    return button;
  }
}
```

When deleting, we remove the item from the table, which in turn delegates the removing to the container. Therefore, we are isolated from the container's type and we can reuse this delete button in many containers, with no knowledge of the underlying container's specific type.

Job select

The job select column generator lets us display the job of a person in the form of a simple select.

The select has two important requirements:

- When initially displayed, it should show the job of the person as it is in the database.
- When its value is changed, the foreign key value in the database should be changed accordingly.

```java
package com.packtpub.learnvaadin;

import org.hibernate.Session;

import com.vaadin.data.Property;
import com.vaadin.data.Property.ValueChangeEvent;
import com.vaadin.data.Property.ValueChangeListener;
```

```
import com.vaadin.data.hbnutil.HbnContainer;
import com.vaadin.data.hbnutil.HbnContainer.SessionManager;
import com.vaadin.ui.Component;
import com.vaadin.ui.Select;
import com.vaadin.ui.Table;
import com.vaadin.ui.Table.ColumnGenerator;

@SuppressWarnings("serial")
class JobColumnGenerator implements ColumnGenerator {

  private SqlContainerApplication application;

  JobColumnGenerator(SqlContainerApplication application) {

    this.application = application;
  }

  @Override
  public Component generateCell(final Table source, final
    Object itemId, Object columnId) {

  HbnContainer<Job> jobContainer = new
    HbnContainer<Job>(Job.class, application.getSessionManager());

    final Select select = new Select("", jobContainer);

    select.setItemCaptionPropertyId("label");

    select.setImmediate(true);

    Property jobProperty =
      source.getItem(itemId).getItemProperty("job");

    Long jobId = (Long) jobProperty.getValue();

    if (jobId != null) {

      select.select(jobId);
    }

    select.addListener(new ValueChangeListener() {

      @Override
      public void valueChange(ValueChangeEvent event) {

        Long jobId = (Long) event.getProperty().getValue();

        Job job = null;

        SessionManager sessionManager =
         application.getSessionManager();

        Session session = sessionManager.getSession();

        Person person = (Person) session.get(Person.class,
          (Long) itemId);
```

```
        if (jobId != null) {
          job = (Job) session.get(Job.class, jobId);
        }
        person.setJob(job);
      }
    });
    return select;
  }
}
```

The previous code just implements the initial value selection and the update process. Some things are worth mentioning:

- We use the application `getSessionManager()` method in order to use the lazy instance provided by it. In this way, we do not store the session and avoid getting stale connections while sharing the session across all containers.

- We easily get the job's ID: there is no coupling to the Hibernate container as we manipulate high-level abstractions. As such, selecting the correct job in the select widget is a no-brainer.

  It consists of getting the person's job property value, which is a foreign key, and setting it on the select, which uses the job's primary key.

- Finally, changing the database to the value of the selected job is just a matter of creating a listener. The latter gets the job and the person, and associates both. The only "difficulty" is managing `null` selection.

 For Hibernate's less seasoned developers, note there's no call to `update()` or `merge()` since we load the `Person` entity from the session. Committing the transaction will flush the session and thus execute the `UPDATE`.

Main window

The main window just has to use a Hibernate container for persons.

Like components we already developed, this one has initialization code separated in two parts: one in the constructor and one in another method so as to access the application.

```
package com.packtpub.learnvaadin;

import com.vaadin.data.hbnutil.HbnContainer;
import com.vaadin.data.hbnutil.HbnContainer.SessionManager;
```

```java
import com.vaadin.ui.HorizontalLayout;
import com.vaadin.ui.Table;
import com.vaadin.ui.VerticalLayout;
import com.vaadin.ui.Window;

public class MainWindow extends Window {

  private static final long serialVersionUID = 1L;

  private Table table;

  public MainWindow() {

    VerticalLayout vLayout = new VerticalLayout();

    vLayout.setMargin(true);

    setContent(vLayout);

    table = new Table();

    table.setPageLength(10);
    table.setEditable(true);
    table.setSizeFull();

    table.addGeneratedColumn("delete", new DeleteColumnGenerator());

    addComponent(table);

    HorizontalLayout hLayout = new HorizontalLayout();

    hLayout.setMargin(true);
    hLayout.setSpacing(true);

    addComponent(hLayout);
  }

  void initialize() {

    SqlContainerApplication app = (SqlContainerApplication)
      getApplication();

    SessionManager sessionManager = app.getSessionManager();

    HbnContainer<Person> personContainer = new
      HbnContainer<Person>(Person.class, sessionManager);

    table.setContainerDataSource(personContainer);

    table.addGeneratedColumn("job", new
     JobColumnGenerator((SqlContainerApplication) getApplication()));

    table.setVisibleColumns(new Object[] { "firstName", "lastName",
      "birthdate", "job", "delete" });
  }
}
```

Note that very few lines (those highlighted) are coupled to the Hibernate container. We could easily provide an implementation that uses the SQL container of *Chapter 7*.

Hibernate configuration

For the sake of completeness, here is the `hibernate.properties` file. It uses HyperSonic SQL database.

```
hibernate.connection.url=jdbc:hsqldb:mem:vaadin
hibernate.connection.driver_class=org.hsqldb.jdbc.JDBCDriver
hibernate.connection.username=SA
hibernate.connection.password=
hibernate.show_sql=true
hibernate.dialect=org.hibernate.dialect.HSQLDialect
hibernate.current_session_context_class=thread
hibernate.hbm2ddl.auto=update
```

Putting it all together

Before using these classes, a few steps are required.

Hibernate

Download Hibernate first: it is available on SourceForge, at `http://sourceforge.net/projects/hibernate/files/hibernate3/`. The latest distribution is 3.6.4. Final at the time of writing.

Open the archive and copy the `hibernate.jar` to the `WebContent/WEB-INF/lib` directory, as well as the content of the `lib/required`.

For Maven users just add the dependency to your POM and you are done!

SLF4J

However, note that Hibernate is dependent on a logging framework named SLF4J.

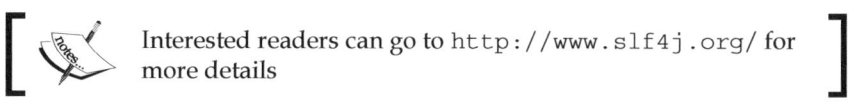 Interested readers can go to `http://www.slf4j.org/` for more details

This framework is available in two JARs, one for the API, the other for different implementations. Although the former is distributed along Hibernate, the latter is a personal choice. Whether we are using Maven or not, we have to decide which implementation to use: Log4j, Jakarta Commons Logging, JDK logging or simple `System.out` and `System.err` calls. In all cases, we will have to download the implementation JAR from `http://www.slf4j.org/download.html`. Moreover, in the two former cases, we will also need to download the right JAR from their respective sites.

>
> **Version match**
>
> It goes without saying that both API and implementation versions have to match. Furthermore, both must also be compatible with the "true" logging framework in the case of Log4j or Commons Logging. Maven will take care of this through the POM but otherwise, it is advised to carefully read the documentation to align versions.

HbnContainer

Additionally, download the Hibernate container itself. This add-on is available at `http://vaadin.com/directory#addon/hbncontainer`.

Final notes

Before closing the door on the Hibernate container, there are some remarks that need to be made.

Serialization exception

When using the Hibernate container, during consecutive restarts, a strange exception may appear in the log: **java.io.WriteAbortedException: writing aborted; java.io.NotSerializableException: org.hibernate.persister.entity. SingleTableEntityPersister**.

Although not impacting application's normal run, this causes data not to be serialized (and thus state loss) during session serialization. In essence, it all boils down to a single `ClassMetadata` field of the Hibernate container. Therefore, we should either subclass the container and provide our own serialization process or live with the stack in the log.

Optimizations

Seasoned Hibernate developers (and less experienced ones) noticed the stack is full of Hibernate queries.

For example, it seems jobs are queried for every line, which is not a very good idea as they are more like a repository table.

In order to reduce the number of queries, it is advised to set up a second level cache, based on your favorite product (see Ehcache or JBoss cache for example) and configure it for the container's usage.

This goes well beyond Vaadin; the lesson here being that using Vaadin should not make you forget parts of the application unrelated to the presentation are also important, if not more so.

Rollback management

Our code does not manage any rollback for the sake of simplicity. In production code however, it is not an option.

What really matters in this case is re-synchronizing the GUI with the data. As such, in case of rollbacks, it is advised to reload the data from the database tier.

Java Persistence API

Although JPA is part of Java EE 6, it merits its own section.

JPA is very similar to Hibernate, in that it is the standardized way to access database, whereas Hibernate is a proprietary approach.

The add-on directory also offers a container able to use JPA 1.0: the Vaadin JPA Container. The add-on is certified by the Vaadin Company, note that it is available under either the AGPL license if your project is compatible or a commercial license.

We won't go into further details here as most concepts are very similar to Hibernate container. Moreover, we also used JPA mappings for our previous example. Anyway, knowing this add-on exists can be a lifesaver.

Summary

This chapter saw us browsing through a variety of third-party products and standards. In all cases, Vaadin could use them to provide the expected service, proving its well-thought design and versatility.

On the service layer, we learned how to use both Spring and CDI, the use of each depending on one's personal taste and one's environment. Both adopt very similar integration strategy, a custom servlet.

On the persistence layer, we discovered how to connect table widgets to databases using the renowned Hibernate framework through the use of the Hibernate Container add-on.

There are two things to keep in mind from this chapter:

1. First, when an integration need arises, be sure to check the Vaadin add-on directory first. Chances are someone already tackled the problem. Before using the add-on however, check the ratings, the comments, the license, and eventually the cost. Carefully evaluate the risk of using a third-party add-on and the cost of developing your own.

2. Second, integration can be done at different levels, depending on the type of third-party product. For service layer frameworks, think about the servlet level, for persistence layer, about the container level for collections (or the item level for single objects).

The next (and final) chapter will be about running Vaadin on different platforms.

10
Beyond Application Servers

Until now, we used Vaadin in a "standard" way, with an underlying application server (or JSP/servlet container). This chapter will show us in detail how to run Vaadin applications on a variety of other platforms encountered in enterprises today:

- Portals, as portlets
- OSGi platforms, as services
- Finally, "in the cloud"

We will take a brief look at what each platform really is, and then see how Vaadin can run on them with more or less tweaking.

First, we will see how to manage multiplatform development and how to build tools to minimize the required effort.

Build tools

Until now, in order to create our WAR, we have used Eclipse's (or another IDE's) export feature, which is nice but not comprehensive enough. During the normal course of a project, builds are executed through standard build tools. There are a few arguments in favor of such tools:

- Nowadays, we need automated and reproducible builds, so that we may have continuous builds. Every time a commit is detected or at fixed times, the build is launched and a bad commit—one that breaks the build—is spotted as early as possible.
- Moreover, if we want our project to be multiplatform, and since some configuration may be in conflict, we need to remove those manual and error-prone configuration changes for each build.

- If our project does not have a single developer, it lets each one develop with its favorite IDE, confident in the fact that a third-party tool will handle the build itself.

- Finally, build tools let us plug in other features such as automated tests.

Available tools

Nowadays, plenty of enterprise-quality build tools are available for free. The problem lies in choosing the right one.

Apache Ant

In Java, the first portable build tool was Apache Ant (http://ant.apache.org/). At the time, it was a revolution that soon engulfed the entire ecosystem: every project worth its salt provided an Ant build file that let users build it regardless of their respective operating system.

However, Ant's limitations soon became apparent:

- The Ant build file is very liberal in its approach. To be simplistic, it just defines targets, whatever those may be: compiles, copies, creates the archive, and so on. As such, no two build files look the same, even if they perform the same thing. In short, build files are not paragons of readability.

- In addition, Ant's compile target needs the classpath definition. As a build has to be consistent, external libraries have to be provided and thus committed to the project's source versioning software which it then bloats, and adds no particular value to.

Apache Maven

In order to correct Ant's flaws, Apache launched a new build tool, Maven (http://maven.apache.org/). It corrected the previous shortcomings with two brand-new ideas at the time:

- Maven brought standardization to builds:
    - A standardized build cycle: compile, copy, archive, and so on. As such, Maven's build file, the famed POM (Project Object Model), does not tell what it does like Ant, but only configures how it does it.
    - Standardized subprojects in the form of modules. Now, two projects using WAR included in an EAR looked alike!
- Maven also brought the concept of a repository where every project should put its artifacts. Then, instead of manually downloading third-party libraries, projects would only need to reference them in the registry.

Fragmentation

Maven's approach was not to every developer's taste. Some argued against XML format verbosity, others against the POM's lack of extensibility, some just wanted to hold onto something they practiced for years, like Ant.

The explosion of languages on the JVM added to the confusion, with every language coming with its own build tool: Gradle for Groovy, Rake for Ruby, Gant for Grails, SBT for Scala, and the list goes on.

Final choice

Choosing a build tool in such a context is hard, yet necessary. In the context of this book, we will use Maven to manage our build. The most important reason is that despite the many criticisms against Maven, it actually is a major build tool, if not the tool of choice.

Tooling

In Eclipse (or Eclipse-based STS), Maven tooling is provided by the Eclipse's m2e plugins, available at `http://download.eclipse.org/technology/m2e/releases/` update sites. Please refer to *Chapter 3* for a reminder regarding the use of update sites.

Troubleshooting

If during the web application testing Vaadin throws `javax.servlet.ServletException`: Failed to load application class, check the deployment folder on the server. Chances are `vaadin.jar` is missing. In this case, it is perhaps because the Maven Integration for WTP is not installed.

NetBeans supplied Maven support out-of-the-box. Enjoy!

Maven in Vaadin projects

In Eclipse, there are basically two ways to build Vaadin projects with Maven: either create a Vaadin project and add Maven features to it or the other way around.

Both are valid depending on our use-cases.

Mavenize a Vaadin project

First, create a Vaadin project just as we did in *Chapter 3* with three important differences:

- For the Java sources folder, click on **Remove** on `src` and then **Add Folder** `src/main/java`

- For default output folder, enter `target/classes`

- Finally, for the web content directory folder, enter `src/main/webapp`

 If these values remind you of the standard Maven folder structure, you are absolutely right! Entering these values will prevent us from manually moving folders around after adding Maven to the mix.

Then, right click on the project directory and select **Maven | Enable Dependency Management**. This opens a window: group id, artifact id, version, packaging, name, and description fields are used by the plugin to create the POM.

Fill the values as you would a brand new POM. However, **Packaging** should be **war** in all cases! Click on **Next**, as shown in the following screenshot:

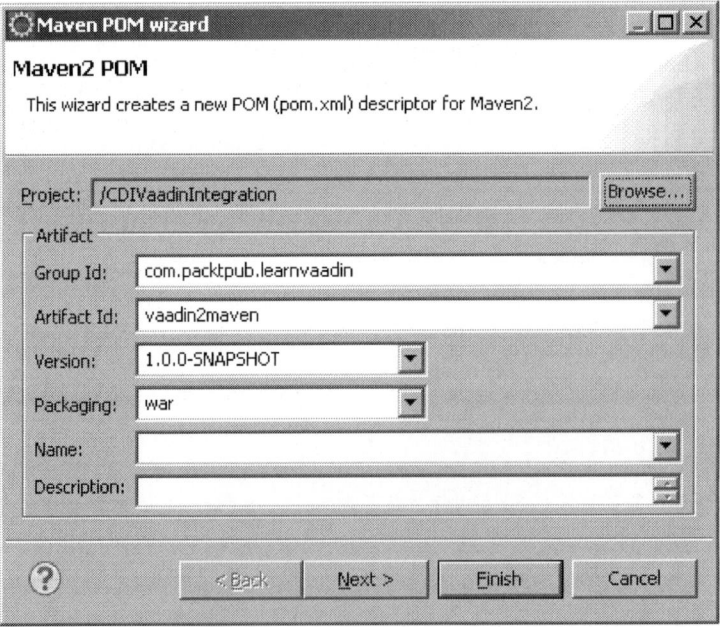

Then, add dependencies. We should at least have Vaadin as a dependency.

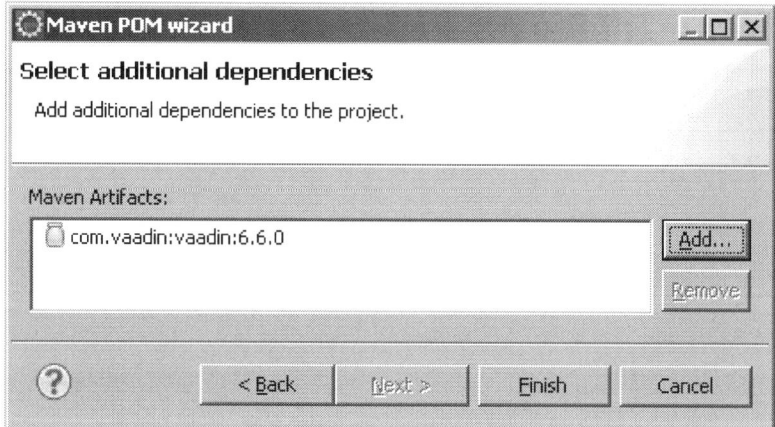

Click on **Finish**.

Now comes the manual part: we have to manually clean up our project. Click on the project and display **Java Resources | Libraries**. Now select Apache Tomcat 6.0 (the server library), EAR libraries and Web App Libraries, right click and click on **Build Path | Remove from Build Path**.

Finally, delete `src/main/webapp/WEB-INF/lib/vaadin-6.7.x.jar`.

Vaadin support for Maven projects

As an alternative, we could also create a Maven project and add Vaadin support.

Go to **File | New | Project**. Locate Maven Project and click on **Next** two times (default values are OK for the first window).

For archetype selection, filter with Vaadin and select **com.vaadin: vaadin-archetype-clean** and click on **Next**, as shown in the following screenshot:

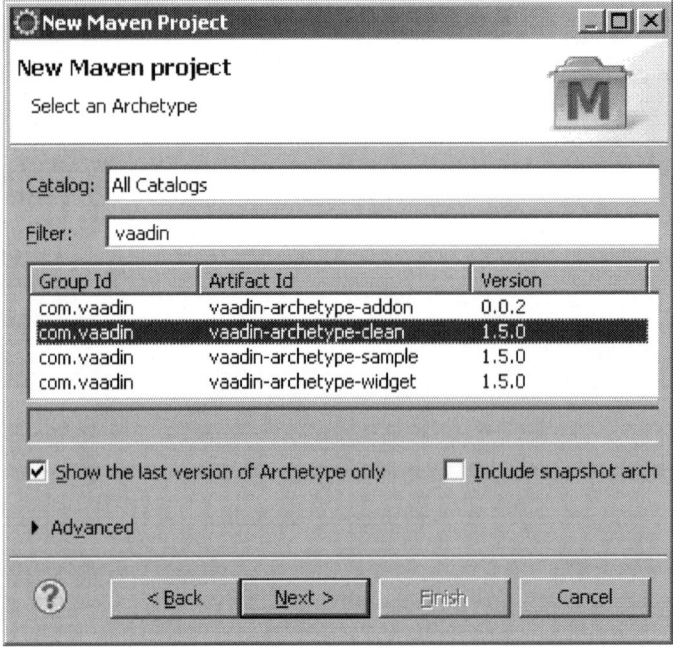

Enter the same values as for section Mavenize Vaadin project above and click on **Finish**.

A quick glance at the POM tells us it is much more furnished as compared to adding dependency management to a Vaadin project:

- The property `project.build.sourceEncoding` avoids making our POM platform-dependent
- The other properties manage versions: Vaadin, GWT, and GWT plugins
- The Maven compiler plugin is configured to use Java 1.5 by default
- The Jetty plugin will let us easily test our Vaadin application with the Jetty servlet container
- Finally, two additional repositories are added besides the main Maven repository: one for Vaadin snapshots, the other for Vaadin add-ons

In order to use Vaadin Eclipse plugin, right click on the project and click on **Properties**. Select **Project Facets** on the left and check **Vaadin Plug-in for Eclipse** as shown in the following screenshot:

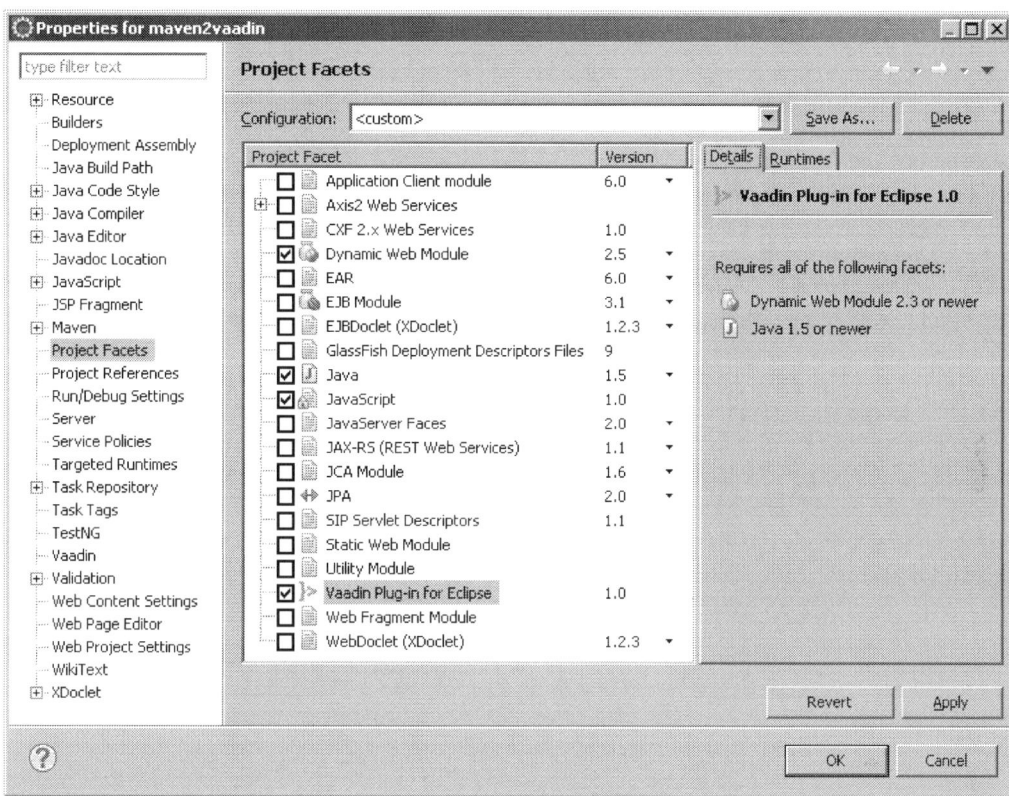

 Version 1.5 of the archetype is the latest version available. Yet, it still uses GWT compiler 2.2.0 (as opposed to 2.3.0 in Eclipse). If this does not suit you, you will have to sully your nails and make manual changes to Eclipse configuration files, which is not recommended unless you know what you are doing.

Mavenizing Twaattin

There is no advantage to migrate Twaattin under Maven at this time, but we will prepare the project now to be ready for the rest of the chapter.

Preparing the migration

Since we are to migrate an existing project instead of creating the right project structure from the beginning, we will need to move directories around:

- First, create the `src/main/java` directory. Move files from `src` to it. Then, right click on the project and select **Properties**. Click on **Build Path**, tab Sources. Remove `src` and add `src/main/java`.

- While we are at it, set the output directory to `target/classes` instead of `build/classes` on the same tab.

- Finally, create folder `src/main/webapp` and move files from `WebContent` to it. Eclipse does not take kindly on this sort of operation, we will need to smooth it somewhat: locate the `org.eclipse.wst.common.component` file under the `.settings` directory. Change the `source-path` attribute of the following tag by the new location:

```
<wb-resource deploy-path="/" source-path="/WebContent"/>
```

Enabling dependency management

Now we just follow the preceding section procedure. Dependencies go well beyond Vaadin:

- Servlet API
- Vaadin SQL Container
- Quartz
- Twitter4J
- SLF4J API and an implementation
- ICEPush and ICEPush GWT

Moreover, in order to add the SQL Container and ICEPush add-ons features, we need to reference the Vaadin Directory repository where those add-ons are registered (they are not in repo1).

```
<project ...>
...
  <repositories>
    <repository>
      <id>vaadin-addons</id>
      <url>http://maven.vaadin.com/vaadin-addons</url>
    </repository>
  </repositories>
</project>
```

Finally, both `icepush` and `icepush-gwt` JAR are in no available repository at the time of the writing. We have to download it at `http://www.icepush.org/downloads.html`. It is mandatory to register, however.

Grab `icepush-gwt-2.0.0-alpha3.zip`, extract the files, and build the JAR with Ant. Calling `ant bin-dist` in the extracted directory is enough; the target will build the needed archives.

When done, install both built archives in your own local repository (or better yet, your enterprise repository):

```
mvn install:install-file -Dfile=dist/icepush.jar -DgroupId=org.icepush
-artifactId=icepush -Dversion=2.0.0-alpha3 -Dpackaging=jar
```

```
mvn install:install-file -Dfile=dist/icepush-gwt.jar -DgroupId=org.
icepush -DartifactId=icepush-gwt -Dversion=2.0.0-alpha3 -Dpackaging=jar
```

Finishing touches

The last step just lets us use Maven dependency management. A few steps are still needed in order to build the entire project outside Maven.

GWT build

As of now, the Vaadin Eclipse plugin takes care of creating the widgetset. We need to enforce this in Maven alone.

First things first, the version of the GWT compiler needed by Vaadin 6.7 is 2.3 and is dependent on Java 6. Configure the Java version in the Maven compiler plugin in the POM as follows:

```xml
<project ...>
...
  <build>
    <plugins>
      <plugin>
        <groupId>org.apache.maven.plugins</groupId>
        <artifactId>maven-compiler-plugin</artifactId>
        <version>2.3.2</version>
        <configuration>
          <source>1.6</source>
          <target>1.6</target>
        </configuration>
      </plugin>
    </plugins>
  </build>
</project>
```

Be sure to right-click on the project, **Maven | Update Project Configuration** so as to let Eclipse know something changed.

This is a prerequisite, but by no mean does it change anything regarding GWT compilation. Moreover, Version 2.3 of the GWT compiler adds a dependency to the Java Validation API (both JAR and sources). Therefore, we need to add these to Twaattin's dependencies—in provided scope so as not to package them in the WAR:

```
<project ...>
...
  <dependencies>
    <dependency>
      <groupId>javax.validation</groupId>
      <artifactId>validation-api</artifactId>
      <version>1.0.0.GA</version>
      <scope>provided</scope>
    </dependency>
    <dependency>
      <groupId>javax.validation</groupId>
      <artifactId>validation-api</artifactId>
      <version>1.0.0.GA</version>
      <classifier>sources</classifier>
      <scope>provided</scope>
    </dependency>
  </dependencies>
</project>
```

 We would expect to put these in the GWT plugin section, but it does not work. Somehow, the GWT plugin needs them to be in the compile classpath.

The following plugins configuration gets the job done:

```
<project ...>
...
  <build>
    <plugins>
      <plugin>
        <groupId>org.codehaus.mojo</groupId>
        <artifactId>gwt-maven-plugin</artifactId>
        <version>2.2.0</version>
        <executions>
          <execution>
            <goals>
              <goal>compile</goal>
```

```
          </goals>
          <phase>compile</phase>
        </execution>
      </executions>
      <configuration>
      <webappDirectory>
        src/main/webapp/VAADIN/widgetsets
      </webappDirectory>
      </configuration>
      <dependencies>
        <dependency>
          <groupId>com.google.gwt</groupId>
          <artifactId>gwt-user</artifactId>
          <version>2.3.0</version>
        </dependency>
        <dependency>
          <groupId>com.google.gwt</groupId>
          <artifactId>gwt-dev</artifactId>
          <version>2.3.0</version>
        </dependency>
      </dependencies>
    </plugin>
    <plugin>
      <groupId>com.vaadin</groupId>
      <artifactId>vaadin-maven-plugin</artifactId>
      <version>1.0.2</version>
      <executions>
        <execution>
          <goals>
            <goal>update-widgetset</goal>
          </goals>
          <phase>compile</phase>
        </execution>
      </executions>
    </plugin>
  </plugins>
</build>
</project>
```

Note that we deliberately upgraded the GWT compiler version from 2.2.0 (the plugin's version) to 2.3.0 in order to be fully compatible with the version from Vaadin Eclipse plugin.

Cleaning up warning messages

There are still some disturbing warning messages that pollute our nice build:

- **The POM for org.icepush:xxx:jar:2.0.0-alpha3 is missing**: This message can be removed by properly installing the JAR in the Maven local repository; please see `https://maven.apache.org/plugins/maven-install-plugin/usage.html` for details.

- **Using platform encoding (Cp1252 actually) to copy filtered resources, i.e. build is platform dependent**: This message appears when developing on Windows. We need to add a property to our POM to specify the file encoding.

```
<project ...>
...
  <properties>
    <project.build.sourceEncoding>
      UTF-8
    </project.build.sourceEncoding>
  </properties>
</project>
```

- **Warning: selected war files include a WEB-INF/web.xml which will be ignored**: This message comes from the newest Version (2.1.1) Maven WAR plugin. Add the following configuration to your POM:

```
<project ...>
...
  <build>
    <plugins>
      <plugin>
        <groupId>org.apache.maven.plugins</groupId>
        <artifactId>maven-war-plugin</artifactId>
        <version>2.1.1</version>
        <configuration>
          <packagingExcludes>
            WEB-INF/web.xml
          </packagingExcludes>
        </configuration>
      </plugin>
    </plugins>
  </build>
</project>
```

Optimizations

Some artifacts versions are the same because they are somehow coupled together, such as Icepush/Icepush GWT, GWT user/dev and validation and its associated source. Those can be factorized in properties in order to DRY (*Don't Repeat Yourself*) the POM.

Finally, notice that the widgetset generation output, either through Eclipse or through Maven, is localized in `src/main/webapp` and not in `target`. This means that we have no need to compile it with each build and it can be safely isolated in an activatable profile. As this plugin takes a good part of the build time, it is worth doing it.

Final POM

The final POM is available on Packt's website.

This may seem quite a struggle for little added value, but it is the prerequisite to effortlessly add additional platforms to run Twaattin on.

Portals

Although not as widespread as some wished them to be 10 years ago, portals are still common enough to be a target of choice for Vaadin web applications.

Portal, container, and portlet

Before going further, one has to understand some essential notions about what a portal is and how it is constituted.

Three different concepts are each attached to a different granularity level.

- **Portlet**: A portlet is a pluggable software component, meant to be displayed inside a portal. As opposed to a servlet, a portlet only generates a part of the rendered page. If we liken it to a wall, a portlet would be a brick.

- **Portal**: A portal is a full-fledged application that aggregates portlets. Most portals will also allow administrators (or individual users) to customize the portlets' layout, as well as the global portal's look-and-feel.

  To continue our wall analogy, the portal would be the wall itself.

- **Portlet container**: A portlet container is the technical layer that manages portlets. It plays the same role for them, as would a servlet container for servlets, including request forwarding, response handling, lifecycle management, and so on.

  In a wall, the container would be the cement that sits between the wall and each separate brick.

Choosing a platform

Currently, there are two different JSRs for portlet API:

- JSR-168 also known as the Java Portlet API, is the first generation specification introducing portlets in Java. As many first specifications go, it has limits which the next JSR tries to address.

- JSR-286 is the Java Portlet API 2.0 and is meant to replace the former specification. It tries to align itself with the OASIS portlet specifications (WSRPS 2.0) and introduces new features such as:
  - ° Inter-portlets events
  - ° Shared rendering parameters
  - ° Non-HTML resource serving
  - ° Portlet filters

In addition, different products implementing these specifications are available. At the time of writing this book, enterprise-grade portals that can be considered for use comprise both commercial products and free/open source ones.

- Commercial products include:
  - ° IBM WebSphere Portal is a part of the many offerings of IBM WebSphere (http://www-01.ibm.com/software/websphere/portal/)
  - ° Oracle WebLogic Portal (http://www.oracle.com/technetwork/middleware/weblogic-portal/)

- Free/open source products consist of:
  - ° Apache Jetspeed 2 (http://portals.apache.org/jetspeed-2/) is a portal relying on Apache Pluto (http://portals.apache.org/pluto/), a raw portlet container. It does not seem very widespread.
  - ° JBoss GateIn (http://www.jboss.org/gatein) is the result of the merging of former projects JBoss Portal and eXo Portal.
  - ° Last but not least, Liferay is a portal commonly found in the enterprise. It is developed by Liferay Inc. which also provides commercial fee-based support for it.

Liferay

Vaadin's demo itself runs in Liferay. Both companies already work together in a partnership to integrate their products with each other, so there is plenty of good documentation on the Web, mostly on `vaadin.com` and on `liferay.com`, that describes how to do that. Interesting articles are:

- Develop Vaadin Apps as Portlets at `http://www.liferay.com/community/wiki/-/wiki/1071674/develop+vaadin+apps+as+portlets/maximized`, oriented toward Liferay 6.0

- Running Vaadin Mail Portlet in Liferay 5.2.x at `http://vaadin.com/wiki/-/wiki/Main/Running%20Vaadin%20Mail%20Portlet%20in%20Liferay%205.2.x`, for Liferay 5.2

Both articles, coupled with sound portal and portlet development knowledge should be enough for one to create and deploy portlets in Liferay, regardless of the version.

> Starting from Liferay Version 6.0, Vaadin widgetsets are included so there is nothing to install on the platform to run Vaadin applications on it.

If one still encounters difficulties running Vaadin apps as portlets, then one should turn to the Vaadin forums, which provide answers to many questions.

GateIn

The platform of choice taken as an example for the rest of this section is GateIn: what is explained in the following sections can be adapted to your portal of choice.

> For enterprise users, GateIn is also available in an enterprise edition, **JBoss Enterprise Portal Platform (JEPP)**. It is a boosted version of GateIn for which JBoss provides support, at a price. For more information on JEPP, visit `http://www.jboss.com/products/platforms/portals/`.

Downloading and installation

GateIn comes bundled with either JBoss AS 5.1.0 or with Tomcat 6.0.20. Using one or the other depends on one's requirements and personal tastes. In the context of this book, we will use Tomcat 6.0.20.

Download the version that is suitable for you from the following URL:

```
http://www.jboss.org/gatein/downloads
```

Installing GateIn is just a matter of unzipping the downloaded archive. For Windows users, take care to extract it under a path that contains no space characters.

Preparing the platform

GateIn uses **HSQLB (Hyper Structured Query Language Database)** as its internal database. If we intend to use data sources instead of a direct connection to the database, experience shows that HSQLDB has unsupported features that will break our applications. Moreover, it will only become apparent during the execution.

Therefore, the wisest course of action would be to configure GateIn to use a more compliant SQL RDBMS. As MySQL is both free and open source and GateIn supports it, we will first configure the portal to use it.

GateIn offers a **Java Content Repository (JCR)** should we need JCR for our portlets. Locate `<GATEIN_HOME>/gatein/conf/configuration.properties` and replace the following lines:

```
gatein.jcr.datasource.driver=com.mysql.jdbc.Driver
gatein.jcr.datasource.url=jdbc:mysql://localhost:3306/gatein
gatein.jcr.datasource.username=gatein
gatein.jcr.datasource.password=gateinpassword
```

This is also the configuration place for the identity management store, that is where identities and credentials are managed. Since we are there, change the configuration to use MySQL:

```
gatein.idm.datasource.name=jdbcidm
gatein.idm.datasource.driver=com.mysql.jdbc.Driver
gatein.idm.datasource.url=jdbc:mysql://localhost:3306/gatein
gatein.idm.datasource.username=gatein
gatein.idm.datasource.password=gateinpassword
```

Finally, put the MySQL drivers, compatible with the version of MySQL in `<GATEIN_HOME>/lib`.

> **Create schemas beforehand**
>
> As opposed to HSQLDB, we will have to create MySQL schemas before first launching GateIn. Use your preferred tool to do that, GateIn will create the tables.

Launch

Finally, navigate to `<GATEIN_HOME>/bin` and type:

`gatein start`

Alternatively, calling `gatein-dev` shell (or bat) instead of plain `gatein` lets us launch GateIn in debug mode, in order to connect Eclipse to it and check our code.

In order to check whether GateIn launched normally, navigate to `http://localhost:8080/portal`. The default portal home page should be displayed.

Now it is done, we are good to go further!

Troubleshooting

If Tomcat runs fine but you get a 404 not found in your browser, then be sure to check that the environment variable `CATALINA_HOME` is not set (or at least set to GateIn extract directory).

Tooling

The good news here is that we already have all the needed tooling at our disposal, as the Vaadin Eclipse plugin has the right parameters to create portlets instead of standard web applications.

A simple portlet

As an example, we will develop a simple portlet that displays a message when a button is clicked.

The development of such an application holds no secret for us, so let's focus our attention on the differences when developing portlets.

Creating a project

Portlet project creation starts like any other Vaadin project: **File | New | Other** and choose **Vaadin Project**.

Fill the wizard as we did in *Chapter 3*. Now in deployment configuration, which is Servlet by default, choose **Generic Portlet**. As a side note, bear in mind that Generic Portlet is Portlet v2.0 (also known as JSR 286) and that Old Portlet is Portlet v1.0 (also known as JSR 168).

In order to configure the context root, enter "hello" during the WebModule step.

In the final step, the Portlet version is asked for again: do not change it as it could have adverse effects on the project's integrity.

> In essence, the Deployment Configuration list-box determines which XML schema will be used in the `portlet.xml` while the Portlet Version list-box is about which Vaadin portlet to inherit from. The plugin pre-selects the portlet version from the deployment configuration, but still allows the user to choose both independently which is not particularly a good idea.

Finishing the wizard, Vaadin creates the project, just like in *Chapter 3*.

Portlet project differences

There are some subtle (and not so subtle) differences however, that we will look into in detail.

Portlet deployment descriptor

The Vaadin Eclipse plugin created a file named `portlet.xml` under `WEB-INF` in our project. Developers familiar with portals know this file as the portlet deployment descriptor. For those unfamiliar, it is very akin to a web deployment descriptor (`web.xml`), but aimed at portals instead of applications servers.

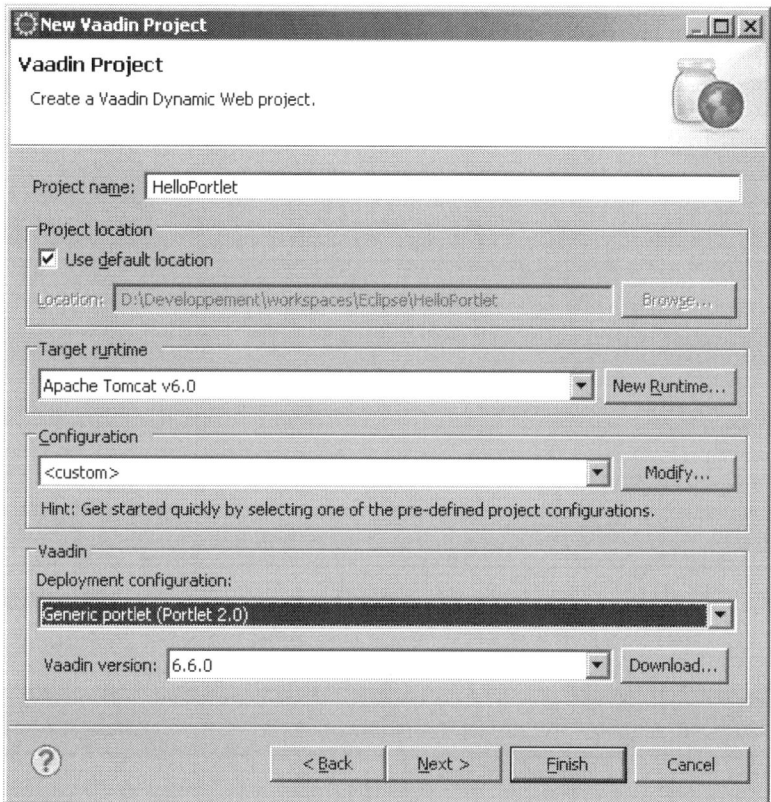

The generated descriptor is as follows (comments excluded):

```
<?xml version="1.0" encoding="UTF-8" standalone="no"?>
<portlet-app xmlns="http://java.sun.com/xml/ns/portlet/portlet-
app_2_0.xsd"
       xmlns:xsi="http://www.w3.org/2001/XMLSchema-instance"
```

```
        version="2.0" xsi:schemaLocation="http://java.sun.com/xml/ns/
portlet/portlet-app_2_0.xsd
        http://java.sun.com/xml/ns/portlet/portlet-app_2_0.xsd">
    <portlet>
        <portlet-name>Hello Portlet portlet</portlet-name>
        <display-name>Hello Vaadin</display-name>
        <portlet-class>
com.vaadin.terminal.gwt.server.ApplicationPortlet2
        </portlet-class>
            <init-param>
                <name>application</name>
                <value>
com.packtpub.learnvaadin.HelloPortletApplication
            </value>
            </init-param>
        <supports>
            <mime-type>text/html</mime-type>
            <portlet-mode>view</portlet-mode>
        </supports>
        <portlet-info>
            <title>Hello Vaadin</title>
            <short-title>Hello Vaadin</short-title>
        </portlet-info>
    </portlet>
</portlet-app>
```

The following describes the differences as compared to a generated web deployment descriptor:

- The XML schema points to a portlet schema, not a web app schema

- The portlet class is `ApplicationPortlet2`. It is compatible with the Portlet 2.0. API. Note that `ApplicationPortlet` is available for Portlet 1.0 API retro-compatibility.

- The support section displays both the output mime-type and the portlet-mode. As a general rule, the former should not be changed since it fits Vaadin's output. As for the mode, the specification defines three modes:

  ○ View displays the portlet; it is the standard mode

  ○ Edit lets the user change/configure/manage the portlet

  ○ Help displays help for the portlet

  In addition to the three standard modes, it is also possible to define custom modes.

Although each of these modes has a semantically unique meaning, nothing prevents us from using the view mode to configure the portlet. By default, the mode is "view" and it matches most of our use-cases.

- Finally, `title` and `short-title` have to be filled. Both Liferay and GateIn will look for these pieces of data and won't display the portlet if they are missing.

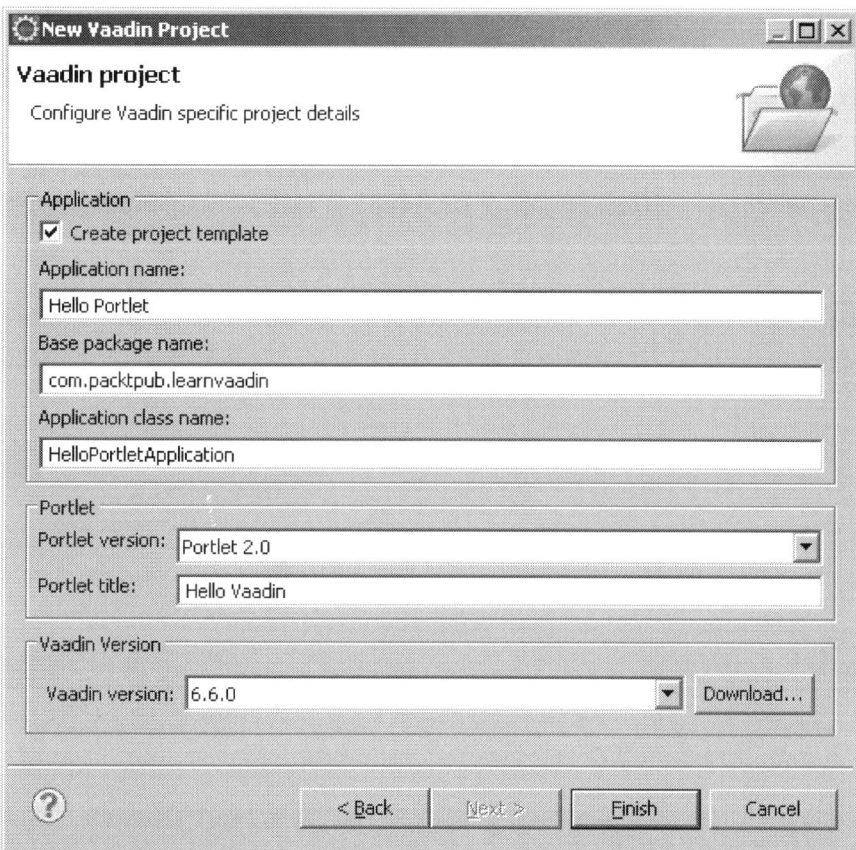

Portal proprietary files

The Vaadin Eclipse plugin also creates the Liferay proprietary files: `liferay-display.xml`, `liferay-portlet.xml`, and `liferay-plugin-package.properties`.

When using GateIn as the portal platform, those can safely be ignored or deleted.

Similarities

Despite the previous differences, keep in mind that there are also a few similarities: the application instance is the same regardless of the deployed platform. This means that we can keep our code, just update the deployment descriptor, and we are good to go on an entirely different platform!

>  There is a slight reservation to this, however, as listeners (if in scope) are context-dependent: see the section named *Handling portlet specificities* in this chapter.

Using the portlet in GateIn

Now all the necessary development tasks are done, we still have to make the portlet available to GateIn and add it in a page.

Deploying in GateIn

Deploying the portlet in GateIn will make it available for further use. In order to do this:

- Export the portlet as a WAR file. Right-click on the project and choose **Export | WAR file**.
- Copy-paste the exported WAR file under `<GATEIN_HOME>/webapps`

If the initial configuration is kept, then Tomcat will automatically and recursively unpack the exported WAR in the `webapps` directory and start the application. This can be verified by the following Vaadin trace in Tomcat's command window:

14 may 2011 00:01:49 com.vaadin.terminal.gwt.server.AbstractApplicationPortlet c

heckProductionMode

WARN:

==

Vaadin is running in DEBUG MODE.

Add productionMode=true to web.xml to disable debug features.

To show debug window, add ?debug to your application URL.

==

Adding the portlet to a page

In order to add the portlet to a page, we need to login in the portal with the credentials to do it.

Sign in

Click on **Sign in** on the left side of the menu bar. It opens a pop-up login window. By default, **root/gtn** will enable us to have enough credentials to make changes to pages (or add new ones for that matter).

Refresh portlets

Before adding the portlet to a page, a user action is needed. Once logged in, navigate to the **Group** menu and choose **Administration | Application Registry**. It opens the complete list of available portlets. At this point, we cannot see our newly deployed servlet.

Click on the **Import Applications** option at the top left corner of the window (just below **Portlet | Gadget**). A confirm dialog opens asking whether portlets should be imported (this will be done in their respective category) and click on **OK**.

A new category appears, matching the deployed WAR's name. Under it, there should be a single portlet that takes its name from the portlet deployment descriptor.

Add portlet

From this point on, portlets exported to GateIn `webapps` directory will be available for use by end users.

Therefore, navigate to the **Site Editor** menu and choose **Edit Page**. This will change the page mode to edit and change the display. On the **Page Editor** tool pane, search for the freshly added category, and drag and drop the child portlet where you want on the main layout.

Saving is achieved by clicking on the disk icon on the **Page Editor** tool pane. The new portlet will be displayed but unfortunately, nothing shows apart from a plain "Done" message. Why is that?

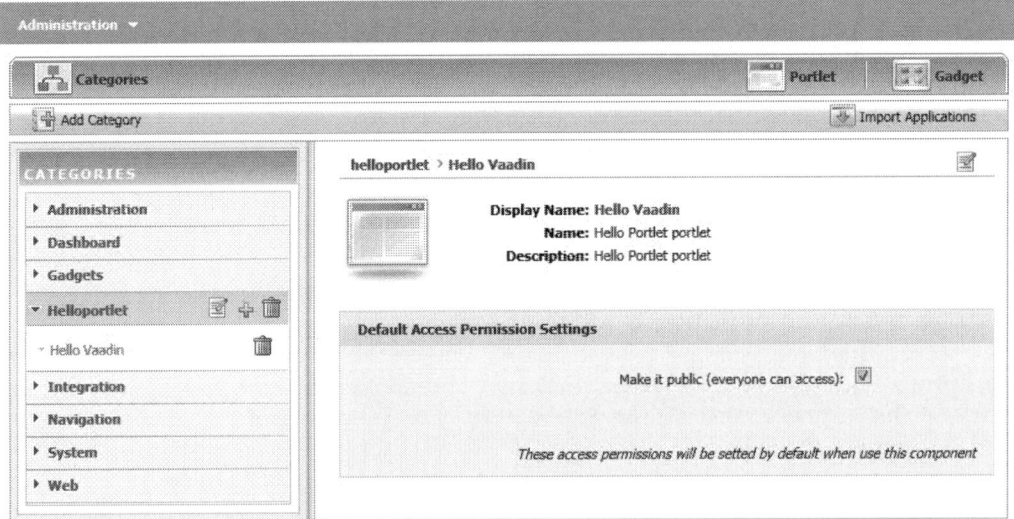

Configuring GateIn for Vaadin

In fact, we missed a crucial step in using Vaadin in GateIn and that is the portal configuration. We will correct this in the following sections.

Themes and widgetsets

Vaadin client's code needs access to the /VAADIN path, where both themes and GWT compiled widget sets lie. When served by a servlet, this path is relative to the root of the web application.

Unfortunately, in the context of a portal, Vaadin has no reference to the servlet context, thus it cannot get the webapp's root. Therefore, the framework will try to access /html/VAADIN **relative to the server's root** to get these files.

There are some options to make this work.

Serve files from the portal

The first solution is to serve files directly from the portal. We need to:

- Put the files from the WAR's /VAADIN directory in the ROOT webapp /html/ VAADIN directory
- Extract files from Vaadin's JAR /VAADIN directory in the ROOT webapp

This has the advantage of putting the default widgetset in a common location, so that all Vaadin's portlets use it. On the other side, this makes the build process more complicated as we have to separate static Vaadin files in one archive from the rest in the WAR.

Serve files from an HTTP server

As an alternative, if we have an HTTP server (Apache HTTP server, Microsoft IIS, or another) in front of our application server, we could serve these files from the HTTP server instead of the application server.

It has the same pros and cons as the previous solution, only with an additional tier.

Configure files location

Another option is to configure the Vaadin static files location. There are two ways to achieve this: either through the portal's own configuration—and we will have to look at each product's documentation to manage that, or through code.

AbstractApplicationPortlet has a getStaticFilesLocation() method that returns html as the default, but we could override the return value. As portlet containers manage WAR, it is a no-brainer to reference the WAR context root. Thus, our portlet would look something like this:

```
package com.packtpub.learnvaadin.twaattin;

import javax.portlet.PortletRequest;

import com.vaadin.terminal.gwt.server.ApplicationPortlet2;

public abstract class AbstractPortalPortlet extends
ApplicationPortlet2 {

  @Override
  protected String getStaticFilesLocation(PortletRequest request) {

    return request.getContextPath();
  }
}
```

Pick a solution and use it here: refreshing the page will display the Vaadin portlet, as shown in the following screenshot:

Advanced integration

Beyond a simple Hello World, we sometimes need advanced capabilities brought by Vaadin. We will check how they work in a portal context.

Restart and debug

We can use Vaadin restart and debug features in GateIn (or any other portal) like we used in standard web applications.

Just append `restartApplication` and/or `debug` query parameters and watch the magic happen.

Be wary that in this case, it will restart all Vaadin portlets displayed on the page at refresh time. Moreover, it will only show the debug window of a single Vaadin portlet, in a non-deterministic way. Hence, it is easier to use these parameters during development when there is only a single Vaadin portlet: that is when they are used for anyway.

Handling portlet specifics

Portlets have some features that are unique, as regards to standard web applications.

First, they have a unique lifecycle. Beyond classical `init()` and `destroy()` methods, two steps are also important: the process action phase and the render phase.

Second, a portlet container also manages for each portlet:

- Its mode: edit, view, and help
- Its window state: normal, minimized, and maximized

Finally, JSR 286 also adds event handling between portlets.

All of these features translate into the portlet API. However, much like the servlet API, the Vaadin framework hides the latter, so developers do not have to worry about it.

In order to let us interact with these elements, Vaadin makes the `PortletListener` interface available which is defined in the `PortletApplicationContext2` class.

 There is a parallel between the `PortletApplicationContext2` and the `WebApplicationContext`, and between `PortletListener` and `TransactionListener`. Among these similarities, note that implementing `PortletListener` should be the responsibility of the application alone, much like `TransactionListener` is for applications running in servlet containers.

Adding a listener to the application is just a matter of checking the context to see the context's type (web, portal 1.0, or portal 2.0). The following snippet illustrates this:

```
public class ListenerPortlet extends Application implements
PortletListene
  @Override
  public void init() {

    // Some initialization code
    if (getContext() instanceof PortletApplicationContext2) {

      PortletApplicationContext2 ctx = (PortletApplicationContext2)
        getContext();

      ctx.addPortletListener(this, this);
    }
  }
}
```

Each of the listener's methods gently maps one of the following request-processing phases:

Phase	Method	Description
Render	`handleRenderRequest()`	Generate HTML
Action	`handleActionRequest()`	Process user actions
Resource	`handleResourceRequest()`	Serve resources
Event	`handleEventRequest()`	Manage events

The Vaadin framework handles the request/response pair in the event phase.

This means that the only method to implement is `handleResourceRequest()`, and eventually `handleEventRequest()` if we need to listen to events. The request parameter for these methods lets us access the portlet mode, the portlet context, the portlet session, and other portlet attributes.

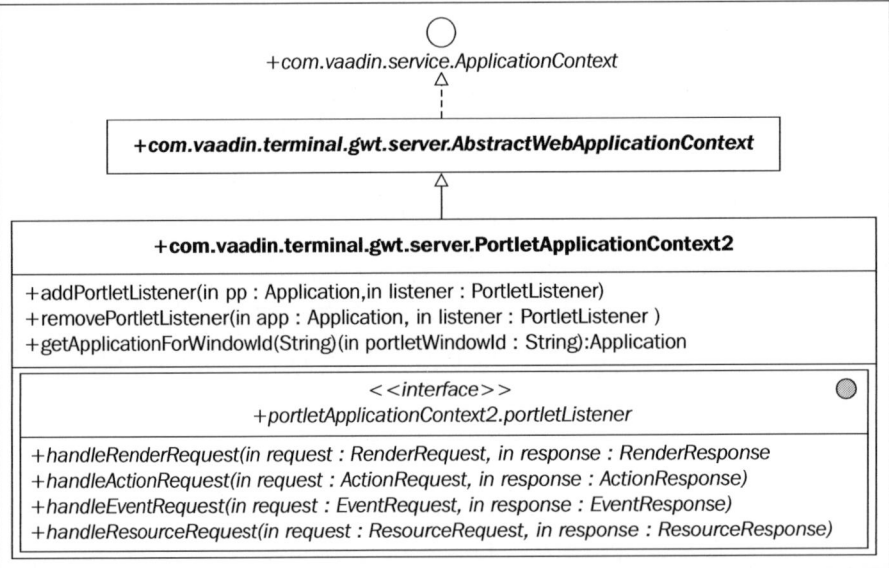

Portlet development strategies

During development, chances are we won't get our portlet right the first time. In order to ease our work, there are some techniques we can use.

Keep our portlet servlet-compatible

As a rule of thumb, portlet development is generally much slower than servlet development because of all the packaging and deployment involved. Tomcat or NetBeans integration in Eclipse, through the WTP plugin, lets us update classes and see changes on the fly. Hence, it is better if we can develop a servlet: it is advised to keep the servlet-compatibility mode the longest time possible to test our portlet in a simple applications server.

Portal debug mode

When this parallel cannot be maintained, for example, in order to add inter-portlet communication features, we will have to deploy our newly developed portlet on the target portal to develop further. In order to be able to debug the portlet, two actions are in order:

- Launch GateIn in debug mode, with the help of the `gatein-dev start` command (instead of the standard `gatein start`)
- In Eclipse, connect to the JVM launched in the debug mode. In order to accomplish this, click on the scrolling menu of the **Debug** button on the toolbar (the one that looks like a bug) and choose **Debug Configurations**.

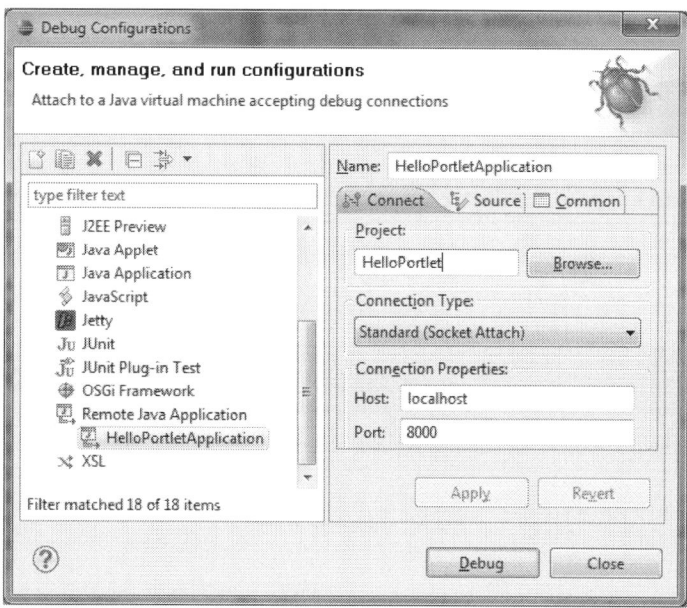

This will open a window: select **Remote Java Application** in the list and click on the **New Launch Configuration** in the upper left corner. Default port (**8000**) is suitable if GateIn also uses the default configuration.

- For NetBeans users, we can also connect to an external JVM. Click on **Debug menu | Attach Debugger**.

  In the opened window, keep the defaults and set the port to 8000, it is done.

From this point on, we can set breakpoints in our portlet and manage the flow from inside the IDE!

Updating a deployed portlet

Finally, successive portlet deployments are likely to be in order. In order to do that, we only have to do as for the first deployment: first export the WAR to GateIn, and then import applications in the portal (see the section name *Deploying in GateIn* in this chapter for a quick reminder).

Integrating Twaattin

In order to integrate Twaattin, we not only need to take the actions described earlier but also tweak somewhat our previous code in order to manage potential mismatches.

In addition to using the context-using portlet, standard updates are localized in the POM and in the deployment descriptors.

Portlet deployment descriptor

Our brand new portlet deployment descriptor looks like this:

```xml
<?xml version="1.0" encoding="UTF-8"?>
<portlet-app xmlns="http://java.sun.com/xml/ns/portlet/portlet-
app_2_0.xsd"
  version="2.0" xmlns:xsi="http://www.w3.org/2001/XMLSchema-instance"
  xsi:schemaLocation="http://java.sun.com/xml/ns/portlet/portlet-
app_2_0.xsd http://java.sun.com/xml/ns/portlet/portlet-app_2_0.xsd">
  <portlet>
    <portlet-name>Twaattin</portlet-name>
    <portlet-class>com.packtpub.learnvaadin.twaattin.TwaattinPortlet</
portlet-class>
    <init-param>
      <name>application</name>
      <value>com.packtpub.learnvaadin.twaattin.TwaattinApp</value>
    </init-param>
    <init-param>
      <name>widgetset</name>
      <value>
```

```
com.packtpub.learnvaadin.twaattin.widgetset.TwaattinWidgetset
    </value>
  </init-param>
  <supports>
    <mime-type>text/html</mime-type>
    <portlet-mode>view</portlet-mode>
  </supports>
  <portlet-info>
    <title>Twaattin Application</title>
    <short-title>Twaattin</short-title>
  </portlet-info>
  </portlet>
</portlet-app>
```

The only Vaadin-specific part lies in the widgetset tag, in order for the framework to locate it (just like in the `web.xml` previously).

Web deployment descriptor

The web deployment descriptor has major changes:

```
<?xml version="1.0" encoding="UTF-8"?>
<web-app version="2.5" xmlns:javaee="http://java.sun.com/xml/ns/
javaee"
  xmlns:xml="http://www.w3.org/XML/1998/namespace" xmlns:xsi="http://
www.w3.org/2001/XMLSchema-instance"
  xsi:schemaLocation="http://java.sun.com/xml/ns/javaee http://java.
sun.com/xml/ns/javaee/web-app_2_5.xsd ">
  <display-name>Twaattin</display-name>
  <context-param>
    <param-name>productionMode</param-name>
    <param-value>false</param-value>
  </context-param>
  <servlet>
    <servlet-name>ICEPush for Portlets</servlet-name>
    <servlet-class>org.vaadin.artur.icepush.ICEPushServlet
    </servlet-class>
    <load-on-startup>1</load-on-startup>
  </servlet>
  <servlet-mapping>
    <servlet-name>ICEPush for Portlets</servlet-name>
    <url-pattern>/*</url-pattern>
  </servlet-mapping>
  <listener>
```

```
        <listener-class>
          com.packtpub.learnvaadin.twaattin.DataInitializationListener
        </listener-class>
      </listener>
    </web-app>
```

Note there is no more declaration or mapping for the Twaattin Servlet as it is now handled at the portlet level.

On the other hand, we have to let the ICEPush servlet respond to asynchronous calls from the client. It cannot be handled by portlets in any case, so we must fall back to the standard servlet. Note that the `load-on-startup` tag **has to be filled** in all cases or we will run into a nasty `NullPointerException`.

Maven changes

Maven updates come from adding/removing dependencies but also making Twaattin run in both portals and standard application servers.

Dependency changes

As we directly use the portlet API, we need to add the `javax.portlet:portlet-api:2.0` dependency, in scope `provided` of course.

In addition, GateIn provides some dependencies we previously included in the WAR, so the following dependencies are to be removed:

- HSQLDB (and use MySQL instead)
- JTA and the SLF4J API from Quartz transitive dependencies
- SLF4J runtime as well

Those can be handled in the POM. The next section will show us another option though.

Multiplatform build

Multiplatform build is a little difficult to manage. Basically, there are two ways to achieve this:

- A single Maven project with assemblies created with the Maven Assembly Plugin, one for each platform
- A Maven parent project and one module for each platform

Both are equally valid: we will go with the former because an assembly is both easier to do and to explain than multimodule projects.

Assembly descriptor

The assembly plugin lets us create an assembly descriptor for each additional artifact attached to a main artifact. It looks like this:

```xml
<?xml version="1.0" encoding="UTF-8"?>
<assembly
  xmlns="http://maven.apache.org/plugins/maven-assembly-plugin/
assembly/1.1.2"
  xmlns:xsi="http://www.w3.org/2001/XMLSchema-instance"
  xsi:schemaLocation="http://maven.apache.org/plugins/maven-assembly-
plugin/assembly/1.1.2 http://maven.apache.org/xsd/assembly-1.1.2.xsd">
  <id>portlet</id>
  <formats>
    <format>war</format>
  </formats>
  <includeBaseDirectory>false</includeBaseDirectory>
  <fileSets>
    <fileSet>
      <directory>src/main/webapp</directory>
      <outputDirectory>/</outputDirectory>
      <excludes>
        <exclude>**/web.xml</exclude>
      </excludes>
    </fileSet>
    <fileSet>
      <directory>
        ${project.build.outputDirectory}
      </directory>
      <outputDirectory>/WEB-INF/classes</outputDirectory>
    </fileSet>
    <fileSet>
      <directory>src/main/assembly/gatein</directory>
      <outputDirectory>/WEB-INF</outputDirectory>
    </fileSet>
  </fileSets>
  <dependencySets>
    <dependencySet>
      <outputDirectory>/WEB-INF/lib</outputDirectory>
      <excludes>
        <exclude>*:war</exclude>
        <exclude>javax.transaction:jta</exclude>
        <exclude>org.slf4j:slf4j-api</exclude>
        <exclude>org.slf4j:slf4j-simple</exclude>
      </excludes>
    </dependencySet>
  </dependencySets>
</assembly>
```

This recreates the WAR as the Maven WAR plugin does, only we are able to both remove dependencies and add GateIn files, such as the portlet deployment descriptor and a specific web deployment descriptor.

Final POM

Changes in the POM are found in two parts:

- First, we have to activate assemblies, through the Maven Assembly plugin in the POM. We do this as follows:

```
<plugin>
  <groupId>org.apache.maven.plugins</groupId>
  <artifactId>maven-assembly-plugin</artifactId>
  <version>2.2.1</version>
  <configuration>
    <descriptors>
      <descriptor>src/main/assembly/gatein.xml</descriptor>
    </descriptors>
  </configuration>
  <executions>
    <execution>
      <goals>
        <goal>single</goal>
      </goals>
      <phase>package</phase>
    </execution>
  </executions>
</plugin>
```

- We should exclude portlet specific classes and configuration files from the "plain" WAR. As of now, it only includes our portlet. This is easily resolved in the Maven WAR plugin configuration.

```
<plugin>
  <groupId>org.apache.maven.plugins</groupId>
  <artifactId>maven-war-plugin</artifactId>
  <version>2.1.1</version>
  <configuration>
    <packagingExcludes>WEB-INF/**/TwaattinPortlet.class
    </packagingExcludes>
  </configuration>
</plugin>
```

Congrats! With just these two minor updates, we made Twaattin available as a webapp and a portlet.

OSGi

OSGi is a very promising technology that aims to resolve some deficiencies in Java. Despite its inherent structure, OSGi concepts are straightforward and aim to work at three different levels.

- First, OSGi comes with the concept of a **bundle**. Bundles are JARs, but provide additional information in their manifest: most notably, a bundle expresses which packages it exposes to the outside world (read which ones have public visibility) and which one it needs in order to fulfill its dependencies. Optionally, it may also define an activator class, which is a listener used on the next level. This defines the **modularity layer**.

- OSGi also provides the way to manage a bundle's lifecycle. Basically, a bundle may be in six different states and transitions between states are well defined. The six states are as follows:

State	Description
INSTALLED	Platform aware of bundle
RESOLVED	Checked for OSGi-correctness
STARTING	Being started. If an activator is defined for the bundle, calls its `start()` method.
ACTIVE	Running and available in the OSGi platform to be used by other bundles
STOPPING	Being stopped. If an activator is defined for the bundle, calls its `stop()` method.
UNINSTALLED	Final state

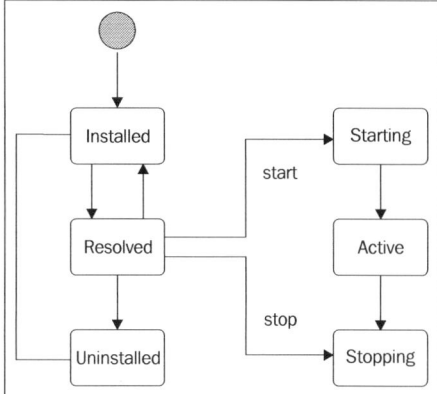

This layer is known as the **lifecycle layer**. A major benefit of this layer is hot deployment of bundles.

- Finally, some common capabilities are described in the **service layer**, each in the form of a Java interface. These interfaces are grouped in three different sets:

  ° System, like logging, deployment and admin

  ° Protocol, like HTTP and Universal Plug-and-Play

  ° Miscellaneous, like XML parsing

  Bundles may implement those services and register in the services registry for other bundles to discover and use them.

Also, note that OSGi is a standard promoted by the OSGi Alliance, which includes notable members IBM, Oracle Red Hat, and VMware. For a deeper insight into OSGI, visit the OSGI Alliance site at `http://www.osgi.org/`.

Choosing a platform

Some OSGi platforms are available to add our own bundles to the following:

- Knopflerfish (`http://www.knopflerfish.org/`), an independent OSGi implementation

- Apache Felix (`http://felix.apache.org/`), a small yet compliant OSGi platform

- Eclipse IDE manages its plugin architecture with the help of OSGi. The Equinox project (`http://www.eclipse.org/equinox/`), a whole OSGi implementation was started to achieve that.

Many applications servers also run on top of OSGi in order to manage complexity through modularization: Oracle Glassfish 3, Oracle WebLogic, IBM WebSphere, Red Hat JBoss, and OW Jonas 5 are such application servers.

> Another way to use OSGi is to embed a compatible container in the application. As one should probably tweak the application server the application will run into, chances are that it won't be considered as a viable option in the enterprise. Thus, we will focus on the "running in an OSGi container" way.

In order to illustrate OSGi, we will use Oracle Glassfish in the rest of this document. Glassfish uses Felix under the cover. In most cases, however, it should play no part as OSGi is a specification and Felix is only an implementation among others.

Glassfish

Like many other providers, Oracle supplies two distributions of its Glassfish application server: Glassfish Server Open Source Edition (available under CDDL or GPLv2 license) and Glassfish Server which is available under a commercial license.

In order to stay true with the open source approach, we will use the Open Source distribution.

Deploying bundles

There are basically three ways to deploy an OSGi bundle to Glassfish. However, for the first two, we will need to update Glassfish configuration in order to enable them. These are worth the effort.

Prerequisites

Edit the file `<GLASSFISH_ROOT>/domains/domain1/config/domain.xml`. Locate the JVM options line starting with `-Dorg.glassfish.additionalOSGiBundlesToStart`.

Append `org.apache.felix.fileinstall,org.apache.felix.shell.remote` at the end of the line. The first parameter is for the file system deployment and the second is for telnet.

The final line should look like this:

```
<jvm-options>-Dorg.glassfish.additionalOSGiBundlesToStart=org.apache.
felix.shell,org.apache.felix.gogo.runtime,org.apache.felix.gogo.
shell,org.apache.felix.gogo.command,org.apache.felix.shell.remote,org.
apache.felix.fileinstall</jvm-options>
```

Start (or restart) Glassfish.

> There are other ways to change Glassfish configuration. They include the `asadmin` command line, as well as the Glassfish console. Please refer to the appropriate documentation if the need be.

Telnet deployment

Once the configuration is updated, we can type the following in the command prompt:

```
telnet localhost 6666
```

The command prompt will display the following text.

```
Welcome to Apache Felix Gogo


g! help
```

 For security-minded readers, Glassfish should only allow local telnet connections by default. We should not worry too much about letting remote users access the console.

Installing an OSGi bundle is just a matter of typing on the prompt:

```
install file:///path/to/bundle
```

Glassfish will neatly return the newly installed bundle's ID:

```
Bundle ID: xxx
```

Just remember to then start the bundle (pass the start command the returned ID).

```
start xxx
```

To be sure everything went OK, type lb on the command prompt. It displays the whole list of all installed bundles, as well as their current status: it should show the new bundle (probably as the last item) as ACTIVE.

File system deployment

The second way to deploy a bundle to the Glassfish server is the simplest: just put the bundle in the <GLASSFISH_HOME>/domains/<MY_DOMAIN>/autodeploy/bundles folder.

A look at the log can confirm it works:

```
Installed <GLASSFISH_ROOT>/domains/domain1/autodeploy/bundles/vaadin-
6.7.x.jar
```

In addition, we can check the Felix console just like with the previous method.

Web console deployment

Navigate to Glassfish administration panel at `http://localhost:4848/`.

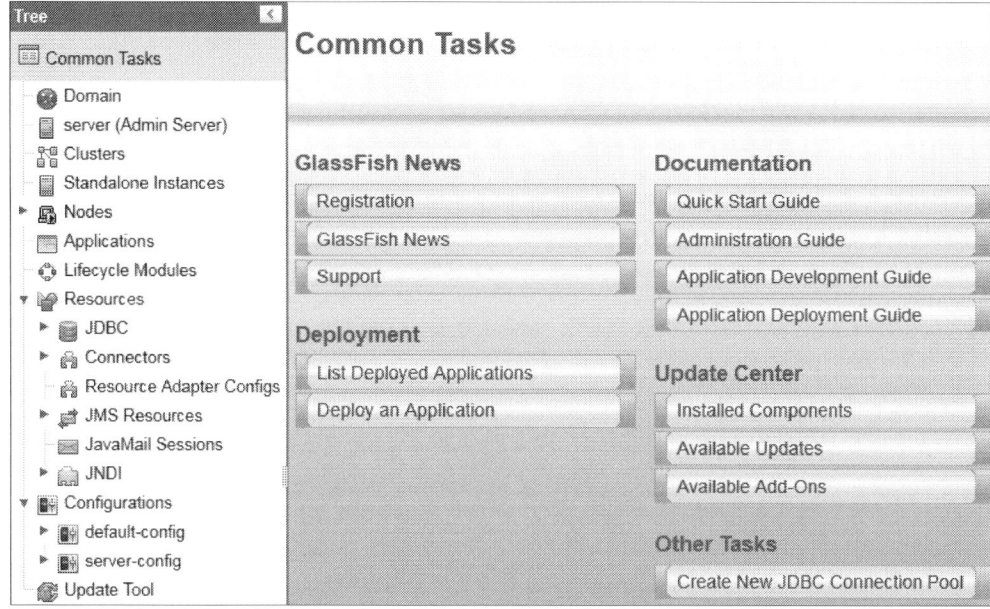

Click either on **Deploy an Application** on the homepage or on the **Applications** menu on the left.

Fill the opening window as follows:

- Select the bundle to deploy
- **Type**: **Other**
- **Status**: check **Enabled**
- **OSGi Type**: check
- **Run Verifier**: check
- **Force Redeploy**: check if the bundle is already deployed

Click on **OK**; this will deploy the bundle. The preceding options are depicted in the following screenshot:

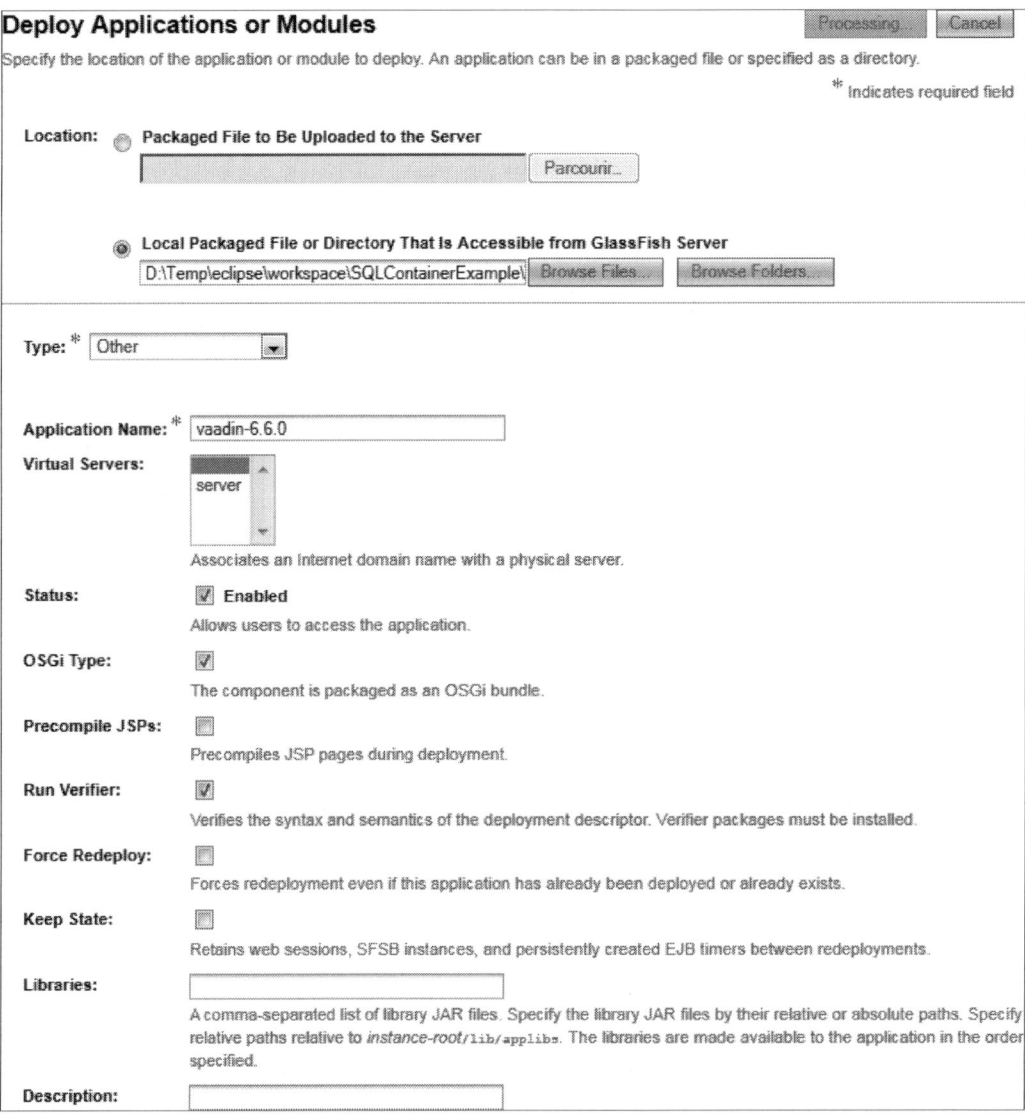

Logs should display the operation's status as follows:

INFO: Installed xxx.yyy [242] from reference:file:/<GLASSFISH_ROOT>/domains/ domain1/applications/yyy-s.t.v/

INFO: Started com.vaadin [242]

INFO: yyy-s.t.v was successfully deployed in 11 555 milliseconds.

Whatever the method used, the result would be the same, that is, separating the Vaadin JAR from the WAR.

Tooling

The good news here is that there is no need for further tooling beside what we already installed: we will keep Eclipse (or NetBeans) as our IDE and Glassfish will serve as an OSGi container.

The bad news is that the many OSGi advantages come at a price: OSGi makes development more structured. Whereas we previously could use a build tool or not, now we have to use one in order to reproduce builds through automation. In order to be consistent with former sections of this chapter, it is advised to use Maven: how to do it is the goal of the following sections. Alternatively, one could choose Ant, SBT or even Make if one is really desperate.

Vaadin OSGi use-cases

Benefits from OSGi are varied and depend on what layers are used.

Vaadin bundling

Strategies regarding libraries in an application server context come in three different flavors, each having pros and cons:

- Often, every web application comes with its libraries bundled in its `WEB-INF/lib` folder. The good part is that each is then independent; the bad is that even with similar libraries in the same versions, it adds to the WAR size, but also unnecessarily increases the memory load since each WAR's class loader has to load an instance of the library.

- Another approach is to put libraries in the application server's shared libraries folder. In this case, WAR can be very lightweight. Moreover, only the application server class loader has to load the library: it is done once. On the downside, applications have no choice on the version of these libraries, and have to use the one provided by the application server (much like the servlet API library).

- Finally, most application servers allow administrators to add libraries to the classpath of single applications; some even allow the defining of groups of libraries to ease that. This strategy gets the best of both worlds— independency and memory optimization—at the cost of much higher administration cost.

With OSGi, the administrator could deploy different versions of Vaadin on the OSGi platform and each deployed application would specify which version it needs. The platform would then resolve dependencies for us.

Modularization

A non Vaadin-specific use-case for Vaadin we could benefit from is modularization. We could decouple an application in modules, and then manage each one's lifecycle independently from one another.

A good example of module granularity would be application objects, in the case of multiple Vaadin application per WAR. A slightly more convoluted—yet still a possible case would be Vaadin windows: one could conceive an application, so that screens could be upgraded separately.

Hello OSGi

As an example, we will deploy a simple application as an OSGi bundle.

First, we will need to create a Vaadin project that we will make OSGi-compatible. Proceed as usual or refer to the description in *Chapter 3*.

Making a bundle

As can be expected, making the JAR OSGi-compliant is just a matter of putting the right information in the manifest.

At the very least, manifest headers should include

Header	Value	Description
Bundle-ManifestVersion	2	OSGi version compatibility. 2 means OSGi R4
Bundle-Name	hello-osgi	Human readable name
Bundle-SymbolicName	com.packtpub.learnvaadin.osgi	System name
Bundle-Version	1.0.0	Bundle version
Require-Bundle	com.vaadin;bundle-version="6.1.0"	Bundle dependency. Here, we only use Vaadin 6.1.0
Web-ContextPath	/osgi	context root
Export-Package	com.packtpub.learnvaadin	Exposed package entry points

Header	Value	Description
Import-Package	javax.servlet, javax.servlet.http	Package dependency
Bundle-ClassPath	WEB-INF/classes	Classpath. Since it's not a standard webapp but a bundle, we have to redefine the classpath the OSGi way

 For a complete list of headers, visit the following URL:

http://www.osgi.org/Specifications/ReferenceHeaders

The complete manifest looks like the following:

```
Bundle-ManifestVersion: 2
Bundle-Name: hello-osgi
Bundle-SymbolicName: com.packtpub.learnvaadin.osgi
Bundle-Version: 1.0.0
Bunlde-Vendor: Nicolas Frankel
Require-Bundle: com.vaadin;bundle-version="6.1.0"
Web-ContextPath: /osgi
Export-Package: com.packtpub.learnvaadin
Import-Package: javax.servlet, javax.servlet.http
Bundle-ClassPath: WEB-INF/classes
```

 Note that the formatting should be taken care of precisely since there is a limit of 72 characters for a line, according to the JAR specifications (visit http://download.oracle.com/javase/1.4.2/docs/guide/jar/jar.html#Name-Value%20pairs%20and%20Sections for more information).

Export, deploy, run

The previous manifest is enough. Now is time to run the application.

First, we need to export it: right-click on the project and choose export as WAR. As Eclipse has no hint that we want an OSGi bundle, we need to use our favorite ZIP tool, open the exported archive and remove the WEB-INF/lib directory as it will be available in Glassfish as a bundle dependency.

 Removing the WEB-INF/lib directory is not mandatory *per se* because we did not configure Vaadin to be available on the classpath but it's proper to do so.

Then, just like the Vaadin JAR in section named *File system deployment* in this chapter, put the JAR in the `<GLASSFISH_HOME>/domains/<MY_DOMAIN>/autodeploy/bundles` folder and it is done.

Finally, point your browser to `http://localhost:8080/osgi` and watch the magic happen.

Correcting errors

Actually, the magic consists of two errors that make the developed application unusable. Let's correct them.

Application class

First, OSGi dynamic class loading specifics make the standard Vaadin code throw the following runtime exception:

```
javax.servlet.ServletException: Failed to load application class: com.packtpub.learnvaadin.HelloOsgiApplication
```

In fact, the `newInstance()` method in our good old `ApplicationServlet` class is unusable in an OSGi context. In order to correct this, we have to throw away the servlet and create our own that just returns a brand-new application instance with no fancy stuff around.

```
package com.packtpub.learnvaadin;

import javax.servlet.ServletException;
import javax.servlet.http.HttpServletRequest;

import com.vaadin.Application;
import com.vaadin.terminal.gwt.server.AbstractApplicationServlet;

@SuppressWarnings("serial")
public class OsgiApplicationServlet extends AbstractApplicationServlet
{

  @Override
  protected Application getNewApplication(HttpServletRequest request)
    throws ServletException {

    return new HelloOsgiApplication();
  }
```

```
    @Override
    protected Class<? extends Application> getApplicationClass() throws
        ClassNotFoundException {

        return HelloOsgiApplication.class;

    }
}
```

This bare servlet code is not generic and cannot be factorized but just works.

Accessing the widgetset

The previous servlet lets us see the loading indicator, but then an information box complains about the widgetset failing to load:

```
Failed to load the widgetset: /osgi/VAADIN/widgetsets/com.
vaadin.terminal.gwt.DefaultWidgetSet/com.vaadin.terminal.gwt.
DefaultWidgetSet.nocache.js?1307388448247
```

What happens is that the default widgetset is contained in Vaadin's JAR and our servlet cannot access them due to OSGi class isolation. Like always, there is more than one solution, but a single one can be implemented with no action except to our project.

We just have to add the widgetset to our project:

1. Compile the widgetset, which has the default widgetset as its only widgetset
2. Reference the widgetset in the web deployment descriptor

```
    <servlet>
      <servlet-name>Hello OSGi Application</servlet-name>
      <servlet-class>
        com.packtpub.learnvaadin.OsgiApplicationServlet
      </servlet-class>
      <init-param>
        <param-name>widgetset</param-name>
        <param-value>
          com.packtpub.learnvaadin.widgetset.HelloosgiWidgetset
        </param-value>
      </init-param>
    </servlet>
```

This configuration lets us bundle the widgetset along with the JAR and access it from within the Vaadin's code.

Integrating Twaattin

Now it is time to go beyond a simple example and update Twaattin to be an OSGi bundle in its own right. Naturally, we will keep our previous compatibility, offering three artifacts: one standard, one GateIn, and one OSGi.

Bundle plugin

In the previous Hello OSGi example, we manually created the OSGi manifest. As Twaattin already uses Maven, much information is already available in the POM. As such, it is a good idea to also let Maven handle the OSGi manifest.

To this end, the Apache Felix project provides the `maven-bundle-plugin`, which is based on the Bnd utility. The complete documentation of the plugin is available online at `http://felix.apache.org/site/apache-felix-maven-bundle-plugin-bnd.html`.

 Bnd is a free tool (provided by the aQute company) that can generate a project's OSGi manifest from its classes and libraries. More information can be found at `http://www.aqute.biz/Bnd/Bnd`.

The plugin takes Bnd one step further and uses all Maven provided data, including dependencies, which suits our purpose just fine. Goals are provided not only to generate the OSGi bundle, but also to just generate the manifest.

Like with the rest of the Maven ecosystem, the plugin infers reasonable defaults for most pieces of information, meaning we only need to configure specific parts.

It translates like so for Twaattin:

```
<plugin>
  <groupId>org.apache.felix</groupId>
  <artifactId>maven-bundle-plugin</artifactId>
  <version>2.3.4</version>
  <extensions>true</extensions>
  <configuration>
    <supportedProjectTypes>
      <supportedProjectType>war</supportedProjectType>
    </supportedProjectTypes>
<manifestLocation>${bundle.manifest.dir}</manifestLocation>
    <instructions>
      <Bundle-ManifestVersion>2</Bundle-ManifestVersion>
```

```
  <Require-Bundle>com.vaadin;bundle-version="6.7.0"</Require-
    Bundle>
  <Web-ContextPath>/${project.artifactId}</Web-ContextPath>
  <Import-Package>javax.servlet,
    javax.servlet.http,javax.naming,javax.sql,javax.crypto,
    javax.crypto.spec</Import-Package>
  <Bundle-ClassPath>.,WEB-INF/classes</Bundle-ClassPath>
  <Embed-Dependency>*;scope=compile|runtime;artifactId=!vaadin
  </Embed-Dependency>
  <Embed-Directory>WEB-INF/lib</Embed-Directory>
  <Embed-Transitive>true</Embed-Transitive>
  </instructions>
</configuration>
<executions>
  <execution>
    <phase>package</phase>
    <goals>
      <goal>manifest</goal>
    </goals>
  </execution>
</executions>
</plugin>
```

This configuration does many things; we will have a look at each part.

The first thing to know is that by default, the plugin only operates on `jar` and `bundle` packaging types. It does not work for other artifact types (it fails silently). Nevertheless, it can be configured to allow other packaging: the first thing to do is to instruct the plugin we understand it is a WAR, but we still want the OSGi manifest. This is done with the `supportedProjectType` tag in the previous XML snippet.

Then, the goal is only to create the manifest, so that we may include it in our bundle. In order to achieve this, we isolate it in a specific folder, defined as a Maven property so we don't have to hard-configure it in the assembly.

Finally, the `instructions` tag references individual headers we will find in the OSGi manifest. The following two things are of particular interest:

1. Although our own code only requires some packages, we absolutely have to import `javax.crypto` and `javax.crypto.spec` packages for Twitter4J uses them. **These additional packages can only be found empirically** (that is, running the application and reading the ensuing error).

2. OSGi specific class loading system disregards the standard WEB-INF/ classes and WEB-INF/lib folders, meaning we have to configure them in the manifest. Moreover, whereas folders can be used for classes, they cannot be used for JAR: luckily, the plugin handles the writing of each dependency. The *;scope=compile|runtime;artifactId=!vaadin expression reads as "any Maven dependency of scope compile or runtime that is not Vaadin".

The previous fragment produces the following OSGi manifest (for readability purposes, the presented manifest does not respect the 72 characters per line limit):

```
Manifest-Version: 1.0
Export-Package: com.packtpub.learnvaadin.twaattin;uses:="javax.
servlet,javax.sql,javax.naming,com.packtpub.learnvaadin.
twaattin.service,com.packtpub.learnvaadin.twaattin.ui",com.
packtpub.learnvaadin.twaattin.persistence;uses:="com.packtpub.
learnvaadin.twaattin.service",com.packtpub.learnvaadin.twaattin.
service;uses:="com.packtpub.learnvaadin.twaattin.ui",com.packtpub.
learnvaadin.twaattin.ui;uses:="com.packtpub.learnvaadin.twaattin,com.
packtpub.learnvaadin.twaattin.service,com.packtpub.learnvaadin.
twaattin.persistence"
Embed-Directory: WEB-INF/lib
Bundle-ClassPath: .,WEB-INF/classes,WEB-INF/lib/quartz-2.0.1.jar,WEB-
INF/lib/slf4j-api-1.6.1.jar,WEB-INF/lib/twitter4j-core-2.2.2.jar,WEB-
INF/lib/slf4j-simple-1.6.1.jar,WEB-INF/lib/icepush-0.2.1.jar,WEB-INF/
lib/icepush-gwt-2.0.0-alpha3.jar,WEB-INF/lib/jta-1.1.jar,WEB-INF/
lib/vaadin-sqlcontainer-1.1.0.jar,WEB-INF/lib/icepush-2.0.0-alpha3.
jar,WEB-INF/lib/c3p0-0.9.1.1.jar
Built-By: frankeln
Tool: Bnd-1.15.0
Bundle-Name: Twaattin
Created-By: Apache Maven Bundle Plugin
Web-ContextPath: /twaattin
Require-Bundle: com.vaadin;bundle-version="6.7.0"
Build-Jdk: 1.6.0_24
Bundle-Version: 1.0.0.SNAPSHOT
Bnd-LastModified: 1307519252812
Embed-Transitive: true
Bundle-ManifestVersion: 2
Bundle-Description: Twaattin is a Vaadin Twitter client
Embed-Dependency: *;scope=compile|runtime;artifactId=!vaadin
Import-Package: javax.crypto,javax.crypto.spec,javax.naming,javax.
servlet,javax.servlet.http,javax.sql
Bundle-SymbolicName: com.packtpub.learnvaadin.twaattin
```

Note that metadata such as Bundle-Name, Bundle-SymbolicName and the like are automatically taken from the POM's artifactId, groupId, and version. Although it is possible to override these values, defaults are good enough for Twaattin.

Moreover, the Export-Package header is taken care of by the plugin (and Bnd underneath) and read from our source code.

 If crafted by hand, take care that OSGi expects the version to be in MAJOR.MINOR.MICRO.QUALIFIER format. These components have to be separated by dots, so Maven -SNAPSHOT qualifier should be replaced.

Multiplatform build

In order for our build to be truly multiplatform, we now just have to provide an assembly descriptor for the bundle (as well as configure it in the POM).

```xml
<?xml version="1.0" encoding="UTF-8"?>
<assembly
  xmlns="http://maven.apache.org/plugins/maven-assembly-
    plugin/assembly/1.1.2"
  xmlns:xsi="http://www.w3.org/2001/XMLSchema-instance"
  xsi:schemaLocation="http://maven.apache.org/plugins/maven-assembly-
    plugin/assembly/1.1.2 http://maven.apache.org/xsd/assembly-
    1.1.2.xsd">
  <id>bundle</id>
  <formats>
    <format>jar</format>
  </formats>
  <includeBaseDirectory>false</includeBaseDirectory>
  <fileSets>
    <fileSet>
      <directory>src/main/webapp</directory>
      <outputDirectory>/</outputDirectory>
    </fileSet>
    <fileSet>
    <directory>${project.build.outputDirectory}</directory>
      <outputDirectory>/WEB-INF/classes</outputDirectory>
    </fileSet>
  </fileSets>
  <dependencySets>
    <dependencySet>
```

```
        <outputDirectory>/WEB-INF/lib</outputDirectory>
        <excludes>
          <exclude>*:war</exclude>
          <exclude>javax.transaction:jta</exclude>
          <exclude>com.vaadin:vaadin</exclude>
        </excludes>
      </dependencySet>
    </dependencySets>
  </assembly>
```

We see that OSGi packaging is not more complex than for our previous portlet, the real piece of work was done in the bundle plugin.

We just have to take care to remove the Vaadin JAR from the `WEB-INF` folder, for it is provided by the OSGi container.

Build and deploy

With only these two changes, we made Twaattin an OSGi bundle in its own right. Moreover, this also reinforces the fact that using Maven was a good step towards true multiplatform build.

Cloud

What is dangerous with the word "cloud" nowadays is that it is a relatively young approach, so that not everyone necessarily has the same.

In order for certain terms to have the same meaning in the scope of this book, some definitions are in order.

Cloud offering levels

Currently, there is some agreement however, that there are three different service levels offered by clouds. This should be the shared understanding for our following work on clouds.

1. **Infrastructure as a Service (IaaS)**: In IaaS, only the hardware is dematerialized. In effect, this only affects system administrators and only in that they interact with a server whose location they don't know, as opposed to one they know of. The net gain here is a decrease on hardware costs as it is mutualized. We still have to install JVM, application servers, and the rest.

2. **Platform as a Service (PaaS)**: PaaS goes one step further and also provides the platform, for example, the JVM and the application servers, on top of the distant hardware. In this case, the cloud vendor completely isolates users from the underlying infrastructure behind a façade, which also offers a user interface to configure the different platforms.

3. **Software as a Service (SaaS)**: The last level of cloud offering is the SaaS, which is an application hosted distantly.

What is common in all three levels is the virtualization of hardware. One never knows on which physical server one runs the OS, the platform, or the software.

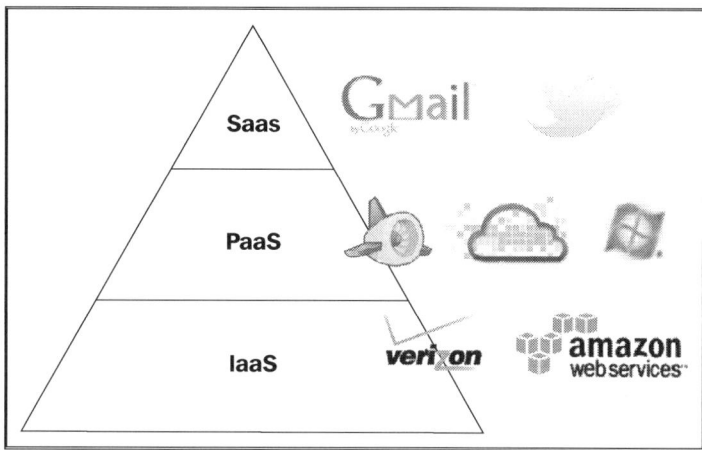

For our purposes, the needed offering is situated on the PaaS level: In this case, we will just deploy our software "in the cloud".

State of the market

This field being relatively new, things are changing fast. In the Java ecosystem, however, there are three stable players providing a cloud platform for our software to run on:

- Google was the first major company to provide a "free" cloud platform for Java web applications in the form of Google App Engine.

  This approach has some disadvantages, including a reduced scope of the Java API that prevents some tasks such as thread launching, file creation, and so on. Moreover, persistence can only be achieved through JPA or JDO, and only so with the help of the DataNucleus product, thus forcing us to use it locally as well.

Finally, although free at the entry level, there are some fees when one goes above some quotas (but these are quite high; for an up-to-date reference on these limits, refer to `http://code.google.com/intl/fr/appengine/docs/quotas.html`).

- The second Java offering comes strangely from Microsoft in the form of its Azure platform. Though not free in the true sense of the term—the trial is free and ends on September 30—the initiative is unique enough to be cited.

  In fact, for Java apps anyway, Azure is not PaaS enough as we need to deploy the application server on our own.

- Finally, the newest player on the scene is VMware which supplies the Cloud Foundry software. This software is provided as an open source project (for private clouds), as well as a platform to deploy on.

As Google was the first, Vaadin provides a specific servlet to run on GAE. Yet, GAE put too many constraints:

- Only a subset of the Java API is available (no threads, no files, and so on)
- Persistence has to be used through the Java Data Object API (JDO—for details, see `http://www.oracle.com/technetwork/java/index-jsp-135919.html`)
- Every object put in session has to be serializable
- Finally, deployment time is lengthy, even on the local testing platform

Therefore, the winner is Cloud Foundry in the scope of this book.

Tooling

We will see in the following section that we can run a standard webapp with no changes in Cloud Foundry. However, the deployment of the application to the cloud can be eased with the help of the right tool.

In our case, the right tool is SpringSource Tools Suite that we discussed in *Chapter 2*. Beginning with Version 2.5.1 from STS, we can install the Cloud Foundry plugin from inside the IDE. Alternatively, we can also install the plugin within a simple Eclipse 3.7. The update site address is `http://dist.springsource.com/release/TOOLS/market-place/e3.7/`. The Cloud Foundry feature is located under Core / Cloud Foundry integration.

Hello cloud

In this section, we will deploy our first web application to Cloud Foundry. Please first create a Vaadin project as we have done before.

Registration

If you intend to use the Cloud Foundry platform, then you need to register on the website to get an account first. Go to `http://cloudfoundry.com/` and come back when it is done. Be warned that it takes a couple of days to get an answer.

Cloud setup

In a standard environment, we would need to create a new virtual server. In the cloud, we need to configure it, but the steps are the same.

1. Locate the **Servers** tab. Right-click and select **New | Server**.

2. With the Cloud Foundry plugin installed, there should be a new entry named **Cloud Foundry** under the **VMware** folder. Select it and click on **Next**, as shown in the following screenshot:

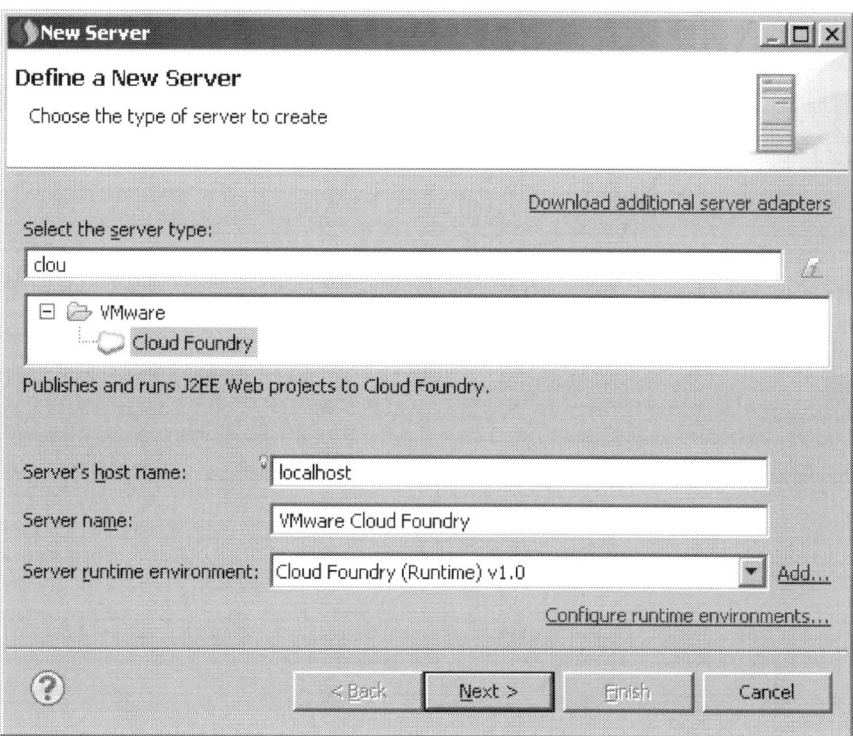

3. Now, fill in the information sent by Cloud Foundry and validate the account. Then, click on **Next**, as shown in the following screenshot:

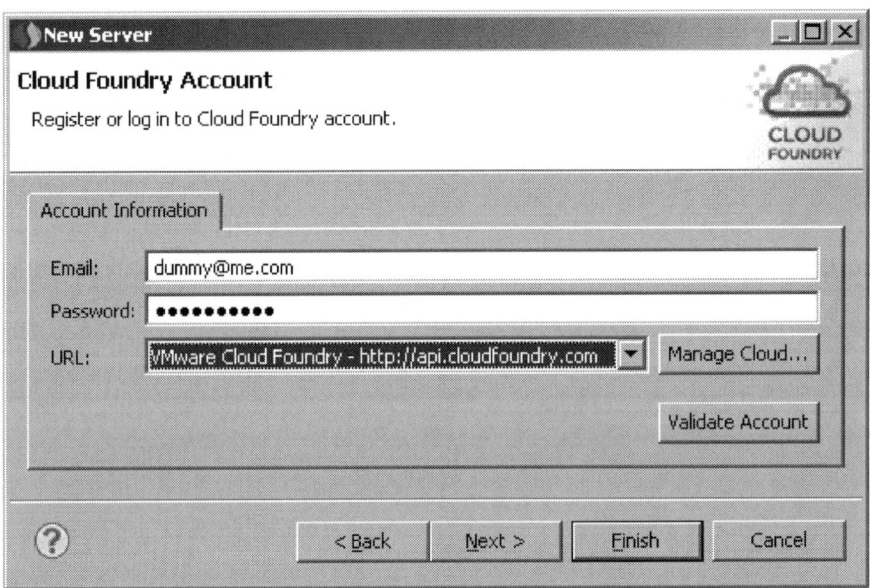

4. Finally, select the project to setup and click on **Finish**. Notice a new "server" appeared in the tab. Under it, there should be our project with the status **Not Deployed**. Now, we have to upload the application.

Application deployment

In order for the application to be deployed "on the cloud", we will need to configure it first. This can be done easily: select the newly available application, right-click on it, and select **Start**.

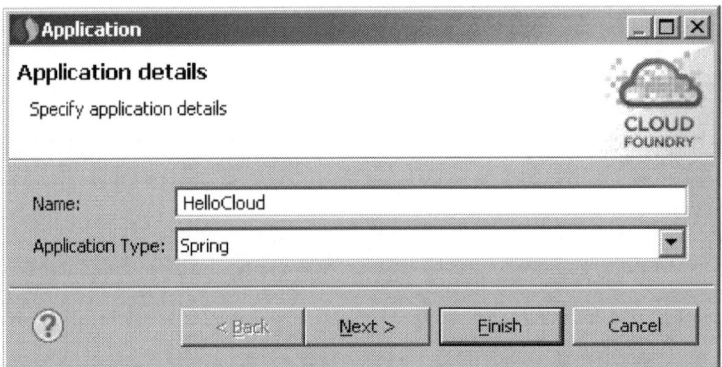

Even though ours is not a Spring application per se, we keep the default values. Click on Next, as shown in the following screenshot:

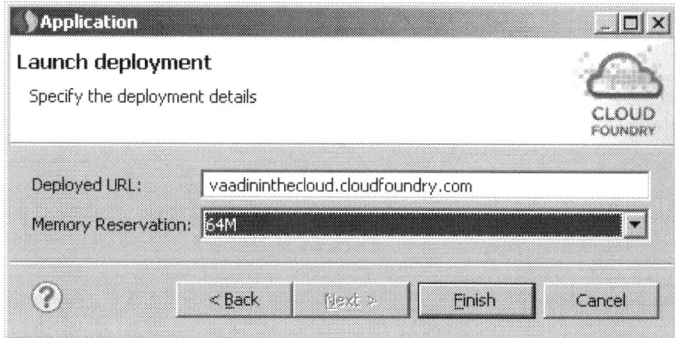

In this step, we can customize the URL and the memory. The URL suits us just fine. As for the memory, we can use the minimal value (64M) as there is no real need for more.

Click on **Finish** and watch the magic happen.

Troubleshooting

Be extra-careful when choosing the URL because it must be unique among all applications (mine, yours, and everyone's). If a 400 error with the message "**The URI xxx. cloudfoundry.com has already been taken or reserved**" occurs, be sure to change the URI accordingly. Don't be afraid to choose a long one!

Finally, navigate to your chosen URL and be amazed!

Alternative deployment

The IDE is not the only solution to deploy our applications in Cloud Foundry. The latter comes with a command-line interface (CLI) named **vmc**. This client can be installed as a Ruby gem, meaning we have to have Ruby installed on our system, and is well beyond the scope of this book.

Readers interested in deploying with the CLI should refer to the documentation available online at the following URL:

```
http://support.cloudfoundry.com/attachments/token/
dyizykvkgocs7yb/?name=Getting_Started_With_VMware_Cloud_Foundry_
using_vmc-u3.pdf.
```

Integrating Twaattin

Regarding the previous section, integrating Twaattin should be painless. In fact it is: still, we need to change the way we get the reference on the datasource.

Creating the datasource

Before using the datasource, we have to create one and associate it with our application. In Cloud Foundry, datasources are services. In order to create such a service, double click on the Cloud Foundry virtual server and select the Services section in the **Application** tab.

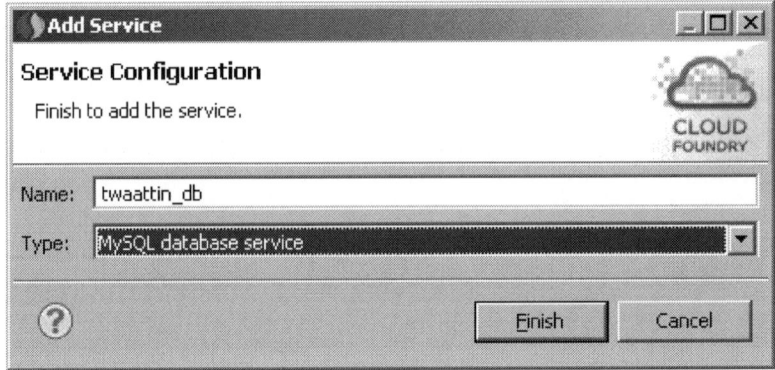

Click on the **Add service** button. In the opening pop-up, fill the fields as follows:

- **Name**: anything you like
- **Type: MySQL database service**

Click on **Finish** and then select the Twaattin application in the Applications section and drag the newly created service in the Application Services section. This is it!

Using the datasource

Cloud Foundry makes information on services available as JSON entities in an environment variable. As getting the variable and then parsing the JSON is somewhat bothersome, Cloud Foundry also provides a library to access it through an API.

This library is available in the Spring Maven repo. In order to use it, the POM has to be updated as follows:

```
<repository>
  <id>Spring</id>
  <url>http://s3.amazonaws.com/maven.springframework.org/milestone</url>
</repository>
```

Then, we just add the dependency as follows:

```
<dependency>
  <groupId>org.cloudfoundry</groupId>
  <artifactId>cloudfoundry-runtime</artifactId>
  <version>0.6.0</version>
</dependency>
```

The last step is to use the datasource. This is how we got it:

```
CloudEnvironment env = new CloudEnvironment();

ApplicationInstanceInfo instanceInfo = env.getInstanceInfo();

MysqlServiceCreator creator = new MysqlServiceCreator(env);

ServiceNameTuple<DataSource> snt = creator.createSingletonService();

DataSource ds = snt.service;
```

Finishing touches

As we may run Twaattin in a variety of environments, we need to introduce a service locator that knows how to get the datasource no matter where. In Cloud Foundry, it will be using the utility API we just saw, otherwise (in GateIn or in GlassFish) it will be from a JNDI resource.

```
package com.packtpub.learnvaadin.twaattin;

import javax.naming.InitialContext;
import javax.naming.NamingException;
import javax.sql.DataSource;

import org.cloudfoundry.runtime.env.ApplicationInstanceInfo;
import org.cloudfoundry.runtime.env.CloudEnvironment;
import org.cloudfoundry.runtime.service.AbstractServiceCreator.
ServiceNameTuple;
import org.cloudfoundry.runtime.service.relational.
MysqlServiceCreator;

public class ServiceLocator {
```

```
    private static transient DataSource ds;

    private ServiceLocator() {
    }

    public static DataSource getDataSource() {

      if (ds == null) {

        CloudEnvironment env = new CloudEnvironment();

        ApplicationInstanceInfo instanceInfo = env.getInstanceInfo();

        if (instanceInfo != null) {

          MysqlServiceCreator creator = new MysqlServiceCreator(env);

          ServiceNameTuple<DataSource> snt =
            creator.createSingletonService();

          ds = snt.service;

        } else {

          try {

            ds = (DataSource) new
              InitialContext().lookup("java:comp/env/jdbc/twaattin");

          } catch (NamingException e) {

            throw new RuntimeException(e);

          }
        }
      }

      return ds;
    }
}
```

From this point on, Twaattin can be deployed on Cloud Foundry like our first trivial example. It is accessible online at `http://twaattin.cloudfoundry.com/`.

Summary

In this chapter, we have deployed Vaadin applications on exotic platforms that go well beyond simple applications servers: portals, OSGi containers, and the cloud. In each case, we used a product, respectively GateIn, GlassFish, and Cloud Foundry to demonstrate the feasibility of it. Should the need arise; however, we now have all the necessary keys to deploy on other products, for example Liferay, Felix, or Google App Engine.

The lesson here is that Vaadin applications can be run on a variety of platforms without much adaptation.

Index

Maven feature
  adding, to Vaadin 317
Mavenize Vaadin project 318, 319
Maven projects
  Vaadin support, adding to 319-321
Maven tooling 317
maxLength property 101
MethodEventSource interface 77, 126
MethodProperty class 150
Microsoft SQL Server 226
modality 89
mode property 168
modularity layer 349
modularization 356
module granularity
  example 356
multi-implementations listeners 125
multiSelect property 167
MySQL 226

N

name column generator 195, 196
NetBeans
  about 18
  distributions, downloading 38
  setting up 38
  Spring support 284
  Vaadin 38
NetBeans Vaadin project
  creating 43, 44
  testing 46
newInstance() method 358
newItemHandler property 167
new items
  handling 169
newItemsAllowed property 167
nominal embedding
  about 210
  configuring 211
  div element 211
  loading 211
  stylesheet 211
non-editable text content 90
noteworthy add-ons
  about 222
  cross-site embedding 222

server push 238-241
  SQL adapter 225
notification
  about 84
  displaying 86
  methods 87
  properties 86
notification class 84, 85
notification, types
  error type 85
  information 84
  tray 85
  warning 85
notify() method 118, 119
null items 169
nullRepresentation property 101
nullSelectionAllowed() method 169
nullSelectionAllowed property 167
nullSelectionItemId property 167
nullSettingsAllowed property 101
null value, text field 101

O

OAuth
  about 189
  URL, for info 189
ObjectProperty 146
object serialization 265
observer pattern
  about 77, 117, 118
  enhancements 118
observer pattern, enhancement
  event 119
  event details 119
  event types 119
onMessage() method 119
open(ExternalResource) method 202
Oracle 16, 226
Oracle WebLogic Portal
  URL 328
ordered container 161, 162
OSGi
  about 349
  platform, selecting 350
  tooling 355
  Twaattin, integrating 360

Red Hat JBoss Application Server 40
refresh() method 227
refreshRenderedCells() method 180
RegexpValidator 94
regular subwindows 89
remarks, Hibernate
  about 312
  optimizations 312
  rollback management 313
  serialization exception 312
removeListener() method 125
renderer component 144
RequestContextListener 289
request-response model
  about 238
  accessing with 202
  brute force approach 202, 203
  integrated approach 204, 205
Require-Bundle header 356
requiredError property 99
required property 99
resizable property 88
Resource interface 82, 83
reusable dialog box
  example 252
rich clients 15
rich clients approaches
  Ajax 15
  GWT 19
  JWS 17, 18
  plugins 16, 17
Rich Internet Application (RIA) 8
rootItemIds() method 188
row header column 176
ROW_HEADER_MODE_EXPLICIT con-
    stant 176
ROW_HEADER_MODE_EXPLICIT_DE-
    FAULTS_ID constant 176
ROW_HEADER_MODE_HIDDEN constant
    176
ROW_HEADER_MODE_ICON_ONLY
    constant 176
ROW_HEADER_MODE_ID constant 176
ROW_HEADER_MODE_INDEX constant
    176
ROW_HEADER_MODE_ITEM constant
    176

ROW_HEADER_MODE_PROPERTY con-
    stant 176
Ruby on Rails 52
RuntimeException 214

S

SaaS 365
SBT, for Scala 317
scriptlets 12
script tag 211
Scrollable 79
secondComponent property 109
sendRedirect() method 217
Serializable interface 76, 77
server client communication, Vaadin GWT
    architecture
  about 265
  descending communication 266, 267
  object serialization 265
  UDIL 265
  YouTube viewer example 267, 268
Server push
  about 238
  example 239, 241
  installation 239
server-side code, Vaadin architecture 56, 57
server side, Vaadin GWT architecture 264,
    265
server side widget 264
service layer 350
service levels, Cloud
  IaaS 364
  PaaS 365
  SaaS 365
Service Locator 282
service() method 302
servlet
  committing 302, 303
servlet class
  about 48
  declaring 48
servlet code, Java EE 6 293, 294
servlet code, Spring 286, 287
servlet context 202
servlet mapping
  adding 47

Thank you for buying
Learning Vaadin

About Packt Publishing

Packt, pronounced 'packed', published its first book *"Mastering phpMyAdmin for Effective MySQL Management"* in April 2004 and subsequently continued to specialize in publishing highly focused books on specific technologies and solutions.

Our books and publications share the experiences of your fellow IT professionals in adapting and customizing today's systems, applications, and frameworks. Our solution based books give you the knowledge and power to customize the software and technologies you're using to get the job done. Packt books are more specific and less general than the IT books you have seen in the past. Our unique business model allows us to bring you more focused information, giving you more of what you need to know, and less of what you don't.

Packt is a modern, yet unique publishing company, which focuses on producing quality, cutting-edge books for communities of developers, administrators, and newbies alike. For more information, please visit our website: www.packtpub.com.

About Packt Open Source

In 2010, Packt launched two new brands, Packt Open Source and Packt Enterprise, in order to continue its focus on specialization. This book is part of the Packt Open Source brand, home to books published on software built around Open Source licences, and offering information to anybody from advanced developers to budding web designers. The Open Source brand also runs Packt's Open Source Royalty Scheme, by which Packt gives a royalty to each Open Source project about whose software a book is sold.

Writing for Packt

We welcome all inquiries from people who are interested in authoring. Book proposals should be sent to author@packtpub.com. If your book idea is still at an early stage and you would like to discuss it first before writing a formal book proposal, contact us; one of our commissioning editors will get in touch with you.

We're not just looking for published authors; if you have strong technical skills but no writing experience, our experienced editors can help you develop a writing career, or simply get some additional reward for your expertise.

open source *
community experience distilled

jQuery Mobile First Look

ISBN: 978-1-84951-590-0 Paperback: 216 pages

Discover the endless possibilities offered by jQuery Mobile for rapid Mobile Web Development

1. Easily create your mobile web applications from scratch with jQuery Mobile

2. Learn the important elements of the framework and mobile web development best practices

3. Customize elements and widgets to match your desired style

4. Step-by-step instructions on how to use jQuery Mobile

Java EE 6 Development with NetBeans 7

ISBN: 978-1-84951-270-1 Paperback: 392 pages

Develop professional enterprise Java EE applications quickly and easily with this popular IDE

1. Use features of the popular NetBeans IDE to accelerate development of Java EE applications

2. Develop JavaServer Pages (JSPs) to display both static and dynamic content in a web browser

3. Covers the latest versions of major Java EE APIs such as JSF 2.0, EJB 3.1, and JPA 2.0, and new additions to Java EE such as CDI and JAX-RS

4. Learn development with the popular PrimeFaces JSF 2.0 component library

Please check **www.PacktPub.com** for information on our titles

Inkscape 0.48 Essentials for Web Designers

ISBN: 978-1-84951-268-8   Paperback: 316 pages

Use the fascinating Inkscape graphics editor to create attractive layout designs, images, and icons for your website

1. The first book on the newly released Inkscape version 0.48, with an exclusive focus on web design

2. Comprehensive coverage of all aspects of Inkscape required for web design

3. Incorporate eye-catching designs, patterns, and other visual elements to spice up your web pages

jQuery 1.4 Reference Guide

ISBN: 978-1-84951-004-2   Paperback: 336 pages

This book and eBook is a comprehensive exploration of the popular JavaScript library

1. Quickly look up features of the jQuery library

2. Step through each function, method, and selector expression in the jQuery library with an easy-to-follow approach

3. Understand the anatomy of a jQuery script

4. Write your own plug-ins using jQuery's powerful plug-in architecture

5. Written by the creators of learningquery.com

Please check **www.PacktPub.com** for information on our titles